MW00514128

A. HOFFER, M.D., Ph.D., F.R.C.P.(C),
Suite 3A - 2727 Quadra St.
Victoria, B.C.   V8T 4E5

# Orthomolecular Medicine For Physicians

*Keats Titles of Related Interest*

1986: A Year in Nutritional Medicine, edited by Jeffrey Bland, Ph.D.

The AIDS Fighters by Ian Brighthope, M.D. with Peter Fitzgerald

B6: The Natural Healer by Alan Gaby, M.D.

Brain Allergies by William H. Philpott, M.D. and Dwight K. Kalita, Ph.D.

Cancer and Its Nutritional Therapies by Richard A. Passwater, Ph.D.

Diet and Disease by E. Cheraskin, M.D., D.M.D., W. M. Ringsdorf, Jr., D.M.D. and J. W. Clark, D.D.S.

Environmental Medicine by Natalie Golos, James F. O'Shea, M.D. and Francis J. Waickman, M.D.

The Healing Nutrients Within by Eric R. Braverman, M.D. with Carl C. Pfeiffer, M.D., Ph.D.

Medical Applications of Clinical Nutrition by Jeffrey Bland, Ph.D.

Mental and Elemental Nutrients by Carl C. Pfeiffer, M.D., Ph.D.

Nutrients to Age Without Senility by Abram Hoffer, M.D., Ph.D. and Morton Walker, D.P.M.

The Nutrition Desk Reference by Robert H. Garrison, Jr., R.Ph. and Elizabeth Somer, M.A.

Orthomolecular Nutrition by Abram Hoffer, M.D., Ph.D. and Morton Walker, D.P.M.

Your Family Tree Connection by Chris Reading, M.D. and Ross Meillon

# Orthomolecular Medicine For Physicians

ABRAM HOFFER, M.D., PH.D.

Keats Publishing, Inc. New Canaan, Connecticut

The information in this book is presented for education and information only and does not contain treatment recommendations for the public. The treatment of illness must be supervised by a physician or other licensed health professional.

**ORTHOMOLECULAR MEDICINE FOR PHYSICIANS**

Copyright © 1989 by Abram Hoffer

All Rights Reserved

No part of this book may be copied or reproduced without the written consent of the publisher.

Library of Congress Cataloging-in-Publication Data
    Hoffer, Abram
        Orthomolecular medicine for physicians.

        Includes bibliographies and index.
        1. Orthomolecular therapy. I. Title. [DNLM:
1. Orthomolecular Therapy. WB 330 H698o]
RM235.5.H64      1989      615.8'54      88-34192
ISBN 0-87983-390-4

Printed in the United States of America

Keats Publishing, Inc.
27 Pine Street, New Canaan, Connecticut 06840

DEDICATION

To Humphry Osmond, Margaret J. Callbeck and Irwin Kahan, friends and colleagues. Together we explored the usefulness of large doses of niacin and niacinamide in the treatment of schizophrenia, using the first double-blind, controlled study in psychiatry. Jointly we coauthored the first report describing the results of our studies.*

And to Dr. Arthur M. Sackler for his foresight in publishing our paper in his journal.

And, finally, to all my colleagues and associates in the United States, Canada and Australia, who have added so much to orthomolecular medicine. Without their dedicated work, this book would not have been possible.

## ACKNOWLEDGMENTS

I wish to thank Frank Murray for his assistance and enthusiasm in the publishing of this book.

Especial thanks go to Frances Fuller for her skill, dedication and industry in preparing this material for publication.

*Hoffer, A., Osmond, H., Callbeck, M. J. & Kahan, I. (1957). Treatment of schizophrenia with nicotinic acid and nicotinamide. *J. Clin. Exper. Psychopath.*, 18:131–158.

## TABLE OF CONTENTS

# INTRODUCTION

Orthomolecular psychiatry began soon after vitamin B3 was identified as nicotinic acid, or nicotinamide. These chemicals were merely items in organic chemistry until they were identified as the antipellagra factors. Following this, clinical nutritionists began to treat a wide variety of psychiatric diseases with doses then considered very large, i.e., up to 1 gram per day. Before 1950, a small number of reports showed that patients with depression, senile or presenile deterioration, or with some toxic psychoses, recovered when given this vitamin. By 1949, Dr. William Kaufman had published two books summarizing his studies on arthritis. These are very careful, clinically controlled experiments on many hundreds of arthritics, in which he showed that most of the patients given the vitamin became normal, or so much better that they were no longer seriously handicapped. But all these reports were ignored, probably because, by 1950, which ushered in the era of the wonder drugs ACTH and cortisone, medical schools forgot about nutrition, and what little teaching had been available was dropped from their curricula. Since then medical interest in nutrition has been quiescent or sporadic, but there is evidence that the medical community is currently showing consistently more interest in clinical nutrition.

I became interested in vitamin B3 in 1951, when Dr. Humphry Osmond and I began to formulate the adrenochrome hypothesis of schizophrenia. We concluded that vitamin B3 in large doses might be therapeutic for schizophrenics because it had properties which indicated it would be an antidote to adrenochrome. We tested this idea in a pilot experiment, and soon after we completed the first double-blind, controlled experiment in psychiatry. (It should be noted that in England physicians had used this type of test to measure the therapeutic effects of aspirin and steroids on arthritis.)

One of the earliest references to a controlled experiment in American literature was the study by Cowan, Diehl and Baker. They reported that "the students were assigned alternately and without selection to an experimental and to a control group. The students in the control group were treated exactly like those in the experimental groups except that they received placebos instead of the vitamin preparations." But this was not a randomized study. Modern biostatisticians are very unhappy with their procedure for selecting the two groups. Further, there is no statement to prove the study, which was undoubtedly single-blind rather than double-blind. With a single-blind design the investigators know the treatment code. Again this is not considered a good experiment.

With positive results we launched a number of similar controlled studies and a large number of clinical, nonblind studies. We confirmed Kaufman's arthritis studies, corroborated that the vitamin helped recover senile confusional states, and discovered that nicotinic acid (but not nicotinamide) lowered cholesterol levels. This was fortunate for all American physicians using large doses of nicotinic acid, because nicotinic acid was subsequently cleared by the Food and Drug Administration as a hypocholesterolemic substance and thus can be used freely by physicians without having to obtain individual FDA approval.

Since our early findings, a large number of psychiatrists have developed what is now known as orthomolecular psychiatry. Most of the medical literature, therefore, was written by psychiatrists for psychiatrists, or for the public interested in psychiatric problems. Over the past fifteen years a large number of physicians—not psychiatrists—have developed orthomolecular medicine. But medical literature in this instance is more diffuse. A large number of books have appeared dealing with nutrition or with special diets, but there are very few which describe physical diseases and how they can be treated.

A physician who wishes to become familiar with orthomolecular medicine may do so by simply beginning with a sugar-free diet and one or two vitamins. Even with this simple approach, physicians who have used this treatment are so persuaded by the results that they have become orthomolecular physicians. I know of none who, after one year of practice, have reverted to their previous methods. Another way is to take one of the training courses provided by organizations such as the Huxley Institute for Biosocial Research, the Academy of Orthomolecular Psychiatry and the Orthomolecular Medical Association.

Unfortunately, physicians do not have a single volume which contains the information they need to practice orthomolecular medicine. They could assemble such a book, but they would have to spend much time gathering material from the medical literature; this deters many from starting. For this reason I have prepared this book for general practitioners.

The basis for all medical practice is clinical nutrition. I have thus included a section on orthomolecular, or clinical, nutrition. General practitioners practicing orthomolecular medicine can treat many psychiatric patients successfully; there is a section on orthomolecular psychiatry for them.

The main body of this book contains descriptions of how orthomolecular medicine is used to treat diseases of the various organ systems—such as gastrointestinal disorders, arthritis, autoimmune diseases, and even cancer. I will not repeat information already taught in medical schools and already available in standard medical books. This book is not a replacement for information already known dealing with pathology, course of the disease, etc. It is to be used in conjunction with the standard core of information already established. Nor is orthomolecular treatment a replacement for standard treatment. A proportion of patients will require orthodox treatment, a proportion will do much better on orthomolecular treatment, and the rest will need a skillful blend of both.

I have discussed a small number of diseases, avoiding those which I have not treated personally. Nor have I attempted to describe all the conditions which some have found treatable by orthomolecular methods. I have never used chelation therapy so I have not discussed this, even though it is a very important method of treatment. It is undeservedly controversial. In my opinion, this is another example of a debate—not scientific but emotional—precipitated by physicians who are ignorant of the method and its results. Morton Walker and Garry Gordon have published an excellent review. *The Chelation Answer*, (M. Evans and Co., Inc., 216 East 49th St., New York, NY 10017, 1982). Nor have I discussed the treatment of viral diseases including AIDS. I have had no experience treating viruses in general and have treated only one AIDS case, diagnosed by his physician. He recovered on a combination of ascorbic acid, B vitamins, diet, and Mycostatin.

Nor have I given any space to candidiasis. This is described in a most comprehensive way by the following colleagues and friends:

Truss, C. O., *The Missing Diagnosis*, C. O. Truss Publishing, 2614 Highland Ave., Birmingham, AL 35205, 1983.

Crook, W. C., *The Yeast Connection*, Professional Books, P.O. Box 3494, Jackson, TN 38301, 1983 and 1984.

Trowbridge, J. P., & Walker, M., *The Yeast Syndrome*, Bantam Books, Inc., 666 Fifth Ave., New York, NY 10103, 1986.

## CHAPTER REFERENCE

Cowan, D. W., Diehl, H. S., & Baker, A. B. Vitamins for the prevention of colds. *JAMA* 20 (16):1268–1271. December 19, 1942.

# CHAPTER 1

## NUTRITION

The basis for good health is nutrition. When malnutrition or starvation are present, it is impossible to respond effectively to any medical treatment. Few medical schools provide their students with a useful understanding of the importance of nutrition in generating disease and how to correct diet when they treat patients. Physicians have abdicated their responsibility in favor of nutritionists, who are usually biochemists, and to dieticians. Very few clinical nutritionists practice in hospitals. It is not surprising that hospitals are so naive about nutrition, and that most of their patients suffer more from malnutrition on discharge than they do on admission.

Medical students pay little attention to nonclinical nutritionists. In no other medical specialty is the basic teaching left to nonmedical specialists. It is clear to many of them that nutrition must be unimportant in the hierarchy of medical specialties. It is equally clear to them that it plays no role in medical practice. But orthomolecular physicians have adopted nutrition as a main component of any medical, surgical, or psychiatric treatment.

### WHAT KIND OF FOOD DO WE NEED?

We must live on food that our bodies can digest and which will provide us with the essential nutrients we must have. These are nutrients which cannot be made in the body. In other words, we must eat food to which we have adapted during our evolution.

Animals are divided into three main groups according to their major food source. Carnivores live primarily on meat. Herbivores live primarily on vegetation. The third group is called omnivores because they can live on, and in fact require a large variety of, foods from animal and vegetable sources. The last group includes man, apes, gorillas, bears, etc.

Herbivores have adapted to their food supply by developing a digestive system which can break down the cellulose-rich foods and digest them. Carnivores have different digestive tracts. Omnivores have systems which can deal with some vegetable food and all flesh, but which cannot break down grass, for example, to its elementary glucose. It is not difficult to understand why forcing cows to live on meat or feeding lions grass would make them ill. In other words, our health depends upon eating food to which we have been adapted over 100,000 years of evolution.

Unfortunately, most of our food is processed and has been so altered that it bears little resemblance to the food consumed by our caveman ancestors. For most of our evolutionary development we lived on food which is similar to food consumed by animals and fish, who still live in a natural state. The best zoos try to follow this principle in feeding their animals.

We, as omnivores, are not all alike. We differ physically in stature, in personality, in blood types, and in fingerprints. We also differ in our nutritional requirements. The range is enormous, sweeping across the omnivore spectrum from people who are almost entirely carnivores and well to people who are almost entirely vegetarian and well. Most are somewhere in between. There is no single diet which is "the" diet for everyone. When anyone recommends "the" diet for everyone, it is a lie. Many may be helped, but not all. So far there is no generally accepted way, except by trial and error, of determining an individual's optimum diet.

Our food requirements also vary with age, activity, sex, stress, and presence of disease. An infant can digest human milk but he may be lactose intolerant when he becomes an adult. A pregnant woman must have a diet which is different from her nonpregnancy diet. Most people are dimly aware of this.

Requirements for supplements also vary. The need for any one nutrient may vary a thousandfold, though usually a narrower range of variation exists. The need for supplements decreases as the nutritional quality of all the food on our plates increases.

## WHAT KIND OF FOOD HAVE WE BEEN ADAPTED TO?

Although we cannot be certain of it, the evidence is overwhelming that our ancestral food was of much higher quality than is our modern, high-tech food. Evidence is available from anthropological studies, from studies of people still living on food little damaged by food technology, and from studies of animals in zoos and their optimum requirements. This primitive food can be described by six adjectives: whole, alive, nontoxic, variable, indigenous and scarce. In sharp contrast, modern food to a large degree, as consumed by most people, can be described as artifact, dead, toxic, monotonous, exotic and overly abundant. Any diet which can be described by the

six positive adjectives, whether it is mostly vegetarian or meat, will be suitable for people.

### Whole

Animals in their native state eat whole foods. Deer graze on leaves and berries. Wolves eat other animals. Bears eat fish, animals, insects and vegetation. Our ancestors seldom luxuriated in too much food. Scarcity is a great motivation not to waste food. They ate all the edible portions of animals, cracking bones to get at the marrow. They ate whole grains when they could get them. The advantage of whole foods is that they contain all the nutrients needed to keep life going. But whether there was an initial advantage or not, we have been locked into a system that demands we eat foods we have adapted to, and we have adapted to whole foods.

### Alive

In the native state animals, especially carnivores, eat food which is alive or has recently been alive. The advantage is that this food has not deteriorated by loss of nutrients, by oxidation, and by contamination with bacteria and fungi. When food does not have to be stored, there are no storage problems.

### Nontoxic

Most plant species are poisonous for man. Our ancestors used two main guidelines. Did the plant taste neutral, sweet, or bitter? And did it make one sick or dead? By trial and error we discovered which plants and which portions of plants we could eat. Theoretically there is no nontoxic food, since every species is foreign and can induce injury in some. However, food plants are relatively nontoxic and will do no harm if our diet adheres to the six rules described by the six adjectives.

### Variable

Our ancestors' diet depended upon time of day and season as well as on geography. They were wanderers who followed their food supply, as did the !Kung in the Kalahari

Desert until recently. When we eat a large variety of foods, we are less apt to become allergic to any one food. This variability also increases the nutritional quality of the diet, since one food's surplus of some nutrients can compensate for other foods' deficiencies. The American Indian formerly ate a much larger variety of foods than we or they do today.

### Indigenous

Animals and plants adapt to cold weather by changing their ratio of omega-3 to omega-6 essential fatty acids. Omega-3 EFAs are more liquid, freeze at lower temperatures and, as antifreeze protects our cars, they protect our bodies. If we eat foods grown locally, we already start with a ratio of omega-3 to omega-6 suited to that climate and we need to do less work biochemically to try to create the correct ratio in our bodies. It is difficult to correct this ratio without using the right foods. People who live on indigenous (locally produced) foods will be healthier and adapt more readily to their climate.

### Scarce

It is unlikely that there was any surplus of food until agriculture developed about ten thousand years ago. The best proof is that the world's population did not begin its explosive increase until agriculture developed. There always was and always will be a strict relationship between the number of people and the supply of food—famine victims in Africa will attest to that. We have not adapted to a superabundance. We have adapted to temporary abundance followed by temporary starvation. I doubt there were many obese cavemen and -women.

These are the main attributes of the food to which we have adapted, the kind of foods animals eat in their native state and the kind of foods fed to their animals by the best zoos (Hoffer 1983). It is not the kind of food we feed people in hospitals, nursing homes, restaurants, cafes, and in most of our homes.

## WHAT KIND OF FOOD DO WE EAT?

The food we feed patients in hospitals (and everywhere else) is accurately described by the six negative adjectives. I do not mean to imply that our ancestors were wiser than we are today. They ate more nutritiously because they had no choice. In the same way, animals eat wisely when they have no choice. When cavemen and -women began food technology by inventing fire and cooking, they could not have foreseen how this would eventually destroy the quality of our food. But we do know better.

Yet the professionals to whom society entrusted the quality of our food, the physicians and the nutritionists, have failed to behave responsibly, often advocating junk diets when they knew this was wrong. Society believed that the physicians and nutritionists knew something about clinical nutrition. Therefore, we must have a new profession, a group who will understand the connection between good food and health, between sick food and disease.

### Artifact

Food is fractionated. The better or more nutritious fractions are discarded or fed to our livestock. The protein, fat and carbohydrate are isolated and then recombined into material that looks, smells, and tastes like food but is not. It is possible to make caviar from starch, black dye, and salt. No natural food is safe from exploitation. Even fish is now being processed to appear like it is another, more desirable, fish material. Artifacts do not contain the nutrients present in the original food and often contain chemicals not present in the original food.

### Dead

Modern food has to be stored because there is such a long distance between the farm and the kitchen. Store-bought must be kept free of bacteria and fungi and its enzymes must be removed or suppressed; this is difficult to do with whole food. Thus, it is easier to store white flour than whole-wheat flour. To be prepared for storage, food may have to be heat-treated, pasteurized, canned, cooled or frozen. The most devitalized foods keep best. The longer food is stored, the less nutritious it becomes.

### Toxic

Modern food, especially processed food, contains two types of additives—chemicals used to enhance preferred qualities such as taste, smell, color, stability, etc. The best known are the cosmetic additives. But processed foods also contain trace or hidden additives—chemicals used in preparing the artifacts that are used in preparing the final processed food artifact. The final food processor is probably not even aware these additives are present, and they are not listed on the final label.

Modern foods are not toxic immediately, although when one sees how sugar can turn a normal child into a hyperactive tyrant in an hour, it is difficult not to consider it as toxic as any poison. Modern foods are insidious and they can destroy over several years. That is why it is so difficult to establish a cause and effect relationship.

### Monotonous

The high-tech food industry depends upon having large amounts of a few plant foods—our staples, including sugar, wheat, oats, corn, milk and cheese. These few food sources are reworked and recombined into an amazing variety of processed foods. A modern supermarket may contain 10,000 to 20,000 different items. There may be a hundred different boxed breakfast cereals, yet all are made from sugar, wheat, oats or corn, plus additives. It is this monotonous, repetitive attack on our bodies by the same artifact foods that is responsible for a huge proportion of all allergies.

### Exotic

These are foods grown in one climatic area and sent to another; usually north or south. Bananas are exotic to Canada, while flaxseed or wheat in the Sahara would be equally exotic. There is some reason to believe the most dangerous movement is from tropical to cold climatic areas, because tropical plants do not contain enough of the omega-3 essential fatty acids needed in the cold areas, while they are not needed in tropical areas and probably are not harmful.

### Surplus

Not only is our food bad, we have too much of it, so that perhaps one-quarter of the people in high-tech societies are obese. The problems of obesity and the other diseases caused by excessive consumption of food, especially sugar, are enormous. The term "the Saccharine Disease" has been coined to describe these diseases (Cleave 1975).

## A FEW SIMPLE RULES

Most patients will not appreciate being told they must eat food which is whole, alive, nontoxic, variable, indigenous, and scarce. Once they are interested in the possible connection between malnutrition and their discomfort, they want to know as simply as possible which foods they should eat and which foods they should avoid. Yet, most physicians do not have enough time or interest in nutritional counseling, nor do they have available nutritionists to whom their patients can be referred. Fortunately, one need know only a few simple rules. These are: (1) no junk food; and (2) avoid any food you know makes you sick. Junk food is defined as any food which contains added sugar and additives. The no-junk diet is easy to understand and relatively easy to follow. Later on, as the patient becomes more familiar with diet, more specific information will be given.

## WHAT IS THE HARM IN EATING FOODS TO WHICH WE ARE NOT ADAPTED?

The food industry, most doctors and most nutritionists advise us there is no harm in eating modern food if our diet is "balanced." The term *balanced meal* has been a favorite one used by nutritionists for many years. It means that the optimum proportion (balance) of all necessary food components is provided. But it has come to mean something else. Most nutritionists, in the name of a balanced meal, consider that even larger quantities of sucrose in a meal are fine provided that it is balanced against some protein, fat and the essential vitamins and minerals. This leads to the preposterous statement that junk cereal and milk are nutritious, whereas in reality the cereal has diluted the nutritional quality of the milk. Some nutritionists consider the doughnut made from white flour, oil and sugar plus a tiny quantity of vitamins a good food, presumably because it is balanced. The U.S. Department of Agriculture advises that a couple of doughnuts plus a glass of milk provide a balanced meal.

The concept of balance was originally useful, but it has been corrupted by our food technology and no longer serves any useful purpose. However, there is no better word, and I will use it in its original sense—to denote the importance of using optimum quantities of all the essential nutrients. This is best achieved by obtaining these from a variety of foods, which are more apt to satisfy our needs than is a dependence upon any one food.

Food should be balanced in itself, within each meal, and over the entire day. The best way to ensure balance in a food is to use only whole food which nature has already balanced. Balance in a meal is achieved by eating several foods from different groups, such as meats, fresh vegetables, fruits, dairy products, nuts and seeds. Balance over the whole day is ensured by eating balanced meals every time a meal is consumed. Snacks need not be made from a variety of foods as they are minor components of our diet, but they must be whole foods, not doughnuts, chocolate bars and other junk.

Clinical nutritionists, orthomolecular physicians, and some clinical ecologists have seen how correcting a patient's diet leads directly to their recovery. It does not require a major leap in logic to conclude that had the patient followed the optimum diet all along, that disease would not have occurred.

Modern diets differ from diets we have adapted to in a number of ways. Protein levels, fat and lipid levels, and carbohydrate levels may be too high or too low. This applies to vitamin and mineral levels as well. But it is too simplistic to talk about too much or too little of any food component. One individual can eat only so many calories. If the amount of one is increased, there must be a reduction in the quantity of another. If one increases the protein level there must be a decrease in fats and carbohydrates. For this reason, studies that take into account only fats and their relation to coronary disease but ignore carbohydrate levels will yield very low correlation or association, even if there were a high association.

I will describe the most common fault with modern food, and what that fault does to people. This is the low-protein, high-sugar, low-fiber diet which causes the Saccharine Disease.

## CARBOHYDRATES

There is a common belief that all carbohydrates are the same and that all sugars are the same. Nutritionists have fallen into the same serious error. They reason that, since carbohydrates are eventually broken down into simple sugars such as glucose and fructose, they are all the same. They do not recognize the importance of the bulk of the food, nor the presence of other essential nutrients in the carbohydrate-rich foods, nor the importance of the rate at which sugar is released in the digestive tract and absorbed into the blood. Nor do they recognize that artifacts such as sucrose (table sugar) are not absorbed and metabolized as are the complex carbohydrates.

It is, therefore, essential to understand a bit of the chemistry of the carbohydrates.

Carbohydrates are divided into complex long-chain carbohydrates and into short-chain carbohydrates or sugars. Each carbohydrate is composed of a large number of molecules, which have five, or more commonly six, carbon atoms in a chain. These are sugars such as glucose, fructose or lactose. The sugar glucose consists of individual molecules attached to one another in a chemical bond. Glucose is called a monosaccharide. Monosaccharides are usually glucose, fructose and galactose. The main sugar in the blood and body is glucose. It is the sugar given usually in 100-gram amounts before the common sugar tolerance test is done. It is an essential sugar in the body but it is not essential as a pure substance in our food. All the cells of the body depend upon glucose, the brain more so than the rest of the body. Glucose is made in the body by splitting complex sugars or carbohydrates into their basic units, yielding mostly sugar. This process begins in the mouth when the saliva is chewed into our food. The saliva contains enzymes that split (hydrolyze) these carbohydrates into simple sugars. Hydrolysis continues in the stomach until the process is inhibited by the acidity of the stomach, but it begins again when the food enters the small intestine, especially after the pancreatic juices are mixed with the food.

Glucose is the energy sugar. But the food industry, when it claims that sugar is a good source of energy, leaves the impression that sucrose, the common table sugar from beets or sugarcane, is a good source of energy. It is, on the contrary, the cause of a large number of physical diseases, all manifestations of the Saccharine Disease, and of a large number of depressions, anxiety states, alcoholism and other addictions. This will be examined later. Glucose in its pure form is probably as dangerous. The apparent paradox arises from the fact that only the slow release of glucose from food, in conjunction with the release of the other nutrients, makes it safe. Pure glucose, devoid of any other nutrients, is nearly as harmful as sucrose. Patients who develop violent reactions after drinking 100 grams of glucose before the sugar tolerance test have no doubt about this. The severe nausea and vomiting, headache, and other equally unpleasant reactions can be very persuasive.

Another monosaccharide is fructose. It is present in fruit. It is probably somewhat less toxic than either glucose or sucrose for two reasons. It tastes sweeter weight for weight, and less is used in order to achieve the same sweetness satiation. And it does not stimulate the pancreas to release insulin. However, consumed in large quantities it is bad since it too does not contain a normal quota of other nutrients. Like glucose, when fructose is released in the body from food, it is not harmful and is a useful source of energy. But there is no physiological need for free fructose from external sources.

Fructose, either in the form of tablets or as a free-flowing crystalline or powdery material, is just as harmful as sucrose, even though it is available primarily in health food stores. It is not a safe substitute for pure sucrose or glucose or for any other pure sugar.

The third common monosaccharide is galactose, present chiefly as one of the components of lactose or the sugar present in milk— milk sugar. It tends to be less sweet than either glucose or fructose.

Disaccharides are sugars which have two monosaccharides linked to each other chemically. The two common ones are sucrose, which consists of one glucose and one fructose molecule, and lactose, which consists of glucose and galactose hooked to each other. These more complex sugars must be hydrolyzed into the simple monosaccharides before they are absorbed into the blood. If they are not split they will remain in the bowel and become a source of calories for bacteria. They can produce serious gastrointestinal upsets. The body has enzymes that split these double sugars, called sucrase (the one that hydrolyzes sucrose) and lactase (the one that hydrolyzes lactose).

Sucrose is by far the most common sugar. The average consumption of this sugar is about 120 pounds per person per year—for men, women and children. This means that half the population consumes more. This figure is arrived at by dividing the total sugar consumption of any nation by the total population. It includes sugar used in confectionaries, candies, soft drinks, breakfast foods, canned soups and so on. It is so ubiquitous that it is very difficult to follow a sugar-free program. It is found even in foods where one would least suspect its presence.

When sucrose is consumed, it is rapidly hydrolyzed and absorbed and then quickly shunted into the liver and converted into triglycerides. These fats are then released into the blood and stored in the fat depots. Of all the common sugars, sucrose is converted into triglycerides the most quickly.

Sucrose is very toxic because it does not carry with it the normal quota of other nutrients and because it is released into the blood too quickly. When sugar beet or cane sugar are consumed they are not nearly as toxic, since they are present in diluted form in a bulky vehicle which cannot be consumed too quickly. The relationship of pure sucrose to the Saccharine Disease and to relative hypoglycemia will be examined further on. In other words, the sucrose present in natural food is not toxic but commercial or household sucrose is. To advertise and promote sucrose as a pure energy-producing food is fraudulent. No drug company would be allowed to promulgate similar misleading information. I am in full agreement that sucrose ought to be barred from human use. It should be converted entirely into alcohol, which could be used as a fuel for our cars. In this way it would conserve our dwindling supplies of petroleum. The protein, vitamins and minerals could be fed to livestock.

These monosaccharides and disaccharides are processed into highly refined sugars, as they do not commonly exist in this pure form in nature. One exception is honey, which contains large quantities of glucose, fructose and sucrose. In the spring, when there is insufficient pollen for the foraging bees, some beekeepers feed them sucrose syrup. This is then deposited into the honey. Later during the year, as more pollen becomes available, less and less sucrose is fed. During summer and fall very little sucrose is found in honey. If one is allergic to beet or cane sugar it would be as reactive in the honey as in the pure state. For this reason late summer and fall honey are preferable, but this means getting honey from a beekeeper and not from the supermarket. In areas where sucrose is never fed, this would not be a problem. Honey is somewhat safer than sucrose because it is sweeter due to the fructose content, so that less is needed, and, because it is not as pure and as refined as sucrose, it contains very small quantities of vitamins and minerals. If used to replace sucrose in the same quantity, it is just as toxic.

The complex saccharides are composed of very long chains of glucose molecules attached to each other, which vary in length from the rather short-chain carbohydrates such as glycogen to the very long, fibrous foods such as fiber. These carbohydrates are called polysaccharides. They have different properties. They are not sweet but tend to be bland like potatoes. They are not easily dissolved in water as are the simple sugars, and they have structural properties not found in simple sugars. They are, therefore, not as toxic as are simple sugars. Because of their bulk it takes more time to eat them, and because they are hydrolyzed slowly in the digestive system, the sugar (glucose) released does not enter the blood as quickly. They tend to produce an even flow of sugar compared to the water-soluble sugars. For example, it would take a while to eat five apples (or potatoes or carrots) one after the other. The mechanical problem of chewing and swallowing slows down the rate of consumption. In addition there is a natural process of becoming satiated. On the other hand, the same amount of glucose or sucrose can be dissolved in a few ounces of water and can be swallowed in ten seconds. An enormous amount of sugar can be dumped quickly into the stomach. Furthermore, since these complex polysaccharides are not sweet they do not pervert one's palate as do the sweet sugars.

Pure complex carbohydrates are also artifacts, as they are not found in a refined state in nature, where they are surrounded and mixed with protein, fat, vitamins and minerals. For this reason the foods naturally rich in carbohydrates are good food, not dangerous. These are called natural, unrefined, or unprocessed carbohydrates. The processed carbohydrates are substances such as starch. They are toxic but not as bad as the mono- and disaccharides. The unprocessed carbohydrates also contain very complex polysaccharides which cannot be hydrolyzed in the body. There are no enzymes that can process them. These substances are the celluloses like wood, husk or bran. As they are not hydrolyzed they soak up liquid as they pass through the digestive tract and there play a very useful role. This will be examined further on.

In general, unprocessed (unrefined) carbohydrates are safe while processed (refined) foods are not. The degree of toxicity depends upon the degree of refinement. Thus, whole wheat is nontoxic unless one is allergic to it. During processing it is cracked and ground and the central portion, the endosperm, is sifted out. The outer coats, bran, germ, and the layers next to the bran and germ are taken away for other uses. When the whole kernel is used, the flour is called a 100 percent extraction flour. If the middle or inner endosperm is used, it is called a 60 or 70 percent extraction. Thus the higher the percent extraction the more germ and bran are present

and the more nutritious is the wheat flour. The wheat kernel's main function is to grow a new plant. Growth starts from the germ. It is, therefore, logical for the essential nutrients of the germinating plant to be as close to the germ as possible.

Many years ago when I was a cereal chemist, I studied the pattern of distribution of thiamine (B1) and riboflavin (B2) in the kernel. The various fractions from the mill were analyzed. The highest concentrations of these vitamins were found in the bran and germ and the lowest in the endosperm, i.e., in white flour. Before the kernel ripens or hardens it is green and the contents of the kernel are fluid or milky. When growth is completed and the kernel begins to mature, the rate of loss of water from the kernel by evaporation into air is greater than the rate of admission from the stem into the kernel. This is why it dries and becomes very hard. It occurred to me that the movement of water from within the kernel to the outer coats and into the air swept the nutrients with it and deposited them near the germ and bran. Mathematical equations I developed from physicochemical laws gave a fairly good approximation of the actual distribution. I examined the effect of two opposing forces: one the force of translocation produced by the evaporating water, and the other a counter force of diffusion, that would tend to equalize the distribution. This work was not published and remains, at least to me, an interesting idea only.

## TOO MUCH CARBOHYDRATE

### Unprocessed

Excessive consumption of carbohydrate foods such as potatoes, wheat, rice and so on will cause obesity and will produce an imbalance associated with an inadequate intake of protein and fat. The dangers of excess are similar to the dangers of taking too much of any food which is deficient in other essential nutrients. Because of the bulk of unprocessed carbohydrate-rich foods, it is difficult to over-consume them.

### Processed

These include all the preparations rich in added sugar or prepared in such a way that they have lost a large proportion of other essential nutrients. This includes polished rice, white flour and a variety of substances made from them.

Excessive consumption of processed (refined) carbohydrates is the major cause of a broad group of neuroses and of a large number of physical illnesses. Until recently these were looked upon as unrelated diseases with no known etiology. However, it has become apparent that they are diseases caused by malnutrition. It may help many people, who suffer from these diseases, to embrace the principles of supernutrition if they become aware why they are ill. I will, therefore, discuss first the neuroses and then the psychosomatic conditions.

## THE NEUROSES

Neuroses or psychoneuroses are psychiatric diseases that mainly alter mood. These changes are quantitatively different in degree from mood changes that are part of the normal reactions of people. Neuroses bring no perceptual changes, *i.e.*, no perceptual illusions and hallucinations, no thought disorder, and therefore no schizophrenia. The distinction between neuroses and early schizophrenia may be very difficult to ascertain. The presence of early perceptual changes can be determined by the use of perceptual tests such as the HOD and the EWI.

Neuroses must also be distinguished from the psychotic depressions. Attempts have been made to distinguish between reactive depressions and endogenous depressions. A reactive depression is said to be present when the feeling of sadness is appropriate to the psychosocial environment. Thus, mourning is normal after a bereavement. This is an example of a reactive depression. An endogenous depression is one which is independent of the environment. The distinction is very difficult to make, since the decision whether a depression is reactive is made by the psychiatrist, who tends to judge this by the way he might react to a similar event or series of events. There is also a tendency to believe depressed patients, who in most cases find some psychosocial explanation for their depression and will find ample reason to be depressed even though there may be no relationship whatever.

In most cases, anxiety and depression co-exist in varying proportions, and it is difficult to determine how relevant each is in the total clinical picture. Depression may be the primary symptom, followed by anxiety over the presence of the depression and the impact it is having upon the person; or anxiety may be the primary symptom, with a responding depression because of the discomfort engendered by the anxiety. In this section I will, therefore, discuss neuroses where anxiety or tension are the primary symptoms.

The neuroses must also be distinguished from psychopathic disorders. The diagnosis of a psychopathic disorder is based on behavioral changes. Psychopathy has been defined as: (1) a failure to learn how to give and take love; (2) an inability to form stable interpersonal relationships; (3) a failure to develop a normal conscience, with possible absence of guilt or remorse. These patients are very impulsive, overreact emotionally, and often engage in antisocial behavior. One might say they are behaviorally inappropriate.

I will consider only those conditions characterized by abnormal anxiety and tension, in the absence of perceptual changes and thought disorder, and with depression secondary to the anxiety. The absence or presence of somatic symptoms will be irrelevant for the diagnosis.

Since this is not a textbook of psychiatry, I will not discuss the various forms of neuroses nor the diagnostic subgroups. Nor will I discuss the psychosocial therapies that have been and are still being used. This information is available in any standard textbook of psychiatry.

Orthomolecular psychiatry has been interested in the biochemical aspects of the neuroses, and these only will be considered. These are the diseases caused by malnutrition or faulty nutrition.

## THE NEUROSES: DISEASES OF MALNUTRITION

One of the difficulties in diagnosing anxiety is that it is a normal reaction to any illness. Any threat to the health and comfort of any person is apt to generate a good deal of anxiety. It is also a product of most forms of malnutrition. The two most common forms of malnutrition that cause anxiety relate to some of the B vitamins and to the excessive consumption of processed and refined foods. Since any vitamin deficiency will produce one or another form of ill health, it would be logical that a deficiency of any vitamin can cause anxiety. However, the B vitamins seem to be more closely related to anxiety than the other vitamins. Perhaps that is because they are most apt to be needed in extra quantities. The B vitamin-related neuroses will be discussed in Chapter Three of this book.

## THE CARBOHYDRATE NEUROSES

Another large group of patients suffering from depression and anxiety are the ones who overconsume sugars and the other processed or refined foods such as white bread, pastries, etc. The conditions produced by this type of malnutrition have been called the Saccharine Disease by Cleave, Campbell and Painter (1969) and more recently by Cleave (1975), at least for the physical manifestations of this disease. These researchers did not include the psychiatric components of this major syndrome, but I have no doubt it is as real and as pervasive, because these components are coexistent in such a large proportion of patients. It is rare to find patients with the physical expression of the Saccharine Disease who do not also suffer from many of the mood changes typically found in the neuroses. It is more common to find many with serious mood disorders who do not have the physical components. The main difference is that patients whose main symptoms are physical will be more apt to receive somatic treatment, whereas patients whose symptoms are mainly psychiatric are more apt to wind up in the psychiatrist's office. In both cases malnutrition is the last thing to be considered, if it is considered at all.

Cleave's arguments supporting his conception of the Saccharine Disease will be presented here. This disease results from an enormous increase in the consumption of refined or processed foods, especially sugar and white flour. The unnatural refined carbohydrates must be sharply differentiated from the complex carbohydrates. It is not the total consumption of carbohydrates which is harmful but the consumption of the refined carbohydrates. The natural carbohydrates such as whole-grain cereals are not harmful. On the contrary, they are very essential. Cleave had considered using the term "Refined Carbohydrate Disease" but found the term "Saccharine Disease" preferable for a variety of reasons. This is defined as a single disease afflicting many different organs, including the brain, as I will later show.

The two chief refined carbohydrates are: (1) sugar, which is a pure chemical (a disaccharide) extracted and refined from sugar beet or cane (left behind are all the other constituents of these plants—the protein, fat, fiber, vitamins, and minerals); and (2) white flour, which has been severely emasculated of its nutritive value. White bread has been used for several thousand years, but it did not become cheap enough for general consumption until about the end of the eighteenth century. Nor was the technology so well developed. In terms of evolution and adaptation, we have had only a moment in a very long history in which to develop any biological adaptation. For example, the Eskimo of northern Canada have probably had only 50 years, and the !Kung of the Kalahari Desert only about a decade.

The situation has been much different with respect to table sugar. In Britain in 1815, about 15 pounds of sugar were consumed per person per year. Today it is close to 125 pounds. Recently I saw a woman complaining of severe anxiety and tension who consumed up to 350 grams of sugar (over half a pound) per day in the form of soft drinks. Her yearly intake of sugar must have been close to 250 pounds per year. The total amount consumed is still rising. There have been two interruptions in this trend. During the wars of 1914 to 1918, sugar consumption dropped to about 65 pounds, as it did again during the last world war of 1939 to 1944. This was due to the blockade that prevented shipment of sugar from overseas. In England during the wars there was a significant improvement in the general health of the nation, something which was very surprising and perhaps even disappointing to the psychosomatic theorists who had predicted that the increased psychosocial stress of the war would increase the incidence of the so-called psychosomatic diseases. But after the wars the consumption of sugar rose rapidly until it reached its present level. There is no reason to suspect that the consumption has reached its maximum, since the massive intake of sugar produces a form of addiction that drives the intake up and up. This phenomenon has been specific for the industrial nations, but the drive to export has expanded to the entire globe. Just as bad money drives out good money, so does bad (sweetened) food drive out good food. Many nations who can ill afford to do so are importing increasing quantities of high-sugar-content foods and decreasing their intake of nutritious natural foods.

A few years ago my wife and I holidayed in Mexico. We enjoyed Mexican food, and in the morning we would often order a breakfast consisting of tortilla made from corn covered by two fried eggs with a side order of beans. This was a very filling and satisfying meal, very inexpensive, and it kept us from being hungry until evening. This was a great advantage when sightseeing. At the same time we would observe the ordering habits of the Mexicans in the same restaurant. To our surprise they would more frequently order the American breakfast consisting of pancakes (white flour) that they covered with syrup, white toast that they covered with jam, and coffee containing ample quantities of sugar. During that week I read a lament by a public health official of Mexico at a medical meeting that up to 40 percent of the tested population of Mexico were prediabetic (probably hypoglycemic). It was obvious that the American food was considered more nutritious and valuable since it cost twice as much.

The average figure of 125 pounds is derived by dividing the total sugar consumption by the total number of people, including infants. This means that the mean intake of adults must be much higher than that. It means that half the population are consuming more than 125 pounds, and many are consuming very much more. There are reports of many young people deriving 50 percent of their calories from sugar. The patient just referred to consumed about half her calories in the form of sugar. Surprisingly, she was not fat.

We live in an industrialized culture permeated and saturated with sugar. For an additional excellent analysis of the toxic effects of sugar, see Yudkin (1972). Professor Yudkin recommends that it be banned. Anyone who reads his work carefully must agree, even though it seems almost impossible for this to happen. However, if we were to decrease our consumption to about half of what it is today, to about the level forced upon England by the two wars, there is little doubt there would be a major improvement in our national health.

As with refined flour, there has been no time to adapt to this newer diet. I do not see how one could ever adapt unless a few humans develop a gastrointestinal system and bacterial flora which will be able to synthesize vitamins, protein and fat from the sugar. But this system could not make the minerals that are required. Even if such a development were possible, it would require many hundreds of thousands of years. During this time the toll on human life and the degree of disease will have been enormous. I do not think we should wait for nature; we should instead use our intelligence and our newer knowledge of nutrition. By simply reverting to the type of food to which we have been adapted we can immediately begin to save humanity from a very large fraction of the diseases it will otherwise continue to suffer.

Technology can be used in two ways. It can be used as it has been in Western society to enhance the palatability of food, *i.e.*, to make it colorful, tasteful, easily served, and stable for long storage while more or less ignoring its nutritional quality; or it may be used to improve the quality of natural foods by skillful preparatory techniques. The undesirable techniques have been amply described and documented. Examples of the beneficial technological methods are less well known.

The preparation of corn (maize) by the alkali processing technique was known for at least 2,000 years. Corn, as prepared by most white people, is an inadequate food, and heavy reliance upon it as a main food was responsible for the pandemic of pellagra present in the United States until vitamin B3 was added to wheat products at the beginning of the last war. Tortillas are a food made from corn cooked with alkali. Rats and pigs fed on tortillas are healthier than those fed with ordinary corn. Tortillas in Central America are made by heating dried corn to almost boiling in a 50 percent solution of lime in water for 30 to 50 minutes. It is then cooled, the solution remaining is poured off, and treated corn

is washed thoroughly and drained. It is then ground finely and cooked into pancakes. Apparently this process increases the availability of some of the essential amino acids, increases the ratio of isoleucine to leucine, and increases the availability of vitamin B3, which in corn is almost unavailable otherwise. People living on tortillas are, therefore, less apt to develop pellagra.

Researchers have concluded that people who had not discovered this method of preparing corn would be more apt to suffer malnutrition. A careful examination of 51 different societies proved that corn remained a major source of food only for those societies that were using the alkali preparing method. Seven societies were high consumers and cultivators of corn and used the alkali technique. None of the 12 societies that were both low cultivators and consumers used alkali. The mean difference was statistically highly significant. Katz concluded that maize became an extensive part of the diet only when alkali cooking techniques were used. This practice developed at least by the year 100 B.C. Lime-soaking pots were already in use then at Teotihuacán, the first urban center in Mesoamerica.

It is highly unlikely that people who turned to the alkali technique would be aware of the nutritional benefit produced by their discovery. Certainly huge numbers of people living within several hundred miles of Mexico, in the U.S.A. seemed unaware that perhaps some of the ravages of pellagra which killed them by the hundreds could have been prevented by this simple procedure. Over the centuries, people who adopted the alkali process must have been dimly aware that they felt better or that they were healthier, and they associated this improved health to the new way of preparing corn. Later the technique would become part of the cultural tradition or even given religious values. Once the technique became generally used it would in an evolutionary way produce a superior race of people biologically. The alkali users must have gradually displaced those who, either through ignorance or due to opposing views, did not follow such a technique. The interesting thing about this development is that primitive people were able to improve their nutrition by depending solely upon very gradual improvements in health. This, then, is in contradistinction to the other evolutionary mechanism by which animals learn to avoid foods that make them sick within the next few hours.

The best recent example of using modern technology to improve food originated during the last war, when enrichment of flour was brought into general use. It was generally conceded that whole-wheat flour was more nutritious than white flour, but for many reasons whole-wheat bread was not generally available or used. Perhaps only 10 percent of the population used whole-wheat bread. This percentage may be much higher now, following some valuable new information about its benefits. I am certain that the manufacturers will meet the demand once they become aware of it, even if they will not spend much money extolling its better nutritional quality. It was agreed in 1941 that the addition of small quantities of thiamine (B1), riboflavin (B2), and niacinamide (B3) to white flour would restore some of the loss resulting from the milling process. In 1961 Dr. Norman Joliffe was honored by the American Bakers Association and the American Institute of Baking. The meeting was addressed by Dr. W. H. Sebrell, Jr. Dr. Sebrell stated that the introduction of enrichment was a major event in the history of nutrition because it not only contributed to making the people of the United States stronger and healthier, but it also marked a great new step forward in preventive medicine that has spread to many other countries. He pointed out that the great concern of the medical and public health professions was over the high incidence of vitamin-deficiency disease; the health professionals believed that "it was impossible to get the people who need them most to buy or to use vitamin pills regularly."*

Dr. Sebrell concluded that the enrichment program had significantly improved the health of the nation. Certainly it has decreased the prevalence of pellagra. But it is also true that the enrichment program developed nearly 50 years ago is not necessarily the best one, and that it could have been much improved by paying more attention to the recent developments in nutrition. However, no amount of enrichment would be as good as going back to the original whole-grain product. In other words, the white flour would have to be enriched not only with the vitamins, all those that have been removed, but also with the minerals and with the fibrous part of the kernel which has been removed. Dr. Sebrell was aware of the need for revision of the program when he added: "The present program was developed more than twenty years ago based on nutritional needs and knowledge at that time. Is there any need to consider revision in the light of new knowledge and changed conditions today? It is my own feeling which I think is shared by many others, that nutritional knowledge is accumulating so fast and still changing so rapidly that we cannot answer the question at this time. New and important information is coming to light on the functions and value of vitamin B6. It is possible that further research will show that this nutrient should be added to the enrichment formula." Sebrell concluded: "It is my opinion that guidance for changing the required ingredients should be the demonstration of a health need for which this is the best method of prevention. Optional ingredients should be allowed when it is shown that such ingredients result in improving the nutritional value of bread. It is unlikely that we are now going to find any new clear-cut deficiency disease like beriberi and pellagra, but we can rather

---

*Ironically, the situation seems quite different today, with the official medical societies opposing the use of vitamin tablets by the general population, probably spurred, aided, and abetted by the FDA.

expect to find health situations that are more difficult to prove and analyze from a nutritional view point, *e.g.,* increased growth, greater resistance to disease, decreased disability, shorter convalescence, better mental activity, delay in the onset of aging."

Refining of carbohydrates is harmful in three different ways: (1) it removes fiber from our diet, which affects the gastrointestinal system from the teeth to the colon; (2) it causes overconsumption of calories due to overconcentration and to the increased ease of overconsumption; (3) it removes protein, which is required to neutralize hydrochloric acid in the stomach. The way these three attacks on our nutrition cause disease will be the subject of the next section.

## PHYSICAL MANIFESTATIONS OF THE SACCHARINE DISEASE

### Effects of the Removal of Fiber

This causes two sets of conditions:

(1) Simple constipation with its complications of venous ailments (varicose veins, deep-venous thrombosis, hemorrhoids, diverticular disease, and cancer of the colon); and (2) dental caries and periodontal disease.

When normal quantities of fiber (bulk) are consumed, the normal transit time of the feces is about 24 to 48 hours, as against the 48 to 96 hours found in people who live on low-fiber diets. As a result, constipation is very common. In Britain up to 15 percent of the population regularly take laxatives. This is most common among the elderly, who have had much more time to damage their bowels by their defective nutrition. I have seen a large number of elderly who use daily laxatives and as a result suffer from a variety of complications, including malabsorption.

Two serious consequences arise from constipation: (1) diverticulosis, and (2) diverticulitis (an inflamation of the diverticuli). Cleave

(1975) suggests that the slow passage of the colon's contents leads to increased absorption of water from the feces and to greater viscosity of the contents, necessitating excessive contraction of the bowel. Whatever the reason, there is a clear association between constipation, diverticulosis and absence of a diet containing adequate quantities of fiber. The evidence is provided in Cleave's 1975 book.

Diverticulitis is ascribed to a combination of the constipation due to the lack of fiber and the deleterious effect of the high sugar intake that accompanies it. There is an undesirable pathological effect on the bacterial population of the gut due to the surplus of the sugar. The effects on the bowel do not come on quickly and may require up to 40 years before they are fully developed. The evolutionary mechanism developed for rejecting foods that are harmful to us does not come into play.

Another manifestation is the irritable colon (simple colitis) due to the same two factors. Therefore, simple addition of bran while continuing to eat large quantities of sugar may not be helpful. One of the most dangerous conditions is cancer of the colon, which may derive and probably does from the same set of causes.

The other conditions such as caries, periodontal disease and the many varicosities due to back pressure from the constipation will not be discussed here. Although they are debilitating conditions, they are not as closely related as the afflictions of the bowel to mood disorders. It is rare to be free of depression, tension, and anxiety when these conditions are present. In fact, ulcerative colitis was—and may still be—considered one of the classic psychosomatic conditions when psychosomatic medicine was in vogue. As a rule, *psychosomatic* meant that physical factors were ignored and that psychosocial factors were considered predominant. I can recall many years ago studying the psychosomatic profile for the seven conditions popularized by Flanders Dunbar.

As a matter of fact, I soon realized that the same dynamics were being invoked for every one of these psychosomatic conditions. This is probably why psychoanalysts were never able to show from a knowledge of the dynamics only that they could ever predict which psychosomatic condition was present.

### Effects of Overconsumption

The refining of food leads to an unnatural concentration of carbohydrates, which deceives the palate, our sense of taste, and leads to overconsumption. This is the sole immediate cause of obesity. A large appetite is not the cause nor is a dislike of exercise. For example, it would be highly unusual for anyone to consume six apples over a five minute period. The bulk of this natural food prevents this from happening. But it would not be unusual to consume the equivalent amount of calories in the form of sugar in one's tea or coffee or soft drink. Obesity is very closely linked with diabetes mellitus and with the even more common condition called relative hypoglycemia. I believe that a large number of the so-called diabetes, especially of the adult-maturity type or late-onset type associated with obesity, are not really diabetes but one of the variants of relative hypoglycemia. Any patient who does not require insulin, in my opinion, does not suffer from true diabetes. This will be discussed under the psychiatric aspects of the Saccharine Disease.

Obesity is very often associated with severe mood disorders or more accurately with relative hypoglycemia. The evidence showing how increased consumption of refined food causes diabetes is reviewed by Cleave.

The other saccharine conditions listed by Cleave as manifestations of the Saccharine Disease will not be discussed. They are: (1) coronary disease; (2) primary E. Coli infection of the bowel; and (3) gallstones.

### Effects of the Removal of Protein. Peptic Ulcer.

Usually the stomach is stimulated to secrete gastric juices containing hydrochloric acid when food is consumed. For perhaps 99 percent or more of man's existence on earth, his food contained the natural admixture of protein plus the other constituents. When the food reached the stomach, the acid quickly was bound by the protein which it helped digest. Therefore, there was no surplus amount of acid lying around in the stomach, and the inner lining of the stomach, the mucosa, remained intact. The protein buffered the acid against the stomach wall. However, in today's nutrition very often food is consumed that contains less protein than was originally present, or it may contain no protein at all. When one drinks a bottle of soda pop, one places in the stomach what might appear to be food to the stomach because it is attractive in appearance and tastes sweet. There will be the same increased excretion of acid, but there will be no protein present and the soda pop will remain free in the stomach. The only buffering protein will then be the mucosa itself and the protein exudates on its surface.

Refined foods such as flour and polished rice have lost perhaps 10 percent of their protein, but the refined sugars have lost it all.

Peptic ulcer is another of the classic psychosomatic diseases, but I will spare the reader the description of the causal dynamics that has been postulated.

Thus two of the main psychosomatic diseases turn out to be aspects of the Saccharine Disease. Nutritious food turns out to be much more important than thousands of hours of skillful psychoanalysis. Think of the enormous sums of money spent in researching these conditions by patients in receiving what they assumed was treatment. Think of the fantastic hypotheses, fantasies spun by analysts and psychologists in determining personality on the basis of the frequency of bowel movements while totally ignoring nutrition. A constipated person is not a person with an anal personality who is a miser and wishes (subconsciously, of course) to hoard. Remember that feces is the same as gold to many analysts. This person is merely ignorant of the importance of good nutrition and would soon cure his condition, and I suppose his personality problems, by adding fiber and removing refined sugars from his diet.

## ALLERGIES

The first rule is to avoid junk food, and the second basic rule is to avoid food that makes you sick. Whether one is dealing with an allergy or a toxicity is irrelevant. The patient suffers just as much. Clinical ecologists have specialized in detecting these foods and in developing treatments. The subject is very complex. It is described by clinical ecologists such as Dr. Marshall Mandell (1979).

However, physicians need not be clinical ecologists before they can begin identifying foods that patients are allergic to. They can become pretty good clinical ecologists later on. The foods are identified by history and by a number of tests. Patients are asked about their diets, their food preferences and about foods that have made them sick. Foods most likely to be a problem are those consumed in large amounts—the staples. People generally are very fond of these foods. If a patient loves cheese there may be a cheese allergy. If that same patient hates milk, it is almost certain an allergy is present. These patients have learned that milk causes unpleasant symptoms such as plugged sinuses, runny nose, and stomach pain, while the cheese, to which they are just as allergic, causes only fatigue and depression. They may also love milk and consume up to eight glasses per day. The cause of trouble may be any food.

Once the diet history is completed, it may be possible to identify all the allergic or toxic foods. These foods are then avoided for at least six months. If the diagnosis has been correct, these patients will be much better or well. After six months it may be possible to eat these foods infrequently, perhaps not more often than every four days. However, some allergies are fixed and are never lost.

If the history does not elicit all the allergic or toxic foods, elimination diets can be used. There are a large number of these and they range from four-day water fasts to specially selected diets which use only foods seldom or never consumed. If the elimination diet is successful the patient will be better. Then individual foods can be introduced. If a food causes a reaction, that food is again eliminated for six months as before.

A number of other tests are used, such as sublingual tests with food extracts, titered intradermal tests and blood tests for immunoglobulins and for cytotoxicity. For these tests the patient may need to be referred to an allergy specialist, especially if the specialist is also familiar with clinical ecology.

The nutritional literature is full of long-term studies which show the damaging effects of chronic malnutrition. Perhaps more attention will be paid after the report by Robert Ross (1987) becomes known. He reviewed Dr. J. R. Galler's studies of chronic malnutrition over several generations. Dr. Galler is director of the Center for Behavioral Development and Mental Retardation at Boston University School of Medicine. She studied the effect of constant malnutrition on many generations of animals. She used descendants of a colony of malnourished rats begun in the mid-1960s. Animals born of undernourished mothers were smaller, weighed less, had behavioral problems, and were more susceptible to disease. On the same diet there was a steady decline for eight generations. After that there was no further deterioration. When the animals were given an adequate diet it took four generations before they were rehabilitated.

Her human studies showed the deterioration within one generation when children were living on poor diets. One human generation is about 20 years. This suggests that on a steady poor diet deterioration will continue for over one hundred years. Can any society afford to wait so long, especially when the rat studies suggest it will take 80 years to recover? I believe we are already seeing our third generation of malnourished populations. The massive destruction of our national diet began about 40 years ago.

## CONCLUSION

Clinical nutrition need not be very complicated. For millions of years our ancestors and our present wild animals did pretty well in knowing what to eat, without any training. They were not more intelligent, they simply had no choice. They ate what they had adapted to.

We have introduced a choice by damaging our diet and providing what appears to be food but is not. To return to our previous state of consumption, what we can be healthy with, there are two simple rules: (1) eat no junk; and (2) avoid foods that make you sick. The skillful physician will help patients achieve this objective. The price of not doing so is disease. The reward of doing so is good health.

## CHAPTER REFERENCES

Carlson, L. A., Levi, Lennart and Oro, L. (1967), Plasma lipids and urinary excretion of catecholamines in man during experimentally induced emotional stress, and their modifications by nicotinic acid. The Laboratory for Clinical Stress Research, Department of Medicine and Psychiatry, Karolinska Institute, Stockholm, Sweden.

Cleave, T. L. (1975), *The Saccharine Disease.* New Canaan, Conn.: Keats Publishing.

Cleave, T. L.; Campbell, G. D. and Painter, N. S. (1969), *Diabetes, Coronary Thrombosis and the Saccharine Disease.* Bristol, England: John Wright and Sons, Ltd.

Hoffer, A. (1983), Orthomolecular nutrition at the zoo. *J. Ortho. Psych.*, 12:116–128.

Mandell, M. and Scanlon, L. W., *Dr. Mandell's 5-Day Allergy Relief System.* New York: Thomas Y. Crowell.

Ross, R. N., The hidden malice of malnutrition. *Bostonia* 61(2): 49–52, February/March 1987.

Shute, W. E. and Taub, H. J. (1969), *Vitamin E for Ailing and Healthy Hearts.* New York: Pyramid House Books.

Yudkin, J. (1972), *Sweet and Dangerous.* New York: Peter H. Wyden.

# 2

# *FOOD SUPPLEMENTS*

• • • • • • • • • • • • • • • • • • • • • • • • • • • • • • •

Food supplements are those essential constituents of food which are present in very small amounts, do not provide calories, and are essential components of enzymes. They are needed in relatively small amounts because enzymes are able to transform much larger quantities of substrate; there is little wastage.

Plants and animals differ in their need for food supplements, but all living tissues share the same basic nutrients. This is how animals can live on plants and other animals. Plants synthesize every organic molecule, the final product and the enzymes. A plant requires only water, carbon dioxide, oxygen, the necessary minerals, light and some stability in order to make every natural compound present, except vitamin B12, which can be made only by bacteria. Animals are not able to make the same nutrients—this is why they must have organic foods.

The first major evolutionary change occurred when cells began to engulf other cells. The predator cells become the unicellular animals—our ancestors. The other cells remained as plant ancestors. This was advantageous to the predator cells, since they immediately found a ready source of food which they did not need to make. The saving in energy and in chemical synthetic apparatus was enormous. A plant cell which must make everything has no energy left for locomotion. The energy saved by the ready food supply led to locomotion. Animals could not have existed without this separation into plant and animal life. Vitamins are needed by plants, but they make what they need, and only mineral supplements are required by both plants and animals.

In the natural state vitamins and minerals are combined with other food constituents into a complex, three-dimensional form. For example, pure vitamin B3 is not found in nature; it is present in nucleotides. These may be so firmly bound that the vitamins are released very slowly and sometimes in inadequate amounts when they are consumed. This is one of the problems with a monotonous corn diet. However, when the corn is treated with calcium in an alkaline medium, some of the vitamin is released. Adding vitamins to food does not simulate natural food; vitamins and minerals are released slowly from natural food in the gastrointestinal tract, while vitamins and minerals added to food are released quickly. Thus, niacinamide added to flour may be absorbed into the blood long before the wheat starch is converted into sugar and absorbed. This is not harmful but it is important to know.

Vitamins and minerals are food artifacts and therefore must be used with care. They are generally helpful, in contrast to sugar, but they can be abused and they too contain trace additives. Thus, niacin made from nicotine will contain traces of nicotine, to which a few people may be sensitive. Ascorbic acid made from corn will contain traces of corn, to which some are allergic.

Vitamins are organic molecules necessary for a large variety of chemical processes which occur in every tissue of the body, including the brain. Recently it has been found that vitamin C and niacinamide have a direct relationship with receptors in the brain. By definition, vitamins cannot be made in the body, are required in very tiny amounts and serve to catalyze reactions in the body. A few vitamins do not meet this definition but have been thought of as vitamins for so long that it is hardly likely they will ever be reclassified. Ascorbic acid is required in large or gram doses, which is not characteristic of a vitamin, nor should it be so considered according to Stone (1972). Nicotinic acid and nicotinamide can be made in the body; about 60 milligrams of tryptophan will yield one milligram of vitamin B3 by means of the nucleotide cycle. Therefore B3 is by definition not a vitamin. Vitamin D3 is made in the skin by the influence of ultraviolet light and should not be listed as a vitamin. It is more aptly looked upon as a hormone. Perhaps the whole vitamin concept should be dropped and each vitamin be designated by its name only or as an accessory factor or food supplement. The vitamin concept has served its purpose. Today it is detrimental to orthomolecular nutrition and to medicine.

Minerals are divided into two main classes: toxic, such as mercury, and essential trace minerals, such as selenium or zinc. No mineral can be generated in the body—all have to be provided by our water and food.

People using vitamins have been confused by claims that natural vitamins are healthier than synthetic ones. It is important to understand what these various terms really mean. Vitamins are all organic molecules, whether made by plants or man; they are in every way identical. The only difference is that vitamins made by plants and still present in the plant do not contain trace additives, which are present in man-made vitamins. But when plant-made vitamins are extracted and purified and made into a crystalline powder or into tablets, they also contain traces of all the chemicals used in the process. They differ from synthetic vitamins only in having different trace additives. The only way to insure additive-free vitamins is to use food only, but this is unreasonable advice for those who require more than food can supply.

A food extract or dried preparation rich in a particular vitamin would also contain minerals, vitamins and enzymes related to the metabolism of the vitamin, but all would be present in small amounts. For example, a dried powder made from acerola or rose hips will contain some vitamin C plus the enzymes, minerals and other vitamins which helped create it and help metabolize it. But for a person needing large doses of vitamin C, too much of the powder would have to be consumed.

Further confusion is generated by labeling laws. A product may have no synthetic or extracted vitamin in it, yet the label may show a large number of vitamins. For example, yeast tablets contain small amounts of most vitamins. They are not vitamin tablets but are a food source. Rose-hip powder is a relatively poor source of vitamin C and must be reinforced with a lot more to make 100-mg or stronger tablets, and therefore is a mixture of synthetic and natural-source vitamin C. It would be better if the terms "natural" and "organic" were dropped and if the label simply indicated the source of the vitamin.

Laboratory tests for determining which vitamins are required and in what quantities have only been moderately helpful. The main reason is that measurable changes occur long after a very serious deficiency is present. In pellagra, a killing disease, vitamin B3 blood levels are normal at onset and it also appears in the urine. Total nucleotides in the red blood cells are also normal. There is, however, an increased proportion of mononucleotides that may rise from 2 or 3 percent to around 12 percent of the total. The dinucleotide (NAD) is the active antipellagra factor, while mononucleotides have no vitamin function. The ratio of mono- to dinucleotides is not measured in clinical laboratories. If one waits for definite abnormalities, one has waited too long. It is not good medical practice to allow patients to develop beriberi, pellagra, pernicious anemia or scurvy before instituting vitamin therapy.

A second reason vitamin assays have been inefficient is that a measurement of body fluids gives only a very crude indication of the levels present within the tissues and cells. We can only guess how much vitamin C is present in the brain, the humors of the eye, or the adrenal cortex by the amount in blood or by the amount that spills into the urine.

Vitamin levels in blood are not helpful in determining how much should be taken each day. Very low levels certainly are proof that a deficiency is present, but normal values do not mean that no supplements should be used. I have seen many patients with normal blood values who became well after supplementation with the vitamin apparently present in normal quantities.

Another way is to measure reactions that depend upon vitamins—with a deficiency this reaction becomes abnormal. However, these reactions are not nearly sensitive enough. The deficiency must be very severe before the abnormal reactions become apparent.

A number of laboratory procedures (tests) are available from a few specialized laboratories. They will help the nutritionally oriented physician be more precise in formulating the nutrients required. They are also helpful in persuading patients that they should try the treatment program. Some of these tests are given in the Appendix to this book.

Until these problems are solved by finding measures which parallel the state of health, we will have to depend upon clinical judgment, an awareness of the need for vitamins and a therapeutic response to determine the optimum quantity. Fortunately vitamins are so safe that there is hardly any danger to the person in determining the best dose. This is done by increasing the dose slowly until there is no further improvement. Once this has been achieved the person can test which is the best continuing dose by decreasing the quantity. If he remains in good health, the newer dose can be used; if symptoms reappear the dose can be increased. Each vitamin has unique properties that must be known since they are helpful in establishing the correct dose.

Before dealing with the nutrients that are most commonly used in orthomolecular medicine, I will discuss in general some of the issues of vitamin and mineral side effects and toxicity. A few critics of orthomolecular medicine have greatly exaggerated these properties, of vitamins especially, and these have even gotten into official, government-issued literature. Several years ago the FDA distributed 100,000 copies of a pamphlet which contained a number of serious and incorrect charges. When Linus Pauling challenged the FDA to cite their sources for these claims, they long delayed answering him; they later reported that the writer of the pamphlet was no longer working for them. Still later, the FDA apologized and admitted they had erred seriously and had ordered that the pamphlet be withdrawn. The pamphlet itself was really no worse than are many articles written by a few people with one thing in common: None has ever treated a single patient with orthomolecular medicine and so they have no first-hand experience with either the therapeutic or toxic effects of large doses of vitamins. What was significant about that pamphlet is that the FDA experts were so ignorant of vitamins that they would allow such an article to be released. Or did they think that the misinformation would go unchallenged?

The few critics of orthomolecular medicine have had easy access to the medical journals, such as the *Journal of the American Medical Association*, which has consistently refused to publish any rebuttal to attacks on orthomolecular theories. The critics charge: (1) that any quantity of vitamins above the recommended doses is unnecessary and therefore wasteful, and (2) that these dosages can be toxic. The first criticism is merely a statement of the vitamin theory, which has remained unmodified for 80 years. Orthomolecular practitioners have found through clinical experience extending over 30 years that many patients do not get well until they are given these larger doses. These patients do not agree that larger doses are not necessary, and they are pleased to pay the price of the vitamin. Being well is much cheaper than remaining sick. Using large doses is not novel to vitamins; every drug has a therapeutic, effective level which varies from person to person. The amount required for maximum response may require a much larger dose; thus tranquilizers given by injection are much more effective than the same tranquilizers given by mouth. For some diseases, 40 grams per day or more of an antibiotic are used in order to achieve an effective blood level. This is not considered wasteful even if most of the antibiotic appears in the urine. It is an illogical requirement of vitamins that only doses that cause no spillover into urine should be used, and it is one no physician can accept for any medication, including vitamins.

Anything used by man may be toxic, food may be toxic, water may be toxic. I have treated a patient who spent his whole day at a water fountain and gained 60 pounds. Within a few weeks after this fountain was closed he lost his extra water. In every case, when a treatment is recommended it is necessary to balance the risks. These are: (1) the risk of the disease not treated, or treated by other drugs,

and (2) the risk of the ratio of benefit to side effect. When the disease is life-threatening or threatens to leave the patient chronically ill, any treatment will be used, provided the side effects or toxic reactions are less than the threat of the disease and can be dealt with by the physician. Tranquilizers can be and often are very toxic, yet they must be used. Insulin can be and often is very toxic, but must be used. The basic question then is not the toxicity but the efficacy. If a drug is effective, toxicity must be considered, but the drug will be used until equally effective, less toxic drugs become available. If a drug is not effective, then it should never be used, so toxicity is not a main factor. However, critics refuse to accept any of the evidence of the effectiveness of vitamin therapy and they emphasize toxicity as a way of deterring physicians and the public from using vitamins. They understand that vitamins are relatively safer than any other preparations available in a drugstore, but they search for potential toxic reactions. They finally conclude that certain toxicity is possible or can occur, but they never point to any studies indicating that actual patients have been damaged by any vitamin toxicity, or that show an estimate of the proportion of people from the huge number now taking vitamins who have suffered side effects or toxicity.

Under each nutrient I will list the side-effects and toxicities which have been reported and that I have seen in clinical practice, and I will give an estimate of the frequency of these reactions.

## VITAMIN SUPPLEMENTS

Vitamins are organic molecules normally found in living tissue in very small amounts. They are essential for most of the metabolic reactions in the body wherein they act as catalysts, or as portions of catalysts called enzymes. They do not contribute calories as do carbohydrates and fats, nor do they contribute to the structural integrity of tissues.

As catalysts they are used over and over. By definition they cannot be made in the body, but this definition was made before enough was known about vitamins. Some of the vitamins, by this definition, are not vitamins: Vitamin D3 is made in the body by the effect of light on the skin; vitamin C is a vitamin only for man and a few other species and is made in the bodies of most animals in large quantities; vitamin B3 (niacin and niacinamide) is made in the body from tryptophan. But these three substances have been classed as vitamins for so long that it is highly unlikely they will be classified as anything else.

Nutritionists have been concerned about the optimum amount of vitamins the body needs. When they were first identified, it was recognized that very small amounts were needed to prevent the typical terminal or deficiency disease. The vitamins were discovered and identified by measuring the effect of various food fractions on animals, plants, or bacteria that were fed a diet lacking that vitamin. To detect thiamine, food extracts were fed to pigeons made to suffer beriberi by a specially prepared, thiamine-free diet. Very little thiamine is needed to prevent and cure beriberi; this is also true of other deficiency diseases such as scurvy and pellagra. Scientists assumed that no additional vitamins were needed if these deficiency diseases were absent. If a patient did not have pellagra, he needed no additional vitamin B3. Later on, nutritionists realized that patients had symptoms of deficiency that were not severe enough to be diagnosed as the fully developed disease. Pellagrologists diagnosed patients as having subclinical pellagra. These patients were not near death as are pellagrins, but they were not well either, and they did become normal when given additional quantities of vitamins. The Recommended Daily Allowances (RDA) reflect the view that very minute quantities of vitamins are required, but they also recognize that requirements vary with age, physiological state and degrees of stress. Nevertheless, the maximum doses recommended in the RDA tables are little higher than the minimal doses required to prevent classical deficiency diseases. The tables also reflect the quantity of vitamins obtainable from food. They do exclude the use of vitamins for most people to supplement the diet. Supporters of the RDA believe that a balanced and varied diet will be adequate for the vast majority of people. Even if this were true, it still ignores a huge number of people who are not well and who are patients at one time or another. There are no recommended dose tablets of vitamins for patients. I will present such a table—a Therapeutic Daily Allowance (TDA) table further on.

Many patients have recovered when treated with large doses of vitamins, doses that are 100 to 1,000 times those recommended to prevent the terminal deficiency diseases. A few patients require one milligram per day of vitamin B12, which is 1,000 times the average daily dose. To lower cholesterol and triglyceride levels, patients require 3,000 mg (three grams) of niacin per day, which is several hundred times the pellagra-preventive dose. Some schizophrenic patients have needed 30 grams per day or more. The term *megavitamin therapy* was developed to describe these larger doses. Irwin Stone first used the term *mega ascorbic acid* for the use of large quantities of vitamin C; from this it spread to cover all vitamins used this way. But the term *megavitamin therapy* is not particularly useful; it confuses many into thinking there is something called a "megavitamin." The term *megadose vitamin therapy* is better, as it focuses on the use of large quantities.

Physicians using these large doses recognize that individuals have different vitamin requirements and that the range of variation is much greater than we had suspected several decades ago. We now recognize that the range of vitamin needs for optimum health varies from those quantities present in good, whole food, to doses up to a thousand times greater. The main problem for an orthomolecular physician is to determine what that optimum level is.

Deficiency diseases occur when individuals with average vitamin requirements live on food deficient in that vitamin. Usually such a diet contains several vitamin and mineral deficiencies. There is a relative deficiency as the diet fails to provide what is required. When the requirements are so high even a perfect diet cannot provide it, we find exactly the same relative deficiency, but as the problem is the body's requirements and not in the diet, it is called a dependency. A dependency is also a relative deficiency. In both deficiency and dependency disease, the net result is the same although the mechanisms are different.

A dependency may be present at birth or may be acquired. Genetic factors are involved, for no pathology can express itself except in the context of chromosomal needs failing to be met by one's chemical environment. Genetic factors determine the optimum vitamin requirements. Vitamins have to be delivered to the cells. This requires the transfer of vitamins across several membranes, through certain tissues, and requires the presence of the correct mechanism, of which the vitamin is a part. If a person has an efficient mechanism for absorbing a vitamin, the consumed optimum dose will be less than for a person with a less efficient mechanism. Individuals develop pernicious anemia because they cannot absorb vitamin B12 efficiently. They must be given this vitamin by injection to bypass the gastrointestinal tract.

Vitamin dependencies can be acquired. This follows a prolonged period of deficiency of that vitamin, usually due to severe malnutrition combined with stress. I have seen patients develop a dependency following a few weeks of stress before, during and after surgery, when combined with severe malnutrition. Modern hospitals are almost unaware of the importance of special nutrition for their patients. Within the past four years I have seen many elderly men and women who dated their fatigue, tension and depression from such an episode in a hospital. They had been given intravenous fluids but no food for many days. One was not fed for two weeks, and when food was offered it was junk—colored gelatin and a soft drink. These made her so ill she insisted she would sooner be back on I.V. fluids. These patients required large doses of several vitamins before they began to recover. But the most striking proof arose from an "experiment" conducted in the last World War. This was a catastrophe in which Allied members of the armed forces were Japanese prisoners of war for several years. The Canadians suffered from a deficiency of protein, fat, calories, vitamins and minerals. A combination of serious diseases arising from a deficiency of calories and nutrients, combined with severe psychological stress, produced a clinical syndrome characterized by accelerated aging. These soldiers were made vitamin B3 dependent and recovered only after they were given large doses of nicotinic acid and remained well only if they continued to take these large dosages. It is possible they developed other nutrient dependencies. Because nearly all these veterans improved so significantly by taking nicotinic acid, it is likely their dependency on vitamin B3 was the main one. One year in these camps aged each prisoner the equivalent of five normal years of aging. That is, a veteran age 60 in Canada, having been a prisoner four years, would be as old physically and mentally as an 80-year-old Canadian who had not been in these prisons.

Forty-five years ago, pellagrologists observed that a few chronic pellagrins did not recover on the usual low-dose vitamin treatment. To their surprise they needed 600 milligrams per day; on a smaller dose their pellagra symptoms did not go away. They could not explain this discrepancy between theory and observation. It is clear chronic pellagra caused a vitamin B3 dependency. Experiments with dogs support this conclusion. Dogs given black tongue (canine pellagra) were cured by small doses of vitamin B3 if they were given the vitamin soon after pellagra developed. If black tongue was allowed to remain for one-third of their life span, they required much larger amounts to become well. The evidence is strong for vitamin B3. I have no doubt other vitamin dependencies are caused by chronic deficiencies.

Vitamin Nutrition Information Service (VNIS), Volume 2, No. 2, 1981, put out by Hoffmann-La Roche, described what used to be subclinical deficiencies as a "marginal vitamin deficiency," the gray area of nutrition. At last vitamins have a parent to defend them. Patented drugs have parents who promote and defend them. Vitamins are not patentable and so have languished as orphans often have. The use and promotion of vitamins in high doses has depended upon the energy and enthusiasm of physicians who have seen what they do, and patients who have been helped when all else failed.

Marginal vitamin deficiency is a middle ground between health and frank deficiency. As there are no specific symptoms, this in-between state is not apparent. Vitamin deficiency comes on slowly. During a prelimininary stage, body stores of vitamins and minerals are slowly depleted. The second stage, the biochemical stage, occurs when these micronutrients are depleted. Enzymes whose activity depends upon having adequate amounts of vitamins work less efficiently, but the individual still appears well in growth and appearance. The third stage is the physiological stage; now enzyme activity is sufficiently impaired to cause personality and behavioral changes. These are nonspecific, including anorexia, depression, irritability, anxiety, insomnia and somnolence. The final stage is the classical deficiency, a stage near death. The clincal and anatomical changes are now clear. The first three stages comprise the gray area, marginal deficiency or subclinical area, the first term used 50 years ago.

These conclusions were not written by or-thomolecular physicians, and were based upon a bibliography of 71 reports by scientists published in the usual scientific journals. We orthomolecular physicians can take heart from this, for it shows there is a vast body of supportive evidence about which we have heard little. This evidence does not make headlines as do the statements of a few vociferous critics, so well loved by a few medical journals and many colleges of medicine.

The author of the Hoffmann-La Roche pamphlet concludes: "We support the efforts of nutrition researchers who are probing for answers to such questions as: What are the long-term effects of marginal vitamin deficiencies in terms of survival, performance, wound healing, resistance to disease, etc.?

Are suboptimal intakes contributing to subtle behavioral effects that are escaping detection by the usual parameters of physical and laboratory examinations?

What functional impairments at the cellular level might result from suboptimal intakes?

How do marginal deficiencies affect the immune competency of the body?

What is the relationship, if any, of the body's nutritional status to the development and progression of chronic disease such as arteriosclerosis?

Have all the signs of malnutrition been discovered, or are we still missing some?

In future years, the VNIS hopes to see improved nutrition become a significant contributor to the overall health of the population. We urge all members of the nutrition community to foster a climate of awareness and discovery—open to new knowledge, but judicious in its application."

## HOW MUCH VITAMIN IS NEEDED?

With such wide range of vitamin needs among individuals, and even for the same individual throughout life, how do we find out what is the optimum amount? The most effective way is through trial and error, for there are no laboratory tests which help us decide. Is it possible to determine levels of vitamins in body fluids that indicate a deficiency is present or will soon appear. If there is no vitamin B3 or ascorbic acid or thiamine in the urine, it is certain there is very little in the body. But no clinician should wait until these deficiency states develop, for the mortality from these classic deficiency diseases is too great. The same biochemical tests are of less value for individuals who are not suffering from the deficiency disease but who have subclinical variants of these deficiency diseases. The test which might be helpful will be described under each vitamin.

Patients and their physicians can determine what the optimum doses are. I define the optimum dose as that quantity which restores health without causing either unpleasant or dangerous side effects. This definition also contains the clue to determining the optimum dose; one starts with a dose that long experience has shown is the most effective starting dose for that condition. Our work with schizophrenia shows that one gram three times per day is a useful starting dose. Once it has been established that there are minimal or no side effects, one continues to see if there is an adequate therapeutic response. If both patient and doctor are satisfied with the rate of improvement, the dose is not increased. If the improvement rate is too slow, the dose is increased slowly, i.e., an increase every few weeks or months until the therapeutic rate is accelerated or until side effects develop. One of the common side effects of too high a dose of vitamin B3 is nausea. It is possible to take higher doses of niacin. If nausea does develop, the dose must be reduced or vomiting may develop. Uncontrolled nausea and vomiting can be dangerous, causing dehydration and loss of electrolytes. The optimum dose is the subnauseant dose, that dose 1 or 2 grams below the nauseant dose. Other vitamins have different side effects. Vitamin C, for example, has another end point—it causes intestinal gas (flatuence) and diarrhea. The optimum dose is the sublaxative dose, which is also therapeutic. Usually healthy people require less vitamin C and develop the laxative effect at lower doses than do individuals who are under stress or ill. Normally I require 1 to 3 grams of vitamin C per day, but on one occasion when I had been bitten by sand flies I took 30 grams per day with no laxative effect. Vitamin C can be used as a laxative; one that is much safer than any commercial laxative—probably because it does not interfere with bowel absorption. When I describe each vitamin I will indicate how the optimum amount can be determined.

The optimum dose required to restore health may be too high once the patient has recovered; maintenance doses may be much lower. They should be determined even if there are no side effects. The health maintenance optimum dose is usually smaller and is that dose required to keep the person healthy. Again, it will have to be determined by trial and error. The dose is decreased very slowly, using lower increments for several months before the next move down is made. If there is any recurrence of symptoms the dose is raised immediately. Some vitamins have a maintenance dose which should not be reduced. Usually lower doses are not as effective in maintaining health for these vitamins. This will be discussed under the respective vitamins.

Orthomolecular physicians will pay little attention to the official RDAs. But as inadequate as these minimal standards are, even officially, there is a caveat in these requirements, which are recommended only for almost "all healthy persons in the United States." This immediately excludes every person who consults a physician except for those few who seek annual physicals. Arthur M. Sackler in *Nutrition Reviews*, page 23, Fall 1985, points out that most people, many of whom never consult physicians, are not well. Five conditions alone—alcoholism, allergies, arthritis, diabetes, and hypertension—affect up to 110 million U.S. citizens. Nor is there any meaning in averages as far as patients are concerned. Every patient is unique. A physician who depends only on averages will be a much less than average physician. Sackler concludes: "The common belief that RDAs are generally applicable to all sectors of our population as a standard is a misleading chimera. As standards they are more often fallacies than facts."

## ARE THERE UNIQUE SUBCLINICAL VITAMIN DEFICIENCY SYNDROMES?

The classical deficiency syndromes are rare in technologically advanced nations, but these syndromes were so striking and so devastating that they still remain the main theme of professors of biochemistry who teach medical students. Who has not heard of scurvy, pellagra, etc.? Because they are so infrequently seen, most physicians would fail to recognize them. These deficiency states arise from monotonous diets with very few varieties of food, such as the corn diet that causes pellagra, or from starvation. One deficiency may be predominant but many more are present. The only examples of pure deficiency states may be those produced in experiments on man and animals and in individuals who are vitamin dependent. Thus, a person who is vitamin B3 dependent on a good diet may have ample quantities of every nutrient except vitamin B3 because he requires so much. In my opinion some acute schizophrenics have such a pure deficiency (dependency) state. The mental changes are much more prominent and the obvious physical changes of pellagra are missing.

Subclinical vitamin deficiencies produce a variety of symptoms and signs that can mimic an amazing variety of medical and psychiatric syndromes that may be due to other diseases such as infections, immune deficiencies, etc. Physicians confronted with these syndromes consider them to be manifestations of these diseases. When they do not respond to treatment they tend to give them up as psychiatric. Many physicians do not think of any

possible connection to nutritional problems. A proper examination of patients' diets would provide the essential diagnostic clues. When these patients do recover on vitamins they have selected on their own or which have been recommended by others, the recovery is ascribed to faith, to a placebo reaction or to a natural remission. I have often remarked that nutritional therapy has the remarkable effect of suddenly enhancing the placebo effect.

Nutritional deficiencies affect all cells and all organs of the body. With the cells operating at subnormal levels, the whole body must be suffering. Systemic or general symptoms include fatigue, inertia, tension, generalized pain and muscle irritability. In addition, organs operating at subnormal efficiency will add symptoms and signs unique to that organ. In thinking of causes of the discomfort, physicians should remember that in the absence of readily recognized diseases such as hyperthyroidism, infection, the presence of fatigue, anxiety and depression should suggest a thorough search for nutritional factors, especially when the major symptoms develop after severe and prolonged stress. Such stress is common before, during and after surgery if patients stay very long in a hospital. This is more common following gastrointestinal complications, severe loss of weight, chronic infection, cancer and other debilitating diseases.

## VITAMIN A

Symptoms of both vitamin A deficiency and toxicity were known long before vitamins were recognized. Night blindness, xerophthalmia and keratomalacia were described over a century ago. Arctic explorers knew that polar bear liver was dangerous, since explorers in the sixteenth century lost their skin after eating polar bear liver—one pound would contain over 30 million units of vitamin A.

Vitamin A is found mainly in animal and fish livers, milk, butter and eggs. Yellow, orange and green plants contain carotene, which is converted to vitamin A in the body. Beta-carotene is the most common one. Alpha carotene is found in a few species only. Vitamin A aldehyde is found in citrus fruits and green vegetables.

In the body vitamin A esters are converted to alcohol, which may be stored as vitamin A palmitate or converted to its aldehyde. Carotenes are converted to aldehyde, which is transformed to vitamin A acid or incorporated in visual purple. About 50 percent of the vitamin A in the body comes from carotene.

Vitamin A is stored in the liver and is transported as a lipoprotein. Carotene is stored in body fat and colors it yellow. People who eat too many carrots will have carrot-colored body fat. Both vitamin A and carotene are easily oxidized. This process is inhibited by antioxidants, especially the fat-soluble vitamin E.

Vitamin A is essential for normal vision. It forms the visual pigments rhodopsin and iodopsin. It is essential for epithelial tissue. I consider it a surface membrane vitamin, as it is essential for the health of the skin and its appendages, mouth, gastrointestinal tract, and genitourinary tract.

### Pathology of Vitamin A Deficiency

*Eye Lesions*: Night blindness, xerophthalmia and keratomalacia, which can lead to severe degeneration and perforation of the cornea.

*Body Surfaces*: Skin becomes dry, itchy and susceptible to infection. Secretions may decrease. In the gastrointestinal tract there is malabsorption. The respiratory system is more susceptible to infection by decreasing mucous secretion. In the genitourinary system there is an increased tendency for stone formation.

### Pathology of Vitamin A Excess

Since vitamin A is fat-soluble, it can be stored in the body. If the daily dose exceeds the amount utilized or destroyed, the amount in the fat stores will build up and may reach toxic levels. It is not inherently toxic but may cause toxic effects simply because too many molecules are circulating. It is comparable to having too many friends in a room. It is an overcrowding phenomenon. Nevertheless, this property has allowed some nutritionists to exaggerate grossly its toxicity. Even government regulatory agencies have become concerned and in Canada have limited vitamin A levels to a maximum of 10,000 international units (IU) per capsule for over-the-counter sales. There are very few well documented clinical reports of vitamin A toxic reactions. In over 30 years of practice I have seen only one case. This woman with breast cancer, unresponsive to all standard treatment, had been started on 500,000 IU per day as part of an alternative program. About six months later her hair fell out and her liver enlarged. A few weeks after the vitamin A was stopped she began to recover and her hair again began to grow. After several months her hair growth was normal but her liver was still slightly enlarged. One other person on 50,000 IU per day developed a slight erythema between her fingers. This cleared rapidly when the dose was reduced. It is dishonest to exaggerate grossly the toxic effects as a way of discouraging physicians from becoming orthomolecular physicians.

Intoxication has been reported with 50,000 IU per day. Symptoms included itchy skin, muscle stiffness, and a variety of neurological changes; but very large doses taken for long periods generally are required for toxicity. The changes are reversible. Carotene excesses will discolor skin.

Reich (1971) routinely uses high doses of vitamin A in combination with vitamin D3 for treating asthma and arthritis. He also combines these with calcium, phosphorus, and magnesium in the form of bone meal or dolomite. He uses either cod or halibut liver oil or the synthetic equivalent as a vitamin A source. The best sources of the vitamin are fish oils.

The optimum dose is determined by the response of the lesions and in subjective feeling. One can start with 10,000 IU per day and increase it slowly. I have seldom used more than 50,000 IU per day. Once the optimum response is recognized the dose may be decreased to the appropriate maintenance dose. (One International Unit [one IU] = 0.3 micrograms.)

Generally one should suspect a vitamin A deficiency whenever there are problems with the body's surfaces: skin, hair, nails, mucosa, or night blindness. Another indication is repeated colds that are not responsive to ascorbic acid. The normal serum level ranges around 50 mcg. per 100 ml.

Beta-carotene, a vitamin A precursor, and synthetic vitamin A analogues are showing a lot of promise as anticarcinogens. Populations low in vitamin A blood levels are more prone to develop cancer.

### Indications for Using Vitamin A

1. For vitamin A deficiency.
2. For cancer. Willett and MacMahon (1984), Nettesheim (1980) and Prasad and Rama (1985) reviewed the relationship between vitamin A, vitamin A analogues (retinoids), carotene and cancer. These compounds have inhibited tumor induction, inhibited the promotion phase and caused some tumors to regress. Some of the synthetic retinoids are most potent in prevention and treatment.
3. For colds. Vitamin A is necessary to maintain the integrity of body surfaces. A deficiency may decrease mucous secretion and increase susceptibility to colds.
4. For asthma.

### THIAMINE (VITAMIN B1)

Thiamine was the first micronutrient called a vitamin by Casimir Funk in 1912. The concept that foods could be deficient in nutrients was as improbable then as are many orthomolecular views to physicians today. Sir Patrick Manson was convinced beriberi was a contagious disease, even though he was aware that the Japanese navy had eliminated it by improving the sailors' diets. People who ate polished rice developed beriberi while their neighbors who ate brown or parboiled rice did not. Parboiling drives the thiamine into the kernel from the bran and germ. Thiamine was synthesized in 1936 by R. R. Williams.

Carbohydrates cannot be metabolized in the absence of thiamine. Pyruvic acid accumulates to toxic levels, leading to lactic acidosis in some cases.

While beriberi is endemic to the Far East, it can also occur in alcoholism, in malabsorption, severe diarrhea, and uncontrolled vomiting.

Early signs of deficiency are fatigue, loss of weight and loss of appetite. Later gastrointestinal and neurological signs appear, such as tingling, pain and paresthesia in legs and feet. Such a diet followed for many years causes a chronic, dry, atrophic type. Patients showed neuromuscular pathology, ankle or foot drop, toe drop and paralysis of the vocal cords. Tachycardia is always present.

Breast-fed infants in beriberi countries are at grave risk. They suffer constipation, occasional vomiting, and tympanites, with attacks of crying and restlessness. There may be convulsions.

### Thiamine in the Diet

In Canada and the U.S.A. thiamine is added to white flour. The aim is to raise the levels to what is normally present in whole wheat: around 4 micrograms per gram. My first job as a research chemist in a flour mill laboratory was to develop a method for measuring thiamine in cereal products and to monitor the amount of this vitamin in the flour after it had been added.

Beriberi is rare in the U.S.A. and Canada, but subclinical (marginal) states probably are not rare. It will be found in people who depend too heavily on alcohol and on sugars and fats.

Thiamine is present in whole and enriched cereals, legumes, meat from well nourished animals and yeast. Subclinical beriberi is thus only found in alcoholics and in people who use too much sugar or fat or who suffer from malabsorption. Patients in modern hospitals are probably at risk.

### Indications for Using Thiamine

Heaviness and weakness of limbs, anorexia, pain and paresthesia in limbs, and prolonged diarrhea should alert one to the need for thiamine. In babies, warning signals are pallor, loss of weight, restlessness, neck stiffness and spasticity of extremities. It is likely subclinical beriberi is much more common than we realize. Thus, in 1962 Sebrell wrote: "The thought still seems to persist that severe thiamine deficiency is a disease of rice-eating people and does not occur in the United States. This leads to a situation where many physicians fail to consider the possibility of beriberi when they are faced with a puzzling diagnostic problem. However in the past severe clinical beriberi was widely found in the United States. . . . New England, Arkansas, Texas and California." This was written about 20 years after enrichment of flour with thiamine was started. It is likely Sebrell would be as pessimistic today, as our food supply has deteriorated even more since then.

Thiamine was discovered because food technology—polishing rice—created the deficiency beriberi. Had man never developed food technology and later chemistry, we might not have discovered thiamine; perhaps it would not have mattered.

After it was synthesized the cost of thiamine came down very quickly. Today all thiamine-containing tablets in drug stores, supermarkets or health food stores are synthetic. It would cost too much to extract and crystallize naturally created thiamine. In 1942 it cost five dollars per gram. Today it costs pennies per gram.

The megadose range for thiamine varies from 100 mg to 3,000 mg per day. The usual range is under 1,000 mg per day. It is available in tablets up to 500 mg in size. The modern anti-stress formulas contain moderate quantities. A popular one contains 15 mg per tablet. It is one of three vitamins added to white flour since about 1942.

Thiamine is nontoxic when used at its optimum level per person. It has an odd, nutlike taste. At higher dose levels a related odor may be evident from the body. The most common side effect is some nausea at high doses but even this is rare. It is also used by injection. For certain conditions, such as alcoholism and its complications, it may be desirable at the onset to use it by injection.

Thiamine is considered the specific treatment for Wernicke-Korsakoff syndrome (Victor and Adams 1961; Victor, Adams, and Collins 1971). Based upon my experience with other toxic or organic psychoses, I have concluded that thiamine is very useful for the neurological component of deliria of many types, while vitamin B3 is more effective for the psychological component. Deliria will be considered later. Ideally every delirium should be treated with adequate doses of thiamine, vitamin B3, ascorbic acid for its antistress properties, and with mineral supplementation, especially zinc. In real life there are no single deficiencies. Any condition that causes an organic, toxic confusional state (a delirium) must cause multiple vitamin and mineral deficiencies and-or dependencies.

Thiamine should be used to treat alcoholics. Cade (1972) used at least 200 mg of thiamine intravenously in his mixture of multivitamins. He found that 86 alcoholic patients died in 1945-1950, but after introducing thiamine eight died between 1956 and 1960, and none thereafter despite an increase in the number of alcoholic admissions. I have seen equally dramatic responses to vitamin B3 and ascorbic acid. Probably all three should be used.

Thiamine has been used by orthomolecular psychiatrists to suppress the craving for amphetamines, and it has been effective in some patients with depression. It is used in very large amounts for treating multiple sclerosis (Klenner (1971, 1973), as part of a multivitamin program, and by a Canadian surgeon, Mount (1973), by itself.

Subclinical beriberi causes typical symptoms of anxiety or neuroses. In deprivation experiments, normal subjects on a deficient diet complained of headache, poor concentration, decreased mental alertness, fatigue and nervousness. On the Minnesota Multiphasic Personality Inventory, scores were elevated on hypochondriasis, depression, hysteria and anxiety. I wonder how many subclinical beriberi patients have spent many psychotherapeutic hours because they were anxious. Of all the physician subspecialties, psychiatrists are the least likely to inquire about the nutritional state of their patients.

### RIBOFLAVIN (VITAMIN B2)

Riboflavin has played little role in orthomolecular medicine, but this may soon change. It may be that one of the side effects of chronic tranquilizer medication is an induced riboflavin deficiency.

Clinically it is difficult to recognize riboflavin deficiency, as there are no symptoms unique to its absence and it is usually found in people suffering other deficiencies as well. White flour has been enriched with riboflavin since 1942. Also milk is no longer left in glass bottles in which the vitamin can be destroyed by light.

One of the more difficult clinical associations of vitamin B2 deficiency is with birth defects, which are more extensive than those caused by thalidomide. This is caused by a deficiency of the riboflavin nucleotides. The relationship is clear in animals. It is more difficult to establish in man. But it is something we must expect, especially in babies born to mothers receiving tranquilizers.

The first symptoms of riboflavin deficiency are sore throat and angular stomatitis. Later,

patients develop glossitis, seborrheic dermatitis of the face and dermatitis on the trunk and limbs. Skin becomes atrophic, hyperkeratotic and hyperplastic. In some the cornea becomes vascularized and cataracts may form. Later a normochromic and normocytic anemia develops. The anemia may be due to the need for riboflavin to assist the conversion of folic acid to N methyltetrahydrofolic acid.

Foods rich in riboflavin are milk, liver, meat, cheese, eggs, and green vegetables. White flour contains added riboflavin. Because it is easily destroyed by light, green foods should be stored in the dark. Sprouting plants when green have much more B2. It seems to keep pace with chlorophyll formation. There is very little B2 in seeds.

Riboflavin is not very soluble in water and cannot be absorbed quickly in the intestine. It is best given in divided dosages. If a rapid action is needed, it should be injected. The yellow color of the urine after giving riboflavin is a good measure of the absorption from the gastrointestinal tract.

Until recently riboflavin appeared to have no special importance in orthomolecular psychiatry. However, Zaslove, Silverio and Minenna (1983) have shown that riboflavin deficiency is produced by the chronic use of high doses of tranquilizers.

### NIACIN, NIACINAMIDE (VITAMIN B3)

Most vitamins were recognized biologically and nutritionally before their chemical structure was determined. In chemistry, compounds are named logically once the structure is finally established. When the first vitamin was purified it was called vitamin B1, later thiamine. The second one was called vitamin B2, later riboflavin. The third one was the antilellagra vitamin, or B3, later recognized to be nicotinic acid and nicotinamide. Nicotinic acid had been synthesized many years earlier but had remained merely one of a large number of chemicals of no biological interest. Once it was found to be vitamin B3, nicotinic acid was renamed niacin, and nicotinamide was renamed niacinamide for medical use. "Nicotinic acid" is too similar to "nicotine." This association suggested the evil effect of nicotine and frightened a few away from the vitamin. Both niacinamide and niacin are components of the nucleotide cycle, which insures the continual production of nicotinamide adenine dinucleotide (NAD). This is the active anti-pellagra factor, a component of the respiratory enzyme system.

The term *vitamin B3* was revived by Bill W. (Bill Wilson), a cofounder of Alcoholics Anonymous, when he distributed his first Alcoholics Anonymous report to physicians, which was entitled "The Vitamin B3 Therapy." The term is, in fact, very useful, as it includes both niacin and niacinamide.

## Pellagra

Pellagra is one of the classical diseases of Western civilization. As long as populations lived on a variety of whole foods, pellagra was very rare. But when farmers began to grow single crops as the main source of cash and for food, diseases due to single cultured crops (monocultures) became epidemic. Farmers and poor people in the southern United States and in several countries around the Mediterranean Sea, e.g., Spain and Italy, began to depend almost entirely on corn. Pellagra is the direct result of excessive corn consumption combined with a lack of other foods. This is not due only to a deficiency of vitamin B3 in corn; it is due to the fact that the vitamin is so tightly bound chemically that too little is absorbed by the body. Curiously, natives of Central America discovered several thousand years ago that corn consumed as tortillas did not cause pellagra. As noted previously, they treated the crudely ground whole corn with calcium-rich alkali, which liberated the vitamin.

Pellagra has several causes. First, it is caused by a deficiency of tryptophan. Normally this amino acid is the major precursor of vitamin B3. About 1 to 2 mg of B3 is made from 60 mg of tryptophan. Some of the rest is eventually converted to serotonin, one of the brain neurohormones. There is evidence that tryptophan deficiency may be the cause of the typical skin dermatitis of pellagra. The dermatitis of pellagrins given tryptophan healed more rapidly than when they were given vitamin B3 only.

Second, pellagra is caused by a deficiency of vitamin B3. This is caused by diets which contain too much corn or which depend too heavily on other food which has been processed (such as flour), or which is naturally low in this vitamin.

A third cause of pellagra is a deficiency of pyridoxine. Pyridoxine must be present before tryptophan can be converted to NAD. Diets deficient in B6 are as pellagrogenic as diets deficient in vitamin B3.

Fourth, pellagra is caused by excessive loss of vitamin B3 in urine. NAD is made from tryptophan, niacinamide and niacin. If too much vitamin B3 is lost, insufficient NAD will be made. The loss of vitamin B3 is under the control of the ratio of isoleucine to leucine. Isoleucine decreases loss of B3, while leucine increases the loss. Ideally, foods should contain more isoleucine, but in fact in most there is slightly more leucine compared to isoleucine. Excessive leucine causes pellagra and isoleucine is an anti-pellagra factor. I found that isoleucine is also an anti-schizophrenia factor.

Corn is the ideal pellagra-producing food for it is: (1) low in tryptophan; (2) low in vitamin B3 which is extracted with difficulty; (3) too high in leucine and too low in isoleucine. Tribes of Indians from Central America and from the southern United States varied their use of alkali-treated corn. Those tribes using corn as a major food item used it mostly as tortillas. Tribes which used corn as a minor diet constituent ate corn as we do, on the cob or cooked directly. A recent sociological study showed there is a direct and significant correlation between the proportion of corn in the diet and the degree of irritability or aggressive behavior in that group of people (Mawson and Jacobs 1978). It would be prudent to add vitamin B3 to all corn products, i.e., corn meal, grits, etc.

### Pellagra's Four Ds

A number of diseases present such a varied set of symptoms and signs that a study of these diseases is almost a study of medicine. Syphilis is one such disease. I consider that pellagra is probably the one condition which can mimic a larger number of physical and psychiatric diseases. Deficiency of the essential fatty acids is another, perhaps because one of the main functions of vitamin B3 is to aid in the conversion of these essential fatty acids to prostaglandins. Rudin (1981, 1982) considers essential fatty acid deficiency substrate-pellagra, i.e., pellagra due to a deficiency of substrate in contrast to the corn-induced pellagra, which is due to a deficiency of vitamin. Both result in a deficiency of prostaglandins.

Classical pellagra has been characterized by the four Ds: dermatitis, diarrhea, dementia and death. It is, after all, a preterminal disease. If a vitamin B3 deficiency is diagnosed only after pellagra is obvious, one is playing Russian roulette with the life of the patient.

Dermatitis is a symmetrical, reddish brown, sometimes black, discoloration of the parts of the body exposed to the sun. It has the appearance of a chronic suntan or sunburn. As I have stated earlier, this is probably a primary tryptophan deficiency. Chlorpromazine, the first major tranquilizer, increases the tendency for this type of dermatitis in schizophrenics.

Diarrhea may alternate with constipation. Of course, it increases malabsorption and aggravates the condition.

Dementia is an organic dementia with confusion, disorientation and memory disturbance. This is the typical terminal psychosis.

Earlier stages are more typically schizophrenic with perceptual changes, thought disorder, and mood changes. Psychotic behavior is common. At one time over 25 percent of spring admissions to mental hospitals in the southern U.S. were psychotic pellagrins. There was no way of distinguishing them from other schizophrenic syndromes until vitamin B3 came into clinical use. If these patients responded quickly to the vitamin, they were diagnosed as having pellagra. If not, they were diagnosed as having schizophrenia. This practical diagnostic test had a very important deleterious consequence; it effectively quenched any interest in using vitamin B3 as a treatment for schizophrenia until Hoffer and Osmond began double-blind, controlled studies. (See Hoffer, Osmond, Callbeck and Kahan 1957.) It would have been more appropriate to recognize the pellagra psychosis as one of the schizophrenia syndromes and to classify these patients as fast or slow responders to small doses or megadoses of vitamin B3.

The intermediate stages of pellagra, i.e., somewhere between normal and pellagrous, is characterized by a variety of syndromes representing any of a large number of psychiatric, nonpsychotic states. Early pellagrologists considered neuroses one of the variants of subclinical pellagra, or this in-between state. Another form is the syndrome affecting children that produces the hyperactive or learning-disordered child.

The severe forms of pellagra take more of a neurological form, i.e., the organic psychoses or toxic confusional states, and these may be a main factor in some senile psychoses. Huntington's disease has been described as one of the expressions of pellagra (Still 1979, 1980–1981).

### Administration of Vitamin B3

Orthomolecular therapists use vitamin B3 in large doses. For a large number of diseases the usual vitamin doses are totally inadequate. Each condition requires its optimum dose, which varies from one to many grams per day. It is usually given in three divided doses, for it is water-soluble and quickly eliminated from the body.

Niacin almost always causes a pronounced flush when it is first taken. This is probably due to the sudden release of histamine. The flush or vasodilation is remarkably similar to the one which follows the injection of histamine, with one major difference—a histamine injection lowers blood pressure, while the niacin flush does not.

The flush starts in the forehead and face and works its way down. Sometimes the whole body turns red to the toes, but this is rare. With the flush the person's face and body turn red and feel itchy and hot. After an hour or so the flush slowly disappears. The first flush is usually the worst. With each dose thereafter there is less and less flush, and in most cases it is almost gone after a few weeks. If the dose is too low flushing may remain a problem. Each person has a minimum dose that must be exceeded before flushing ceases, usually one gram taken three times a day. For awhile it was hoped niacin would be a useful vasodilator, but it is not because the flush is erratic. There is no flushing of the meninges of the brain but some tissues do flush. The intensity of the flush depends upon the subject's state of niacin saturation and upon the rapidity of absorption. To minimize the flush, one reduces the rate of absorption. This is done by taking the vitamin after meals so it will be diluted by the food. Flushing can be increased by dissolving it in hot water and drinking it on an empty stomach. Slow-release (SR) preparations markedly reduce the intensity of the flush and are preferred by many. Also SR preparations are more effective per weight of dose. One-half gram SR may be as effective as one gram of the non-SR preparation. The flush is not harmful, but patients must be warned to expect it or they may become fearful. Physicians who recommend niacin and nurses who hand it out must not fail to let the patient know about the flush. If this is done, patients seldom are concerned. A few patients enjoy the flush and try to regain it by stopping their niacin for a few days. When they resume taking it, the sequence of decreasing flushes is again experienced.

Esters of niacin are generally free of this flushing action because the niacin is released so slowly the flush threshold in the body is not exceeded. Linodil is a preparation of inositol and six molecules of niacin that is available in Canada and Europe but not in the U.S.A. Inositol is a member of the B complex of vitamins. It is present in fruit, whole grains, nuts, milk, meat and yeast. Recently it has been found to have some effect on diazepam receptor sites. Thus, a combination of niacin and inositol seems to be particularly useful. New esters of niacin are being investigated primarily in Europe and Japan. There is no flush with niacinamide in 99 out of 100 people, but every year or so I run into a person who flushes on niacinamide. They may be able to convert it very rapidly into niacin.

The intensity of the flush can be reduced by using either antihistamines or aspirin, or both, either before or at the same time the niacin is taken. Robie (1967) reported that cyproheptadine (Periactin) effectively decreased the intensity of the flush. He also used it to treat a generalized rash which occurs rarely with nicotinic acid. Kunin (1976) found that aspirin, which inhibits prostaglandin production, could moderate the flush. Illingworth, Phillipson, Rapp, and Connor (1981) came to the same conclusion without knowing of Kunin's prior finding. They found that aspirin markedly reduced the flush. Their patients were given 250 mg of nicotinic acid three times daily with meals and increased every two to four weeks, reaching a dose of 3 to 8 grams. For the first four to six weeks they took 120 to 180 mg of aspirin with each dose. One-half of the usual 5-grain aspirin tablet provides 150 mg.

The optimum dose of vitamin B3 is that quantity that will cure the patient in the absence of side effects. The usual side-effect is nausea and later vomiting. If the stage of nausea is reached the dose must be reduced. If vomiting starts the vitamin should be stopped for a couple of days and then started at a lower dose. If this is not done the persistent vomiting will lead to dehydration.

Both forms of vitamin B3 are available in 250-mg, 500-mg, and 1,000-mg tablets or capsules. The usual starting dose for adults is one gram three times per day after meals. This may be increased if the therapeutic response is too slow, until side effects occur. If at 6 grams per day there is nausea, the dose should be reduced to 5 or 4 grams per day. With niacinamide the nausea-producing dose is lower than for niacin. It is seldom possible to go as high as 9 grams per day for niacinamide. For niacin the nauseant dose may be extremely high—a few subjects have taken 60 grams per day with no nausea. When the nauseant dose is low for both forms, both may be needed to reach a therapeutic level of total B3.

Vitamin B3 is considered to be nontoxic by orthomolecular therapists and also by the American Medical Association. There have been no deaths due to taking Vitamin B3. It is impossible to commit suicide by overdosage, a desirable property not present in tranquilizers or antidepressants. Rarely will vitamin B3 cause jaundice. In 25 years I can recall 10 cases, and I have treated up to 10,000 patients with niacin. None died, and some, it was discovered, were jaundiced from tranquilizers—when they were discontinued and the niacin retained, the jaundice cleared. Vitamin B3 is a remarkably safe therapeutic substance even when taken with no medical supervision. With adequate medical supervision it is completely safe.

Many years ago, after the hypocholesterolemic effect of niacin was confirmed by the Mayo Clinic, some physicians became concerned because some of the liver function tests showed liver dysfunction even though no jaundice was present. They therefore took liver biopsies on a number of patients who had used 3 grams per day for one year. Histological examination with electron microscope revealed no evidence of liver dysfunction.

Since then, many have noted that if the test is done while patients are taking niacin, the SGOT and SGPT will be elevated. It is my policy to ignore these findings unless there is clinical evidence of liver dysfunction. No liver function test is valid unless the patient has been off niacin for five to seven days; if there is no jaundice, the tests will then be normal.

Apparently liver function tests remain normal if the dose of niacin is built up slowly. Most internists using niacin for lowering blood lipid levels are not overly concerned. In the Coronary Drug Project, in which over 1,000 patients were given niacin for up to seven years, the incidence of liver dysfunction was very low.

It is likely that niacin interferes with the mechanics of the liver function test, or else niacin has some effect in the liver which tends to exaggerate these effects. Thus, niacin increases bilirubin levels because it competes with bilirubin at the hepatic uptake level via bilitranslocase. It induces hyperbilirubinemia in patients with Gilbert's syndrome. Gilbert's syndrome is a benign condition marked by a mild unconjugated hyperbilirubinemia without severe hemolysis or liver disease.

It might be a good idea to do routine bilirubin values before starting niacin to determine whether Gilbert's syndrome patients are more apt to show abnormal liver function tests on niacin.

The effect of niacin in elevating bilirubin has been suggested as a diagnostic test for Gilbert's syndrome.

### Uses for Vitamin B3

A. PSYCHIATRIC
1. THE SCHIZOPHRENIAS
In 1952 Dr. Humphry Osmond and I began

the first double-blind therapeutic experiment in psychiatry when we compared a yeast nucleotide preparation against placebo. Shortly after, we started a double-blind experiment comparing niacin, niacinamide and placebo on a group of 30 acute schizophrenic patients. The sickest patients from each group (more depressed or more violent) also received a short series of electroconvulsive therapy. One year after discharge each patient was reevaluated. The treatment code was then broken. From the placebo group three were well. The usual or natural or spontaneous recovery rate is considered to be about 35 percent. The other two groups fared better; from each about

75 percent were well. We had doubled the one-year natural recovery rate. Three more double-blind experiments confirmed these conclusions. Since then the use of vitamin B3 has become standard practice for orthomolecular therapists. But it is important to note that vitamin B3 alone is seldom used for treating schizophrenia. It is combined with orthomolecular nutrition, with other vitamins or minerals, and for a while with standard neuroleptic drugs when they are required. This comprehensive program has been used on over 100,000 schizophrenics in North America. The following are the expected results.

| Type of Patient | Duration of Treatment | Outcome |
|---|---|---|
| Acute and subacute | 2 years | 90% recovery, none worse |
| Chronic—ambulant | 2–3 years | 75% recovery, none worse |
| Chronic—in institutions | 2–5 years | 50% recovery, none worse |

When tranquilizers are used, smaller quantities are needed. Eventually, recovered patients do not need to use any tranquilizers. (For a complete review see Hoffer and Osmond 1976.)

## 2. ALCOHOLISM

The use of vitamin B3 for treating alcoholics was first developed by Bill W., cofounder of Alcoholics Anonymous. He had observed its beneficial effect on himself and on 30 of his associates in AA. Because of his interest, its use for treating alcoholics spread rapidly. The best studies on thousands of patients were completed by Dr. Russell Smith (1974).

## 3. DEPRESSION

For some depressions B3 is a valuable adjunct combined with proper nutrition. Dr. Harvey Ross (1975) has an excellent description of how it can be used.

## 4. CHILDREN WITH LEARNING AND BEHAVIORAL DISORDERS

Dr. R. Glen Green noted that these children were remarkably like children described as having subclinical pellagra over 40 years ago. Because they had not developed the typical pellagra skin lesions, Dr. Green (1970, 1974, 1975) called them "subclinical pellagrins." This broad group includes the whole spectrum of learning and behavioral disorders. These children respond well to orthomolecular therapy. Vitamin B3 is an important component. The first person to use the comprehensive program was Dr. Allan Cott (1969, 1971, 1973). He has been confirmed by Dr. Green, by Dr. L. Silverman (1975), Hoffer (1971, 1972), and by a large number of orthomolecular physicians who have been too busy to report their data.

## 5. SENILITY

I have found vitamin B3, especially niacin, to be very helpful in reducing the onset of senility, but it is only one component of a comprehensive program, (Hoffer 1974; Hoffer and Walker 1980). So far no member of my family has been "allowed" to become senile.

## 6. CRIMINAL BEHAVIOR

Vitamin B3 is an important component of orthmolecular treatment with astoundingly good results (see Hippchen 1978, 1981, 1982; Schauss 1979, 1980).

## 7. LYSERGIC ACID DIETHYLAMIDE (LSD) REACTIONS

Vitamin B3 is a very potent agent for reducing the intensity of these reactions. (See Agnew and Hoffer 1955.)

## B. PHYSICAL DISEASES

### 1. ARTHRITIS

By 1950, Dr. W. Kaufman had published two books detailing the beneficial effects of vitamin B3 for a large group of arthritics. These books, now out of print, are still available from the author (395A Ottawa Lane, Stratford, Connecticut 06497).

I have seen similar beneficial results. This does not mean that every arthritic will respond; a number of other vitamins, especially pyridoxine, vitamins A and D3, and a mineral, zinc, have also been shown to be helpful. There is no doubt a large proportion of arthritics are vitamin B3 responsive, using 2 to 6 grams per day.

### 2. HYPERLIPIDEMIA

Prof. R. Altschul, Dr. J. Stephen and I (1955) discovered that niacin, but not niacinamide, lowered cholesterol levels. It also lowers triglycerides. Since our 1955 report, over 2,000 studies have been completed confirming our work and trying to discover how niacin works. Niacin may soon be the only broad-spectrum hypolipidemic substance available. Atromid, its only competitor, has been found in England to increase the death rate, increase the rate of gallbladder disease, and to increase the mortality postsurgically for these gallbladder cases.

A coronary drug study was completed in 1975. The nearly 8,000 survivors were reexamined by Canner (1985) who was interested in determining whether the treatments had caused any deleterious side effects (except for death). To his surprise, the niacin-treated group lived two years longer and had an 11 percent decrease in mortality compared to all other groups. Had these patients remained on niacin after 1975, I have no doubt the mortality would have been decreased even more and might have approached Dr. Ed Boyle's finding of a 90 percent decrease.

The National Institutes of Health, Washington, D.C., recommends that elevated cholesterol levels be decreased by diet, and when this is not adequate, by using substances such as niacin. They recommend Atromid not be used.

### 3. VASCULAR DISORDERS

One of the best accounts of the usefulness of niacin in treating vascular disorders is given in the book *Niacin in Vascular Disorders and Hyperlipidemia* by R. Altschul (1964). According to Condorelli, who contributed a chapter to Altschul's book, niacin has been used on a fairly wide scale for a number of vascular disorders. These studies began in 1938 and were based upon the vasodilation caused by niacin. At the time of Condorelli's writing, in 1964, niacin was in wide use for these conditions in Italy. Very few English-reading physicians are aware of this important work.

Niacin even by intravenous infusion is very benign. During the flush it causes a transient slight increase in blood pressure, which rarely reaches 10 percent above the base line and is normal within 5 minutes. This is followed by a transient decrease in pressure, seldom more than 10 percent. The systolic pressure is more affected. For all practical purposes there is very little effect.

Circulation time is decreased up to 25 percent, and cardiac output is increased due to an increase in systolic stroke volume. Pulmonary resistance is decreased, as is peripheral resistance. Oxygen consumption is increased. But there are no EEG changes.

Condorelli (1964) found a number of indications for niacin, including vasomotor headaches, regional angiospasm, amaurosis caused by spasms in the retina, cerebrovascular spasms and acrospastic syndromes. The type of headache which responded is characterized by spells of nonpulsating pain with paleness and retinal angiospasm. Ergotin makes these headaches worse.

Condorelli also found niacin the treatment of choice for embolism. Thus, 100 mg given intravenously after an embolus in large proximal vessels alleviates the pain within a few minutes. The paleness eases, as do hypothermia and cyanosis. For a few days niacin is given intravenously every two to four hours, then every six to eight hours. Since 1941, in Condorelli's department, no embolectomy was required if the first injection of niacin was started early enough. He wrote: "Nicotinic acid is a wonderful and reliable drug in the treatment of embolism of the extremities and it should never be missing from the first aid remedies of a physician."

Niacin also helps in treating end arteries (cerebral, spinal, renal, mesenteric and retinal), but the results are not as dramatic. One of my elderly patients became blind in one eye following an embolus in the retinal artery. On 3 grams per day of niacin, this suddenly cleared several weeks later and he regained his vision.

Niacin, according to Condorelli, is also the treatment of choice for thrombosing arteriopathies, "as an acute functional treatment to facilitate collateral circulation and thus mitigate ischemic disorders by arterial stenosis or occlusion." He finds it valuable for claudication. It has removed the necessity for amputation following diabetic gangrene.

It is the best treatment for end artery thrombosis, but again its curative effects are not as dramatic as for thrombosis of the extremities.

I have used it for 25 years after strokes and have found it very valuable in restoring brain function. Obviously, necrotic brain tissue will not be replaced, so there is no complete restoration. It appears as if surrounding tissues are able to regain function and take over some of the function of destroyed brain tissue.

It is not surprising it was also found very useful in treating coronary disease. Angina of effort was improved, disorders of the atrioventricular and intraventricular conduction system were improved, as was coronary insufficiency.

Niacin must not be used in acute infarction with shock. But it can be started once circulation is established when it will limit the area of irreversible ischemic damage.

Finally, these Italian physicians found it very beneficial for acute glomerulonephritis. Treatment shortened and sometimes terminated dramatically the hematuric phase, activated diuresis, mitigated albuminuria, and brought uremia to normal. Equally dramatic results were achieved in treating eclampsia.

Recently, a man and his wife, both retired, visited us in Victoria, British Columbia. We had worked together in a Saskatchewan alcoholism treatment program from 1955 on. During dinner the woman reminded me that about 25 years before, she had suffered from severe nephritis that her nephrologist declared untreatable. He began to prepare her for dialysis, as there was no hope that anything else would help. Her nephrologist was one of the best known and admired specialists in the field. I told my friend of the Italian research, advising her to consider using 3 grams per day of niacin in consultation with her physician. He dismissed this idea out of hand. However, when she weighed the alternatives she concluded she would try niacin. Within a month she was well and has remained well.

A second case responded equally dramatically. This was a preteen girl with chronic glomerulonephritis. As there was no treatment, her father, an intelligent teacher, began to read as much nutritional literature as he could obtain and on his own started to give her niacin. She, too, recovered and has been well for over 20 years. After she recovered she consulted Dr. Max Vogel who examined her history and records and confirmed she had had glomerulonephritis and that she was now well.

Now we have animal studies confirming these earlier clinical observations (Wahlberg, Carlson, Wasserman and Ljungqvist 1985). They began their study with the observation that 20 percent of Type I diabetics who are ill more than 25 years do not develop microangiopathy, even without optimal glucose control. This suggested other metabolic disturbances. Earlier reports had already shown these disturbances were in the tryptophan-nicotinamide adenine dinucleotide cycle. They induced diabetes in 60 rats with streptozotocin. One group were given niacinamide for six months and compared to a control group not given any. At the end of the study the niacinamide-treated rats had significantly lower blood sugar levels. Immunofluorescent staining of niacinamide-treated rats was significantly less pronounced. The vitamin retarded development of diabetic nephropathy.

For all vascular conditions, the Italians started with niacin given intravenously, using 100 mg injections. Perhaps similar results could be achieved using the larger oral doses. The advantage of a smaller I.V. dose is that nausea hardly ever occurs.

In North America clinicians were interested in niacin's hypocholesterolemic effect which led to the idea this could be used to protect against coronary vascular disease. The massive multihospital, multimillion-dollar and multidrug study concluded that none of the compounds used for lowering cholesterol—thyroid, estrogen, Clofibrate and niacin—were any better than placebo in decreasing coronary episodes following the first pretreatment one. A reexamination of the published data shows that niacin was slightly more effica-

cious than the other four treatments. However, the effect was so slight it leads to the conclusion that it was of no clinical significance or that the massive research was inadequate. For many years Hoffer and Osmond (1961, 1963) and Hoffer (1967) have been discussing the inadequacies of the double-blind design. Boyle's (1978) work supports our view. He followed a large group of patients for ten years after their first coronary. The death rate was only 10 percent of what would be expected from such a group. Boyle gave each patient individual attention characteristic of the good clinician and was interested in really examining whether niacin could help. No one has yet reported that faith or placebo has reduced the incidence of coronary deaths subsequent to the first attack. There is nothing as dramatic as the bypass operation with all the experiences surrounding it. Yet there is very little evidence that it prolongs life significantly, even though it does relieve pain and discomfort.

I am convinced that niacin can decrease significantly the incidence of coronary disease, but I do not think it by itself is the solution. Ideally, one would use a sugar-free orthomolecular diet, high in fiber, low in fat. One could then add niacin when needed, for its hypocholesterolemic effect. That is the term most commonly used, "cholesterol-lowering," but it is more accurate to say that it *normalizes* lipids. When cholesterol is very low, i.e. below 140 mg., niacin tends to elevate it (Hoffer and Callbeck 1957). On niacin all cholesterol values tend to cluster toward 180 mg, which I consider to be the optimum level. I would balance niacin with pyridoxine, which plays a role in arteriosclerosis, with ascorbic acid, which heals damaged intima, and with essential fatty acids and zinc.

Familial hypercholesterolemia will not respond to dietary management. The only effective combination is Colestipol, a bile acid sequestrant, and niacin, which reduces synthesis of low-density lipoproteins. For the first time it is possible to bring lipid levels down to normal range and to test the effect this will have on premature arteriosclerosis and death (Illingworth et al. 1981; Moutafis, Myant, Maricini and Oriente 1971; Kane, et al. 1981).

Niacin releases histamine and heparinoids from their storage sites. These substances control lipid levels by modulating their transfer across membranes. Niacinamide has no effect on lipid levels, nor does it release histamine or heparinoids (Hoffer 1983).

Niacin ought to decrease the size of lipid storage sites due to excess cholesterol. In fact this has been observed clinically. I have seen cholesterol tags in skin regress in a few months. It is likely that in a similar way cholesterol can be removed from fat plaques which contain too much. It would, of course, have no effect on chronic, fibrotic, calcified lesions not containing excessive cholesterol. Ost and Stenson, in R. Altschul's book (1964), examined niacin. They studied 11 men and five women with intermittent claudication. At the beginning their mean age was 60 years. They were treated 21.5 months (range 13 to 35). Five were also on anticoagulant medication. In 14, walk tolerance improved. None were worse. In three, circulation as measured by plethysmographic and oscillometric recordings improved; none were worse.

Twenty-nine legs were examined repeatedly. In four there was a regression of the lesions in the arterial wall. In 11 legs, blood flow through the femoral artery had deteriorated. This work shows that regression of the lesion is possible, but it is slow and probably requires more time.

Recently, Lewis (1982) found that femoral arteriosclerosis advanced at only one-third the usual rate in subjects treated with Clofibrate, niacin, or Cholestyramine. The rate of arteriosclerosis formation was measured by arteriography at the onset of study and 15 to 24 hours later. Cholesterol levels were down 25 percent and triglycerides were decreased 40 percent.

### 4. DIABETES MELLITUS

By keeping lipid levels normal, niacin should protect diabetics against the most dangerous chronic side effect—arteriosclerosis. But it may have an effect on glucose levels in blood, on the glucose tolerance curve and on insulin requirements. Insulin requirements may be increased or decreased.

Recently, Vague, Vialettes, Lassmann-Vague, and Vallo (1987) concluded that niacinamide given to young adult Type I insulin-dependent diabetics produced a remission in some.

They conducted a double-blind experiment with 16 newly-diagnosed, ketotic, Type I (insulin-dependent) diabetics, ages 10 to 35 years. One week after starting intensive insulin, the subjects were started on niacinamide or placebo, 3 grams per day. If insulin was still required after six months, the vitamin was discontinued.

| Number | Niacinamide | Placebo |
|---|---|---|
| | 7 | 9 |
| At six months, not needing insulin | 5 | 2 |
| At 12 months, not needing insulin | 3 | 0 |

Three of the treated group reached two-year remissions. None of the placebo group were in remission longer than nine months. The researchers concluded: "Our results and those found from animal experiments indicate that, in Type I diabetes, nicotinamide slows down destruction of B-cells and enhances their regeneration, thus extending remission time."

One such animal experiment is described by Yamada, Nonaka, Hanafusa, Miyazaki, Toyoshima and Tarui (1982). These authors summarized their work as follows:

This experiment was undertaken to explore a novel method of therapy for insulin-dependent diabetes mellitus (IDDM), using nonobese diabetic (NOD) mice that had symptoms and histologic changes similar to those of human IDDM patients. We examined preventive and therapeutic effects of large-dose nicotinamide administration on diabetes in NOD mice. Eighteen young female NOD mice without glycosuria were randomly divided into two groups; nine received subcutaneous nicotinamide (0.5 mg/g body wt) injections every day and the other nine were maintained as a control group and not injected. After 40 days, all of the mice given nicotinamide showed almost normal glucose tolerance and only mild insulitis on histologic study. On the other hand, marked glycosuria and severe insulitis were observed in six of the nine mice not injected. Four of six NOD mice given nicotinamide from the day of the first occurrence of marked glycosuria displayed a disappearance of glycosuria and an improvement in glucose tolerance during the therapy; however, urine sugar became negative in only one of the six mice that received nicotinamide from one to two weeks after the onset of marked glycosuria. These results indicate that nicotinamide has preventive and therapeutic effects on diabetes in NOD mice, and suggest the reversibility of B-cell damage, at least at a very early stage of IDDM.

In my opinion, this is a remarkable development in the treatment of juvenile diabetes. Certainly niacinamide is much less toxic than cyclosporine.

## 5. ALLERGIES

Niacin releases histamine from its storage sites, the mast cells. When the histamine levels are reduced the individual is protected to a major degree against allergic shock reactions. Dr. Ed Boyle found that guinea pigs, pretreated with niacin, no longer died from anaphylactic shock. I have observed that patients with food allergies can tolerate and re-quire much larger doses of niacin. When the offending food is no longer eaten, the amount tolerated and required is reduced sharply. I now follow the working rule that any patient who requires 12 grams per day probably has one or more food allergies.

Many years ago the Mayo Clinic reported that 75 percent of all migraine headaches responded to niacin (see Hoffer 1962). Histamine seems to be involved. I also have seen astonishing recoveries from niacin. My most surprising observation was a man who had suffered severe migraines for 30 years. After one month on niacin, 3 grams per day, he remained migraine-free. Ménière's disease has been treated for several decades with niacin by otolaryngologists.

## 6. LUPUS ERYTHEMATOSUS (LE)

The author of *The Sun Is My Enemy*, Mrs. H. Aladjem (1972), describes her search for a treatment for her LE, which had been diagnosed and declared untreatable by Boston's best physicians. She had heard of a physician in Bulgaria who had a treatment, and eventually she found him. He started her on parenteral niacin, which she still takes. She has been in steady remission since. A large number of LE patients use niacin as one of the treatments.

## 7. LEUKOPLAKIA

This is a precancerous condition of the throat. In Sweden it was routinely cured with vitamin B3 and the cancer was prevented (Warburg 1967).

## 8. STRESS

Niacin is a remarkable antistress factor. Dr. L. Levi, Director for Clinical Stress Research, Karolinska Institute, Stockholm (see Carlson, Levi and Oro 1967), found that any excitement, fear or pleasure would release fatty acids into the blood. The adrenaline released fatty acids from the fat storage sites. When subjects pretreated with niacin were exposed to identical stress there was no increase in fatty acids. This may be how it is therapeutic for coronary victims.

Dr. J. Yaryura-Tobias (1971) has also found niacin to be an antistress factor. Rats tied to a restraining board are under severe stress and develop peptic ulcers. Similar rats pretreated with niacin and exposed to the same degree of stress very seldom developed ulcers. Dr. Ed Boyle, in a few preliminary experiments, found that mice pretreated with niacin and thrown into cold water kept on swimming; control mice died from shock.

I have observed this antistress effect on patients over the past 30 years and have myself taken it that long. It has given me at least four more useful hours each day.

### Conclusion

Vitamin B3 is a remarkable vitamin with a multiplicity of uses. There is little doubt it will be used on an ever-increasing scale once physicians become familiar with it. Already it is used on a very wide scale.

### Side Effects

Any chemical used in treatment may have both negative and positive side effects. Positive or advantageous side effects are so rare they are seldom discussed in pharmacology. Toxicology deals only with negative effects. Nutrients, in sharp contrast, have a large number of beneficial effects which are unexpected and had not been considered. The reason is that nutrients are not used for symptomatic treatment only—they have a global effect on health. For example, vitamin B3 cures pellagra. One of the main, but not invariant, symptoms of pellagra is a typical skin rash, especially in areas exposed to the sun. A cured pellagrin has a positive side effect, which is the cure of the skin rash. If a person has a number of symptoms, each one a symptom of a vitamin-responsive condition, each one will respond. If the main symptom is arthritis, using vitamin B3 will cure the arthritis, but positive side effects will include a sense of well-being,

better gums, lower cholesterol and triglyceride levels (if nicotinic acid is used). Using nicotinic acid to lower cholesterol levels will have a positive effect of decreasing the tendency for arteriosclerosis. But there is no point in continuing this type of discussion; vitamins restore health in a global sense and remove all symptoms of the disease being treated.

Negative side effects are the flush already described for nicotinic acid, nausea and occasionally vomiting, headache, excessive release of histamine, an effect on blood sugar tolerance, skin lesions and liver disease (Hoffer 1962, 1969).

### NAUSEA AND VOMITING

Both nicotinamide and nicotinic acid will cause nausea and vomiting if the dose is too high, but a few days are required before this side effect occurs. The first reaction is mild nausea. Later it is more pronounced and if the dose is not reduced it will lead to vomiting. Excessive vomiting can cause dehydration and may be one of the factors in the etiology of liver disease when it does occur. Children may not know how to describe nausea and will simply lose their appetite. When nausea is present, the dose must be reduced. But this may lower the dose below its therapeutic level. If nicotinic acid causes nausea one can change to nicotinamide, or from nicotinamide to nicotinic acid, or subnauseant levels of both may be required; 1.5 grams of nicotinic acid, plus 1.5 grams of nicotinamide provides 3 grams of total vitamin B3. If neither form can be tolerated, one of the esters such as Linodil or Complamin may be used. The nauseant effect can also be reduced or eliminated by using antihistamines and antinauseants. Tranquilizers have antihistamine properties and are also antinauseant and are helpful in controlling nausea.

Nausea induced by vitamin B3 is nearly always gone within 24 to 48 hours after its use is discontinued. This is the best way of determining whether the nausea is coming from the vitamin or from some physical illness. When severe vomiting has developed, it may require two days to clear. Adequate fluid intake, small amounts every hour, will prevent dehydration.

HEADACHE

This is a rare side effect, especially of nicotinic acid. It is probably related to the histamine-releasing properties of nicotinic acid. It is never severe, being usually a mild, prolonged tension headache. It can be controlled by mild analgesics and very rarely the vitamin B3 has to be changed to a different form. Yet nicotinic acid can be very helpful in removing migraine headaches (Hoffer 1962).

EXCESSIVE RELEASE OF HISTAMINE

The name *nicotinic acid* frightens many physicians. They are unaware that, like many natural organic acids, nicotinic acid is a very weak acid. It releases fewer hydrogen ions and is comparable to ascorbic acid or lemon juice. It is much less acid than the hydrochloric acid present in the stomach. But because peptic ulcer has been wrongfully ascribed to too much acid rather than a deficiency of whole food, many believe nicotinic acid will aggravate ulcers by increasing acidity. Nicotinic acid does not increase acidity; on the contrary, it binds hydrogen ions and probably decreases the acidity very slightly. I have given patients nicotinic acid even when they have had a history of duodenal ulcer, with no ill effect.

A few patients with no history of ulcer have experienced excessive secretion of gastric juices, perhaps because the histamine released by the niacin overstimulated gastric secretion.

EFFECT ON SUGAR TOLERANCE

Very soon after I began to study the clinical and physiological properties of vitamin B3, I found that it altered the sugar tolerance curves of a few people (Hoffer 1962). When it did have an effect it was to decrease the sugar tolerance. It is necessary to discontinue the nicotinic acid for at least five days before doing a glucose tolerance test. There is no residual effect. Diabetics may be treated with nicotinic acid and in most cases it has no effect on insulin requirements. These changes are usually small and require minor dosage adjustments. The hypolipidemic properties of nicotinic acid indicate it should be used for diabetics if there is an indication for it. Nicotinamide has no effect on either glucose tolerance tests or on insulin requirements.

SKIN LESIONS

A very small proportion of patients, particularly schizophrenics, develop a dark pigmentation of skin when they are first treated with nicotinic acid. Nicotinamide has no effect. The pigmentation comes on after several months, especially on some flexor surfaces. There are no symptoms associated with it— no itching, no rashes.

## NICOTINAMIDE ADENINE DINUCLEOTIDE

NAD is the antipellagra factor containing nicotinamide. Some years ago, Hoffer and Osmond (1966) obtained a special preparation dissolved in oil and surrounded by an enteric coat. This was done to minimize the hydrolysis of NAD in the stomach. We tested its antischizophrenic properties on a small number of schizophrenic patients located in a university hospital psychiatric ward. Some were chronic ambulatory patients, some were acute, and one was a long-term resident in a mental hospital. The results were amazing and were evident to residents and nursing staff—in a few days patients showed improvement seen after many months on vitamin B3 or not seen at all. The one chronic patient responded so well she was placed in a special home. Her psychiatrist from the mental hospital had never seen her so well. But then we ran out of supplies because the company which had agreed to provide the NAD sent no more. Within a few days, all the patients had relapsed. The chronic patient was then readmitted and treated as vigorously as possible, but was not responsive to any treatment and died within a year in that mental hospital.

Our report generated a controversy but did not generate any serious attempt to reproduce our work. One study by Kline used chronic, back ward patients only from Rockland State Hospital in Orangeburg, New York. They saw no clinical improvement. But the HOD scores of their treated patients became much lower, while their placebo controls showed no change. However, Kline et al. (1967) ignored the HOD findings. In our experience we have never seen such a discrepancy between a significant decrease in HOD scores in a few weeks and no clinical response. The HOD test is more objective. Nor did Kline use the same type of NAD we had used. Another study used only chronic patients with the correct NAD and concluded it did not help this particular chronic group. A third study used only I.V. NAD and saw no results.

Pfeiffer (1975) examined the effect of various NAD preparations with his quantitative EEG. Our preparation was the only one with major activity. The way Kline prepared it, it showed very little activity.

As I could not obtain any more, there the matter rested. Hoffer and Osmond (1966) reported what we saw.

One theoretical objection to our finding was the commonly held view that large molecules could not pass membrane barriers, and there was no rationale to explain how it could work. Richards, Snell and Snell (1983) may have provided both a rationale and a method for testing. They used transverse slices of hippocampus as a bioassay to screen extracts of fresh brain tissue. They were searching for that fraction of fresh brain tissue which reversibly depressed synaptic transmission in the dentate gyrus of the hippocampus. They found it was NAD that was active at a concentration range of 1 to 10 uM. The degree of depression was related to the concentration of NAD. This was due to the adenosine portion of the NAD. They concluded that NAD exerted its powerful depressant effect by reducing the release of a transmitter, i.e., by exerting a negative feedback control.

Niacinamide acts like a diazepine provided it penetrates into the brain. Mohler, Polc, Cumin, Pieri, and Kettler (1979) isolated niacinamide from brain tissue and found it was an endogenous constituent that attached itself to benzodiazepine receptors. Nicotinamide had the following effects on cat spinal cord activity: (1) dorsal root reflexes induced by dorsal root stimulation increased up to 50 percent; (2) excitability of primary efferents was not affected; (3) unconditioned monosynaptic ventral root reflexes were not affected; (4) electrophysiological effects very similar in size and latency to benzodiazepine when applied locally; were produced by cat spinal cord; (5) punishment-suppressed behavior of cats was restored; (6) anticonvulsant activity in cats; (7) antiaggressive effect in cats; (8) relaxed muscles; (9) hypnotic effect, prolonging total sleep time and increasing rapid-eye-movement sleep; (10) increased serotonin levels in brain. All these are also benzodiazepine properties.

Only 0.3 percent of nicotinamide penetrates into the brain; therefore, large doses must be given even though it is as potent as benzodiazepine.

Thus, at last we have the beginnings of a mechanism to explain how vitamin B3 (which is converted into NAD) and NAD can be centrally active.

## CHOLINE

Choline is the precursor to the neurohormone acetylocholine. It is a component of lecithin as phosphatidyl choline, a triglyceride containing two fatty acid groups and one phosphoric acid group with an organic nitrogen base. Very little choline is found free in the diet. Some choline is transported into the brain, where acetylcoenzyme A, catalyzed by choline acetyltransferase, forms acetylcholine. Acetylcholine is split by acetylcholinesterase. More choline is released in the brain from phosphatidyl choline.

Choline or lecithin in the food controls the level of choline in blood and in the brain. Increasing choline intake thus elevates levels of acetylcholine in the brain, and diseases associated with deficient levels of acetylcholine in the brain ought to be helped.

### Treatment of Senile Dementia

As with other psychiatric diagnostic terms, *senility* refers to a number of syndromes. It can be caused by multiple cerebral infarcts, or little strokes, or in fact even by single, larger strokes. It can be caused by progressive arteriosclerosis without little strokes. It may follow a number of nutritional deficiencies, including lack of thiamine, vitamin B3 and others. Or it may be due to the accumulation of metals—of these, aluminum has been implicated. I suspect other metals will be found to play a role when they are studied in senile brains. In what is known as Alzheimer's Disease and in subsequent senile dementia activity of choline acetyltransferase has been found. In 1977 a group in Edinburgh gave choline to seven Alzheimer's subjects. For two weeks the subjects received 5 grams of choline chloride per day; then for two weeks they got twice as much. There was some improvement. (See Boyd et al, 1977).

In 1978 another group at the National Institute of Mental Health gave 10 grams of choline or placebo to 10 normal subjects for two days. There was some improvement in memory, more pronounced in the subjects who were the worst.

Berry and Borkan (1983) reviewed studies of choline for Alzheimer's Disease. In one study, 25 grams of lecithin improved three out of seven cases after four weeks. They improved in learning ability, understood instructions better and were cooperative. A second study yielded similar results with 20 grams of choline per day, or 100 grams of lecithin per day.

### Tardive Dyskinesia

This will be discussed further on. It is one of the serious toxicity effects of tranquilizers in schizophrenics. The other major one is that tranquilizers, if required continually, do not permit recovery.

Choline was first used in treatment of tardive dykinesia in 1975. Sixteen grams per day produced significant decrease in abnormal movements. This original observation has been confirmed in several studies, but lecithin has replaced choline because it is more palatable and more physiological. None of the studies examined the role of manganese, which was discovered by Kunin (1976). Manganese is required in very small doses, and the rationale for its use appears to me to be more scientific. Certainly it is easier to take a few milligrams per day of manganese compared to gram doses of choline or lecithin. I suggest lecithin be tried only in those cases where manganese does not work.

### Side Effects

Megadoses of choline may cause nausea, salivation, sweating and anorexia. Bacterial degradation of choline in the gastrointestinal tract causes the "dead fish" odor in sweat and urine.

Lecithin is easier to consume, but in doses over 25 grams per day it may cause anorexia, nausea, bloating or diarrhea. Purer preparations cause fewer side effects. The best lecithin is that which is richest in phosphatidyl choline.

### ASCORBIC ACID (VITAMIN C)

The literature describing ascorbic acid is very large. Here I will give a brief account only, emphasizing its clinical applications. The following books are the most important vitamin C publications, and should be read and studied by physicians. They are:

1. *The Healing Factor. Vitamin C Against Disease*, by Irwin Stone, Grosset and Dunlap, New York, 1972.
2. *Vitamin C and the Common Cold*, by Linus Pauling, W. H. Freeman and Co., San Francisco, 1970.
3. *Vitamin C, the Common Cold and the Flu*, by Linus Pauling, W. H. Freeman and Co., San Francisco, 1976.
4. *Cancer and Vitamin C*, by E. Cameron and L. Pauling, W. W. Norton and Co., New York, 1979.
5. *Vitamin C, Its Molecular Biology and Medical Potential*, by S. Lewin, Academic Press, New York, 1976.
6. *The Vitamin C Connection*, by E. Cheraskin, W. M. Ringsdorf, Jr. and E. L. Sisley, Harper and Row, New York, 1983.

Ascorbic acid resembles glucose in structure, but it is much more reactive chemically. When animals make ascorbic acid they start from glucose. This series of reactions requires the enzyme gulonolactone oxidase, which catalyzes the formation of the last enzymatic reaction. When 2 keto 1-gulonolactone is formed, it changes into ascorbic acid. Humans and a few other species of animals lack this enzyme and so cannot make ascorbic acid. Ascorbic acid can be oxidized to dehydroascorbic acid via an intermediate free radical (Ascorbic Free Radical, or AFR). Ascorbic acid, AFR and dehydroascorbate form an equilibrium, depending on a large number of chemical conditions. Of the three, ascorbic acid is the most stable. Natural stabilizers, such as bioflavonoids and other reducing substances, are present in living tissue.

### Distribution in the Body

The amount of ascorbic acid in various tissues of the body varies markedly; probably this depends upon how those tissues use the ascorbic acid.

The adrenal glands contain more ascorbic acid per unit weight than any other tissues. The medulla synthesizes noradrenalin and adrenalin and the cortex a variety of steroid hormones. Ascorbic acid is involved in both sets of reactions. It not only is essential in the synthesis of these amines, but it is also used to protect them from oxidation to the toxic noradrenochrome and adrenochrome. Noradrenalin and adrenalin can get into the blood only by passing through the cortex by diffusion. They thus pick up and combine with ascorbic acid to form a more stable derivative that can be reproduced in the laboratory. It is likely that an adrenal gland depleted of its ascorbic acid, as occurs during stress, is less able to protect the noradrenalin and adrenalin from oxidation to the highly toxic noradrenochrome and adrenochrome. When the gland is sectioned (cut) in the laboratory and allowed to stand, the medulla turns red. Oxygen converts these amines into noradrenochrome and adrenochrome. The cut tissue does not have enough antioxidant to stabilize the adrenalin.

Leukocytes transport ascorbic acid to damaged tissue, where it is deposited. Thus, concentrations of ascorbic acid can be achieved that are greater than those resulting from plasma alone. Leukocytes also require ascorbic acid for making globulins and for phagocytosis. Leukocytes, rich in ascorbic acid, can ingest many more bacteria per cell. Leukocytes are so avid for ascorbic acid that when too little is present they will retain enough to cause scurvy in other tissues. Many of the symptoms associated with leukemia are due to the sequestration of the body's reserves in the huge volume of white blood cells. Up to 7 grams of ascorbic acid each day may be required merely to satisfy the leukocytes' requirement for vitamin C and to allow the rest of the body to obtain some.

The lens of the eye requires a lot of ascorbic acid to keep it properly fluid and transparent. The amount of ascorbic acid present is decreased when cataract is present. Conversely, large doses of ascorbic acid are useful in preventing and treating cataract (Stone 1972).

The brain is rich in ascorbic acid. With age the concentration goes down. Ascorbic acid is so important to the brain that it accumulates it across the blood-brain barrier at great cost. Even so, less than 1 percent of the ascorbic acid taken by mouth gets across into the brain. Its role there undoubtedly is to protect neurons, especially at transmitter sites, from being destroyed by oxidized derivatives of amines, such as dihydroxyphenylalanine (dopa), or topa, or noradrenaline and adrenalin. The chrome indoles are very toxic. They have been found to inhibit transmission of signals across the synapse.

Ascorbic acid is essential for a large number of reactions in the body and may be the key molecule for life itself (Szent-Györgyi 1972). The reactions listed here provide some examples of how the body concentrates this essential nutrient where it is needed.

## A Few Properties of Ascorbic Acid

1. Ascorbic acid combines with other molecules, such as noradrenalin and adrenalin. With nicotinamide it forms a yellow-colored complex, an ascorbate nicotinamide salt. NAD could complex in the same way.

2. Ascorbic acid destroys histamine. Clemetson (1980) analyzed 437 blood samples for histamine and ascorbic acid levels. When the ascorbic acid falls below 0.7 mg/100 ml, blood histamine levels increase markedly. Giving 1 gram of ascorbic acid each day for three days reduced histamine levels in every case. The accumulation of histamine in the tissues when scurvy is present is due to the deficiency of ascorbic acid.

   Clemetson reported that in nine out of 10 cases of premature separation of the placenta, ascorbic acid levels were very low. Two other patients also had elevated blood histamine levels.

   Ascorbic acid should be used in every condition where elevated blood histamine levels are a factor. These include burns, bites, hives, and a variety of allergic conditions.

3. Ascorbic acid dissolves cholesterol by lowering surface tension, increasing its solubility. It also tends to pull calcium out of the calcium plaques. Other elements are also removed. Three grams of ascorbate in urine carries 0.4 grams of sodium. Potassium, ammonium, magnesium, iron, copper and zinc are also excreted in increased quantities. Smaller amounts of lead, mercury and cadmium are excreted. Essential elements such as zinc should be supplemented when large doses of ascorbic acid are used. It can be used to help detoxify the body of its excess lead, mercury, cadmium, and even copper, when present in excess.

The ascorbic acid molecule probably was present in the primordial soup in which life developed, as was vitamin B3 and perhaps other vitamins. It preceded life by a long time. It would be surprising if it were dangerous, for life developed and accommodated to molecules already present in the fluid. About 450 million years ago, vertebrates developed and flourished for about 100 million years. Then land animals evolved: reptiles, birds and mammals. Fish and amphibians made ascorbic acid in their kidneys; birds are in transition from earlier forms, who used their kidneys, to later forms who used both kidney and liver, and finally to more recent forms who use only liver, as do most mammals.

But about 60 million years ago our ancestors lost the ability to make ascorbic acid. The enzyme l-gulonolactone oxidase, which in other animals converts D-glucuronic acid lacton to 1-gulonolactone, disappeared. The gene that controlled its formation vanished.

Our ancestors lived on diets rich in ascorbic acid. The loss of ascorbic acid synthesis did not destroy the individual because there was enough in food to maintain life. Enough advantage was gained by the release of energy for other biochemical processes that had been required to make ascorbic acid. Pauling (1968) described how this loss of a gene became an evolutionary advantage. But once the ability to make ascorbic acid was lost, it could not be regained. Surviving man paid an enormous price in disease and death from having to live with mild to severe deficiency of ascorbic acid; as our ancestors ranged farther and farther from ascorbic acid-rich foods, the price became more costly. The stage before death is scurvy, a major scourge of mankind. Only man, guinea pigs, and a fruit-eating bat have become totally dependent on external sources of ascorbic acid. I suspect that our domesticated animals, especially cats and dogs, are following our footsteps. Some purebred puppies suffer from hip dysplasia, or canine scurvy.

Classical scurvy is seldom seen in industrialized nations. It usually is first seen as a sallow, muddy complexion in a person who suffers loss of energy, fatigue and fleeting joint pains. Gums become sore and bleed. There are frequent nosebleeds and skin hemorrhages. Eventually the skin becomes dingy and brown. Teeth loosen, old healed scars open, healing ceases, there is shortness of breath and, soon after, death.

Resistance to infections is decreased. According to Stone (1972), the Black Death was so terrible because it was superimposed upon preexisting scurvy. One-quarter of the population of Europe, 25 million people, died. But, even then, folklore associated scurvy with lack of green plants.

The development of large ships which could sail many months brought scurvy to the fore. Ships would sail from home with many more sailors than were required because so many would die at sea from scurvy. Even after Dr. James Lind proved that scurvy could be prevented by eating citrus fruit, it took the British Navy 40 years to start issuing juice. The use of lemon juice, it was estimated, doubled the fighting force of the navy, but the 40-year delay cost it 100,000 casualties.

The Board of Trade waited another 72 years before issuing citrus juice to its Merchant Marine. The U.S. Army became aware of it in 1895. Scurvy finally was beaten when Dr. Szent-Györgyi proved in 1931 that ascorbic acid was vitamin C. At first he tried to call his white crystalline substance extracted from peppers "ignose," because no one knew what it was. The editor of the journal to whom he submitted his paper rejected this and also Dr. Szent-Györgyi's second suggestion, "Godnose." For this discovery and other essential research, he was awarded the Nobel Prize in 1937.

### Clinical Uses

1. TREATMENT OF SCURVY AND SUBCLINICAL SCURVY

Classical scurvy is rare in technologically developed countries, so rare it would probably not be diagnosed even if it did occur. There is no question the only treatment is to provide ascorbic acid as quickly as possible. If the objective is to remove the obvious symptoms and signs, not much vitamin C is required. But if the objective is good health, several grams per day will be used. Subclinical scurvy is much more frequent, but it is as rarely diagnosed as scurvy, for physicians are not accustomed by their medical training to think of subclinical vitamin deficiencies. For most physicians, the absence of scurvy means there is no need for ascorbic acid. Subclinical scurvy cannot be detected by laboratory tests. It should be suspected if a nutritional history suggests that little ascorbic acid-rich food has been consumed, or if the individual has been under severe emotional and/or physical stress and if he has some of the symptoms of scurvy in its earliest stages when no other disease is present.

## 2. STRESS

Ascorbic acid probably is one of the body's most important chemicals for dealing with stress. The medical literature is summarized by I. Stone (1972). Animals increase production of ascorbic acid when under stress. Leukocytes carry and deposit ascorbic acid to locally injured areas at concentrations much higher than can be achieved by blood plasma concentrations. Stress rapidly depletes the adrenal gland of its ascorbic acid and greatly increases the oxidation of ascorbic acid. A measure of stress may be the ratio of ascorbic acid to dehydroascorbic acid—under stress the ratio goes down.

Inorganic poisons stress the body. Large doses of ascorbic acid reduce the mortality of guinea pigs given mercury cyanide, protect against mercury bichloride, and reduce the toxicity of mercurial diuretics. Ascorbic acid reduces the toxicity of lead. In one experiment, as little as 100 mg per day removed symptoms from workers suffering from lead poisoning at a large industrial plant; the symptoms of lead poisoning resemble those of subclinical scurvy. In the same way, ascorbic acid protected patients against undesirable side effects of arsenicals used in the treatment of syphilis and against chromium and gold salts toxicity. Mercury from mercury-silver amalgams used in filling teeth poisons many; ascorbic acid increases mercury excretion.

Ascorbic acid has reversed the toxic changes caused by benzene. Benzene rapidly depletes the body of its ascorbic acid. Rats reacted to benzene injection by increasing production of ascorbic acid. Ascorbic acid has protected mice against the poisonous effect of strychnine. Digitalis side effects have been controlled, aspirin has been less toxic, and too much vitamin A has not produced scurvy-like symptoms when ascorbic acid is used. Ascorbic acid should be given for barbiturate intoxication.

Klenner (1971, 1973) treated a case with 54 grams intravenously the first day.

In 1960 it was shown that 100 mg per kilogram of ascorbic acid abolished the effect of morphine on rats.

Anesthesia is very stressful and reduces ascorbic acid levels. In animals depleted of ascorbic acid, anesthesia came earlier, was more prolonged and they recovered more slowly. All my patients who are given electroconvulsive therapy are on ascorbic acid.

Ascorbic acid inactivates bacterial toxins such as tetanus toxin. Animals treated with this vitamin respond much less severely to tetanus toxin. In 1954 Klenner (1971, 1973) treated one case successfully.

Botulism has not been treated with ascorbic acid, but the remarkable detoxifying properties of ascorbic acid suggest it should be tried in very large doses. It has also been used successfully for treating snakebite.

Physical stress calls for large amounts of ascorbic acid in the same way chemical stress does. Stone (1972) referred to a paper written in 1952, with a bibliography of 242 references, about stress and ascorbic acid. The author concluded that under normal conditions there was enough ascorbic acid to deal with acute stress, but more was required for chronic stress. Stone's review shows that heat (fever) and burns, exposure to cold, physical trauma, fractures, high altitude and radiation all call for large doses of ascorbic acid. I have known two patients given total body radiation for leukemia who also received about 10 grams of ascorbic acid per day. They suffered very little nausea and did not lose their hair. Subjects exposed to nuclear fallout should receive high doses of ascorbic acid. It is likely ascorbic acid mops up the free radicals produced in cells by the radiation and decreases cellular damage. I would also take vitamin E and selenium as an additional precaution.

The most common forms of chemical stress are due to pollution of our air and water and smoking. The deleterious effects of these stressors can be markedly reduced by taking large amounts of ascorbic acid. Stone concluded that smokers suffer from "Smoker's scurvy."

Shock and wounds of every type call for a lot of ascorbic acid. Earlier I referred to the increased oxidation of ascorbic acid to dehydroascorbic acid under stress. Chemical assay methods usually measure total ascorbic acid levels, i.e., the combination of ascorbic acid and dehydroascorbic acid. The latter is toxic in high concentrations. Under severe stress nearly all the ascorbic acid is oxidized to dehydroascorbic acid. These methods will show no change in total ascorbates, even though nearly all of the ascorbic acid is consumed. Hoffer and Osmond (1963) calculated the ratio of ascorbic acid to dehydroascorbic acid; this Stone termed the *morbidity index*. Normal subjects have a ratio of 15, a morbidity index of 15. Those who were critically ill but survived had an index of 1, while those who had died had an index of 0.3 to 0.5. During convalescence the survivors' morbidity index increased to between 3 and 5.

The following values are taken from Stone (1972, 181).

| Disease | Number | Ascorbic Acid | Dehydroascorbic Acid | Morbidity Index |
|---|---|---|---|---|
| Normal | 28 | 0.87 mg/100 ml | 0.06 mg/100 ml | 14 |
| **Meningitis, Tetanus, Pneumonia and Typhoid Fever** | | | | |
| Died | 32 | 0.29 | 0.75 | 0.39 |
| Survived | 67 | 0.45 | 0.45 | 1.00 |
| Convalescent | 53 | 0.64 | 0.16 | 4.00 |
| Cholera | 21 | 0.62 | 0.37 | 1.70 |
| Smallpox | 16 | 0.51 | 0.56 | 0.90 |
| Meningitis | 32 | 0.55 | 0.32 | 1.72 |
| Gonorrhea | 16 | 0.53 | 0.26 | 2.00 |
| Syphilis | 16 | 0.74 | 0.18 | 4.20 |

Healthy tissues contain most ascorbate as ascorbic acid. But it does not cross cell membranes readily. Dehydroascorbic acid does cross membranes more readily and in the cells is reduced back to ascorbic acid. Under severe stress the many biochemical mechanisms that reduce dehydroascorbic acid must fail, leaving too much unchanged. Dehydroascorbic acid in large doses is toxic. Stone's morbidity index appears to be a measure of the redox potential of the ascorbic acid–dehydroascorbic acid system. Health is favored by less oxidation, and during disease excessive oxidation is present.

In speculating about the causes of excessive oxidation, the most commonly associated biochemical reactions with stress should be considered. These are the increase in secretion of adrenalin and noradrenalin with any stress, the increase in secretion of corticord steroid hormones, and increased release of histamine with allergy-induced stress. Each reaction demands ascorbic acid. The synthesis of noradrenalin and adrenalin requires ascorbic acid, but this synthesis is also needed to decrease the oxidation to noradrenochrome and adrenochrome, which, when they are formed, react with ascorbic acid, which is oxidized to dehydroascorbic acid, and the adrenochrome is mostly inactivated to a nontoxic dihydroxy indole. In our research we found this indole to have antianxiety properties.

The production of corticord steroid hormones also requires ascorbic acid. This is another reason why the adrenal glands store so much ascorbic acid. Histamine is destroyed by ascorbic acid. This is why large quantities of ascorbic acid are so effective in treating all histamine-releasing stresses such as insect and snakebites, plant poison contact, allergic reactions, burns, etc. There are other biochemical reactions as well that may require ascorbic acid. There are some reasons why under stress the body becomes more oxidized, which is reflected in decreased ascorbic acid and increased dehydroascorbic acid levels, or decrease in the morbidity index from 15 to under 1.

Clemetson (1980) is very concerned about the presence of dehydroascorbic acid in ascorbic acid. Solutions of ascorbic acid contain traces of metallic ions which enhance oxidation of small quantities of ascorbic acid. Plant polyphenols trap or combine with these ions and so block their catalytic effect. Clemetson recommends that all ascorbic acid preparations should contain small quantities of these natural substances, such as bioflavonoids, for this reason.

The chemical measure for total ascorbic acid takes into account a second inert form, the straight-chain form of ascorbic acid. The usual ascorbic acid and dehydroascorbic acid are lactone rings. Ascorbic acid is delactonized by C-AMP-phosphodiesterase (PDE). The delactorized derivative (del-A) is biologically inactive. Total ascorbate measurement, therefore, are unlikely to be correlated with disease unless all three components of the ascorbate system are measured, for it is possible to have enough total ascorbates with hardly any ascorbic acid—scurvy can be present with normal total ascorbate levels.

## 3. ASCORBIC ACID AND THE VASCULAR SYSTEM

Ascorbates are involved in two of the essential functional components in maintaining normal vessel walls and blood circulation: formation of collagen, which is needed to maintain elasticity and strength of the blood vessels; and the solubilization of cholesterol. This does not suggest that only ascorbates are involved in arteriosclerosis, coronary disease, and strokes. These are very complex phenomena involving the diet—particularly the relationship between fats, complex and simple carbohydrates, and protein—as well as the ability to deal with large amounts of chylomicrons. But ascorbates do play a crucial role.

Ascorbic acid is essential for synthesis and maintenance of collagen. Structurally weak collagen is the cause of the bleeding symptoms of scurvy, such as bleeding gums and capillaries, loose teeth and reopening of old wounds and scars. Blood plasma ascorbic acid levels were made on a large number of consecutively admitted patients (see Paterson 1941). Fifty-six percent of all the patients had low values (under 0.5 mg%) while 81 percent of the coronary patients were low. Other studies found similarly low values. From these and other studies it was concluded that ascorbic acid depletion was due to stress, that segments of arteries most susceptible to mechanical stress had the least ascorbic acid, and that deficiency of ascorbic acid allowed depolymerization (breaking up) of ground substance. Finally, the researchers concluded that ascorbic acid could be used to replenish areas of arteries deficient in ascorbic acid. McCormick (1957), a physician who pioneered the use of large doses of ascorbic acid, recommended it be used rather than anticoagulants to control thrombosis.

Cholesterol is associated with arteriosclerosis. Subjects with high blood cholesterol are more prone to develop arteriosclerosis and coronary disease. Ascorbic acid plays a role in controlling arteriosclerosis: ascorbic acid deficiency greatly increases synthesis of cholesterol. Feeding ascorbic acid decreases cholesterol levels in rabbits, guinea pigs, rats and humans; but in humans the results are not as clear as they are with nicotinic acid. The results were more significant with higher doses in patients with higher cholesterol levels. Feeding cholesterol lowers ascorbic acid levels. Spittle (1971, 1972) found that blood serum levels of cholesterol could be varied by varying ascorbic acid intake. She concluded that arteriosclerosis is a long-term deficiency of ascorbic acid.

Arteriosclerosis induced in guinea pigs by ascorbic acid deficiency was reversed by ascorbic acid. Early lesions were removed more quickly than well-established lesions.

The ascorbate system can remove cholesterol from plaques in two ways. Ascorbates are "detergents," they lower surface tension. Arterial deposits are insoluble complexes of calcium, phospholipids, and cholesterol. Artificial precipitates of these types of deposits can be redissolved by physiological saline containing more than 20 mg ascorbate per 100 ml. The second mechanism is removal of calcium from arterial deposits (Lewin 1976).

Na ascorbate + Ca phospholipid
              cholesterol ⟶
              (insoluble) ⟵
Ca ascorbate + Na phospholipid
(soluble)    cholesterol ⟶
              (soluble) ⟵

Magnesium may tend to replace calcium in the insoluble complex. Lewin suggests it can occur in the arterial plaques as follows:

Ca phospholipid cholesterol + Mg
Ca + Mg phospholipid cholesterol

Generally, magnesium salts are more soluble than are similar calcium salts.

### 4. THE COMMON COLD

The problem with investigating the common cold is that it is not as common as it is thought to be. The term *cold* is applied to any acute, short-lived viral infection of the upper respiratory tract that may be followed by bacterial infection. The characteristic symptoms are a feeling of malaise, a moderate or profuse nasal discharge from swollen and boggy mucosa covering the sinuses, which may become purulent, and often a low-grade fever. Most colds are gone in about six days. A large proportion of people have a profuse discharge which appears to be a cold but which is not caused by a viral invasion. It is an allergic sinus reaction. When any large populations are tested with any anticold preparation, both types of "colds" are present. But as they are different conditions with different causes, it is hardly likely they will respond to the same treatment or be prevented by the same measures. Thus, antihistamines are much more apt to control the allergy-type colds than the viral cold. Antibiotics will effectively control bacterial infections in the nose and throat, while ascorbic acid may operate on all three causes but will be less effective with allergy-type colds. Milk-product allergy is a common cause of the allergy cold. In my own case I suffered from chronic sinus discharge for over two years. Before that I contracted at least three colds each year. During my two-year chronic cold, I treated myself with very large quantities of ascorbic acid with no relief. After a four-day fast I discovered I was allergic to milk. On a milk-free diet for the past 17 years I have been completely free of "colds," unless I inadvertently ingest some milk product.

This heterogeneity of populations with the common cold explains the controversy over the efficacy of ascorbic acid as a treatment and preventative agent. The evidence is described thoroughly by Pauling (1970, 1976) and Stone (1972). I have no doubt that ascorbic acid does prevent many colds and ameliorates the symptoms when it is present, but, in my opinion, it works best for the real common cold, the one that is due to a virus. Even then, because there is an overlap between both types of colds, the results may be unclear. There are, in fact, three types of colds;

(1) the allergy cold; (2) the virus-induced cold; and (3) the mixed cold, wherein an allergic condition predisposes the person to a virus infection. This third type of cold would respond to ascorbic acid, but not as efficiently as the virus-type cold.

Any experiment on the common cold must include the following variables: (1) a distribution of the population into the three types of colds; (2) a dose response test for each group to determine the mean optimum for each group; and (3) prophylactic and therapeutic trials.

Dr. S. Lewin (1976) suffered from repeated attacks of mixed-type colds. From childhood on he had repeated attacks of nasal stuffiness, colds, sore throat, catarrh, and associated respiratory diseases. The colds were heavy, often making breathing through the nose impossible. After starting on ascorbic acid his colds became infrequent and less severe. His symptomatology is typical for the mixed allergy-virus type of cold, which explains the partial response.

The viral cold is caught in two ways: by becoming chilled, which activates quiescent virus in the respiratory tract, combined with lowered interferon and antibody levels; and by contact, via sneeze droplet transmission, with a person having a cold. Ascorbic acid increases interferon levels and increases antibody levels. These effects, plus its other stress properties, should effectively prevent the common cold precipitated by cold. In the same way, it should protect against droplet-induced colds. But ascorbic acid does not protect against infection caused by instilling virus cultures. Lewin considers that this latter procedure is so far from the usual way of catching a cold that conclusions gained in this way have limited clinical significance. Nose droplets contain mucous, which contains virus particles and antibodies; the mucous likely arrests virus movement.

The artificial virus is an ideal way of causing a cold. For this cold scientists must be given credit. If they could not reliably produce a cold on demand their research would be much more difficult. This research must be repeated using nasal droplets known to contain virus, with adequate amounts of ascorbic acid as a pretreatment. When this is done, research physicians will also find that ascorbic acid is an effective tool for preventing and treating the common cold—the viral type—and they will confirm the clinical observations made by large number of physicians and the self-observations made by millions of people who prefer to believe their own response, not the conclusions of a few incompletely controlled clinical studies that have not taken into account the number of variables involved.

Cathcart (1984) "dose-titers" patients to find the optimum amount of ascorbic acid. He discovered that the optimum dose varies enormously, depending upon the disease and the person. The optimum dose is that amount that just fails to cause gas and diarrhea—the sublaxative dose. Each person has an optimum anticold ascorbic acid dose. A person whose effective dose is 1 gram per day will have effective control of his colds and will not need to consult his physician. A person who has an effective dose requirement of 6 grams per day will not respond to 3 grams per day. Such a subject is much more likely to consult his physician, who will hear he had taken ascorbic acid with no response. The ascorbic acid responders have no reason to see the physician, who sees only ascorbic acid failures. The physician's sample is biased against ascorbic acid and his conclusions remain negative. Many more subjects have responded, and their reaction is positive. In the same way a specialist who sees only referrals may unthinkingly conclude that all general practitioners are incompetent, since they see only their "failures."

Mink, Deck, Jennings and Inhorn (1987) used sixteen men in a double-blind, controlled experiment, using placebo or ascorbic acid,

500 mg taken four times per day. For one week the volunteers lived and interacted with eight men infected with laboratory-induced cold virus. Both ascorbic acid and placebo were continued for another two weeks. Seven of the eight given placebo developed colds, as did four of the eight on ascorbic acid. In addition, the signs and symptoms of the colds in the ascorbic acid group were significantly less. They concluded that the data suggested the vitamin also decreased the severity of the disease.

## 5. VIRAL INFECTIONS

Dr. F.R. Klenner (1954) was successful in using large amounts of ascorbic acid for treating all viral diseases. Very dramatic results were found with polio before polio vaccines were developed. In 1954, I visited Dr. Jonathan Gould, a psychiatrist in London, England who had developed a multivitamin mixture of B vitamins for treating deliria. He told me about an experiment on polio he had participated in, but which had not been reported in the medical literature. The control group received the usual treatment and a number of them developed paralysis and its chronic sequelae. The treated group were given large doses of ascorbic acid—not one became paralyzed, and there were no residual defects.

Within a few years after crystalline ascorbic acid became available, Jungeblut (1935, 1937, 1939) was able to conclude that it reduced the severity of polio in infected monkeys and increased resistance to it. But Sabine (1939), using more virus to infect the animals and less ascorbic acid, did not observe a protective effect. Klenner (1954, 1971, 1973), North America's foremost pioneer in megadoses of ascorbic acid, used 27 to 210 grams per day. Most of the larger doses were given intravenously. Stone (1972) reports other positive clinical reports. Polio is under control now, but these early experiments prove ascorbic acid is effective and safe. I suggest that every person should be on ample quantities of ascorbic acid before taking any polio vaccine, in order to remove the chance of undesirable side effects, even though these are very infrequent.

Viral hepatitis should also respond to large doses of ascorbic acid, and, when used has been effective. Scorbutic guinea pigs suffer fatty degeneration of the liver. Ascorbic acid should protect the liver and inactivate the virus.

Recently a physician from Hawaii visited me. We compared our clinical experiences with vitamins. He described a woman who came to him with viral hepatitis who wanted to be cured in three days as she had a reservation to fly to the mainland then. He promptly started an intravenous drip, using 60 grams of sodium ascorbate per 1,000 ml of fluid. In two days she received 180 grams. She made her flight, having recovered. Cathcart (1975) states that viral hepatitis is the easiest disease for ascorbic acid to cure. The dose varies from 40 to 100 grams per day orally, or when the sublaxative level is too low, by injection intravenously. Stools and urine become normal in three days in acute cases, the patients feel well in four days, and jaundice is clear in six days. SGOT and SGPT values quickly fall. Chronic cases respond more slowly.

Herpes can be treated successfully with ascorbic acid. There are three types, causing cold sores, shingles, and genital herpes. Ascorbic acid inactivates herpes virus if enough is used. Lewin (1976) followed 38 people after they started to use 1 to 2 grams of ascorbic acid daily. Each had suffered three to five episodes for several years. On ascorbic acid, 30 had no further attacks. The rest had fewer and less severe episodes. Six of the eight increased the ascorbic acid to 3 or 4 grams per day and noted much more relief. Cathcart reported that acute cases responded promptly. Chronic cases required more time. Zinc, in combination with the ascorbic acid, increased the efficacy.

Shingles also responds. Stone referred to

three physicians who treated 349 cases with cures—in most cases, within a few days. Ascorbic acid was given by injection.

I have seen no report of genital herpes, but it would be surprising if ascorbic acid did not have some therapeutic effect in those cases too.

## 6. BACTERIAL INFECTIONS

Ascorbic acid ought to fight bacterial infections for the following reasons: (1) it is bacteriostatic; (2) it detoxifies bacterial toxins; (3) it controls and maintains phagocytosis; and (4) it can be administered in very large doses, as it is relatively nontoxic. It has been used in treating tuberculosis, pneumonia, whooping cough, typhoid fever, dysentery and other infections. In these early studies megadoses were not used, but even with lower doses ascorbic acid was helpful. Thirty years ago McCormick recommended 2 to 4 grams of ascorbic acid per day.

I consider ascorbic acid an essential adjunct in treating schizophrenia, perhaps because of its antistress effect or because it reduces the production of toxic oxidized derivatives of adrenalin. But I have had a few patients who did not recover until given over 10 grams per day. Recently I treated a chronic schizophrenic patient who had not responded over a period of 10 years to tranquilizers, many series of electroconvulsive therapy, or other orthomolecular therapy, including 3 grams per day of ascorbic acid. She continually complained of a feeling that half her brain was dead. A series of electroconvulsive therapy (ECT) would relieve this partially for a few months. About three years ago she demanded more ECT, as she was very depressed over this problem with her brain. Because the effect of ECT was temporary and partial, I decided instead to increase her ascorbic acid to 12 grams per day (one teaspoon of powder dissolved in juice, given three times per day). One month later she was well. She has remained well and considered taking a job; for the past three years she has been well for the first time in 10 years. The role ascorbic acid plays is reviewed in my book, *Niacin Therapy in Psychiatry* (1962), and in my chapter in *Orthomolecular Psychiatry* (1973), edited by Pauling and Hawkins.

## 7. ASCORBIC ACID AND CANCER

I recommend Cameron and Pauling's book, *Cancer and Vitamin C* (1979), as one of the best and most informative discussions of the cancers—their causes, treatments, and the potential of ascorbic acid in enhancing remissions and recovery. Prof. Pauling's stand in support of ascorbic acid has generated much controversy, but it has also generated a tremendous amount of interest. Unfortunately, Establishment organizations and institutions have taken an unreasonable, and in my opinion unscientific position against his conclusions. Dr. Pauling's enormous scientific stature and moral position are forcing some of these institutions to reexamine their attitudes.

Over the past two years the National Cancer Institute and the American Cancer Society have reversed their previously negative positions on cancer and nutrition, allowing many physicians to present findings they had been fearful of presenting.

I became interested in cancer and better treatment, following an unexpected response in one of my patients to both nicotinic acid and ascorbic acid nearly 30 years ago. In retrospect, I had seen a partial response eight years earlier, in 1952. A middle-aged, psychotic woman was admitted to the psychiatric ward of the general hospital in Regina, Saskatchewan. Her psychiatrist intended to give her a series of electroconvulsive treatments. We had no tranquilizers. I was interested in the antipsychotic properties of ascorbic acid. Her psychiatrist agreed to withhold ECT for three days. I had originally planned on giving her 1 gram three times per day, but the three-day limit forced me to use more. She was immediately started on 1 gram each hour. Over the next 48 hours she received 45 grams. By then her psychosis cleared, she did not require ECT and she was discharged in one week. This patient had had one breast amputated for cancer and later received cobalt radiation. The breast area became infected and ulcerated. At this juncture she became psychotic. By the time she left the psychiatric ward her breast had begun to heal, but she died six months later from her cancer. I had no idea the ascorbic acid might help her cancer, which it might have done had I maintained her treatment.

About 1960, a retired professor from the University of Saskatchewan appeared in the psychiatric ward of University Hospital. He had inoperable bronchiogenic cancer, which was seen in X-ray and bronchoscopic examinations, biopsied and confirmed by histological examination. He also developed psychiatric changes that suggested he had secondaries in the brain. Surgery was therefore contradicted. In its place he was given cobalt bomb radiation over the chest area. He was later admitted to the psychiatric ward because his behavior was totally disorganized.

At that time I was examining a large number of psychiatric cases for the presence of kryptopyrrole (KP, originally called "mauve factor"), in their urine. KP was present in most schizophrenics but disappeared when they recovered. It was also present in about one-quarter of patients suffering from depressions, anxiety states, alcoholism and so on. Fewer than 5 percent of normal subjects had it, and some of this group were first-order relatives of schizophrenics. I also examined a number of physically ill patients; about 10 percent of this group excreted KP, but most of them had cancer. Eight patients with bronchiogenic cancer all excreted large quantities. When this patient appeared with both cancer of the lung and a psychosis, I became very interested in testing his urine— which contained large quantities of KP.

At the end of the week I suggested to his supervising psychiatric resident that the professor start on nicotinic acid and ascorbic acid, 1 gram three times each day. He started on a Friday. The following Monday he was free of his psychosis. When I spoke to him he had no memory of the previous three months. During this time he had been in the psychiatric ward once before and had been discharged as terminal to his home. But his wife had been unable to cope with his psychotic behavior even with the help of a practical nurse. I discussed his cancer with him and suggested he continue to take both vitamins after discharge. My reasoning was that since patients with KP responded well to this treatment whether they were schizophrenic, depressed or anxious, perhaps the vitamins might help him. I wondered whether his excretion of KP also indicated that his cancer might respond, even if not as dramatically as his psychosis had.

He survived two and a half years, dying of a coronary at age 75. The Cancer Clinic followed him regularly. After 18 months of well-being I had a chance to discuss his case with the director of the clinic, who told me that the lesion had disappeared from the X-ray picture. The director added that he was beginning to think they had diagnosed him wrongly, that he never had cancer. This is known as saving the phenomenon, in this case the phenomenon being the statement: "Vitamins cannot cure cancer." If there had been a "cure," it could not have been cancer. By then I had enough follow-up data to conclude that cancer patients who excreted KP lived longer after treatment than did patients who did not excrete KP (Hoffer 1970). I had a chance to try these two vitamins on two other cases of cancer with no effect.

But in 1968 I saw another recovery. A 16-year-old girl was diagnosed as having a highly malignant osteogenic sarcoma in her arm. Immediate amputation had been recommended. I had treated her mother for depression several years before. With her daughter's illness she became depressed again and once more consulted me. She described her daughter's illness. I obtained the results of pathological examination from my colleague, Dr. J. Stephen. Prof. R. Altschul, J. Stephen and I had first reported early in 1955 that nicotinic acid lowered cholesterol levels. The girl's life expectancy was so slim I felt I could not avoid telling her mother about the occasional success I had seen with the two vitamins. She agreed to bring her daughter to see me. I advised her to allow radiation treatment. I was convinced then as I am today that ascorbic acid would protect patients against the side effects of cobalt bomb radiation. But I advised her not to agree to amputation unless there was a definite recurrence. The girl also agreed to take nicotinamide and ascorbic acid, 1 gram three times a day. In 1978 her mother phoned me because a son had become schizophrenic. She also told me that her daughter had remained well.

Since 1960 I have known seven patients treated for cancer with vitamins. The first four, treated before 1970, received 3 grams per day of ascorbic acid. The three treated in the past five years all received more than 10 grams of ascorbic acid per day plus a number of B vitamins. Five of the whole group never received cancer chemotherapy, while two did receive radiation. Four are still well, including the two who were radiated. The other three have died, including the two who received cancer chemotherapy. This small series suggests that chemotherapy decreases the response to ascorbic acid treatment, as has been already proposed by Cameron and Pauling (1979), but that radiation is not as harmful. Ascorbic acid can reverse the undesirable side effects of radiation if it is given while radiation treatment is being received. Another conclusion from this small series is that radiation therapy ought to be combined with ascorbic acid therapy in a much larger series. The radiation would destroy the large cancerous tissue mass, and the ascorbic acid would de-

crease radiation side effects, increase resistance against recurrence, and help destroy other cancerous tissues, which probably are present in other parts of the body.

These cases illustrate the responses of individual patients. There must be many others who will respond in the same way. Mrs. A. B., born in 1919, came to see me in July, 1978. Two months before she had been operated on for jaundice. At operation a tumor the size of a squash ball was seen in the head of the pancreas. It was left intact because of the danger of spreading tumor tissue to other areas, and a new pancreatic duct was created to bypass the obstruction of her natural duct, which was causing the jaundice. After operation the jaundice cleared. She had been worried about cancer for several years following the death of a sister from cancer. She was advised no treatment would be given.

She had read Norman Cousins's book in which he described the effect of ascorbic acid and laughter on himself. She began to take 12 to 16 grams of ascorbic acid per day in water. When she discussed this with her family physician, he referred her to me for general nutritional advice.

I advised her to continue with her sugar-free, junk-free diet; to take 40 grams of ascorbic acid per day; to decrease her intake of animal protein-rich food; and to use enzyme supplements, 500 mg of niacinamide three times a day, 220 mg of zinc sulfate per day, and a multimineral supplement.

In February 1979 she reported that two successive CAT scans revealed that the mass previously visualized and seen directly at operation had vanished. A month later another examination showed her original duct had reopened —now she had two. She now kept her ascorbic acid level at 30 grams per day. She is still well.

## 8. ALLERGIES

Many obvious allergic reactions are mediated by the release of histamine. Excessive histamine causes itching in skin, swelling, hives, vasodilation (flushing) and decreased blood pressure. The most effective antihistamines prevent the tissues that react with histamine from doing so. Other ways of decreasing the effect of histamine is to decrease the histamine concentration in its storage sites (with nicotinic acid) or by destroying it as it is released from its storage sites. This is done by ascorbic acid. *In vitro* histamine and ascorbic acid molecules rapidly react and destroy one another. I have already referred to Clemetson's study that showed this also occurs *in vivo*. I would expect ascorbic acid to be very valuable for dealing with all histamine-mediated toxic reactions such as insect bites, snakebites, poisonous plant reactions, and, of course, more common allergic reactions. Optimum doses are required and should be used as soon as possible after the histamine is released. Prevention is better. A person expecting to be bitten by insects would be wise to take optimum daily doses several days before.

## 9. HEROIN ADDICTION

Recently, Libby and Stone (1977), and Libby et al. (1982 a, b, c) reported that ascorbic acid in large doses combined with protein and vitamin B supplements allowed heroin addicts to stop heroin with no withdrawal symptoms. Smaller doses (10 grams per day) prevented any craving for heroin. They were then able to remain heroin-free. These results were corroborated by Free and Sanders (1978).

It certainly is better to keep addicts well by nutritional therapy than it is to maintain them on another addicting drug such as methadone.

## 10. SUDDEN INFANT DEATH SYNDROME (SIDS)

Kalokerinos, in his book *Every Second Child*, (1981) records the huge infant mortality among the Australian aborigines and how it dropped from 50 percent to under 20 per 1,000 when these infants were given enough ascorbic acid to prevent scurvy. He has concluded that Sudden Infant Death Syndrome (SIDS) is probably due mainly to infant scurvy. Stone agrees (1972).

Scurvy probably remains a major disease in many populations but is rarely diagnosed because of the current preoccupation with the idea that it has been defeated. Stress scurvy must be much more common. I have no doubt most post-surgical patients would heal more quickly if given adequate supplementation with ascorbic acid.

### Is Ascorbic Acid Dangerous?

More accurately, are the optimum dose ranges recommended by orthomolecular practitioners dangerous? Any chemical can be toxic if enough is taken. As I mentioned earlier, I have known a schizophrenic patient who spent many hours each day by the hospital water fountain. Within a few weeks he had gained 60 pounds. When the fountain was disconnected he lost this weight in a few days. He had been well on the way to killing himself with water, yet water is not considered a dangerous nutrient. Any person who describes any substance as dangerous must define the parameters of toxicity, i.e.: (1) the dose; (2) the duration of treatment; and (3) what is meant by toxic reactions.

Critics of vitamin therapy have avoided discussing these parameters, which has freed them of the necessity to be scientifically accurate. But, because their claims have been repeated so frequently in a number of medical journals, it is necessary to review the various claims for ascorbic acid's toxicity and the medical evidence for these claims.

## 1. KIDNEY STONES

It has been suggested frequently that ascorbic acid *may* cause kidney oxalate stones, leaving the unwary reader to believe that *may* and *will* are the same. Nowhere do these critics give an estimate of the proportion of people taking ascorbic acid who have, in fact, gotten kidney stones from ascorbic acid. The reason for this is that there have been no cases reported, and the *may* remains such a remote possibility that it should not deter anyone from using ascorbic acid. The remote possibility is based upon faulty biochemical reasoning. Some of the ascorbic acid is converted to oxalate. At 4-gram doses or less, very small quantities are formed. At higher doses more is formed, but so far it has not increased the probability of kidney stone formation. In over 30 years I have not seen any, nor have many other physicians with vast experience.

It is, in fact, theoretically almost impossible for ascorbic acid to cause oxalate stones for the following reasons: (1) ascorbic acid increases the acidity of urine, and acid urine increases solubility of calcium in urine, and so there is a decrease in formation of calcium in stones; (2) ascorbic acid increases diuresis, which also decreases probability of oxalate stone formation; and (3) ascorbic acid combines with calcium ions, again decreasing the concentration of calcium oxalate. I agree with Cathcart (1985) who concludes that ascorbic acid probably decreases kidney stone formation. I cannot recall a single patient of mine on ascorbic acid who developed stones—out of at least 10,000 patients over 30 years. In a recent review, Cheraskin et al (1983) came to the same conclusion. They quote Prof. S. R. Tannenbaum, who wrote: "The conception that excess amounts of ascorbic acid lead to the formation of oxalic acid in urine is simply not correct."

Victor Herbert, a dedicated antivitamin–antinutritional medicine physician, based his view on one medical student who told him he had an attack of renal colic due to a kidney stone after seven weeks of following his mother's advice to take 1 gram of ascorbic acid per day. Dr. Herbert demands double-blind, controlled studies conducted by critics before he will accept the value of megavitamin therapy. His lectures have generated a nationwide phobia among many physicians that ascorbic acid causes kidney stones.

There probably is no connection between excretion of oxalate and kidney stones. Cheraskin (1983) reports that normal subjects ex-creted 28 mg of oxalate in urine, while patients forming stones excreted 27.5 mg. I suggest that increased oxalate in urine is an indication that the body is excreting it more efficiently, thereby decreasing susceptibility to oxalate-stone formation.

Clinicians looking for a cause of kidney stones will have better luck looking at pyridoxine deficiency. Pyridoxine (B6) decreases oxalate production. In doses of 500 to 1,000 mg per day, vitamin B6 is useful for treating primary oxalosis. This condition is characterized by kidney stones, nephrocalcinosis and renal failure (Will and Bijvoet 1979).

Belfield (1984) is a veterinary surgeon with many years experience treating animals. He does not believe dogs can make enough of their own vitamin C. Wild animals eat food much richer in vitamin C than do pets, and the most important single supplement for domestic dogs is vitamin C, which is safe. Belfield gave 10-pound dogs 20 grams of vitamin C intravenously each day for five days. There were no side effects. One animal with blood in the urine from cystitis recovered after the second injection. Belfield has not seen a single animal on vitamin C maintenance who developed kidney stones. On the contrary, in two animals vitamin C was used to dissolve kidney stones.

The final blow to the ascorbate oxalate-stone idea was delivered by Fituri, Allawi, Bentley et al. (1983), who showed that the apparent increase in oxalate measured by previous authors was a laboratory artifact. The oxalate was developed in vitro by heating the urine at 100°C. for 30 minutes. When a better method was used that avoided heat, there was no increase. These authors concluded: "The increases were due to in vitro laboratory error, not to an in vitro production of oxalate from the vitamin."

Those workers who did find an increase in oxalate used a method which included heating urine for 30 minutes as an intrinsic part of the method. The apprent increase was an in vitro artifact. The recent method used by Fituri et al. (1983) did not require heating the urine. With this method there was no increase in oxalate. Fituri et al. found that heating urine containing ascorbic acid caused the conversion to oxalate.

Fituri et al. concluded: "The increases found by [two previous authors] would seem to have been due to in vitro conversion of ascorbate to oxalate during the assay procedure, rather than any increased in vivo production of oxalate from the vitamin."

Over the past ten years the idea has become established that ascorbic acid in large doses will cause kidney stones. This idea is held most strongly by physicians who are not familiar with vitamin biochemistry but who have heard that this can happen. By constant repetition of a conclusion based entirely on an idea which was theoretical, this idea has become enshrined as a fact. The same thing happened with the erroneous idea that abscorbic acid destroyed vitamin B12.

Herbert and Jacob (1974) reported that ascorbic acid added to a test meal in vitro destroyed vitamin B12, and from this they inferred that ascorbic acid could cause pernicious anemia. However, Newmark, Scheiner, Marcus and Prabhudesai (1976), and Marcus, Prabhudesai, and Wassef (1980), using a method designed for foods, found no loss and concluded that the original work was flawed by use of the wrong method. Pernicious anemia has not been shown to follow ascorbic acid consumption.

The idea that large doses of ascorbic acid can cause kidney stones originated following a few reports that ascorbic acid was partially metabolized to oxalate (Lamden and Chrystowski 1954; Takenouchi, Aso, Ichikawa and Shiomi 1966; Tiselius and Almgard 1977; and Hughes, Dutton, and Truswell 1981). Briggs, Garcia-Webb, and Davies (1973) found one man who was an oxalate former and postulated he might increase the risk for oxalate stones if he took large doses of ascorbic acid.

These papers provided the evidence for the common belief ascorbic acid might cause kidney stones. This has not been reported to have happened, even though millions of people are using substantial doses of ascorbic acid each day. Experts at a symposium on ascorbic acid concluded: "We could find no reports of oxalate stone formation in normal individuals." (See Barness 1977).

Now it turns out that the apparent increase in the excretion of oxalate in urine was due to an error in the clinical method used. According to Fituri, Allawi, Bentley and Costello (1983), 8 grams per day of ascorbic acid for seven days had no effect on serum oxalate levels or excretion values.

Yet the myth that ascorbic acid may create kidney stones runs on and on. Alhadeff, Gualtieri and Lipton (1983), months after Fituri's paper appeared, still caution us that excessive (not defined) intake of vitamin C may also be associated with the formation of oxalate stones. Of the six references, not one is to an original paper—they are all references to textbooks, which usually refer to others' views. Pretty soon we will have a massive bibliography of references to authors referring to one another, with none based on experimental evidence.

There were two ideas which pointed to a connection between ascorbic acid and kidney stones. The first was the idea that ascorbic acid would increase oxalate. The second was that this would increase oxalate kidney stone formation. Both ideas are wrong. The first idea has been shown to have no basis, and the second has not occurred. Will the ascorbic acid—kidney stone myth be put to rest? I doubt it, for these erroneous statements are such an easy way to frighten physicians.

2. WILL ASCORBIC ACID CAUSE PERNICIOUS ANEMIA?

Herbert and Jacob (1974) reported that ascorbic acid added to laboratory gastric meal destroyed vitamin B12 when incubated at 37°C for 30 minutes. They used a radioassay method. From their in vitro results they concluded that "high doses of ascorbic acid popularly used as a home remedy against the common cold destroy substantial amounts of vitamin B12 when ingested with food." Not only did they use an inaccurate method for measuring vitamin B12 levels, but they also drew a clinical inference from an in vitro study. This report was rapidly published in the *Journal of the American Medical Association* and was erroneously summarized under its title. Letters to the editor criticizing this report were rejected.

Two years later, Newmark, Scheiner, Marcus et al. (1976) reported that Herbert had used the wrong assay method. When another official method—known to be accurate—was used, no loss of vitamin B12 could be found. But Herbert continued to make his claim in various journals and during lecture tours, as though Newmark, et al. had never existed. Newmark, Scheiner, Marcus et al. (1976) studied a laboratory meal prepared by Herbert from which samples were extracted and sent blind to Newmark for analysis. No loss of B12 was found when the correct method was used. Even 20 times as much ascorbic acid as Herbert used did not destroy vitamin B12. Their final conclusion has not been refuted, i.e., "appropriate assay methods for vitamin B12 demonstrate that it is not destroyed by ascorbic acid in a mimicked gastric environment." These are exciting laboratory debates. Clinically, the evidence is clear—ascorbic acid has not caused any cases of pernicious anemia out of the many millions of people who use large doses. (See also Marcus, Prabhudesai, and Wassef 1980; and Hogenkamp 1980.)

3. OTHER POSSIBLE TOXIC REACTIONS

A number of other claims have been made, not very seriously and also on theoretical grounds. These are that ascorbic acid may cause miscarriages and that it may cause cancer. There are no clinical reports that these results have ever occurred. There is no doubt that had any physician found reason to suspect this had happened to a patient, it would have been written up and as quickly reported in medical literature. For new treatments which appear to threaten established ideas are eagerly examined for evidence of toxicity, which is eagerly published, while toxic side effects of established treatments are published much more leisurely.

It has been asserted that once a person has been taking high doses of ascorbic acid he becomes dependent and will suffer withdrawal if it is discontinued, as if that person had become addicted. This idea is based upon a single study on infants whose mothers were taking moderate doses of ascorbic acid. The author concluded that these infants for a few weeks after birth suffered from vitamin deficiency. I do not subscribe to this view, i.e., that ascorbic acid predisposes toward scurvy. It is indeed possible that people who have been using adequate amounts of ascorbic acid will not feel as well when they stop if the ascorbic acid has been responsible for the feeling of well-being. In the same way, a pellagrin cured by vitamin B3 and allowed to become sick again is not suffering from a pathological dependency on vitamin B3. We all require adequate amounts of every vitamin and anything less may make us feel worse. In nearly 30 years of experience I have seen no withdrawal effects. I have myself abruptly stopped taking ascorbic acid after having been on 30 grams per day for several weeks, with no subjective discomfort. However, patients on high doses of ascorbic acid for cancer must not suddenly discontinue, for there is evidence the cancer will rebound and grow more quickly.

Nevertheless, anyone taking optimum doses should not stop, because the beneficial effect of ascorbic acid will decrease and the chance of being attacked by virus or bacteria will increase. Every person using ascorbic acid should advise any physician or hospital of this risk and hold them responsible if they are not allowed to continue the ascorbic acid.

The physician's or hospital's dislike of, or bias against, vitamins must not be a reason for decreasing the person's optimum health.

The optimum amount of ascorbic acid is the sublaxative dose (Cathcart 1985). Physicians may be unaware of this and consider that diarrhea and flatulence are serious side effects; this is true, but only if both subject and physician are ignorant of ascorbic acid's properties. Ascorbic acid can be used as a laxative. The intensity of the laxative effect can be set by the dose.

A few people have unusual reactions to ascorbic acid that may be allergic in nature—the reactions may be due to the vitamin or to other ingredients in the tablet.

### Administration of Ascorbic Acid

Ascorbic acid is taken by mouth as tablets or capsules, or is dissolved in liquid and injected into the veins. Oral doses are the common way. Tablets and capsules vary in strength from 100 to 1,000 mg, with 500 mg the most common dose. When very large doses are used, the ascorbic acid crystals are the most practical. The preparations should be free of sugar, starch, colors, flavors or any other additives not essential in the formulation of the product. Tablets and capsules are stable if kept cool and out of light in a reasonably dry atmosphere. When vitamin C is dissolved in water it begins to oxidize rapidly. This reaction is not as fast in juice. Solutions should be drunk as soon as possible. Slow-release preparations achieve a more stable blood level, with a reduction in urinary loss. On the other hand, it may be desirable to achieve very high blood levels in order to drive the ascorbic acid into certain tissues in the body.

Ascorbic acid is a weak organic acid that has very little or no effect on stomach acidity, but a few people cannot tolerate the sour taste. The acidity can be removed or diminished by adding small amounts of sodium or potassium bicarbonate until the solution stops effervescing. The increased quantity of sodium is excreted in combination with ascorbic acid. Mineral ascorbates are available as pure salts or as mixtures.

Free ascorbic acid must not be given parenterally. I.V. preparations contain mineral salts such as sodium ascorbate and calcium ascorbate.

## PYRIDOXINE (VITAMIN B6)

If one judges the importance of a vitamin by the number of reactions in the body in which it is essential, vitamin B6 is one of the most important. But of course this is not a valid measure; for each person the most important vitamin is the one that he most needs to supplement. Pyridoxine is in this sense a most important vitamin for many children with learning and behavioral disorders and for schizophrenics. Since the body must have enough pyridoxine to make vitamin B3 from its amino acid precursor, l-tryptophan, a deficiency will cause pellagra-like symptoms, which will be relieved either by pyridoxine or by vitamin B3.

### Indications

#### INFANTILE AUTISM

Dr. B. Rimland (1964), author of *Infantile Autism* and founder of the Institute for Child Behavior Research, has been the key person in demonstrating the therapeutic usefulness of pyridoxine for treating these seriously ill patients. His early observations (1973) and his continuing interest have stimulated up to 12 double-blind, controlled studies, all showing a significant improvement when B6 is added to the program. See publication list, 1982, #54, Institute for Child Behavior Research, 4182 Adams Ave., San Diego, CA 92116.

#### PYRROLEURIANS

Hoffer and Osmond (1961b) described a substance in the urine of schizophrenic patients that they called the "mauve factor." It was present in the majority of schizophrenics and in the minority of non-schizophrenics. When all patients with this factor in their urine were examined clinically, it became evident that whether they were schizophrenic or not they resembled each other more than they did non-excretors from the same group. A depressed mauve-factor excretor was more like a schizophrenic than like a depressed non-excretor. For this reason we called them *malvarians*, i.e., patients who excreted mauve factor in their urine. Later, mauve factor was identified chemically to be a kryptopyrrole, which produced toxic changes in animals, i.e., it is a psychotomimetic for animals.

Pfeiffer and his colleagues (1974, 1975) confirmed the presence of this factor. Further, they developed a simple urine quantitative test and later showed that the mauve factor, later called *KP*, combined with vitamin B6 and zinc. The complex was excreted. Large amounts of KP in the body produced a double deficiency, i.e., of pyridoxine and zinc. Pfeiffer finally described a new syndrome, diagnosed clinically by the presence of too much KP in urine. Patients with pyroluria require much larger amounts of vitamin B6.

## ARTHRITIS

Ellis (1973) found that even in small doses pyridoxine was helpful in treating some forms of arthritis. In these doses it is so safe I would recommend every arthritic be given some, either by itself in combination with other supplements or in a B vitamin complex containing at least 50 mg per tablet.

## INFANTILE CONVULSIONS

In 1952 an epidemic of infantile convulsions was produced by an infant formula deficient in vitamin B6. I have treated an infant with severe infantile spasms, who was unresponsive to any other treatment, with a multi-B vitamin complex containing B6. This infant stopped convulsing in a month and is beginning to develop.

## PREMENSTRUAL TENSION, NAUSEA, AND VOMITING OF PREGNANCY AND ECLAMPSIA

For these ailments, I know of no better treatment than B6, in combination with zinc.

Usually the premenstrual tension is gone or has diminished to much more tolerable levels within three cycles. The dose is under 1 gram per day, usually 250 mg or less, often at 500 mg per day.

## PREVENTION AND TREATMENT OF ARTERIOSCLEROSIS

Dr. Kilmer S. McCully (1983), while Professor of Pathology at Harvard Medical School, proposed that pyridoxine deficiency was involved in the etiology of arteriosclerosis. The homocysteine theory is described by Gruberg and Raymond (1981). This theory is very appealing and accounts for most of the phenomena.

## TREATMENT AND PREVENTION OF PRIMARY OXALOSIS

Pyridoxine in doses up to 1 gram per day prevents production of kidney stones by decreasing the endogenous production of oxalate (Will and Bijvoet 1979; Mitwalli et al. 1984).

## TOXICITY

Pyridoxine is relatively nontoxic. Very few instances of serious toxicity have been reported, but as with any chemical, if too much is given it can cause problems, either by interfering with other biochemical reactions or by unveiling other nutrient deficiencies. The usual dose is under 2,000 mg per day, but the most frequent dose level ranges between 100 and 500 mg per day. At this level it has made a few children more hyperactive, but only in the absence of enough magnesium.

Recently, Schaumburg and six other physicians (1983) from four U.S. medical schools reported that seven people developed sensory neuropathy from high doses of pyridoxine. All recovered. There was no effect on the brain. Three took 2 grams per day and the remaining four took 3, 4, 5 and 6 grams per day. Six took no other supplements and one took a multivitamin preparation. No information was given about their diet. In rats and dogs, 200 mg to 1,000 mg per kilogram of body weight were required to cause unsteady gait (an adult human weighing 60 kilograms would require 12 to 60 grams per day to be equivalent). I consider this excellent evidence to show how safe pyridoxine is. Had these seven been more aware nutritionally and used zinc and magnesium, they might have been spared their sensory changes, and had Schaumburg et al known how to use other supplements these patients might have recovered more quickly.

Mitwalli et al. (1984) reported that 250 mg to 500 mg per day for up to six years had not caused any problems. They have confirmed every orthomolecular physician. I have seen no toxicity for over 15 years.

Recently, Coleman, Sobels, Bhagavan et al. (1985) showed that very high doses of pyridoxine were toxic only in the presence of a vitamin B3 deficiency.

### VITAMIN E

Vitamin E was first discovered as the substance in lettuce that prevented fetal resorption in animals fed a rancid lard diet. Evans called it tocopherol—*tocos* meaning "childbirth" and *phero* meaning "to bring forth." This early identification of vitamin E with childbirth and later with sexual potency has been unfortunate. Early in its history these claims were made, and since then nearly every critic of megadoses of vitamin E refers to this as a way of showing how only quacks promote vitamin E. Vitamin E's antioxidant properties were known even earlier but have been ignored until recently. Over 35 years ago, Drs. Evan and Wilfrid Shute (Shute, Vogelsang, Skelton and Shute 1948), began to use vitamin E to treat coronary and peripheral vascular disease and by so doing launched a violent controversy that still continues. This is another of the senseless controversies that bedevil medicine. It could have been resolved long ago if the critics of vitamin E had repeated the Shutes' work carefully. But in spite of the criticism and opposition, vitamin E is being used on a wide scale. A company selling vitamin E estimated that about 25 percent of the physicians in Canada were using vitamin E personally, although few would prescribe it for their patients.

The controversy has been discussed by Legge (1971) and more recently is reviewed in Evan Shute's medical memoirs, *The Vitamin E Story*, edited by J. C. M. Shute (1985). Their important contribution to megavitamin therapy is detailed in their books (see Shute and Shute 1956; and Shute and Taub 1969).

There are eight forms of vitamin E, of which the most active is d-alpha tocopherol. Beta, gamma, and delta tocopherols are also present. Four similar tocotrienols occur. Synthetic tocopherol is a mixture of four forms, each in a, d or l form. The mixture is all rac-alpha tocopherol or dl alpha tocopherol.

These forms of the vitamin are unstable when exposed to air, so they are manufactured as acetate or succinate esters.

Dl-alpha tocopherol acetate is the standard, of which 1 mg equals 1 IU; 1 mg of d-alpha-tocopherol is equal to 1.49 IU.

Most living tissue exists in an atmosphere of oxygen. Plants do not burn up—oxidize—because they contain antioxidants. They make tocopherols that protect polyunsaturated fats from oxidizing. Vitamin E plays the same role in animal tissue, where it protects substances such as these fats, vitamin A, and phospholipids.

When animals are deficient in vitamin E many reactions are disturbed, but it is not clear why; vitamin E may have this effect simply because of its antioxidant properties. More is known about the animal requirements for vitamin E. In growing animals it is required for proper development and function of endocrine, muscle and peripheral vascular systems. There have been few human studies. In one study carried on for more than five years, men were kept on 5 IU per day only, and by the end of the sixth year it was evident that there was an increased rate of destruction of red blood cells. In spite of the paucity of human studies, 30 IU per day was recommended in 1968. In 1974 this was lowered to 15 IU. One of the reasons for this reduction was the difficulty nutritionists had in devising a diet which had 30 IU per day. Dr. M. K. Horwitt (1976) considers this reduction unwise. Most recommended doses were adequate to prevent the expression of a disease—enough thiamine to avoid beriberi and so on. No one has estimated a value that would give everyone optimum health. Certainly it is higher than these recommended doses and is highly individual. Orthomolecular physicians use dosages up to 3,000 mg per day for a few deadly diseases.

It takes a long time to saturate the tissues with vitamin E. Blood levels are raised much earlier than tissue levels. One advantage of high doses is that saturation will be achieved more quickly, but with any dose many months of treatment will be required before the full therapeutic effect is realized.

## Uses of Vitamin E

### PROTECTION OF LUNGS AGAINST AIR POLLUTION

Vitamin E has been found to protect rats against ozone in air. In areas characterized by high pollution, it would seem prudent to protect oneself by taking vitamin E.

### PORPHYRINURIA

Dr. P. P. Nair and his colleagues (see Nair, Mezey, Murty, Quartner, and Mendeloff 1971), treated four patients; in every case the biochemical changes were corrected.

### PROTECTION AGAINST THROMBOSIS

Over 25 years ago, Dr. Alton Ochsner, Tulane University (see Ochsner, Debakey and Decamp 1950), began to give his surgical patients large doses of vitamin E. Blood clots became rare. Apparently vitamin E inhibits platelet clumping. In Sweden it was found that 300 mg per day prolonged plasma clotting time after six weeks of treatment. Horwitt

(1976) suggested that vitamin E should be tried out instead of aspirin as an antithrombotic agent and that it might decrease the risk of thrombosis in women using oral contraceptives.

### USE FOR PREMATURE INFANTS

Infants given vitamin E have a lower incidence of retrolental fibroplasia. When infant formulas are deficient in vitamin E, anemia and edema develop.

### MALABSORPTION SYNDROME

These children also benefit from extra vitamin E.

### VASCULAR DISEASE

This indication is the most controversial one. Physicians have divided into two groups: the vast majority who will not advise their patients to use it—even though many are taking it regularly for their own health—and the smaller group who are using vitamin E in doses ranging from 400 to 1,600 IU per day, following the Shute brothers' indications. They have been convinced by the Shutes' studies, by its antioxidant properties, by what they themselves have experienced, and by witnessing what it has done for their patients. Enough must be given for long enough before a decision is made about how effective it is for any particular patient.

### ANTI-AGING

Most theories of aging involve oxygen and excessive formation of reactive molecular fragments called "free radicals," which are caused by either oxygen or by a radiant form of energy such as ultraviolet light or X-ray radiation. If these free radicals are left in the body, they quickly react with other molecules, destroying some or causing abnormal physical changes. If long-chain protein molecules are linked to one another by reaction with these free radicals with sulfhydril bonds, the mobility of the chains is reduced. In the same way, rubber is vulcanized by linking free long-chain molecules to one another. In fact, very aged skin, or sun-burned skin, does have some of the characteristics of overly vulcanized rubber—it loses its elasticity.

Vitamin E will react with free radicals, as will other antioxidants, and in so doing it can reduce the ravages of aging. Perhaps it does this to the vessel walls under strain, and by increasing their elasticity it can reduce the probability of coronary disease.

Graying of hair is one of the manifestations of aging. About eight years ago my hair began to gray. About that time I decided to see if taking vitamin E would produce any change in me generally. I did not think about my hair at all and the fact that it was graying played no part in my decision. About six months later I became aware of the fact that the hair on my head had become its normal dark color again. However, the hair on my chest did not become wholly repigmented. This does not mean that everyone with gray hair will respond, but it does suggest that those like myself who need vitamin E will note a similar response.

BURNS

Vitamin E is applied to the surface of burned areas. It is effective in reducing pain and in accelerating healing. I have seen deep, small burns heal so well no trace or scar remained. Many people routinely place it on any burn, including sunburn.

## INOSITOL

Myoinositol is the active form of nine known isomers. Free inositol is a benzene ring compound with a hydrogen and a hydroxyl ion on each carbon. Inositol phosphatide has one or more phosphate groups on each carbon. If all six carbon groups are united with phosphate, the compound is phytic acid or inositol hexaphosphate. Phytin, the calcium or magnesium salt, is insoluble.

Germinating seeds release phosphate from phytic acid, which is present in grains, legumes and other foods. Fermentation by yeast releases phosphates and metals bound to phytic acid. This is why unleavened bread is more apt to cause zinc, calcium, and magnesium deficiency problems.

A specific need in man for inositol hexaphosphate has not been demonstrated, but it would be surprising if it were not essential, as it is present in nearly all tissues, being in greatest concentration in the brain and heart. Inositol lowers serum lipids and cholesterol if given in doses of 3 grams per day.

Pfeiffer (1975) found inositol had antianxiety properties and has used it in patients withdrawing from Valium. He has also used it for treating schizophrenics and in high-serum copper, low-zinc patients.

The average diet provides 300 to 1,000 mg per day of inositol, but large amounts of caffeine may deplete the body of it.

Recently it was found that inositol phosphatides play an important role in a wide variety of neurotransmitters, hormones and growth factors (Marx 1984). Activation of polyphosphoinositide releases two second messengers that evoke cell responses: (1) diacylglycerol; and (2) inositol triphosphate. Increase in intracellular calcium ions was once believed to be due to binding by the receptors of their specific activating agents, i.e., acetylcholine and noradrenalin, and the calcium ions were believed to be the second messenger that transmitted the signal into the cell. But now it is believed that the second messengers are diacylglycerol and inositol triphosphate. The calcium ions have been relegated to a third messenger role. This new role for inositol phosphatides was first suggested 30 years ago.

Inositol takes part in a phosphate cycle. Lithium inhibits the removal of phosphate to form inositol, i.e., it must decrease the quantity of inositol available for phosphorylation. Such a deficiency should slow down all reactions that are mediated by inositol phosphatides. Preliminary evidence suggests that the cells most sensitive to lithium's effects are those being most actively stimulated. Is this why lithium controls mania? Perhaps we have an explanation for the activity seen by Pfeiffer. As lithium controls mania, can we use inositol to control depression? One should try using 1 gram t.i.d., but it might negate the antimanic effect of lithium.

In Canada and elsewhere, except in the U.S.A., inositol is combined with niacin in a proportion of one molecule of inositol combining with six molecules of niacin. This compound, Linodil, is slowly hydrolyzed in the body. The niacin so released very seldom causes any flushing. Linodil has all the beneficial properties of niacin, but perhaps it may have more since it also provides some inositol.

## BIOFLAVONOIDS

These are widely distributed in flowers, fruit and vegetables. A large number have been identified and several thousand are possible. Coumarin (not dicoumarol) is the prototype bioflavonoid. Rutin is extracted from buckwheat. At one time the U.S. Department of Agriculture studied rutin in depth because it wanted to create an additional use for buckwheat.

Bioflavonoids are antioxidant, perhaps because they bind metals such as copper. Combined with ascorbic acid the vitamin is stable. Pfeiffer (1975) found that rutin removed zinc and copper, but not iron, from the body. He also found it had mild sedative activity as measured by the quantitative electroencephalograph.

Bioflavonoids are used medically as anti-inflammatory agents and as an antiallergy preparation. But its most exciting use may be for schizophrenia.

Casley-Smith (1983) reported that his son, a young schizophrenic who was not responding to tranquilizers, was greatly improved within a few days when given a mixture of two benzopyrones—these are bioflavonoids such as rutin and coumarin; they have no effect on blood coagulation. His son has remained nearly well for almost three years on

400 mg per day of coumarin combined with 12.5 mg of fluphenazine decanoate per week. Before adding coumarin the tranquilizer had no effect.

Casley-Smith et al. (1984) have now reported the effect of benzopyrones on chronic patients. Sixteen chronic patients living with their parents were tested. Schizophrenia had been present for over five years in 85 percent of these patients. Patients were matched in pairs and assigned at random to placebo and treatment groups. They were given 3 grams per day of Paroven in three divided doses for 12 weeks. Paroven is a mixture of O-B-hydroxyethyl rutosides, in common use in Europe and other places, to control high protein edema. The treated group were significantly improved over placebo. Their scores on the brief psychiatric rating scale were 27 percent higher, but when patients showed improvement in three rating scales the improvement was closer to 50 percent.

One patient responded very well to active treatment, but after five weeks on placebo relapsed and had to be admitted to the hospital. The staff at the hospital refused to continue the trial. One patient became normal, except he had no insight and refused to take any more treatment. I have seen many patients react the same way. Even schizophrenics who have become normal may develop the idea that they are so well they could not possibly become ill again. Some do remain well for years, but others relapse within days or weeks, and often the relapse is so insidious that they are the last to recognize they are getting sick again. Manics have the same pattern of reaction.

All 11 patients in this double-blind trial considered they were better while on Paroven (P<0.0001 this was due to chance). Casley-Smith et al. listed a number of possible mechanisms of action: (1) by increasing proteolysis by macrophages any virus would be removed more quickly; (2) by improving immune defenses; (3) by its antioxidant effect, which would reduce formation of oxidized derivatives of noradrenalin and adrenalin; (4) by potentiating the effect of vitamin C; and (5) by restoring prostaglandin activity.

In North America these bioflavonoids are not available. Health food stores do have bioflavonoids in 1-gram doses. One gram three times per day could be used.

## PANTOTHENIC ACID

Pantothenic acid is a constituent of coenzyme A, which is involved in the transfer of acetyl groups. Thus it is essential for the synthesis of acetylcholine. This vitamin was discovered by Roger Williams and it is present in all cells—thus the Greek term *panthos*, meaning "everywhere" has become part of its name. Best sources are meats, fish, whole cereals and legumes. The amount we require is not yet established. It is difficult to produce deficiencies of pantothenic acid in animals. Any diet deficient in pantothenic acid is also deficient in many of the other B vitamins.

Pfeiffer (1975) found no activity with 500 mg per day as measured by the quantitative EEG. He recommends 30 mg per day; this dose elevates histamine levels. Large doses, he reports, have lowered sensitivity to pain. I have seen a number of patients using up to 750 mg per day without seeing any side effects.

Pantothenic acid is not one of the B vitamins more commonly used by orthomolecular therapists. It has been found to prolong life in animals and has been used for allergies. One can accurately sum up its role in large doses by the statement that there are no known conditions where it is useful in large doses, i.e., over 250 mg per day. But it is safe. Perhaps in the future more specific indications will be found. It should be useful in preventing senility and for people suffering allergies.

In this century, with increasing stress caused by malnutrition and environmental pollution, every antistress nutrient should be taken in optimum amounts. Pantothenic acid is needed by the adrenal gland and by the immune defense system. In *The Complete Book of Vitamins*, Rodale Press, Emmaus, PA (1977), two reports are summarized. A group of men were stressed by immersing them in freezing water for long periods. They were given various stress tests before and after the immersion. After six weeks on pantothenic acid the tests were repeated. After taking this vitamin the subjects were better able to withstand stress. For example, they were much less depleted of vitamin C. For a long time the loss of vitamin C from adrenal glands in animals has been used as a good measure of stress.

## FOLIC ACID AND VITAMIN B12

Vitamin B12 includes a number of compounds called cobalamines. Hydroxocobalamin is the most active and is the major form present in the body. It is also the form most suitable for therapeutic use.

Physicians are more knowledgeable about vitamin B12 and folic acid than about any other vitamins. They use megadoses of B12, i.e., 1-mg injections, which is 1,000 times the daily requirement. Historically this has arisen because it was so effective against pernicious anemia and was used frequently with no side effects for general fatigue states. In my experience, orthodox physicians have used B12 much more than have orthomolecular physicians.

Deficiency of B12 is rare but is more often found in pure vegetarians, but even with this group it is rare. The most important indications may be motor and mental, even when there is no pernicious anemia and when blood levels are normal.

Many psychotic patients may require B12; up to 50 percent of patients admitted to mental hospitals may be deficient even when no pernicious anemia is present. Reading (1975) recommends that chronically depressed, neurasthenic, or psychotic patients; those with periodic psychosis or atypical manic-depressive psychosis; or manic-depressives with a family history of cancer, premature graying, autoimmune disease, and psychiatric disturbances (especially senile dementia or recurrent depressions) should have serum B12 done. Carney (1969) found that 53 out of 374 psychiatric patients diagnosed organic psychosis, endogenous depression, schizophrenic and neurotic depression were low. It was most common in very old and very young. Nineteen of the low B12 group were also low in folate. Few had pernicious anemia.

Folic acid is required with B12 in transmethylation reactions and both are best used together. See Pfeiffer's (1975) discussion of the important functions of these two vitamins and how they relate to each other and to important biochemical factors.

The average person needs about 0.5 mg of folic acid per day. An average diet provides half that. Best sources are liver, yeast, and dark green leafy vegetables. Many surveys have shown folate deficiency is very common in the following cases: (1) in pregnant women; (2) in old age; (3) in malabsorption syndromes; (4) in excessive alcohol consumption; (5) in the presence of anticonvulsant use; (6) in the use of contraceptive pills; (7) in pernicious anemia; and (8) in many psychoses, especially schizophrenia.

Carl Pfeiffer (1975) found that histapenic (low blood histamine) patients were low in folic acid. Giving folic acid can accelerate recovery. He uses 1 to 2 mg orally per day. But sometimes folate may drive histamine too high.

Folic acid is available over the counter in 1-mg tablets in the United States and was available in up to 5-mg tablets in Canada. I usually use 5 mg per day in the few cases I have treated. Carl Pfeiffer, who has done so much work with folate, recommends that lower doses be used.

## VITAMIN D

Physicians are more familiar with this vitamin than with most of the other vitamins. It is more likely they have seen rickets, at least once. Two sterols have vitamin D activity: calciferol (D2) and cholecalciferol (D3). Ultraviolet radiation converts ergosterol (found in plants) to vitamin D2, and 7-dehydroergosterol (found in animals) to vitamin D3. Moon and Reich (1975) concluded that almost all published accounts of vitamin D toxicity dealt with vitamin D2. These accounts began to appear shortly after irradiated ergosterol became available commercially. Vitamin D2 was used in **all** vitamin D-fortified foods as well as in most multivitamin supplements. A number of physicians have provided evidence that vitamin D2 excess is implicated in atherosclerosis, arthritis, peripheral vascular disease, hypercalcemia, imbalances in magnesium and phosphate metabolism and in heavy metal poisoning. Vitamin D3 present in fish oils apparently has not been implicated in these toxicities. There have been few accounts of fish liver oil toxicity.

The RDA for vitamin D3 is about 400 IU per day. This estimate, however, applies to healthy people. For patients, requirements vary widely, as they do for any nutrient. The physician must determine what is the optimum dose for each patient, not what is the mean dose for the entire practice.

Since vitamin D3 is synthesized in skin from its precursor, the amount required is sun-dependent or, more accurately, ultraviolet dependent. More is needed in winter, in areas where ultraviolet is filtered out by smog, or at high latitudes; here, ultraviolet is filtered out by our atmosphere, since the rays have to travel through more atmosphere before reaching us.

Reich (1971) reported that a combination of vitamin D3 and vitamin A with the minerals calcium and phosphate helped chronic asthmatics. His series was very large, about 5,000 patients. Nearly all had been on traditional treatment before.

For adults Reich recommends 5,000 to 14,000 IU per day of vitamin D3 and 28,000 to 75,000 IU per day of vitamin A. This is combined with bone meal tablets, six to eight tablets per day. Once the desired therapeutic response is obtained the doses are reduced to one-half or one-third these dosages.

Reich claimed a nearly 90 percent improvement rate. I have seen some of his patients, and there is no doubt they had been helped. Other physicians have confirmed that his patients have improved. Since I seldom see asthmatics I have very little experience with this treatment. He has not seen evidence of toxicity with these dosages. Minor intolerances have been noted rarely; they clear once the dose is reduced. D3, the human vitamin D hormone, is much less toxic than D2.

## CHAPTER REFERENCES

Agnew, A., & Hoffer, A. (1955), Nicotinic acid modified lysergic acid diethylamide psychosis. *J. Ment. Sci.* 101:12-27.

Aladjem, H. (1972), *The Sun Is My Enemy.* Englewood Cliffs, N.J.: Prentice-Hall.

Alhadeff, L., Gualtieri, T., & Lipton, M. (1983), Toxic effects of water-soluble vitamins. *Nutrition Reviews* 42 (2): 33-40.

Altschul, R. (1964), *Niacin in Vascular Disorders and Hyperlipidemia.* Springfield, Ill.: Charles C Thomas.

Altschul, R., Hoffer, A., & Stephen, J. D. (1955), Influence of nicotinic acid on serum cholesterol in man. *Arch. Biochemistry and Biophysics* 54:558-559.

Belfield, W. O., (1984), Vitamin C toxicity and the kidney stone myth. *Let's Live,* page 79, June.

Berry, I. R., and Borkan, L. (1983), Phosphatidyl choline—its use in neurological and psychiatric syndromes. *J. Ortho. Psych.,* 12:129-141.

Boyd, W. D., Graham-White, J., Blackwood, G., Glen, T., & McQueen, J. (1977) Clinical effects of choline in Alzheimer's senile dementia. *Lancet* 2:711.

Boyle, E. (1968), "Niacin and the heart." In *The Vitamin B3 Therapy: A Second Communication to A.A.'s Physicians from Bill W.,*

Briggs, M. H., Garcia-Webb, P., & Davies, P. (1973), Urinary oxalate and Vitamin C supplements. *Lancet* 2:201.

Cade, J. F. J. (1972), Massive thiamine dosage in the treatment of acute alcoholic psychoses. *Aust. N.A. J. Psychiatry,* 6:225-230.

Cameron, E., & Pauling, L. (1979), *Cancer and Vitamin C.* New York: W. W. Norton.

Canner, P. L. (1985), Mortality in Coronary Drug Project patients during a nine-year post-treatment period. *J. Am. Coll. Cardiol.* 5:442.

Carlson, L. A., Levi, L., & Oro, L. (1967), Plasma lipids and urinary excretion of catecholamines in man during experimentally induced emotional stress, and their modification by nicotinic acid. *Report of Laboratory for Clinical Stress and Research,* Department of Medicine and Psychiatry, Karolinska Sjukhuset, Stockholm 60, Sweden.

Carney, M. W. P. (1969), Serum Vitamin B12 values in 374 psychiatric patients. *Behavioral Neuropsychiatry,* 1:19-22.

Casley-Smith, J. Letter, October 18, 1983. Results of coumarin double-blind study.

Casley-Smith, J.R., Casley-Smith, Judith R., Weston, F. and Johnson, P. C. (1985), A double-blind trial of benzo-pyrones in chronic schizophrenia. *Psychiatry Research,* accepted for publication.

Cathcart, R. F. Clinical trial of Vitamin C. Letter to the Editor, *Medical Tribune,* June 25, 1975.

———(1984), Vitamin C in the treatment of acquired immune deficiency syndrome (AIDS). *Med. Hypotheses* 14:423-433.

———(1985), Vitamin C: The non toxic, non rate-limited, antioxidant free radical scavenger. *Med. Hypotheses* 18:61-77.

Cheraskin, E. Ringsdorf, Jr., W. M., & Sisley, E. L. (1983), *The Vitamin C Connection.* New York: Harper and Row.

Cleave, T. L. (1975), *The Saccharine Disease.* New Canaan, Conn.: Keats Publishing.

Clemetson, C. A. B., (1980), Histamine and ascorbic acid in human blood. *J. of Nutrition,* 110:662-668.

Coleman, M., Sobels, S., Bhagavan, H. N., Coursin, D., Marquardt, A., Guay, M., & Hunt, C. (1985), A double-blind study of Vitamin B6 in Down's syndrome infants, Part 1, Clinical and biochemical results. *J. Ment. Def. Res.,* 29: 233-240.

Condorelli, L. (1964), "Nicotinic acid therapy in the cardiovascular apparatus." In *Niacin in*

*Vascular Disorders and Hyperlipidemia*, ed. R. Altschul, 156-207. Springfield, Ill. Charles C Thomas.

Cott, A. (1969), Treatment of schizophrenic children. *Schizophrenia* 1:44-59.

—— (1971), Orthomolecular approach to the treatment of learning disabilities. *J. Ortho. Psych.* 3:95-105.

—— (1973), Orthomolecular approach to the treatment of children with behavioral disorders and learning disabilities. *J. Appl. Nutr.* 25:15-24.

Davidson, A. R., Rojas-Bueno, A., Thompson, R. P. H., & Williams, R., Reduced caloric intake and nicotinic acid provocation tests in the diagnosis of Gilbert's syndrome. *British Med. J.* May 31, 1975, Vol., 1. p. 480.

Ellis, J. (1973), *Vitamin B6. The Doctor's Report.* New York: Harper and Row.

Fituri, N., Allawi, N., Bentley, M., et al. (1983), Urinary and plasma oxalate during ingestion of pure ascorbic acid: A re-evaluation. *Eur. Urol.* 9:312-315.

Free, V., & Sanders, P. (1978), The use of ascorbic acid and mineral supplements in the detoxification of narcotic addicts. *J. Ortho. Psych.* 7:264-270.

Gentile, S., Tiribelli, C., Persico, M., Bronzino, P., Marmo, R., Orzes, N., Orlando, C., Rubba, P., & Coltorti, M. (1966), Dose dependence of nicotinic acid-induced hyperbilirubinemia and its association from hemolysis in Gilbert's syndrome. *J. Lab. Clin. Med.* 107 (2):166-171.

Green, R. G. (1970), Subclinical pellagra: its diagnosis and treatment. *Schizophrenia* 2:70-79.

—— (1974), Subclinical pellagra—a central nervous system allergy. *J. Ortho. Psych.* 3:312-318.

—— (1975), "Subclinical pellagra." In *The Hoffer Osmond Diagnostic Test*, Ed. A. Hoffer, H. Kelm & H. Osmond. Huntington, New York: Robert E. Krieger Publishing.

Gruberg, E. R., & Raymond, S. A. (1981), *Beyond Cholesterol: Vitamin B6, Arteriosclerosis and Your Heart.* New York: St. Martin's Press.

Herbert, V., & Jacob, E. (1974), Destruction of Vitamin B12 by ascorbic acid. *JAMA* 230: 241-242.

Hippchen, L. J. (1978), *Ecologic Biochemical Approach to Treatment of Delinquents and Criminals.* New York: Van Nostrand Reinhold.

—— (1981), An exploratory study of the use of nutritional approaches in the treatment of suicide-prone persons. *J. Ortho. Psych.* 10: 147-155.

—— (1982), *Holistic Approaches to Offender Rehabilitation.* Springfield, Ill.: Charles C Thomas.

Hoffer, A. (1962), *Niacin Therapy in Psychiatry.* Springfield, Ill.: Charles C Thomas.

—— (1964), Faith, hope and chemotherapy. *Chemother.* 9:263-274.

—— (1966), Enzymology of hallucinogens. In:*Enzymes in Mental Health*, Ed. G.J. Martin & B. Kisch. New York: J.B. Lippincott.

—— (1967), A theoretical examination of double blind design. *Can. Med. Assn. J.* 97:123-127.

—— (1969), Safety, side effects and relative lack of toxicity of nicotinic acid and nicotinamide. *Schizophrenia* 1:78-87.

—— (1970), The psychophysiology of cancer. *J. Asthma Research* 8:61-76.

—— (1971), Vitamin B3 dependent child. *Schizophrenia* 3:107-113.

—— (1972), Treatment of hyperkinetic children with nicotinamide and pyridoxine. *Can. Med. Assn. J.* 107:111-112.

—— (1974), Hong Kong veterans study. *J. Ortho. Psych.* 3:34-36.

—— (1983), Why nicotinic acid lowers lipid levels. *Can. Med. Assn. J.* 128:372.

Hoffer, A, & Callbeck. M. J. (1957), The hypocholesterolemic effect of nicotinic acid and its relationship to the autonomic nervous system. *J. Ment. Sci.* 103:810-820.

Hoffer, A., & Osmond, H. (1961a), Double-blind clinical trials. *J. Neuropsychiat.* 2:221-227.

—— (1961b), The relationship between an unknown factor (US) in urine of subjects and HOD test results. *J. Neuropsychiat.* 2:363-368.

—— (1963), Some problems of stochastic psychiatry. *J. Neuropsychiat.* 5:97.

—— (1963), Malvaria: A new psychiatric disease. *Acta Psychiatrica Scand.* 39:335-336.

—— (1966), Nicotinamide adenine dinucleotide. *J. of Psychopharm.* 1:79-95.

—— (1966), Nicotinamide adenine dinucleotide (NAD) as a treatment for schizophrenia. *J. of Psychopharm.* 1:79-95.

——(1976), *In Reply to the American Psychiatric Association Task Force Report on Megavitamins and Orthomolecular Therapy in Psychiatry.* Regina, Saskatchewan, Canada: Canadian Schizophrenia Foundation.

Hoffer, A., Osmond, H., Callbeck, M. J., & Kahan, I. (1957), Treatment of schizophrenia with nicotinic acid and nicotinamide. *J. Clin. Exper. Psychopath.* 18:131-158.

Hoffer, A., & Walker, M. (1980), *Nutrients to Age Without Senility.* New Canaan, Conn.: Keats Publishing.

Hogenkamp, H. P. C. (1980), The interaction between Vitamin B12 and Vitamin C. *Am. J. Clin. Nutr.* 33:1-3.

Horwitt, M. K. (1976), Vitamin E: A re-examination. *Amer. J. Clin. Nutr.* 29:569-578.

Hughes, C., Dutton, S., & Truswell, A. S. (1981), High intakes of ascorbic acid and urinary oxalate. *J. Human Nutrition* 35:274-280.

Illingworth, D. R., Phillipson, B. E., Rapp, J. H., & Connor, W. E. (1981), Colestipol plus nicotinic acid in treatment of heterozygous familial hypercholesterolemia. *Lancet*: Feb. 7, 296-298.

Jungeblut, C. W. (1935), Inactivation of poliomyelitis virus in vitro by crystalline Vitamin C (ascorbic acid). *J. Exptl. Med.* 62:517-521.

—— (1937), Further observations on Vitamin C therapy in experimental poliomyelitis. *J. Exptl. Med.* 66:459-477.

—— (1939), A further contribution to Vitamin C therapy in experimental poliomyelitis. *J. Exptl. Med.* 70:315-332.

Kalokerinos, A. (1981), *Every Second Child.* New Canaan, Conn.: Keats Publishing.

Kane, J. P., Malloy M. J., Tun, P., Phillips, N. R., Freedman, D. D., Williams, M. L., Rowe, J.S., & Havel, R. J. (1981), Normalization of low-density-lipoprotein levels in heterozygous familial hypercholesterolemia with a combined drug regimen. *NEJM* 304:251-258.

Kaufman, W. (1943), *The Common Form of Niacinamide Deficiency Disease: Aniacinamidosis.* New Haven: Yale University Press.

—— (1949), *The Common Form of Joint Dysfunction: Its Incidence and Treatment.* Brattleboro, VT.: E. L. Hildreth.

Klenner, F. R. (1954), Recent discoveries in the treatment of lockjaw with vitamin C and Toluenol. *Tri-State Med. Journal*, July.

—— (1971), Observations on the dose and administration of ascorbic acid when employed beyond the range of a vitamin in human pathology. *J. Appl. Nutr.* 23:61-88.

—— (1973), Response of peripheral and central nerve pathology to mega doses of the vitamin B complex and other metabolites. *J. Appl. Nutr.* 25:16-40.

Kline, N. S., Barclay, C. L., Cole, J. O., Esser, A. H., Lehmann, H., & Wittenborn, J. R. (1967), Controlled evaluation of nicotinamide adenine dinucleotide. *British J. of Psych.* 113:731-742.

Kunin, R. A. (1976), Manganese and niacin in the treatment of drug-induced dyskinesias. *J. Ortho. Psych.* 5:4-27.

—— (1976), The action of aspirin in preventing the niacin flush and its relevance to the antischizophrenic action of megadose niacin. *J. Ortho. Psych.* 5:89-100.

Lamden, M. P., & Chrystowski, G. A. (1954), Urinary oxalate excretion by man following ascorbic acid ingestion. *Proc. Soc. Exp. Biol. Med.* 85:190-192.

Legge, R. F. (1971), *Resolving the Vitamin E Controversy.* Canadian Research and Development, Toronto: Maclean Hunter.

Lewin, S. (1976), *Vitamin C: Its Molecular Biology and Medical Potential.* New York: Academic Press.

Lewis, B., Sixth International Symposium on Atherosclerosis. Abstracted *The Medical Post*, Sept. 7, 1982.

Libby, A. F., Day, J. L., Starling, C. R., MacMurray, D. K., & Josefson, F. H. (1982a), A study indicating a connection between paranoia, schizophrenia, perceptual disorders and I.Q. in alcohol and drug abusers. *J. Ortho. Psych.* 11:50-66.

Libby, A. F., Starling, C. R., Josefson, F. H. & Ward, S. A. (1982b), "The Junk food connection:" A study reveals alcohol and drug life styles adversely affect metabolism and behavior. *J. Ortho. Psych.* 11:116-127.

Libby, A. F., Starling, C. R., MacMurray, D. K., & Kline, R. E. (1982c), Abnormal blood and urine chemistries in an alcohol and drug population: Dramatic reversals obtained quickly from potentially serious diseases. *J. Ortho. Psych.* 11:156-181.

Libby, A. F., & Stone, I. (1977), The hypoascorbemia-Kwashiorkor approach to drug addiction therapy: A pilot study. *J. Ortho. Psych.* 6:300-308.

MacMurray, D. K., & Josefson, F. H. (1982), A study indicating a connection between paranoia, schizophrenia, perceptual disorders and I.Q. in alcohol and drug abusers. *J. Ortho. Psych.* 11:50-66.

Marcus, M.; Prabhudesai, M., & Wassef, S. (1980), Stability of Vitamin B12 in the presence of ascorbic acid in food and serum: Restoration by cyanide of apparent loss. *Amer. J. Clin. Nutr.* 33:137-143.

Marx, J. L. (1984), A new view of receptor action. *Science* 224:271-274.

Mawson, A. R., & Jacobs, K. W. (1978), Corn consumption, tryptophan and cross national homicide rates. *J. Ortho. Psych.* 7:227-230.

McCormick, W. J. (1957), La thrombose coronarienne: nouvelle théorie de son mécanisme et de son étiologie. *Union Méd. Canada* 86: 509-514.

Mink, K. A., Dick, E. C., Jennings, L.C. and Inhorn, S. L., Amelioration of rhinovirus colds by vitamin C (ascorbic acid) supplementation. Paper presented at the 1987 International Symposium on Medical Virology, Los Angeles, California, November 12-14, 1987.

Mitwalli, A., Blair, G., & Oreopoulos, D. G. (1984), Safety of intermediate doses of pyridoxine. *Can. Med. Assn. J.* 131:14.

Mohler, H., Polc, P., Cumin, R., Pieri, L., & Kettler, R. (1979), Nicotinamide is a brain constituent with benzodiazepine-like actions. *Nature* 278: 563-565.

Moon, J. Y., & Reich, C. J. (1975), The Vitamin D problem; An important lesson in orthomolecular medicine. *J. Ortho. Psych.* 4:123-131.

Mount, H. T. R. (1973), Multiple sclerosis and other demyelenating diseases. *Can. Med. Assn. J.* 108:1356-1358.

Moutafis, C. C., Myant, N. E., Mancini, M., & Oriente, P. (1971), Cholestyramine and nicotinic acid in the treatment of familial hypercholesterolemia in the homozygous form. *Atherosclerosis* 14:157-268.

Nair, P. P., Mezey, E., Murty, H. S., Quartner, J., & Mendeloff, A. I. (1971), Vitamin E and porphyrin metabolism in man. *Arch. Intern. Med.* 128:411-415.

Nettesheim, P. (1980), Inhibition of carcinogenesis by retinoids. *Can. Med. Assn. J.* 122:757-765.

Newmark, H. L., Scheiner, J., Marcus, M., et al.

(1976), Stability of Vitamin B12 in the presence of ascorbic acid. *Am. J. Clin. Nutr.* 29:645-649.

Ochsner, A., Debakey, M. E., & Decamp, P. T. (1950), Venous thrombosis. *JAMA* 144:831-834.

Ost, C. R. and Stenson, S. (1964), Regression of atherosclerosis during nicotinic acid therapy: A study in man by means of repeated arteriographies, pp. 245-262 in: *Niacin in Vascular Disorders and Hyperlipidemia.* Edited by R. Altschul, Springfield, Ill.: Charles C Thomas.

Paterson, J. C. (1941), Some factors in the causation of intimal hemorrhage and in the precipitation of coronary thrombi. *Can. Med. Assn. J.* 44:114-120.

Pauling, L. (1968), Orthomolecular psychiatry. *Science* 160:265-271.

——— (1970), *Vitamin C and the Common Cold.* San Francisco: W. H. Freeman.

———(1976), *Vitamin C, the Common Cold and the Flu.* San Francisco: W. H. Freeman.

Pauling L., & Hawkins, D. (1973), *Orthomolecular Psychiatry.* San Francisco: W. H. Freeman.

Pfeiffer, C. C. (1975), *Mental and Elemental Nutrients.* New Canaan, Conn.: Keats Publishing.

Pfeiffer, C. C., Sohler, A., Jenney, M. S., & Iliev, V. (1974), Treatment of pyroluric schizophrenia (malvaria) with large doses of pyridoxine and a dietary supplement of zinc. *J. Applied Nutr.* 26:21.28.

Prasad, K. N., & Rama, B. N. (1985), "Nutrition and cancer." In *1984–85 Yearbook of Nutritional Medicine,* ed. J. Bland, 179-211. New Canaan, Conn.: Keats Publishing.

Reading, C. M. (1975), Latent pernicious anemia: A preliminary report. *Med. J. Australia* 1:91-94.

Reading, C. M. and Meillon, R. (1988). *Your Family Tree Connection.* New Canaan, Conn.: Keats Publishing.

Reich, C. J. (1971), The vitamin therapy of chronic asthma. *J. Asthma Research* 9:99-102.

Richards, C. C., Snell, C. R., & Snell, P. H. (1983), Nicotinamide adenine dinucleotide depresses synaptic transmission in the hippocampus and has specific binding sites on the synaptic membranes. *Br. J. Pharmac.* 79:553-564.

Rimland, B. (1964), *Infantile Autism: The Syndrome and its Implications for a Neural Theory of Behavior.* New York: Appleton-Century-Crofts.

———(1973), High dosage levels of certain vitamins in the treatment of children with severe mental disorder. In *Orthomolecular Psychiatry*, eds. D. Hawkins & L. Pauling, 513-539. San Francisco: W. H. Freeman.

Robie, T. R. (1967), Cyproheptadine: an excellent antidote for niacin-induced hyperthermia. *J. Schizophrenia* 1:133-139.

Ross, H. (1975), *Fighting Depression*. New York: Larchmont Books.

Rudin, D. O. (1981), The major psychoses and neuroses as Omega-3 essential fatty acid deficiency syndrome: substrate pellagra. *Biol. Psychiatry* 16:837-850.

—— (1982), The dominant diseases of modernized societies as Omega-3 essential fatty acid deficiency syndrome: substrate beri beri. *Med. Hypotheses* 8:17-47.

Sabine, A. B. (1939), Vitamin C in relation to experimental poliomyelitis. *J. Exptl. Med.* 69:507-515.

Schaumberg, H., Kaplan, J.; Windebank, A., Vick, N., Rasmus, S., Pleasure, D., & Brown, J. (1983), Sensory neuropathy from pyridoxine abuse. *NEJM* 309:445-448.

Schauss, A. (1979), Differential outcomes among probationers comparing orthomolecular approaches to conventional casework counselling. *J. Ortho. Psych.* 8:158-168.

—— (1980), *Diet, Crime and Delinquency*. Berkeley, Calif.: Parker House.

Shute, J. C. M. (1985), *The Vitamin E Story*. Burlington, Ont.: Welch.

Shute, E., & Shute, W. (1956), *Your Heart and Vitamin E*. Detroit: The Cardiac Society.

Shute, W. E., & Taub, H. J. (1969), *Vitamin E for Ailing and Healthy Hearts*. New York: Pyramid Books.

Shute, E. V., Volgelsang, A. B., Skelton, F. R., & Shute, W. E. (1948), The influence of Vitamin E on vascular disease. *Surgery, Gynecology and Obstetrics* 86:1-8.

Silverman, L. B. (1975), Orthomolecular treatment of disturbances involving brain function. *J. Ortho. Psych.* 4:71-84.

Smith, R. F. (1974), A five-year field trial of massive nicotinic acid therapy of alcoholics in Michigan. *J. Ortho. Psych.* 3:327-331.

Spittle, C. R. (1971, 1972), Atherosclerosis and Vitamin C. *Lancet* 2:1280-1281: 1335.

Still, C. N. (1979), Nutritional therapy in Huntington's chorea concepts based on the model of pellagra. *The Psychiatric Forum* 9:74-78.

—— (1980–81), Sex differences affecting nutritional therapy in Huntington's disease—an inherited essential fatty acid metabolic disorder? *The Psychiatric Forum* 9:47-51.

Stone, I. (1972), *The Healing Factor: Vitamin C Against Disease*. New York: Grosset and Dunlap.

Szent-Györgyi, A. (1972), *The Living State*. New York: Academic Press.

Takenouchi, K., Aso, K., Ichikawa, H., & Shiomi, T. (1966), On the metabolites of ascorbic acid, especially oxalic acid, eliminated in the urine following the administration of large amounts of ascorbic acid. *J. Vitamin.* 13:49-58.

Tiselius, H. G., & Almgard. L. E. (1977), The diurnal urinary excretion of oxalate and the effect of pyridoxine and ascorbate on oxalate excretion. *European Urology* 3:41-46.

Vague, P., Vialettes, B., Lassman-Vague, V., & Vallo, J. J. (1987), Nicotinamide may extend remission phase in insulin-dependent diabetes. *Lancet* i:619, 1987.

Victor, M., & Adams, R. D. (1961), On the etiology of the alcoholic neurologic diseases with special reference to the role of nutrition. *Amer. J. Clin. Nutr.* 9:379-397.

Victor, M., Adams, R. D., & Collins, G. H. (1971), *The Wernicke-Korsakoff Syndrome*. Philadelphia: F. A. Davis.

Wahlbwerg, G., Carlson, L. A., Wasserman, J., & Ljungqvist, A. (1985), Protective effect of nicotinamide against nephropathy in diabetic rats. *Diabetic Research* 2:307-312.

Warburg, O. (1966), The prime cause and prevention of cancer. Lecture at meeting of the Nobel-Laureates on June 30 at Lindau, Lake Constance, Berlin-Dahlem. English edition by Dean Burk, Konrad Triltsch, Würzburg, Germany, 1967.

Will, E. J., & Bijvoet, O. L. M. (1979), Primary oxalosis: Clinical and biochemial response to high-dose pyridoxine therapy. *Metabolism* 28:542-548.

Willett. W. C., & MacMahon, B. (1984), Diet and cancer—an overview. *NEJM* 310:633-638; 697-703.

Williams, H. E. (1978), *Idiopathic Urinary Bladder Stone Disease*. Ed. R. Van Reen. Washington, DC: U.S. Gov't. Printing Office.

Yamada, K., Nonaka, K., Hanafusa, T., Miyazaki, A., Toyoshima, H., & Tarui, S. (1982), Preventive and therapeutic effects of large-dose nicotinamide injections on diabetes associated with insulitis. *Diabetes* 31:749-753.

Yaryura-Tobias, J. A., & Diamond, B. (1971), Levodopa-nicotinic acid interaction in psychiatric patients. *Schizophrenia* 3:177-180.

Zaslove, M., Silverio, T., & Minenna, R. (1983), Severe riboflavin deficiency: A previously undescribed side effect of phenothiazines. *J. Ortho. Psych.* 12:113-115.

# MINERAL SUPPLEMENTS

· · · · · · · · · · · · · · · · · · · · · · · · · · · · · · ·

A large number of minerals are present in the body. It would be surprising if they were not there, since life originated in the seas, which contain almost all the minerals. It would require too much of the cell's energy to keep the cell interior free of minerals. It would be energy-conserving to incorporate minerals into enzyme reactions that could co-ordinate with the protein molecules. Minerals present in the greatest amounts in the primi-tive seas would most likely have been used, while very rare elements would play a minor role. Theoretically, every mineral element could have been used, with each having an optimum range. Below this level the mineral would have no particular effect. In the opti-mum range it would play the role life had shaped for it. In excess it would be toxic.

When the optimum range is very close to zero, these elements are needed in trace amounts. When the optimum range is greater, milligram and gram amounts are needed. The optimum is determined by the ease with which these elements can be eliminated and by the presence of mechanisms developed to deal with them. For example, copper is required in 2 mg doses per day; less than this will cause a deficiency, and more will cause cop-per toxicity. Zinc is required in doses of 15 mg per day; less will result in a deficiency, but as zinc is water-soluble and easily ex-creted, the body can tolerate fairly large amounts. A man needs 10 mg of iron a day.

Giving 20 mg a day for many years may cause a problem, but a woman needs 20 mg a day, as she loses more iron with her menstrual periods.

Dr. Carl Pfeiffer has written two very valu-able books (1975, 1978) describing these min-erals and their relation to health. In this chapter I will discuss only a few minerals—the ones most apt to be needed or to be toxic. Orthomolecular medicine pays particular at-tention to these. As this newer medicine de-velops, more minerals will undoubtedly become very important to clinical practice.

## ZINC

### Metabolism

An adult contains 2 to 3 grams of zinc, mostly stored in bones, where it turns over slowly. Serum zinc levels are relatively con-stant, ranging normally between 80 to 110 mcg percent.

An adult needs 15 mg of zinc per day. Most diets provide somewhat less—8 to 11 mg per day. Foods are deficient in zinc for the following reasons: (1) being water-soluble, zinc is leached out of our soil. Soils cropped for centuries, as in Egypt and Iran, have no zinc; (2) processing removes those portions of food richest in zinc, such as germ and bran; (3) cooking disolves zinc, which is then lost in the discarded water; and (4) foods contain chemicals such as EDTA that chelate zinc.

Zinc is a component of 80 metalloenzymes. Yet, even when the body is deficient in zinc, these enzymes seem relatively intact. Perhaps a slight reduction in the activity of a large number of enzymes is as dangerous as more substantial decreases in a few enzymes.

## Deficiency of Zinc

The first deficiency symptoms discovered were dwarfism, hypogonadism, and failure to mature sexually. Other signs are:

1. Skin—striae (stretch marks) in both men and women, retarded growth in hair and nails, brittle nails, and white, opaque spots in nails. Acne is common.
2. Endocrine—interference with the menstrual cycle, premenstrual tension.
3. Increased blood pressure.
4. Joint pain and cold extremities.
5. Retarded wound healing.
6. Loss of taste and sense of smell.
7. Birth defects.
8. Psychiatric symptoms.
9. Acrodermatitis enteropathica.

## Excess Zinc

No known diseases are associated with above-normal zinc levels, but toxic doses can be taken. More than 2 grams per day can be toxic. Fortunately, there is no indication for such large doses. Dr. C. Pfeiffer (1975, 1978) described a 16-year-old boy who took 12 grams of pure zinc over a two-day period. For the next week he was excessively drowsy but then made a complete recovery. The largest dose used clinically was zinc sulfate, 220 mg, taken three times per day for arthritis. At this dose it may cause diarrhea. Usually one tablet per day or less is used of either zinc sulfate, zinc gluconate, chelated zinc tablets, or a liquid preparation developed by Pfeiffer. Only a small proportion is absorbed. Zinc gluconate, 50 mg, provides 15 mg of zinc.

## Zinc and Copper

Zinc supplements decrease copper levels. In combination with ascorbic acid, zinc is used to decrease high serum copper levels. Pfeiffer maintains that normal copper and zinc levels are 90 to 100 mcg per 100 ml and 120 to 140 mcg respectively. The ratio of copper over zinc is a useful index of morbidity. Pregnancy, Hodgkin's disease, oral contraceptives, infections, and leukemia increase the ratio, i.e., elevate copper and lower zinc. Pyrrolleuria, due to excessive quantities of kryptopyrrole in the body, causes a deficiency of pyridoxine (B6) and zinc. Both supplements are used together.

Preliminary evidence shows that senility is associated with a surplus of copper and a deficiency of zinc. For example, the mean ratio of copper over zinc for 23 patients, ranging in age from 60 to 85, was 1.74. They all had memory problems. The mean ratio for seven patients in the same age range with no memory problem was 1.47.

The best clinical reviews of the roles of zinc and copper and other important trace elements are given in C. C. Pfeiffer's excellent books: *Zinc and Other Micro-Nutrients* (1978), and *Mental and Elemental Nutrients* (1975).

## COPPER

Copper is essential for the formation of hemoglobin. It is a constituent of several enzymes and is involved in the development and function of most organs. Copper deficiency is rare. We are more apt to suffer from excessive copper consumption. C. Pfeiffer (1975, 1978) examined over 20,000 patients without finding one case of copper deficiency.

The body contains about 125 mg of copper. The average person ingests 3 to 5 mg per day. Since only 2 mg is required, there is a tendency for copper to accumulate. Copper may accumulate because: (1) zinc levels are too low; or (2) soft acid water dissolves copper from copper pipes. Copper levels in the human brain may double, in contrast to levels of manganese, zinc, or magnesium. Pfeiffer (1984) reported that 5 mg of copper had the same stimulant effect as 5 mg of Dexedrine in normal subjects, as measured by the quantitative EEG. It also caused insomnia. Also, many elderly hypertensives had elevated copper levels. When the copper levels were reduced, the need for antihypertensive medication was decreased.

Excess copper is associated with pregnancy, where ceruloplasmin, a copper-carrying protein, increases. Serum copper may increase from a normal range of around 100 mcg percent to around 250. This may be a factor in postpartum psychosis, in toxemia of pregnancy and in depression that sometimes follows use of birth control pills.

Excess copper has been related to psychoses, heart attacks, and, of course, is present in Wilson's disease.

### Treatment of Excess Copper

1. Zinc and manganese in a ratio of 20:1, i.e., 50 mg zinc and 2.5 mg of manganese.
2. Ascorbic acid in the usual dose ranges.
3. Toxic chelators, such as penicillamine and EDTA.
4. High-fiber diet.
5. Selenium.

## SELENIUM

I first became interested in selenium as a toxic component of wheat grown in certain parts of North Dakota. I was working on my M.A. in cereal chemistry. One of my jobs was to analyze wheat from these areas. There was a brief nutritional scare until it was realized that South Dakota wheat was seldom the sole food for inhabitants of that area. It entered the immense wheat stores in the U.S.A. and was diluted to a safe level. Animal feeds of South Dakota are diluted by forage grown elsewhere.

Soils rich in selenium are found primarily in the Great Plains and the Rocky Mountain states, particularly in the Dakotas and Wyo-

ming. The Northeast, East, and Northwest parts of the United States are very low in selenium. Livestock fed on produce from these soils are apt to be selenium-deficient. In China, Keshan Disease, a myocardial disease was eradicated by using selenium supplements.

Selenium is absorbed primarily in the duodenum and is bound to cysteine or methionine. It can replace the sulphur part of these compounds.

Selenium is present in traces in living tissue. Hemoglobin has 0.65 ppm, alpha-2 globulins, 5.4, and insulin 4 ppm. It is the only trace element active in glutathione peroxidase.

Males require more selenium than females. It is required to promote growth and has a protective action against mercury, cadmium, arsenic, silver and copper, and against cancer. People living in low selenium areas have an increased incidence of cancer. Selenium is an antioxidant and potentiates the action of vitamin E. Human milk contains six times as much selenium as does cow's milk.

Foods from animal sources are richer in selenium than are vegetarian foods. Good sources are brewer's yeast, garlic, liver, and eggs. As selenium is richest in germ and bran, milling and refining grains removes most of the selenium.

The absorption of selenium is affected by a number of variables. The bioavailability varies in foods. Thus, it is more available from wheat than from tuna. Protein decreases its toxicity. Bacteria in the bowel, such as E. coli, bind selenium and make it inaccessible to the body. Also it is difficult to absorb if iron deficiency anemia is present. With severe malnutrition it is absorbed slowly. The need for selenium is increased by polyunsaturated fatty acids and by stress.

In animals selenium deficiency has been associated with muscular dystrophy, pancreatic atrophy, liver necrosis and infertility.

### Indications

These are suggested indications based upon

research on animals and on epidemiological studies.

1. Anticancer—*i.e.*, prevention and treatment.
2. Antiaging—in cataract lens, selenium content is one-sixth that of a normal lens. Normally selenium should increase with age.
3. Antitoxic to heavy metals—arsenic, silver, mercury, cadmium, and copper.

Prudent physicians will not wait for another 40 years until our professors have stirred themselves to do the clinical studies required. Several years ago, a prominent professor of medicine, during a debate on vitamin therapy, declaimed that *no* physician should use vitamins until their use had been sanctified by the professors of medicine. Since most professors of medicine know very little about nutrition, we cannot expect much encouragement from them. Each physician must become an investigator until that day, if ever it comes, when we know everything. Nutrients are so safe used in the therapeutic range that patients will not be harmed.

*Doses*
1. Recommended daily range—50 to 200 mcg per day.
2. Supplements—200 to 500 mcg per day, either in selenium-enriched yeast or, for yeast-allergic patients, as sodium selenite.

## CALCIUM

Without calcium we would be like jellyfish. Ninety-nine percent of our calcium is in our bones and teeth. Each day 700 mg of calcium enter and leave the bones. The 1 percent in the rest of the body is essential for controlling clotting and muscle function, nerve conduction, cell-wall permeability and enzyme activity, of which the best example is ATPase (adenosine triphosphatase).

Only 20 to 30 percent of calcium present in food is absorbed. Absorption is increased by vitamin D (D3 in humans), by protein, by lactose, and by an acid medium. It is decreased by a ratio of calcium to phosphorous from 1.5:1, by phytic acid, oxalate and fiber, which bind it; by excess fat, by alkalinity, and by stress. Calcium deficiency causes rickets in children and osteomalacia in adults. Osteoporosis, most common in women, is related to calcium deficiency, but other factors are active, eg., the ratio of calcium to magnesium. Acute calcium deficiency, when serum levels drop, causes tetany.

Excess calcium is related to formation of kidney stones.

The best single source of calcium is milk and its derivatives. It is also available in whole grains. People allergic to milk can use calcium supplements such as dolomite and calcium salts.

Adults need about 1 gram per day. Pregnant and lactating women need more.

### Osteoporosis

No discussion of calcium and magnesium can ignore osteoporosis. Interest in using calcium supplements in North America is at an all-time high. Annual sales of calcium supplements approached $200 million 1987. Almost everyone is now in favor of its use. *Newsweek*, January 27, 1986, featured calcium on its front cover. It started with the National Institutes of Health Consensus Development Conference on Osteoporosis in April 1984. The conference cited calcium and estrogen as mainstays of prevention and management of osteoporosis. Martin and Houston (1987) have reviewed the relationship between calcium and osteoporosis.

Osteoporosis affects between 15 to 20 million adults in North America. Of these, 1.3 million suffer fractures each year. Mortality and morbidity are enormous. Of over one-quarter million fractures of the neck of the femur, only one-quarter recover fully, while 5 to 15 percent die. The incidence of fractures is increasing.

Osteoporosis is a weakening of the bone due to loss of bone, which increases with age, primarily in women. Bone loss is present in men and before the menopause in women, but then increases more rapidly in women. The rate per 10 years increases from 3 percent to 10 percent from trabecular bone and 1 to 2 percent for cortical bone. Damage to the vertebra is most common. By age 70, one-quarter of women have some vertebral fracture. When the front part of the vertebra fractures, the back curves forward, producing the so-called "dowager's hump." Other compression fractures lead to loss of height—about 1.5 inches over 10 years.

Bone mass depends upon age, sex, race, hormonal state, nutrition, and muscular activity. Of course, there is nothing we can do about the first three. Hormones play a role; it is the decrease in estrogens that increases the development of osteoporosis. But there is still debate about whether or not estrogens will reverse osteoporosis after it is established. It should be helpful in decelerating the further development. Vitamin D3 is classed as a vitamin but should be classed as a hormone. It increases absorption of calcium and phosphate from the gastrointestinal tract by releasing them from bone. The most important vitamin D3 metabolite is calcitriol, which has properties similar to parathyroid hormone, i.e., it decreases bone collagen synthesis and increases bone resorption. But osteoporotic patients are not deficient in calcitriol. I believe patients should have optimum levels of vitamin D3, which should be beneficial as a preventive, even if it has less effect as a treatment.

The relationship between calcium deficiency and osteoporosis is not established, according to Martin and Houston (1987). (Note this in spite of the national Consensus Development Conference conclusion.) Thus there is no relation between calcium consumption by populations and incidence of osteoporosis.

Populations in Third World countries have low calcium intake and little osteoporosis. In their review, Martin and Houston summarized research that again showed no relationship. Three groups of subjects were compared: those with a daily intake of less than 550 mg; between 550 mg and 1,150 mg; and over 1,150 mg for two years. The average bone loss was 3.8 percent, 3.2 percent, and 4.0 percent. They concluded that calcium supplementation had no effect on bone loss in postmenopausal women with or without osteoporosis.

Unfortunately, there have been no studies relating both calcium and magnesium and osteoporosis. Perhaps this is one explanation for the low correlation between osteoporosis and calcium, for, with every additional variable, it becomes more difficult to show a correlation between the casual variables and the condition that results (osteoporosis). There is a reciprocal relationship between calcium and magnesium, which must be examined as it affects bone structure.

There is another reason why the correlation of calcium deficiency to osteoporosis is so poor. This may be because the most important factor is manganese deficiency. Strauss and Saltman (in press) examined the role of a few trace elements. They became interested because a prominent professional basketball player suffered frequent fractures, joint pain, and slow healing. He was on a very poor vegetarian diet. He had no detectable serum manganese. Copper and zinc were low. On dietary supplementation with trace elements and calcium he recovered. Several other patients who healed slowly were also low in manganese, copper and zinc.

Their review of the literature suggested that trace elements affect growth and development of bone, directly and indirectly. Thus, copper is required in cross-linking of collagen and elastin, manganese in synthesis of micropolysaccharides, and zinc in maintenance of osteoblastic activity.

To examine the effect of copper and man-

|                                | Normal          | Osteoporotic     |
|--------------------------------|-----------------|------------------|
| Bone calcium, mg/g             | 149.7 ± 17.3    | 113.7 ± 28.4     |
| Trabecular bone, volume %      | 23.4 ± 5.9      | 12.6 ± 1.7       |
| Bone mineral content, g/cm     | 5.7 ± 0.5       | 3.7 ± 0.5        |
| Bone mineral density, $g/cm^2$ | 1.0 ± 0.3       | 0.7 ± 0.1        |
| Serum manganese, mg/l          | 0.04 ± 0.03     | 0.01 ± 0.004     |

ganese, these investigators placed three groups of rats on three diets: (1) normal, i.e., 66 ppm Mn and 5 ppm Cu; (2) low Mn, low Cu, i.e., 2.5 ppm Mn and 0.5 ppm Cu; (3) low Mn only, i.e., 0 Mn and 5 ppm Cu, for twelve months. Serum calcium was higher in deficient rats, and serum copper was low in both experimental groups. The concentration of calcium in the femur was low, as was manganese. Osteopenic-like lesions were seen. The deficiency of manganese and copper decreased osteoclast activity and bone density decreased. Then they examined mineral levels in serum and bone in a group of osteoporotic, postmenopausal women and a group of normal women. There were no differences in bone copper, manganese or zinc; or in serum copper, zinc, and 1.25 dihydroxy vitamin D3. However, there was a significant difference in serum manganese.

Strauss and Saltman carefully conclude: "It may be prudent to consider the possibility that trace element deficiencies particularly of Mn may be of significiance" (in press).

My conclusion is much stronger. I believe Strauss and Saltman have discovered what will be the most important element in the control of bone integrity and the prevention of osteoporosis.

Dr. C. C. Pfeiffer (1975, 1978) has been using a mixture of zinc and manganese for many years for schizophrenia, rheumatoid arthritis, and several other conditions. For several years I had existed with moderate low-back pain, especially on arising in the morning. Following Pfeiffer's lead, I began to add manganese, 15 to 30 mg per day, to my program. Within six months I was freed of pain. I have seen several of my patients lose low-back pain

after supplementation. Perhaps both are end results of a trace element deficiency, especially manganese. I had been taking enough zinc.

It is prudent to treat osteoporosis with the diet described in this book, supplemented by calcium, 1 to 2 grams per day; magnesium, 500 to 1,000 mg per day; zinc, 10 to 50 mg per day; manganese, 15 to 30 mg per day. Most of us have enough copper.

### Sources of Calcium

A number of calcium-containing compounds are available and should be used when it is not possible to obtain enough from food. The amount of calcium which really counts is that amount that is absorbed. However, even the calcium that remains in the intestinal contents perhaps plays a useful role because it decreases the absorption of lead. Tablets which do not disintegrate in the intestine are, of course, useless.

The amount absorbed depends on vitamin D3, on lactose, which increases absorption—except in lactose-intolerant people for whom it decreases it. Oxalates, fiber (phytates), and fat malabsorption decrease the absorption of calcium. Too much protein (over 142 grams per day) increases calcium excretion. Alcoholics often lose calcium from bones.

### Natural Sources

Natural calcium sources are bone meal, dolomite and oyster shell. A few people make their own supplement, dissolving dried egg shells in vinegar, since they are concerned about lead contamination. Dr. Richard Jacobs, Chief of Nutrient Toxicity of the U.S. Food and Drug Administration, reported 6 ppm of lead

**Synthetic Sources**

| Chemical Name | Commercial Name | Amount of Calcium/mg | Caution |
|---|---|---|---|
| Calcium carbonate | Generic | 250 + 500 | Constipating for some; |
| 40% calcium | Biocal | 250 + 500 | G.I. irritation; |
| 60% carbonate | Caltrate | 600 | May increase |
| | Tums | 200 | blood tetra-cycline levels; |
| | Oscal | 250 + 500 | No more than 4 per day. |
| Calcium phosphate | Calcium AD tab | 126 | |
| Calcium lactate calcium 30% lactate 70% | Generic | 84 | May cause gastric irritation, cannot be used by milk-allergic people. |
| Calcium gluconate calcium 9% gluconate 91% | Generic | 60 | |
| A few food sources: ½ cup canned salmon | | 200 | |
| 8 ounces milk | | 300 | |

*Source:* B.C. Dairy Foundation (1985), Calcium absorption: food and supplements. *Nutrition Action Line*, Fall/Winter 1985.

in these sources. But we should take this into perspective. If we assume the average adult uses 1 gram of dolominte per day, this will add 6 mcg of lead per day. But the average diet provides about 300 mcg per day. Since calcium decreases the absorption of lead, it is possible that these natural sources, even with 6 mcg per day, will result in a net decrease in lead absorption. In my opinion, there is no need to be concerned with these low levels. I routinely recommend dolomite to my patients.

Heaney (1986) examined the bioavailability of different calcium sources. He and his colleagues found that absorption from all sources, natural and supplements, is about the same. However, there is a difference in absorption when calcium sources are taken with water only or with food. With water only, calcium is poorly absorbed. With food, even with lack of HCl, absorption is about the same. As with all supplements, calcium sources are best taken in close association with food.

But even more is required. One of the most effective ways of reshaping bone is mechanical strain. Bone tissue is very dynamic. Thus, with disuse, bone mass is lost quickly. Astronauts lose bone at a rate of 4 percent per month for trabecular and 1 percent for cortex.

Bed rest and immobility from casts are equally detrimental. When gravitational forces are resumed, bone mass builds up again but more slowly. In animals, weight bearing increases bone mass. Athletes have greater bone density than nonathletes. Regular strenuous exercise increases bone mineral content. Martin and Houston (1987) summarized the results of six prospective studies of the effects of exercise on bone mineral content of weight-bearing lumbar vertebrae and the calcaneus. There was some effect on the radius. They conclude: "Regular physical activity, started early in childhood, can increase the peak bone mass of early adulthood, delay the onset of bone loss and reduce the rate of loss; all of these factors will help to delay the onset of fractures. In addition weight-bearing activity, if done carefully, currently provides a safe effective form of therapy for those at risk for osteoporotic fracture" (Martin and Houston 1987).

Do obese men and women have less tendency for developing osteoporosis? They engage in weight-bearing exercise, unless they spend too much time sitting.

### Conclusion

The best prevention and therapeutic program for osteoporosis is the orthomolecular diet supplemented with calcium, magnesium, zinc, and manganese, combined with a moderate weight-bearing and other exercise program. Walking is beneficial, for each step transfers weight from one leg to the other.

## MAGNESIUM

The adult body has about 20 to 30 grams of magnesium, half locked into our bones. Only three other cations are present in greater abundance. Yet magnesium has been ignored by the vast majority of clinicians. Of the 50 percent not in the bones, 99 percent is intracellular. One-third of the plasma magnesium is bound to protein. Serum levels range from 1 to 3 mg per 100 ml.

The average diet contains about 250 mg per day, but many people are deficient. The RDA is 350 mg. Soils may be low in magnesium. Modern gardeners do add magnesium to improve the yield. Processing removes a lot of magnesium from whole grains and more is lost by cooking in water. Some foods with phytic acid bind magnesium. Magnesium is the metallic component of chlorophyll.

Magnesium is absorbed anywhere in the bowel, but chiefly in the small intestine. Usually only one-third of the magnesium in food is absorbed, but when the body requires more, the amount absorbed increases. Absorption is also related to calcium levels. Excessive quantities of one decrease absorption of the other. Absorption is interfered with by excess oxalic acid, phytates, and long-chain saturated fatty acids.

Magnesium is reabsorbed by the kidneys. Many substances increase loss into urine by inhibiting the reabsorption. These compounds include gentamicin, cisplatin, thyroxine, calcitonin, growth hormone, aldosterone, high sodium intake and hypercalcemia.

Because magnesium stored in bones is released very slowly, blood levels can drop on deficient diets, even though total quantities in the body are normal. On the other hand, normal serum levels may be present when total body stores are low. The most accurate measure of magnesium deficiency is a 24-to-48-hour urinary excretion study. Clinicians who do not have these tests available to them should use their clinical judgment and check the patient's response to treatment with magnesium.

### Causes of Hypomagnesia

This is due either to dietary deficiency, to defective absorption, or to excessive loss. Graber et al. (1981) list 36 reasons. The most common are chronic alcoholism, chronic liver disease, uncontrollable diabetes mellitus, excessive use of diuretics, excessive use of cardiac glycosides and malabsorption syndromes.

Alcohol inhibits reabsorption of magnesium by the kidneys. Chronic liver disease causes secondary hyperaldosteronism, which also increases excretion of magnesium.

### Clinical Results of Deficiency

The earliest symptoms are loss of appetite, nausea and vomiting, diarrhea, and mental changes. Hyperirritability is common, with spontaneous or induced muscle spasms. Seizures may occur. There are no syndromes specific to magnesium, which is why it may be overlooked unless one is suspicious that it is lacking. Neurologic and cardiac symptoms may be due to too little calcium and potassium as well as magnesium.

Fouty (1978) maintains that magnesium deficiency should be suspected in any situations associated with potassium deficiency, even though serum levels are normal, as they are in half the subjects. A few cases have been diagnosed as multiple sclerosis. A clinical background of diuretics, steroid treatment, hypercalcemia, diarrhea, alcoholism, hypokalemia and liquid protein diets should lead one to suspect magnesium deficiency.

Perhaps magnesium deficiency is another factor that predisposes people to cancer. *The Sacramento Bee*, on August 22, 1978, carried the story of a Modesto man who cured his own terminal liver cancer by taking magnesium supplements. His cancer was diagnosed in the fall of 1976. The colon was resected followed by chemotherapy until July 1977. The following fall the cancer had spread to his liver, where two inoperable tumors were found. He was given more chemotherapy. He became depressed, weak, fatigued and jaundiced. In November he started on 350 mg of a magnesium compound. One month later he was better.

Rubin (1981) found that magnesium plays a major role in controlling growth of cells. Alternative treatments for cancer generally emphasize green vegetables; chlorophyll is a magnesium-containing molecule. In Poland it was found that there were fewer cases of leukemia when magnesium was plentiful in soil and water.

Magnesium and calcium are involved in the causes of hypertension. Sodium is apparently much less involved and is being dethroned as the chief villain. Apparently the chloride ion in sodium chloride is still an important factor, but other sodium salts, such as sodium ascorbate, are not involved. A series of hypertensive patients on antihypertensive medication were given 1 gram of calcium per day. After a few months half of them no longer required their antihypertensive medication. Since calcium and magnesium interrelate, this means both ions are important. This relationship was examined by Attura, Attura, Gebrewold, Ising and Gunther (1984). Magnesium is decreased in hypertension. The incidence of hypertension is high in areas where drinking water is soft or where there is little magnesium in the soil. It has been known since 1925 that magnesium salts lower blood pressure. Magnesium also plays an important role in regulating vasomotor tone. Low magnesium increases it.

Rats made moderately magnesium deficient suffered an increase in blood pressure from 111 to 131. With more severe deficiency, it went up to 143, an increase of 29 percent. There was a decrease in capillary, postcapillary, and venular blood flow combined with reduced terminal arteriolar, precapillary sphincter and venular lumen sizes.

### Treatment

The diet described in this book ought to contain enough calcium, magnesium, and potassium. Where magnesium supplements are needed, they can be given parenterally when rapid replacement is necessary, or by mouth. Magnesium compounds may cause diarrhea. A large number of magnesium preparations are available. One of the better ones is dolomite, which contains two parts calcium to one part magnesium. Nuts and whole grains are also good sources, as are green vegetables and seafood. People drinking hard water get appreciable amounts of calcium and magnesium from their water. Richest food sources are almonds, sesame seeds, cashews, soybeans, peanuts, bran, and wheat germ.

The control of blood pressure may be the most important indication for calcium and magnesium supplementation.

## MANGANESE

Pfeiffer and LaMola (1983) summarized the relationship of zinc and manganese to schizophrenia. Manganese was first used in 1927, when it was given intravenously. The early results were promising but interest waned when Hoskins used manganese dioxide suspended and injected intramuscularly. Even though he did not follow the procedure of earlier investigators, his conclusions prevailed. This is another example of a failure to replicate that was used to destroy an efficacious treatment. Nutritients are especially prone to this type of sloppy research.

The body has 10 to 20 mg of manganese. Best sources are nuts, seeds, and whole-grain cereals. About 45 percent is absorbed from the diet. A healthy person excretes about 4 mg per day. The average diet contains 2 to 9 mg per day. It is stored in bones, muscles, and skin. In blood it is bound to transmanganin, a protein carrier.

Manganese deficiency is associated with growth impairment, bone abnormalities, diabetic-like carbohydrate changes, incoordination and increased susceptibility to convulsions. About one-third of epileptic children have low blood manganese.

Food grown in manganese-deficient soil is deficient in manganese. Soil erosion, leaching and overcropping reduce soil levels. The apparent health of crops is no guarantee the plant has enough manganese. Obviously, plants do not grow with man's nutritional requirement as an objective. Thus, alkaline soil decreases manganese uptake.

Pfeiffer (1975, 1978) and his colleagues found that oral zinc increased excretion of copper threefold in schizophrenics. Adding manganese increased it even more. They used Ziman drops (10 percent zinc sulphate and 0.5 percent manganese chloride). Six drops b.i.d. provides 10 mg of zinc and 3 mg of manganese. This has been very helpful in treating schizophrenics. The researchers also found that using zinc alone can induce a deficiency of manganese. Epileptics, hypoglycemics, pyrolurics and schizophrenics have the lowest manganese levels.

Normal serum level is around 1.2 parts per billion (ppb). Ninety percent is in the red blood cells.

Pfeiffer (1975, 1978) recommends that high zinc not be used alone, since it can decrease blood manganese levels. He described one case—a severely allergic man under treatment for 15 years with zinc alone—who was given 50 mg of manganese gluconate b.i.d. Soon he felt better. He increased the dose to 100 mg. t.i.d. On starting manganese his manganese level was 6 ppb. After three months it was 11, where it remained for the next 1.5 years. During this period he gained 11 pounds, which he needed, and was able to tolerate foods that had previously made him depressed. He could also tolerate small amounts of zinc, which also used to cause depression.

Excesses of all the heavy metals, including manganese, mercury, copper, cadmium, and lead cause abnormalities in the brain. Perhaps senility is a toxic reaction to a number of these metals, including aluminum; not just aluminum alone. But a deficiency of manganese caused by tranquilizers leads to the disease tardive dyskinesia. In many patients it is irreversible as well as it may be for all patients of doctors who are not familiar with manganese. Kunin (1976)) reasoned that as phenothiazines can bind manganese, and because manganese is found in high concentrations in the extrapyramidal system, this was the cause of tardive dyskinesia. Kunin used

20 to 60 mg of manganese per day. From his series of 15 schizophrenics with tardive dyskinesia, seven were completely cured and only one did not respond. Most responded within a few days. Niacin was also required for some. Corroboration came quickly by orthomolecular physicians. I have seen similarly dramatic responses. Tardive dyskinesia has not been any problem in my large schizophrenic practice. Tkacz and Hawkins (1981) found no cases of tardive dyskinesia in 10,000 patients treated over 10 years. They used vitamins B3, B6, and ascorbic acid.

In general, tardive dyskinesia will almost disappear when vitamin therapy is used, and if it should appear it will be easily treated by manganese supplementation. Ideally, each tranquilizer tablet should contain enough manganese to prevent chelation of the body's manganese. This would have to be determined, but I would guess that 1 to 3 mg per day in the daily supply of tablets would prevent tardive dyskinesia. It is likely that vitamins may decrease the chelation of manganese by tranquilizers; this would explain the Tkacz and Hawkins findings.

Manganese plays a role in seizures. Sohler et al. (1979) found that a group of epileptics had a manganese blood level of 9.9 ppb, compared to the normal level of their controls of 14.8 ppb.

Manganese is relatively safe in doses up to 300 mg per day. Usually doses under 100 mg per day are adequate. Occasionally manganese will elevate blood pressure and produce tension headaches. When this occurs the manganese should be stopped. Pfeiffer recommends using dried or fresh tropical fruits and tea as sources of manganese. Do schizophrenics in England develop tardive dyskinesia? They probably drink more tea than does the average North American schizophrenic.

## IRON

### Metabolism

The average adult has 3 to 4 grams of iron in the body. Seventy percent is in the blood hemoglobin. The rest is stored in marrow and spleen. Red blood cells are recycled every 120 days.

Most of the iron from food is absorbed from the duodenum and jejunum. Only 10 percent of the iron from a mixed diet is absorbed (30 percent from meat). Heme iron is absorbed most easily.

Absorption depends upon the ferritin curtain, the amount of heme iron in the food, by the body's need for iron, by vitamin C levels, and by the amount of calcium. It is decreased by foods high in nonheme iron; by too much iron in the intestinal mucosa ferritin curtain; and by excess amounts of phosphates, phytate oxalate, and tannic acid. EDTA also inhibits absorption. (This chemical is added to foods to remove metals from enzymes to prevent food deterioration due to enzymes.) Foods are allowed to contain 25 to 800 mg of EDTA per kilogram. But 50 to 100 mg per kilogram will inhibit iron absorption. Iron absorption is decreased in patients after gastrectomy and in malabsorption syndromes. Iron is lost by excessive blood loss and during menstruation.

An average man loses 1 mg of iron a day, the average woman 1.5 mg. Ten to 25 percent of our population, mostly women, are deficient in iron.

### Sources

The best food sources of iron are whole-grain cereals, liver, eggs, and meat. There is very little iron in milk products, oils, fruit or vegetables. Cast-iron cooking vessels provide iron, but these are not used routinely.

Many multimineral preparations contain iron. This is beneficial for people who are deficient, but may be harmful for people—mostly men, but also women after menopause—who already have enough iron. A test for serum iron or ferritin will help determine whether multimineral preparations should be used.

## Deficiency

A lack of iron causes iron-deficiency anemia, but a deficiency is rarely missed by modern physicians. The symptoms are vague, but a routine blood examination will demonstrate its presence. Whenever hemoglobin levels are too low, one should suspect an iron deficiency problem, with or without a history of excessive loss of blood. The average man should consume about 10 mg of iron a day, the average woman 20 mg.

## Excess

Iron accumulates in a few patients who have idiopathic hemochromatosis, or in people who consume too much. Emulsifiers in food increase the absorption of iron. Men are more apt to absorb too much.

Iron is one nutrient that is not used in large doses by orthomolecular medicine. So far there are no diseases or conditions that require above average doses, and it is too difficult to excrete excessive amounts; but, as with any nutrient, the optimum amount should be used. This is a narrow range—from 5 to 20 mg per day.

## ALUMINUM, LEAD, MERCURY AND CADMIUM

Following C. C. Pfeiffer's views (1975, 1978), I will consider lead, mercury and cadmium together, but I will also add aluminum. It is likely that some degenerative diseases are caused by an accumulation of these four elements, along with copper and perhaps bismuth. Perhaps senility is such a disease, i.e., caused by a heavy burden of one or more of these metals, not just aluminum. Dr. Pfeiffer suggests that copper, lead and cadmium accumulation are related to reduced memory.

For a long time aluminum was considered nontoxic, but it is present in so many items that we eat or place on our bodies that it is likely some people do suffer from aluminum poisoning. It is present in antacids, toothpaste, baking powder, antiperspirants, cooking vessels, dental amalgams, food additives, food wrappers and cosmetics.

Aluminum encephalopathy has been linked with Alzheimer's Disease, the most common form of senility. These patients have brain neurofibrillary tangles, cell degeneration and too much aluminum in the brain and spinal fluid. Local applications of aluminum to exposed surfaces of the brain caused similar changes.

None of these heavy metals are used in treatment, but many patients will require therapy to reduce the amounts present in their bodies. Elevated lead levels in hair and teeth are associated with behavioral disturbances in children. The lead accumulates from car-exhaust emissions, drinking water in soft-water regions when lead plumbing is used, lead-based paint, certain lead-containing pottery glazes, and lead-soldered cans—especially those containing fruit juices. Lead-soldered cans provide about 14 percent of the total human burden of lead. Canned juice left in open tins will reach five times the U.S. EPA standard for lead. Another source of lead is household dust. In some areas there is so much lead in the surface of soils from car emissions that vegetables grown in these soils will cause lead poisoning, if soil particles are not washed off carefully.

Mercury is another toxic metal. It has long been associated with madness. I have treated three schizophrenics who were psychotic from excessive levels of mercury. This type of poisoning from industry is not as common as is the contamination most of us carry in our mouths, i.e., from amalgam fillings that are called "silver amalgams" when they really should be called "mercury amalgams," since mercury is the major component. Dentists and dental assistants are especially at risk. Mercury is also present in some fish.

Cadmium is very toxic. It is present in water flowing from old galvanized iron pipes that contained cadium contaminants. It is also present in burning coal and tobacco smoke.

Excess cadmium is related to hypertension, kidney damage and atherosclerosis.

All these toxic metals, including copper, can cause psychosis, hyperactivity, convulsions and fatigue. Perhaps they all work by increasing the burden of free radicals, i.e., they increase the amount of highly reactive molecular fragments that are very avid to combine with everything. They are thus enzyme poisons that bind molecules that should remain free together in cross linkages. This is how they may be related to aging and senility.

Treatment for poisoning is similar for all these metals. First, the source of the poisoning must be determined and eliminated. Then one should remove all additives from the diet. Removing the burden allows the body to excrete these metals more effectively. Third, one should increase fiber intake. Fiber tends to bind heavy metals. Birds fed high fiber are much more able to tolerate high cadmium levels. Fourth, one should use chelating substances; the safest is ascorbic acid, which binds to these metals. Then one can use EDTA and penicillamine. Since these chelate many essential minerals, one should make sure they are replaced. If penicillamine is used, pyridoxine (B6) should be added to decrease penicillamine toxicity. Fifth, selenium decreases toxicity of cadmium and mercury, while zinc and manganese help bring copper levels down. Zinc also antagonizes cadmium.

There is no specific syndrome associated with single-metal toxicity. The best diagnostic test is a case history, especially environmental, and curiosity. Hair analysis is very helpful, and is best done serially, i.e., to determine if one's therapeutic measures are decreasing elevated minerals in hair. When available, blood tests, as for zinc and copper, are very useful. It is very difficult to measure mercury. No tests should be run unless one is sure the laboratory knows how to gauge precise mercury levels.

## CHAPTER REFERENCES

Altura, B. M., Altura, B. J., Gebrewold, A., Ising, H., & Gunther, T. (1984), Magnesium deficiency and hypertension: Correlation between magnesium deficiency diets and micro-circulatory changes in situ. *Science* 223:1315–1317.

Consensus Conference: Osteoporosis. *JAMA* 252:799–802, 1984.

Fouty, R. A. (1978), Liquid protein diet, magnesium deficiency and cardiac arrest. *JAMA* 240:2632–2633.

Graber, T. W., Yee, A. S., & Baker, F. J. (1981), Magnesium: Physiology, clinical disorders and therapy. *Ann. Emerg. Med.* 10:49–57.

Heaney, R. P. (1986), *First International Symposium on Calcium and Human Health Proceedings*. Montreal, Canada: Dairy Nutrition Information Bureau.

Kunin, R. A. (1976), Manganese and niacin in the treatment of drug-induced dyskinesias. *J. Ortho. Psych.* 5:4–27.

Martin, D. D., & Houston, C. S. (1987), Osteoporosis, calcium and physical activity. *Can. Med. Assn. J.* 136:587–593.

Pfeiffer, C. C. (1975), *Mental and Elemental Nutrients*. New Canaan, Conn.: Keats Publishing.

—— (1978), *Zinc and Other Micro-Nutrients*. New Canaan, Conn.: Keats Publishing.

—— Personal communication, June 19, 1984.

—— & LaMola, S. (1983), Zinc and manganese in the schizophrenias. *J. Ortho. Psych.* 12:215–234.

Rubin, H. (1981), Growth regulation, reverse transformation and adaptability of 3T3 cells in decreased $Mg^2+$ concentration. *Proc. National Acad. Sci.* 78:328–332.

Sohler, A., Pfeiffer, C. C., & Casey, K. (1979), A direct method for the determination of manganese in whole blood: Patients with seizure activity have low blood levels. *J. Ortho. Psych.* 8:275–280.

Strauss, L. & Saltman, P. In press. "The role of manganese in bone metabolism." In *American Chemical Society Monograph Series: Manganese Metabolism*, ed. C. Kies.

Tkacz,. C., & Hawkins, D. R. (1981), A preventive measure for tardive dyskinesia. *J. Ortho. Psych.* 10:119–123.

# 4    GASTROINTESTINAL DISORDERS

The gastrointestinal tract developed from a single tube, which has become specialized in structure and in function. Its function is to admit food, prepare it for digestion, digest it, extract the essential nutrients, and pass the wastes from the body. The GI tract begins at the mouth—the grinding end that passes the food into the stomach, small intestine, large intestine, rectum, and out through the anus. The whole GI tract is one organ and should be treated clinically as such. It is illogical to consider that the stomach can be diseased while the rest of the tract is healthy. When one portion is diseased, one must assume the whole system is diseased, until it has been shown that the disease is, in fact, localized in one section. The health of the mouth (gums, teeth and tongue) gives one a good idea of the health of the rest of the GI tract. Dentists probably know more about the health of a person's GI tract than do those patients' doctors.

The GI tract has a number of accessory glands either inside or outside the GI wall. These include the liver, which secretes bile juice into the intestine; the pancreas, which secretes pancreatic enzyme into the intestine; the secretory cells in the intestinal wall; the salivary glands; and the stomach, which secretes hydrochloric acid and pepsin.

Since the main function of the GI tract is to digest and assimilate food, it is not surprising that most diseases of the GI tract involve food. The large number of diseases of the gastrointestinal system—such as ulcers, colitis, appendicitis, diabetes, obesity and cancer—are merely symptomatic reactions of the gastrointestinal tract to our low-fiber, high-sugar diets. They are all symptoms of the Saccharine Disease (Cleave, Campbell and Painter 1969), which has been described earlier in this book.

The typical American diet causes the following diseases in the gastrointestinal system:

1. In the mouth: gum disease and caries.
2. In the stomach: peptic ulcer and hiatus hernia.
3. In the intestine: constipation, colitis, appendicitis, cancer, diarrhea, vitamin deficiencies.
4. In the rectum: cancer and hemorrhoids.
5. In the accessory glands: diabetes mellitus from pancreatic pathology, and gallstones from fat and lipid pathology.

## SYMPTOMS OF THE SACCHARINE DISEASE

### In the Mouth

Cleave, Campbell and Painter (1969) and Adatia (1975) summarized the evidence that caries and periodontal disease are caused by our modern diet, which is too rich in sugars and too low in fiber foods. There is a clear relation between tooth and gum disease and diet, whether one compares disease and diet going back several thousand years, or whether one compares various peoples as they are today. In Great Britain in neolithic times, 4 percent of the teeth are carious. These teeth were worn in areas exposed to the grinding effect of fibrous food; modern teeth develop caries where they touch each other. During the Roman occupation of Great Britain, the incidence of caries was 12 percent. The Romans introduced finely ground floor and made sweet delicacies available. Several hundred years later, after the Romans left, the prevalence of caries dropped to 5 percent. In the sixteenth century it rose again as sugar became cheaper and more available. Today, half the population in Great Britain have lost all their teeth by age 50.

Populations who do not eat highly processed foods have little caries, but within a few years of adopting our diet the prevalence of caries goes up dramatically. Gum or periodontal disease is associated with caries.

Weston A. Price, D.D.S. (1989) is one of the early and major contributors to research that established how malnutrition leads to physical degeneration. *Nutrition and Physical Degeneration: A Comparison of Primitive and Modern Diets and Their Effects* was published in 1938 and republished in 1970, and has now been reissued in a 50th anniversary edition by the publishers of the present work, Keats. *Nutrition and Physical Degeneration* is a remarkable book. It details by photographs and description the effect deteriorated food has on a large number of physical characteristics. Being a dentist, Dr. Price paid special attention to mouth, teeth, and gums.

In spite of clear evidence, there are many who remain unconvinced and dispute the idea that the type of food determines the presence of caries and gum disease. Even though Aristotle suspected stagnation of food, especially sweet food, was the cause of caries 2,000 years ago, a small portion of any population avoids sugars to protect their teeth. The craving and addicting potential of the sugars is so great that it is inconceivable to many people that they are harmful. The price they pay in pain, discomfort and ill health is enormous. Perhaps without the sugars in our diet, we would not have needed most of our dentists.

The first stage in tooth and gum disease is the formation of plaque. This is a very dense collection of several varieties of bacteria in a film of gelatinous polysaccharides and proteins adherent to the tooth. The bacteria break down sugar to acids which etch the enamel. The three factors in production of caries and gum diseases are: (1) the bacteria; (2) resistance against the bacteria; and (3) the diet. Certain foods are very cariogenic, i.e., very effective in causing disease. The worse is sucrose—table sugar. White flour is not as bad, but it is worse than whole-wheat flour. Some foods are anticariogenic, i.e., whole wheat, possibly because of its phytate levels.

Preventive measures must, therefore, include mouth sanitation: cleansing and regular removal of plaque, avoidance of cariogenic junk foods, use of whole-grain, fibrous foods and general measures which improve resistance against bacteria. One of my objections to the use of fluoride in water is the exaggerated attention to caries and total neglect of gum disease. Fluoride in water may reduce tooth decay slightly, but it does nothing for gum disease. Reliance on fluoride leads to a feeling of confidence that allows the continuing use of sugar to excess.

Gum disease and caries lead to the loss of teeth. This starts a lifelong problem due to inadequate chewing of food and continual difficulty with artificial teeth. Improperly chewed food is a factor in leaving undigested fragments in the digestive tract.

Other causes of gum disease include insufficient ascorbic acid and vitamin B3. A characteristic symptom of classical scurvy is bleeding, puffy, and sore gums. Classical scurvy is rare, but subclinical scurvy is much more common. Many people note improved health of their gums when they use extra ascorbic acid. However, the use of nicotinic acid is not known by many. I discovered this by accident in 1954.

My gums had begun to bleed. Repeated dental care and ascorbic acid did not help, but after two weeks of nicotinic acid, 1 gram after each meal—taken for other reasons—I discovered to my surprise that my gums had become healthy. It was this observation which led me to suggest to Prof. R. Altschul that he use this vitamin to protect his experimental rabbits against atherosclerosis induced by heated egg yolk. I had assumed that in the same way that nicotinic acid had healed my gums, it might heal the inner lining of the rabbits' blood vessels. Prof. Altschul soon found that it lowered cholesterol levels in his rabbits, and later Alschul, Hoffer and Stephen (1955) found that it also lowered cholesterol levels in people. Since then I have seen other people whose gums recovered with nicotinic acid treatment. It will not replace good dental care and sanitation (plaque removal), but when dental care and hygiene do not cure periodontal disease, vitamin therapy should be considered.

Many forms of malnutrition cause symptoms in the mouth. Riboflavin (B2) deficiency causes a painful, reddish lesion in the corner of the mouth (cheilosis) and inflammation of the tongue (glossitis). Vitamin B3 deficiency causes puffiness and bleeding of the gums. Pyridoxine deficiency also causes cheilosis and glossitis, characteristics of riboflavin deficiency. Scurvy and subclinical scurvy cause bleeding gums and loose teeth. A good physical examination must include a visual examination of the mouth, teeth, gums and tongue.

### In the Stomach and Duodenum

Gastric and duodenal ulcers appear to be different pathological leisons. Of the two, the duodenal ulcer is more clearly linked to faulty diet. Cleave et al. (1969) conclude that peptic-

ulcer is "an unequivocal manifestation of the Saccharine Disease" that occurs mainly in the pyloric end of the stomach and in the duodenum.

Evidence linking prevalence of peptic ulcer with deterioration of our food is powerful, but there are still many anomalies in the relationship, probably because the epidemiology of peptic ulcer is uncertain, and even more because it is so difficult to study the epidemiology of junk food. Most nutritionists have ignored the impact of junk food on health, but it is clear that, as with the other symptoms of the Saccharine Disease, peptic ulcer has become more prevalent in peoples who eat refined foods. In London, England, the prevalence of peptic ulcer was between 0.1 to 0.3 percent before 1900. Incidence was around 1 percent at the turn of the century, and since 1913 has been between 2.2 and 3.9 percent. The main complications are hemorrhage, perforation and pyloric stenosis. Its prevalence increases with age. Up to 20 percent of some populations suffer symptoms of peptic ulcer.

Cleave et al. (1969) maintain that hyperacidity in itself will not cause peptic ulcers, because our digestive tract has developed a process of digesting food that requires a lot of acid. Acid is at best a secondary factor. Cleave et al. discount stress as a main factor.

Psychiatry went through a psychosomatic phase, which lumped peptic ulcer with the seven so-called "psychosomatic" diseases. The attempt to locate psychodynamic factors that could determine whether stress would lead to an ulcer or to arthritis has petered out. Psychodynamic and personality factors undoubtedly play a role in determining how patients deal with their ulcers, but these play an insignificant role in its cause compared to food.

Cleave et al. conclude that lack of protein in the stomach is the main reason for ulcer formation, "because if the natural buffering by the food is reduced, and still more of it is removed altogether, it is clear that the mucous membranes are exposed to a much more serious attack from the acid than they are designed to support."

Man adapted to whole, living foods consumed at frequent intervals. As gatherers and hunters, our ancestors could eat as they foraged or hunted. The vegetation required no preparation, and most of the animal food was small, consisting of worms, bugs, and small animals. Large animals were not a main staple for most people. Food was eaten when it was available and when one was hungry, but, when cooking came into use, this introduced a time factor—the food had to be cooked. Later, with the domestication of man on farms and in cities, the need to work made three meals per day more practical. This is still a common pattern, with liquid and high-sugar snacks in between. Our gatherer/hunter ancestors usually had some nutritious food in their stomach at all times.

The same conclusion was reached by Eaton and Konner (1985) in a recent review of paleolithic nutrition. They wrote:

> The human genetic constitution has changed relatively little since the appearance of truly modern human beings about 40,000 years ago. . . . Accordingly, the range of diets available to pre-agricultural beings determines the range that still exists for men and women living in the 20th century—the nutrition for which human beings are in essence genetically programmed. . . . The diet of our remote ancestors may be a reference standard for modern human nutrition and a model for defense against certain 'diseases of civilization.' (Eaton and Konner 1985)

For a review of the relationship between the degree of civilization and disease, see also Trowell and Burkitt (1981).

Eating fresh or living food *ad libidum* was the pattern of eating to which our GI tract adapted. The mechanics of such a system are quite different from one in which large quantities of food are consumed in a few minutes a few times over the 24-hour day. The ideal situation is a steady stream of small quantities of living food while awake. Digestion continues slowly, releasing nutrients so slowly that there is no overload on the digestive apparatus.

The style of eating has a major effect on one component of the GI tract, the bacterial flora. Living food has a low bacteria count—there has been little time for bacteria to grow. The number of bacteria is further reduced by the hydrochloric acid in the stomach. Acid-tolerant bacteria, such as acidophilus, are able to survive passage through the stomach. Once the food has passed into the small intestine, its pH becomes alkaline. The warm body temperature, moisture, and ample food provide an ideal medium for bacteria; they thrive. The further down the GI tract, the more bacteria are present. The upper intestine should have fewer bacteria than 10,000 per ml. The bulk of the weight of feces is bacteria.

The body has a number of ways of keeping the bacteria count down, at least in the upper part of the GI tract. The first one is the strong acid in the stomach. People who lack acid are at a major disadvantage and are much more apt to suffer bacterial overgrowth. The same applies to organisms such as yeast cells. Another device is the ileocecal valve, which prevents reflux of material into the upper intestine. The bacteria are also suppressed by the secretion of bile and pancreatic juices into the duodenum. These are sterile and help digest bacterial cells. The GI immunological defenses are also important. The final step is the steady peristalsis, which propels GI contents onward. Everything is designed to keep bacterial growth at a minimum. There is thus a gradient of bacterial growth which is lowest in the duodenum and highest in the colon and rectum.

Bacteria interfere with the absorption of nutrients. They produce toxins that injure the intestinal walls, thus interfering with absorption of nutrients and water. From the viewpoint of our bacteria this is a desirable adaptation, since it ensures that nutrients and water are available. The body has adapted to the inevitable bacterial growth by allowing its maximum growth in an area where there is the least absorption, i.e., in the colon. By the time food reaches the colon most of the soluble nutrients have been extracted. Once in the colon, where the bacterial count is at its greatest, much less harm comes to the body. A high-fiber diet stimulates peristalsis, moving the food through within a day or so. The colon is evacuated normally about twice a day. Constipated people may require three days or more, and some have one bowel movement once every seven days, providing much more time for bacterial growth.

Ideally, we have a GI mechanism that minimizes bacterial contamination at minimum cost in terms of energy required in areas of the gut where bacteria can do the most damage, and that allows bacteria to grow in areas where it can do little damage—in the colon. But this requires the use of food and water that is free of bacterial contamination, and this was possible only when man ate living food.

All living matter begins to spoil as soon as life ceases. Storing food, then, becomes a problem of minimizing the bacterial contamination. Perhaps the ancient religious taboo against blood practiced by Moses and his followers was such an attempt, since blood is more apt to contain contaminants. Maybe bled meat stores better. Another ancient technique is cooking, which almost eliminates bacterial contamination. Perhaps this is the reason cooking developed—cooked meat spoils more slowly. This must have been recognized by our first food technologists. A liking for cooked meat developed later. To the people eating cooked meat for the first time, it must have been as repulsive as it is for most people today to eat raw meat. A child fed only raw meat will love it and will have trouble adjust-

ing to cooked meat. All the modern techniques of converting food into junk originated from the need to store food and to preserve it against spoilage—bacterial contamination.

By and large we have succeeded in providing a continuous supply of food that is relatively free of bacteria. The price is great, however, since it is the conversion of living food into long-shelf-life food artifact. But at least that artifact is free of bacterial contamination. Many people living in underdeveloped countries must contend with severe bacterial contamination. They do not have the technological resources for storing and preserving food and their water is contaminated. The bacterial count in their upper intestine is very high, to the point where they suffer from chronic diarrhea. A combination of junk food combined with contaminated food and water practically destroys the ability of the GI tract to contain bacterial contamination. Of the main mechanisms for controlling infection—acid, immunological defenses, secretion of juices, ileocecal valve and continuous peristalsis—the immunological defenses are weakened due to malnutrition, and peristalsis is slowed and weakened due to lack of fiber. This increases the bacterial count in the bowel. Thus, these technological underdeveloped people live in double jeopardy: from bacterial overgrowth in their food and GI tract, and from our modern junk food.

Today, "one meal per day" patterns are not uncommon. The stomach contains no food for long periods of time. This would be tolerable, as in fasting, if the repeated stimulation of acid secretion did not occur. However, the high intake of low-fiber, high-sugar foods provides a constant stimulus for acid secretion.

Normally, when food is chewed, signals from the brain initiate secretion of gastric juices so that food and juices meet in the stomach at the same time. The hydrochloric acid is promptly bound by the protein portion of the food and digestion begins. There is no surplus acid left to irritate the stomach and duodenal walls. But when food artifact is swallowed, this secreted acid is not bound, as there is no, or too little, protein present. Sugar and starch do not bind hydrochloric acid. Even worse, soft drinks contain large quantities of acid which must be neutralized. One protein meal per day provides only partial protection against acid.

Cleave et al. (1969) described the effects of living in prisoner-of-war camps in the Far East during World War II. These camps were horribly stressing to the prisoners. Out of 2,500 Canadian soldiers captured in Hong Kong, 25 percent were dead 44 months later. Yet in these camps there was a low prevalence of peptic ulcer when whole foods were used. In Singapore and Thailand camps, highly milled rice was the main food. By 1944, duodenal ulcer, which had been rare, became a plague. But prisoners taken from Singapore to Thailand to work on the Burma Railway project almost never suffered from ulcer; they were given whole rice or rice bran to supplement their diet.

In Hong Kong, prisoners were fed milled rice and many had peptic ulcers. After two years many were moved to Japan and fed barley, millet, and whole rice. Ulcers vanished. Out of 13,000 prisoners, only one had peptic ulcer. But in Japan where they ate milled rice, the incidence doubled. Even more striking was the experience of German soldiers on the eastern front. At the beginning of the war in 1939, peptic ulcer was so common that "ulcer battalions" were formed. Later, when highly refined food became hard to get, the incidence fell considerably. At the eastern front, peptic ulcer almost disappeared. The closer the soldiers were to home, the more ulcers there were: 3.2 percent of admissions in rear hospitals were due to ulcers, 1.5 percent in field hospitals and none in the front line. Stress theory predicted that just the opposite should have been found because at the front the soldiers suffered anxiety, cold, fatigue, ultracoarse food and deficiency of animal protein.

What happened was that the German army was unable to ship enough food to the front lines 1,250 miles from home. Eventually, food was obtained locally and consisted mostly of turnips and potatoes that were not cooked. On this rough diet ulcers disappeared. Soldiers incarcerated in Russian war camps also remained free of peptic ulcer, since their food was rough, high-fiber and whole-grain.

One factor Cleave et. al. (1969) did not take into account was food allergies. Every food will cause trouble for a few people. The foods we become allergic to are most often those foods we consume in the greatest amounts, i.e., the staples. In Western peoples these are the common grains, especially wheat, meat, and milk products in high dairy areas such as the United States and Canada. Sugar is a universal problem.

The allergic reaction can affect any part of the gastrointestinal tract, causing any reaction from swelling and edema of the mouth to pruritus of the anus. The usual reaction is edema, swelling and congestion of the mucosa, and either increased or decreased muscular activity. The specific symptoms will depend upon which area is most affected. In the throat there is excessive mucous. Health food literature is full of references to mucous-producing foods like milk. The stomach may become atonic or empty too quickly. Peristalsis may become excessive, causing severe diarrhea, or slowed, causing constipation—or these conditions may alternate. Patients often complain of abdominal swelling after eating a food they are allergic to. This must be due to increased edema in the gastrointestinal tract.

Symptoms of food allergy are not always unpleasant. The person allergic to a food often becomes addicted to it and is uncomfortable if it is not eaten at regular and frequent intervals. If it is not eaten, withdrawal symptoms develop that include anxiety, tension, intense feelings of hunger, and often craving for a specific food. The craving for sweets and milk is particularly common. Eating these foods quickly relieves the symptoms until the next withdrawal symptoms appear. The typical after-meal pain of peptic ulcer is often one of the withdrawal symptoms, and it can be very severe. I have seen patients with anxiety become deeply depressed after an abrupt withdrawal from sugar or milk. One of my patients became so depressed that it was necessary to admit her to a psychiatric ward to prevent suicide. This deep depression came on the second day of the sugar-free diet. I now withdraw patients slowly if their consumption of any one food is very gross. A patient who drinks 12 glasses of milk per day, for instance, or 30 cups of coffee, or 12 glasses of soft drink should be withdrawn slowly to prevent severe withdrawal reactions.

The milk diet commonly used for treating peptic ulcer does neutralize excess acid, which binds to the protein, but it prevents many ulcers from healing. I have seen several patients with peptic ulcer whose ulcer did not heal until they discontinued all milk and milk products.

Treatment of peptic ulcer is simple; it includes a food-only diet with major emphasis on whole-grain cereals and uncooked vegetables. Three small meals with snacks in between should be eaten. An allergy history should be obtained. Special tests may be required to determine whether allergies are present, and these foods should be avoided for at least six months and then used infrequently. Antacids will seldom be necessary. Analgesics should be used when discomfort from pain is excessive. The vitamins and minerals with special healing properties include vitamin B3, pyridoxine, ascorbic acid, vitamin E, zinc and perhaps manganese. So many people equate their ulcer with acid that they are fearful of taking acids. They are worried about ascorbic acid and nicotinic acid. Both of these vitamins are very weak organic acids, much weaker than the hydrochloric acid in the stomach. They do not add to the acid burden. On the contrary, nicotinic acid has been shown

to bind acid and therefore decrease the acid burden. Occasionally too much histamine is released by nicotinic acid and this causes too much gastric secretion. The flush caused by nicotinic acid is a histamine flush. I have never withheld giving patients with peptic ulcer nicotinic acid when they needed it. I can only recall one or two who could not tolerate it.

Hiatus hernia is as common as peptic ulcer. A sliding hernia causes symptoms when gastric juices reflux into the esophagus. The main symptoms are pain behind the sternum, hemorrhage and ulceration, which may be followed by fibrosis and stricture. The overall incidence is about 30 percent in a population of patients given X-ray examination for other reasons. The incidence rises with age, from 9 percent in those under age 40, to 69 percent in those over 70. In developing countries it is very rare. Thus, in 1966 only one case of hiatus hernia was found in a series of 1,319 barium examinations in Kenya.

Burkitt (1975) favors the hypothesis that hiatus hernia is caused by increased intraabdominal pressure due to straining at stool because of constipation. It is a direct result of the low-fiber, high-sugar diet.

### In the Accessory Digestive Organs

#### PANCREAS

Cleave et al. (1966) summarized evidence linking diabetes mellitus to diet. They considered diabetes to be one of the main symptoms of the Saccharine Disease, that global disease caused by too little fiber and too many refined carbohydrates, especially sugar. There are two ways that overconsumption of refined sugars damages the pancreas. Too much is consumed too rapidly—with sugar it is easy to consume the day's supply in a few minutes. Then the pancreas has to deal with the massive concentration of sugar in the blood as well as with an overall consumption that stresses the entire digestive apparatus.

The overall incidence of diabetes in India has been traditionally around 1 percent, varying from 2.56 percent in Vellore in Madras to 0.6 percent in Jaipur. Peptic ulcer is also more common in Madras. Madras consumes more milled rice than other areas. Generally the areas that eat more whole-grain cereals have a lower incidence of diabetes. More striking is a comparison between Indians who went to Africa (Natal) in 1860 as indentured laborers and Indians of the same genetic stock who remained in India. In India the incidence of diabetes in adults over age 20 was 5.5 percent and in the over-30 group 8.8 percent. The incidence in Natal was 10 times as great. In Natal the Indians consumed more calories, more animal protein, and more fat, but the main difference was in their intake of sugar: 110 pounds per person per year in Natal compared to 12 pounds in India. This is striking evidence that increasing sugar intake tenfold also increases frequency of diabetes tenfold. Today in North America, sugar intake is about 125 pounds per person per year.

Similar differences were found among other African dwellers. Among native Zulu living on their customary pretechnology diet, diabetes was almost nonexistent. In one hospital, out of 12,669 consecutive admissions from 1962 to 1964, there were 10 patients with diabetes— less than 0.1 percent. Even Zulu cane cutters, who eat large amounts of natural sugarcane— about 4.5 pounds per day, or three-quarters of a pound of refined sugar equivalent—did not become diabetic. These people also consume large quantities of corn, beans and other unrefined carbohydrates. They expend huge amounts of calories in cutting, moving and stacking sugarcane. In 1929, Banting observed the same phenomenon in laborers who worked on the construction of the Panama Canal. They were natives of Dominica who ate large quantities of sugarcane, but only two out of 5,000 had sugar in their urine. However, wealthy Spaniards in Panama, who also ate large amounts of cane sugar, had a high incidence of diabetes. Cleave et al. (1966) conclude that any level of consumption over 70

pounds per person per year places that nation in jeopardy of developing Western nations' incidence of diabetes. But it takes about 20 years after a group of people adopt the Saccharine Disease-producing diet to develop the full-blown syndrome.

In any population, a certain proportion is more vulnerable than the rest. When the diet deteriorates, this group is more apt to develop diabetes. When the same total population reverts to a better diet, fewer people will become ill, and those who have already been injured will be under better control. Diabetic regimes should, and often do, call for sugar-free diets, but do not often call for a diet free of refined carbohydrates.

Obesity is very common; it follows overconsumption of refined sugars and is associated with reduced sugar tolerances. I doubt if any obese person has a normal sugar tolerance. Many are diagnosed as suffering from late onset, maturity-type or adult-onset diabetes. They do not need insulin. In most cases reducing weight to the normal range will remove this type of diabetes. I prefer to restrict the diagnosis of diabetes to patients who must have insulin. These obese people have relative hypoglycemia or hyperinsulinism. The best treatment is a sugar-free diet or, better still, a junk-free diet.

Obesity is considered undesirable medically and is associated with a variety of symptoms. Some of these symptoms are directly attributable to the extra burden of fat or weight which must be carried, but other symptoms may arise, not from the obesity, but from the diet responsible for the obesity. Both obesity and symptoms arise from a diet too rich in refined carbohydrates and too low in fiber. Perhaps this is why there is still a good deal of debate about the dangers of obesity. I have seen a number of obese patients with a variety of physical and psychiatric complaints. On an orthomolecular program they often begin to feel much better before there is any appreciable weight loss.

I consider it undesirable to be too thin or too fat, but there must be a very wide range in between. A person who is 10 to 20 pounds away from the average of a similar sample, i.e., the same height and build, would do well to try to get closer to the mean. The best way is an orthomolecular diet plus sufficient exercise. Weight loss should be slow so that by the time the person's ideal weight has been reached there will have been enough time to become used to the new lifestyle of exercise and nutrition. The question of treatment for the severely obese will be discussed later.

## GALLBLADDER

The main disease of the gallbladder is stones (Burkitt and Trowell 1975). The main component of stones is cholesterol, which comprises about 60 percent of the average stone in England, 74 percent in the U.S.A., and 88 percent in Sweden. Calcium compounds are minor components. The sequence of events is production of supersaturated bile followed by precipitation of cholesterol microcrystals and growth of crystals.

Gallstones are common in all Western countries, having reached epidemic proportions since World War II. Frequency of gallbladder operations increased twofold in many areas in 20 years. Gallstones were rare several hundred years ago. They have become more frequent and are affecting the poorer and younger populations.

This condition is not as common in developing countries. A review of 4,395 autopsies in Ghana between 1923 and 1955 failed to show one case. When gallbladder disease is present, it is more frequently seen in the wealthy and obese eating the white man's diet. When these people change over to our diet the incidence of gallbladder disease increases. The Canadian Eskimo rarely had gallstones, but now operations for gallbladder stones have outnumbered all other operations. Africans living in cities have more disease than Africans living in rural areas.

Gallstone formation is caused by the following factors: First, there is a decrease in the secretion of bile—diets rich in refined carbohydrates reduced bile salt formation in animals. Second, there is an increase in the formation of cholesterol. Clofibrate lowers blood cholesterol levels and increases the flow of cholesterol into bile, making the bile supersaturated. This increases the incidence of gallbladder disease. Nicotinic acid lowers blood cholesterol by a different mechanism, probably by preventing release of fatty acids from fat depots by adrenaline. Nicotinic acid does not increase formation of gallstones.

The main cause of too much cholesterol is the overconsumption of refined sugar, particularly sucrose, and a deficiency of fiber. Increasing fiber decreases cholesterol levels.

It is clear that gallstones are symptoms of the Saccharine Disease and could be prevented by a diet free of junk food. Once the stones have developed, they may require removal by surgery or by dissolving the cholesterol. Their recurrence will be minimized by eating only good food, i.e., a diet free of all refined carbohydrates that is high in fiber.

## INTESTINAL DISORDERS

The theory of the Saccharine Disease has been described in the earlier sections of this book. But in this section on the gastrointestinal symptoms of the Saccharine Disease, it is appropriate to review the digestive relationship to food and junk. The gastrointestinal tract ingests food, digests it, and allows digested nutrients to pass into the blood.

In the state natural to our ancestors, food was the whole food, living food diet. It had to be chewed thoroughly before it could be swallowed. Modern refined food can be swallowed easily with little chewing and therefore contains little saliva. Sugars require no chewing whatever. Whole foods are fed into the stomach much more slowly. In contrast, sugars are dumped in so quickly that the digestive tract cannot deal with them properly.

Fiber (i.e., whole food) is a natural preventive of overnutrition.

In the stomach, refined food is less bulky than whole food and empties more slowy. Heaton (1975) suggests this lack of distension may be responsible for gastroesophageal reflux, i.e., heartburn and regurgitation. Because sugars are soluble in water, the solution in the stomach is very strong and has high osmotic activity, unlike other food components. After a meal of steak in one test, osmolality of stomach contents was 250, while after milk and doughnuts it was 450. Solutions this strong are damaging to cells and also slow the emptying of the stomach.

There is no doubt that the amount of fiber in diet controls the amount of bulk, controls transit time and determines whether the individual will suffer from chronic constipation. It has long been known that bran is one of the best and safest laxatives. The apt phrase "Hard in—soft out; soft in—hard out" well describes the effect of food.

Fiber or bulk have the following functions in the bowel. In fact, the intestine must include its contents as a functional structure—it can only be normal when its contents are normal. These fiber functions are: (1) to stimulate normal peristalsis and normal transit time. With the common sugar-rich, fiber-deficient diet, transit time is greatly prolonged. When I was a medical student 30 years ago, we were taught that the normal frequency of bowel movement varied from seven per day to one every seven days. In fact, the normal range is probably one to three movements per day. The fecal mass should have the consistency of toothpaste so it is expressed easily without the need for exessive strain by the abdominal wall. If the feces are very hard, that person is constipated even with three movements per day. Perhaps physicians should examine stools as carefully as do pediatricians when they give babies a proper examination, or as carefully as does Dr. D. Burkitt (1975).

When intestinal contents remain in transit too long, the fiber and other constitutents can no longer function normally. Recently it has been found that most of the fiber can be broken down and is replaced by bacteria. The major portion of stool is bacterial matter. If there is little fiber left, it is difficult to understand how it can be of any help. With normal (short) transit time, more fiber is still available in the stools; (2) fiber provides a medium for bacteria to grow on; and (3) fiber absorbs bile pigments and other residues that the body does not need. It also absorbs toxic minerals such as cadmium.

When there is too little fiber, these functions are performed imperfectly. The sluggish peristalsis allows fecal matter to accumulate in the colon. This will press on the large veins that return the blood and increase back pressure. This is one of the main factors causing hemorrhoids and varicose veins. By staying longer in the gut, more and more bile pigment is absorbed on the smaller volume of fecal material, which stays in longer contact with the bowel wall. This is believed to be a main factor in the high incidence of bowel cancer, especially in North American men. People on normal food, i.e., high in fiber, have a very low rate of bowel cancer. With a long transit time it is more likely that carcinogenic chemicals will be formed.

A second main factor in intestinal disorders is food allergy. In some people, merely placing food they are allergic to in their mouths will immediately cause peristalsis. Diarrhea is a very common allergic reaction and even more common is the alternation between diarrhea and constipation. Staple foods such as milk and bread are most apt to be involved. Even when diarrhea is an allergic response, it is best to have a high-fiber diet that will reduce the amplitude of swings between diarrhea and constipation.

Several years ago I was asked to see a young woman who suffered from severe diarrhea, to the point that she could not be far from a toilet. She had been investigated with a large variety of tests at University Hospital, but no reason was found and she was no better on discharge. It, therefore, became a psychiatric problem. Her history suggested relative hypoglycemia. There was the typical exacerbation after meals, which were low in fiber and high in sugar. The five-hour glucose tolerance test was the only one not done at the hospital. On the basis of her history, I advised her to start the special high-protein, sugar-free, frequent feeding program I was then following. Within a few days her diarrhea stopped. I believe she had an allergy to refined carbohydrates and sugar; when these were removed her diarrhea cleared. This was helped by the high fiber which came with the therapeutic diet. Both factors made her well. I suspect that colitis is due to a combination of food allergy and a low-fiber, high-sugar diet.

The most common tissue response to allergy is swelling and secretion. Lips and tongue swell, mucosa in sinuses become boggy from secretion. It is likely that the intestinal mucosa also become boggy and irritate the intestines. Is appendicitis due to allergic edema and hypersection of the bowel? In South Africa many years ago, it was said that only people who were blond and spoke English developed appendicitis. They were the ones who lived on the typical Saccharine Disease-producing diet.

There must be some relation between this diet and allergies. Alcohol, which resembles sugar in the way it is metabolized, potentiates the effect of any other allergy. The sugars may have similar properties. This is something which should be investigated.

Many of the diseases of the large intestine come from the fiber-deficient diet. Appendicitis is very rare in people who eat normal food and is very high in those who eat our Western diet. It can, therefore, be prevented by good nutrition. By the time treatment is required, nutritional therapy is too late. Chronic pain over the appendix area (right lower quadrant), if it does not come from diet, could still be prevented and perhaps healed by an immediate return to the healthy high-fiber or whole-food diet.

Diverticular disease of the colon is a major symptom of the Saccharine Disease. It was very rare before 1900, but within 20 years it became common in the Western world. By 1930, it was estimated that about 5 percent of people over 40 had diverticula. It is now the most common disease of the colon. By age 80, two-thirds of the population have it. In sharp contrast, it is very rare among people who still eat a high-fiber diet, but even here its incidence goes up quickly when they adopt our low-fiber, sugar-rich diet. During World War II, the rising incidence was halted when the use of high-fiber flour was made mandatory and when less sugar was available.

Diverticulosis develops when the intestinal wall is squeezed between muscle fibers. When the bowel contents are large and soft there is less pressure and the colon does not segment as severely. Less pressure and work are required to move the contents on. Why, then, was the bland, soft diet used for so long in treating bowel disease? It was believed that coarse particles would either irritate or get into the diverticula and cause perforation. Coarse food and fiber were associated with an irritable bowel. In fact, the majority of diets were already soft and low-fiber, and these diets could hardly be used as treatment since they were the cause. These diets could only make the condition worse and ensure its chronicity.

Cancer of the colon and rectum are associated with the Saccharine Disease diet. In North America and in many European countries, this cancer is responsible for more deaths than any of the other cancers. In the U.S., 70,000 new cases are reported each year. It is rare in developing countries. Polyps are also very rare in developing countries and very common in Western nations. When people from developing nations adopt the low-fiber diet, either in their own country or by moving to a Western nation, the incidence of polyps and cancer increases. According to Burkitt (1975), a number of factors play a role:

1. The amount of carcinogen formed or present due to the bacterial action and/or the quantity and concentration of bile salts.
2. The retention of carcinogen in the large bowel. This is influenced by prolonged transit time, frequency of bowel evacuation, and inhibition against immediate evacuation when desire is felt.
3. Concentration of carcinogens.

A fiber-rich, bulky stool with rapid transit time minimizes all the risk factors for producing cancer of the bowel.

Ulcerative colitis is another common problem of Westernized peoples. As with the other symptoms of the Saccharine Disease, its presence is associated with the low-fiber, high-sugar diet. It is very rare in developing countries still living on high-fiber diets and is very common in developed nations. Crohn's disease has the same association.

The living diet as I have described it will prevent these diseases from appearing. Once these diseases have been established, the use of diet alone will not be as effective, but it should be initiated according to the following rules: (1) whole food only (no junk); and (2) no foods that cause allergic reactions. In addition, supplements should be used for two main reasons: first, because a sick gastrointestinal system is not able to absorb nutrients very efficiently even when they are present, while the typical junk-rich diet is usually very low in essential vitamins and minerals; second, because increased quantities of nutrients are required with any disease to restore the normal repairative processes of the body.

The B vitamins should be given in ample amounts, using some of the modern high-dose multivitamin tablets. They contain 50 to 100 mg quantities of most of the water-soluble B vitamins. Ascorbic acid in these doses softens the stools, controls constipation and helps heal tissues. Vitamin E in doses of 800 IU to 4,000 IU should be used. De Liz (1975) used very large amounts of vitamin E to help cure a severe case of Crohn's disease, which had not responded to any other treatment. Multimineral tablets should also be used, supplemented with ample amounts of zinc and manganese. None of the modern treatments to control pain or infection should be ignored, and when pathology is irreversible, surgical and other treatment will be required.

RECTUM

Varicose veins, deep-vein thrombosis and hemorrhoids are all caused by constipation and all are very common. Varicose veins are troublesome and may be painful, as are hemorrhoids, but deep-vein thrombosis is the most important cause of pulmonary embolism. About half the people who develop ileofemoral thrombosis have some degree of pulmonary embolism. Pulmonary embolism causes about 5 to 9 percent of all hospital deaths. Hemorrhoids always precede the other two conditions. All are rare in developing countries, become more common as the diet deteriorates, and reach their peak in developed countries where the diet is almost entirely processed.

The main cause is constipation. To evacuate the hard stools, intraabdominal pressure must be raised. This pressure is transmitted to the vena cava and its tributaries, and to the veins of the leg when their valves are incompetent. Repeated increases in pressure gradually lead to enlargement of the diameter of these veins until the valves can no longer close them. Any factor that increases stasis (increases the difficulty of the blood in returning to the heart) will aggravate the enlargement of the veins. This includes sitting too much, increased pressure from a loaded colon pressing on the veins, pregnancy, and perhaps very tight clothing.

Treatment must include orthomolecular nutrition (the high-fiber, sugar-free diet), which will relieve the chronic constipation. If constipation is not relieved by the high-fiber diet, the amount of ascorbic acid should be increased until stools are soft. This will also increase healing of the irritated tissues. The other healing nutrients should also be used, with ample quantities of vitamin E. If the hemorrhoids are already well established, other medical treatment will be necessary to relieve pain and infection. Surgery may be required. However, development of future hemorrhoids and varicose veins should be avoided by orthomolecular treatment.

## TREATMENT

Basic treatment must include restoration of the kind of food to which our digestive tract has been adapted, the avoidance of foods to which one is allergic, and the use of nutrients in optimum quantities when they are needed. The specialized regions of the digestive tract will, however, react in special ways and will require additional special treatment.

### Mouth and Throat

Dentists diagnose and treat teeth, periodontal tissue and sometimes the position of the jaw (temporomandibular joint dysfunction). Once their services are necessary, except in the case of trauma, malnutrition has already been present too long.

To maintain oral health, the mouth must be clean and free of pathogenic organisms. The virtues of oral care are well known. Less well known is the need for food which requires work before it can be swallowed. Food should contain enough fibrous matter to be self cleansing. Food which is whole, alive or recently alive, variable, and nontoxic will meet this criteria.

A number of lesions of the mouth require nutrient supplements as well:

1. Periodontal disease such as puffiness and bleeding. Bleeding gums are common in scurvy, but flagrant scurvy is rare today in economically developed nations. Bleeding may also be treated by improving the ability of gum tissue to repair itself.

   In 1954, my gums began to bleed when I brushed my teeth. Ascorbic acid did not help, nor was my dentist able to suggest anything. At that time, and quite independently of this problem, I began to take nicotinic acid, 1 gram three times a day, to see how I would respond in general. To my surprise, six weeks later, with no further dental treatment, my gums stopped bleeding. I concluded that the vitamin had so improved the rate of repair that my gum tissue was able to repair itself as fast as I damaged it by chewing. On examination, my dentist found my gums healthy. Since then I have persuaded a few dentists to try it with good results. Obviously it cannot be used to restore gums when teeth are coated with plaque—this must be treated directly, but if bleeding still continues I consider nicotinic acid a treatment for this kind of periodontal disease.

2. Vitamin deficiencies. Cheilosis indicates a need for riboflavin (B2). Other deficiencies will be reflected in the tongue but, in my opinion, they are not specific for any one vitamin deficiency. Vitamin B2 and vitamin A are necessary for the integrity and health of all body surfaces, including those inside the mouth.

3. Swelling of mucosa, excessive secretion of mucus, and blockage of drainage are usually due to allergies and less often due to infection. Most recurrent runny noses without fever and malaise are allergic reactions and not the common cold. They are best treated by eliminating the offending allergens, but will often respond to large doses of

## DISEASES OF MOUTH AND THROAT
## RESPONSIVE TO ORTHOMOLECULAR TREATMENT

| Condition | Treatment |
|---|---|
| Periodontal disease | Dental Nutrition Nicotonic acid to 3 grams/day |
| Vitamin deficiencies | Vitamin A to 50,000 IU/day Ascorbic acid to bowel tolerance |
| Recurrent colds without fever, rhinitis, sinusitis, excessive phlegm, postnasal drip, ear problems | Eliminate offending allergen Vitamin A and ascorbic acid |
| Leukoplakia | Vitamin B3 to 3 grams/day |

vitamin A and ascorbic acid. Milk is one of the most common food allergies causing chronic sinusitis, difficulty in breathing, recurrent "colds," phlegm and postnasal drip. An amazing proportion of my child patients with learning and/or behaviorial problems, due in part to milk allergy, have had their adenoids and tonsils removed. Are enlarged adenoids and tonsils responses to common food allergies? I think this idea should be examined. Furthermore, these children have a history of frequent earache, infections, and treatment by insertion of tubes.

4. Leukoplakia. This is a potentially precancerous lesion that responds to vitamin B3 therapy, according to Warburg (1967).

### Stomach

The two most common lesions are peptic ulcer and hiatus hernia. Both, according to Cleave et al. (1969), are caused by our modern diet rich in sugar and starches and low in fiber and in protein at the time of eating.

White flour represents a typical diet low in fiber and high in rapidly assimilated carbohydrates. Doughnuts represent to the ultimate the essence of our modern processed foods, since all they contain are white flour, sugar and processed oils. Soft drinks represent a "food" devoid of protein but rich in sugar and devoid of fiber. According to Cleave et al., any food stimulates secretion of peptic enzymes and hydrochloric acid, but protein-poor foods cannot absorb the acid, which is left free in the gastric contents and is thus in a position to irritate and ulcerate the stomach wall. Hiatus hernia is due to increased back pressure from constipation and strain, which has found a weakness in the esophageal-diaphragm junction.

Another common cause of peptic ulcer is food allergy. Since staple foods are most apt to be offenders, it is not surprising that milk is often a cause of peptic ulcer (Mandell and Scanlon 1979). But until recently the bland ulcer diet was heavily loaded with milk, which did cause relief from pain. It is not known how many peptic ulcers were caused by milk allergies and, therefore, could not respond to milk treatment. Milk would be more likely to help peptic ulcers where other foods were the offending allergens. In any event, milk is no longer recommended as the best acid neutralizer for peptic ulcer patients. Milk can relieve pain (without curing the lesion) in the same way that smoking a cigarette relieves momentarily the craving for a cigarette, or heroin removes for a few hours the craving or need for heroin. The basis of food allergy is a physiological addiction. This forces the individual to use that food regularly and frequently in order to control withdrawal discomfort. Patients will consume large quantities of milk (up to 6 quarts daily), bread (up to one loaf per day), doughnuts (12 in one-half hour), and so on.

Treatment is almost entirely nutritional. The orthomolecular diet must be used, i.e., primarily whole foods that are fresh, variable and nontoxic, with special attention to eliminating foods the patient is allergic to. The vitamins which accelerate healing may also be used. These are vitamin A, ascorbic acid and vitamin E. Minerals are also required, especially zinc, which accelerates healing, and

selenium for its antioxidant or anticancer properties.

Excessive hydrochloric acid secretion probably does not exist or is very rare. Patients who appear to have excessive HCl have a relative surplus due to an inadequate supply of good food. People drinking protein-free drinks or eating protein-poor foods are most apt to have relative excess of HCl. Patients complaining of excessive acid, or who have too much when tested, must examine their diet and make the necessary changes. In my opinion the use of antacids is hardly ever necessary. A few are so concerned about acid that the word itself becomes pathological; they will avoid citrus fruits because they contain acid. A few cannot tolerate vitamin C once they know it is ascorbic acid. Usually an explanation of the nature of weak organic acids will allay their fear. A few have been worried about nicotinic acid, which in fact decreases stomach acidity. This is one reason the word *niacin* is preferable. In the same way, we should all call ascorbic acid "hydrogen ascorbate."

## DISEASES OF THE STOMACH
## RESPONSIVE TO ORTHOMOLECULAR TREATMENT

| Condition | Treatment |
| --- | --- |
| Peptic ulcer | Nutrition<br>Vitamin A<br>Ascorbic acid<br>Vitamin E<br>Zinc<br>Selenium |
| Hiatus hernia | Prevent constipation by diet; ample fluid and ascorbic acid. |
| Hyperacidity | Nutrition: quality, quantity, and frequency. |
| Hypoacidity | Restore acid |

Hypoacidity, too little acid, is a more frequent problem, especially in the older population. Once organic lesions, such as cancer or metabolic disorders, are ruled out, hypoacidity is best treated by a diet which tends to be acidic, including foods such as yogurt and citrus fruits; and by using acid, either by sipping weak HCl through a glass tube or, more preferably, by using acid bound to other nutrients, such as glutamic acid hydrochloride. Perhaps this is why the popular folk treatment of apple cider, vinegar, and honey described by Jarvis is still popular, except that it would not work as well for people allergic to yeast.

### Intestines

The most common problems are diarrhea and constipation. Probably one-third of all people over 65 use laxatives.

#### CONSTIPATION

After organic lesions have been ruled out, the most effective treatment is orthomolecular. The most common cause of constipation is lack of fiber. Fiber should be obtained from every food source. Most fiber comes from grains, fruits, and vegetables. The definition of constipation varies enormously. When I was a medical student before 1950, we were given the rule that any frequency between seven bowel movements per day to one every seven days was normal. They confused what is average with what is normal. I consider that any person who does not have one bowel movement per day or whose feces are too hard is constipated.

In addition to ample amounts of fiber, fluid intake must be adequate. About six to eight glasses of fluid per day—not counting alcoholic beverages, tea, or coffee—is recommended. Occasionally, patients with enough fiber and fluid still have a problem. This can often be solved by using ascorbic acid as a laxative, i.e., by increasing the dose until the stools become more fluid.

If none of these measures are helpful, one should look for food allergies, which often cause diarrhea or constipation or an alternation of both. Colitis and other consequences of constipation are treated the same way.

#### DIARRHEA

Chronic diarrhea is present when diarrhea is recurrent or has been present more than two weeks (Phillips 1983). There is no perfect definition, but most people know when they have a problem. It is usually due to increased water in stools, which may arise from osmotic retention of water due to molecules that retain water; from excessive secretion in the small or large intestine; from exudation of mucus, serum or blood into the bowel; and from disorders of contract between chyme and the adsorptive surface.

Osmotic diarrhea is caused by molecules that hold water, such as phosphate, sulfate, and magnesium. Magnesium sulfate (Epsom salt) is a good example. Carbohydrates are a major group of osmotic agents. Patients who cannot hydrolyze lactase will develop diarrhea due to water retention by this disaccharide. Once these carbohydrates reach the colon, where bacterial action is increasingly active, the carbohydrates are broken down, releasing gases and acid. Any food-induced diarrhea can be cured by fasting.

Secretory diarrhea is caused by bacterial endotoxins, bile acids, fatty acids and hormones. One of the most common organisms is E. coli, responsible for half the cases of diarrhea in travelers. The last three forms of diarrhea do not respond to fasting and other causes should be sought.

Treatment is relatively simple. If food reaches the colon without being hydrolyzed sufficiently, the whole digestive process should be examined. The proper diet should be provided, allergic foods identified and eliminated, and measures should be taken to restore normal bacterial flora. This can be done by using antibiotics carefully so as to prevent overgrowth by Candida. I believe that, whenever

## DISORDERS OF THE INTESTINE
## RESPONSIVE TO ORTHOMOLECULAR TREATMENT

| *Condition* | *Treatment* |
|---|---|
| Constipation | 1. Fiber<br>2. Water<br>3. Ascorbic acid<br>4. Remove allergic foods |
| Diarrhea<br>  (a) Osmotic | 1. Diet (remove foods not digestible)<br>2. Fiber (to retain water)<br>3. Ample fluids (prevent dehydration) |
|   (b) Secretory | 1. Antibiotics and antifungals<br>2. Healing vitamins: Vitamin C, vitamin A, vitamin E, B complex |

an antibiotic is used, it should be combined with an antifungal or antiyeast preparation. One should also provide continual reseeding of the flora with lactobacillus, using yogurt or capsules containing these organisms. Travelers' diarrhea might be prevented by using acidophilus capsules, two or three with each meal, beginning a week before starting the trip.

Another way is to use fasting. A four-day fast will empty the colon in most people. This will effectively remove almost all the organisms from the bowel. If this is followed by good, clean food and water, the recolonization of the bowel may consist mainly of the organisms we can live symbiotically with. Perhaps this is why so many people find fasting so helpful, even when they have no food allergies. A one- or two-day fast every month might be very useful in keeping our bacterial friends friendly. However, a normal two to three bowel movements per day should be adequate in maintaining normal bacterial flora.

### DISEASES OF THE RECTUM

The most common rectal disease condition is hemorrhoids. These are caused by increased venous back pressure, usually due to constipation. The best treatment is prevention, i.e., prevent constipation by using ample amounts of fiber and fluid. Once hemorrhoids have developed they may, in the early stages, be treated in the same way. Hemorrhoids which have become infected or fibrous should be treated in the usual medical-surgical ways. Vitamins which accelerate healing should be used, i.e., vitamins A, C and E. These vitamins accelerate healing throughout the entire gastrointestinal tract.

### CASE HISTORIES

As a psychiatrist, I do not see a large number of patients whose complaints are primarily physical. The ones I have seen have been ill for a long time and have failed to respond to any treatment. It is difficult for these physically ill patients to get to see me—in British Columbia, specialists only see patients who are referred by their general practitioners. The GPs are reluctant to refer patients to a psychiatrist who do not have major psychiatric problems. In addition, they are even more reluctant to refer them to me because of my interest in nutritional treatment. Thus, patients who do come to me have either been very persuasive or persistent in asking to be referred. Many have told me that I was their last hope. I do not necessarily agree with this, but this was their view. Each patient is his or her own control, and one should compare the results of previous treatment against the results of orthomolecular treatment. In my opinion they can be their own control, especially since they have already shown they did not respond to any previous treatment and have become more chronic and so less apt to respond to placebo factors.

These case histories include patients seen once with at least one follow-up. A number of patients have been seen only once in consultation and are not given further appointments, or failed to keep their appointments. I have no way of determining what has happened to them. All diagnoses were made by the referring physician.

### G. A.: Crohn's Disease, Year of Birth 1951

G. A. developed severe diarrhea accompanied by severe fatigue following the birth of a child 11 years before. Eight months later she was diagnosed as having Crohn's disease and was started on antibiotics and Prednisone, 5 to 10 mg per day. On the higher dose there was no diarrhea but she had three bowel movements per day on a high-fiber diet.

Because she wished to get off Prednisone, she had slowly improved her diet by eliminating foods she was allergic to, including coffee, beef and eggs. At times she had stopped all milk products and felt much better, but most of the time she drank three to four glasses of milk each day. She often had phlegm in her throat, especially in the morning, and had a runny nose during the day.

She also complained of chronic vaginitis and had been treated with suppositories. Her first infection came on shortly after her pregnancy, and her baby was also infected and required admission to the hospital.

I concluded that she was allergic to milk and that her immune defenses had been weakened by a chronic yeast infection. She was thus advised to totally eliminate milk products and to use Mycostatin, one million units t.i.d., to which I added a moderate multivitamin and multimineral preparation with ascorbic acid three times per day. One week later she was much better. When seen again after one month she was well, having normal energy, no depression and only an occasional episode of diarrhea. She had discovered she was also allergic to chocolate. She was advised to stay on Mycostatin for one year and to slowly eliminate the Prednisone.

*Summary of Treatment*
1. Allergy-free diet.
2. Antiyeast antibiotic.
3. Multivitamin and multimineral supplementation.
4. Ascorbic acid, 3 grams per day.

### Crohn's Disease—Another Case

Mrs. C. L., age 27, had had Crohn's disease for 10 years. It started with severe pain, nausea and vomiting. After that she suffered episodes which began with pain, nausea and vomiting, and sometimes diarrhea. Six months before I saw her she had an intestinal blockage. In between episodes she had been well for up to six months.

I advised her to follow a sugar-free diet supplemented with ascorbic acid, vitamin E, a multivitamin preparation and zinc.

One month later she was much better. Four months later she had suffered three episodes of pain, the last one following three days after drinking wine. I then advised her to use Nalcrom, 200 mg four times per day if she wanted to have dinner out and expected to drink wine. She has been well since.

### L. B.: Chronic Diarrhea, Year of Birth 1910

Mr. L. B. complained of having diarrhea for several years. A few years earlier he had been treated for hiatus hernia and peptic ulcer by a milk diet. Later he became itchy over his body; this came in episodes. This suddenly cleared and was replaced by diarrhea. He was troubled not by the frequency of diarrhea but by its fluidity. The stools were watery, sometimes had mucous, and tended to float.

Just before I saw him he had returned from a holiday in Hawaii, where he had not had any diarrhea. Just before he left for Hawaii, he had started taking aspirin, 600 mg before bed for a sore throat, which he continued to do in Hawaii. At home he ate oatmeal porridge with milk each day, with an additional two glasses of milk per day. In Hawaii he had very little milk.

I concluded he had a milk allergy and started him on a sugar-free, milk-free diet. As well, he was to use niacin, 100 mg t.i.d.; ascorbic acid, 1 gram t.i.d.; pyridoxine, 250 mg o.d.; and zinc sulfate, 220 mg o.d. This is one of my healing programs.

Over the next three months he found: (1) that he was not allergic to milk; and (2) that he could not tolerate even this small dose of niacin. But the other vitamins did not help. Eventually I advised him to use aspirin every evening and very soon he became normal. He obviously suffered from one of the prostaglandin secretory diarrheas.

*Summary of Treatment*
1. Dietary: milk-free.
2. Vitamins, zinc.
3. Aspirin.

### R. B.: *Nausea and Vomiting After Meals, Year of Birth 1946*

R. B. had been suffering from postprandial nausea and vomiting for six months. This was related to the quantity of food consumed at each meal and to the sugar content. Sweets nauseated her immediately. The only food she could eat in any quantity was bread. If she forced herself to keep down the food, she would become very ill. Over six months she had lost more than 12 pounds.

On questioning she reported that ice cream and cheese made her ill, as did garlic and onions. If she did not eat by 4:00 P.M. she developed a severe headache. On the Weight Watchers diet, which is low in milk, she felt much better. She had had a similar episode lasting six months seven years before.

In addition she had arthritis of her fingers and knees, which were painful and swollen. Milk-allergic patients, in my experience, often need pyridoxine and zinc. She had some stigmata of this double deficiency, including stretch marks on her body, white areas on her fingernails, and acne.

I advised her to eliminate all foods containing sugar, all milk products, and beef. She was also given ascorbic acid, 1 gram t.i.d.; pyridoxine, 250 mg b.i.d.; chelated zinc, 30 mg per day; plus a multivitamin tablet.

Six weeks later she had nausea and vomiting only once a day. She found she was allergic to oranges, apples, bananas and peanuts, but she could eat other foods, including chicken eggs and goat's milk. Two and a half months after I first saw her she was normal, but still suffered from arthritis. I then added niacinamide, 500 mg. q.i.d.

*Summary of Treatment*
1. Elimination diet.
2. Vitamins, zinc.

### D. C.: *Colitis, Year of Birth 1956*

Nine months before I saw him, D. C. developed ulcer symptoms for which he was given Tagamet. After one month the pain was much less severe, but he developed diarrhea even after he discontinued the drug. He had three watery stools per day, which gradually subsided to one per day. On occasion he was constipated and suffered pain.

About three months before I saw him he eliminated wheat, milk and eggs from his diet. To his surprise, his sinuses cleared and he had been free of colds for three months.

His optimum weight was 145 pounds. When

I saw him he was 123 pounds. At five feet eleven inches in height this made him dangerously thin. He was not able to work because he was so weak and any physical activity, including bending down, increased his bowel irritability.

Over the previous three months his depression had cleared, although he was still nervous and tense on occasion.

I concluded he had already begun the correct treatment and advised him to maintain his sugar- and milk-free diet. To this I added ascorbic acid, 1 gram t.i.d.; vitamin E, 400 IU b.i.d.; a multivitamin and multimineral preparation and extra zinc.

One month later he was improved to the point he did not require any more visits. He was able to eat yogurt, could not tolerate the mineral preparation, and had little pain.

*Summary of Treatment*
1. Elimination diet.
2. Vitamins and minerals.

### A. K.: Constipation, Diverticulosis, Arthritis, Insomnia, and Malaise, Year of Birth 1913

Seven years before she came to see me, A. K. developed hiatus hernia, diverticulosis, and constipation. For many years she had taken Metamucil and later found that 6 tablespoons of bran per day worked as well. This greatly reduced episodes of severe abdominal pain. Milk and yogurt increased the pain.

Six months before I saw her she developed arthritis in her left thumb and right wrist. Finally, she complained of chronic insomina for 12 years, which she controlled with sleeping medication.

This patient had already dealt well with her constipation and needed help for her arthritis and insomnia.

I advised her to follow a strictly milk- and sugar-free program and to add niacinamide, 500 mg q.i.d. for her arthritis; sodium ascorbate, 500 mg t.i.d.; small quantities of zinc and vitamin B6, folic acid (because of her age), and vitamin A.

One month later she was much better, having colic only once per week. She was more active physically but had noted no improvement in her arthritic pain or insomnia. After another two months she still complained of arthritic pain and insomnia.

*Summary of Treatment*
1. Elimination diet.
2. Vitamins and zinc.

### P. L.: Colitis, Year of Birth 1933

Fifteen years before I saw her, this patient lost her child, age two. She had a nervous breakdown, for which psychiatric treatment was recommended, but her husband would not allow her to do so. Her colitis came on at the same time. Over the next 10 years she suffered another four breakdowns. About three years ago she started herself on a B vitamin program and discontinued her antidepressant medication. She left her alcoholic husband one and one-half years ago.

Her colitis consisted of alternating diarrhea and constipation, which came on if she became very nervous or after eating certain foods. The bouts of diarrhea would last up to two weeks accompanied by flatulence and pain.

I recommended she follow her present vitamin program, which she believed had been very helpful, and told her to avoid all foods containing added sugar and to add ascorbic acid, 1 gram b.i.d.

Two weeks later she was almost well. Four months later she remained well. Under increased anxiety she would have loose movements, but this was rare. She then reported that the arthritis that had started had cleared. I then added niacinamide, 500 mg t.i.d., to stabilize her arthritis.

*Summary of Treatment*
1. Elimination diet.
2. Vitamins.

### P. P.: Chronic Diarrhea, Year of Birth 1944

P. P. complained of clear mucous discharge and grey stools with flatulence for the previous six months. He had one soft movement per day. He also complained of chronic draining of his sinuses, postnastal drip and clogging of his sinuses. He was very tired and found his work stressful. His diet was good except that he drank six to eight cups of coffee per day, each containing one-quarter cup of cream.

He was advised to test his diet by first eliminating milk products, then wheat. To this I added ascorbic acid, 1 gram t.i.d.

One month later he reported he was almost well. He was not allergic to wheat but on several occasions small amounts of milk made him feel sick.

*Summary of Treatment*
1. Elimination diet.
2. Ascorbic acid.

### E. S.: Chronic Diarrhea and Flatulence, Year of Birth 1908

Thirty years before she saw me this patient had lived in the Middle East for three winters, suffering dysentery, which cleared when she came home. A few years later she developed frequency of bowel movement with a lot of gas and liquid. This remained with her until she saw me, in spite of frequent investigations with no physical basis apparent. She was on a sugar-free, high-fiber program, but the more closely she adhered to it, the worse was her diarrhea. She also reported that milk and wheat made her sneeze. Arthritis was becoming troublesome.

I did not alter her diet but advised her to take the following vitamins: (1) niacin, 1 gram t.i.d.; (2) ascorbic acid, 2 grams b.i.d.; (3) folic acid, 5 mg o.d.; (4) vitamin B12, 25 mg o.d.; (5) vitamin E, 400 IU b.i.d.; and (6) vitamin A, 10,000 IU o.d., and a multimineral preparation.

One month later she was better. She had discovered she was allergic to fish and eggs. She remained well for about one year. She then began to use dilute HCl, which made her worse. She lost weight. She, therefore, discontinued the entire program so I could see her as she was with no supplements. Her appetite was poor and her skin was dry.

She was started again on: (1) niacin, 1 gram t.i.d.; (2) ascorbic acid, 1 gram t.i.d.; (3) zinc gluconate, 100 mg o.d.; plus the rest of the vitamins she had discontinued. One month later she had regained four pounds and felt well.

*Summary of Treatment*
1. Elimination diet.
2. Vitamins, zinc.

### J. S.: Ulcerative Colitis, Year of Birth 1912

About eighteen years ago, J. S. suffered a double tragedy, the loss of a son and a daughter. He was very depressed and had his first attack of ulcerative colitis. He and his wife provided each other excellent support. One year ago his wife died, again leading to severe anxiety and depression, and his ulcerative colitis once more became very severe, leading to bowel obstruction. He was treated surgically and was left with a colostomy, but it was hoped this could eventually be reversed. However, the lesions healed only partially, leaving enough scar tissue to make reversal less probable.

Six months before he saw me, he had started on his own vitamin program, which he found helpful. Two months before I saw him he was started on a tricyclic antidepressant. He had also improved his diet and had eliminated red meats.

I advised him to try eliminating milk products and to continue his vitamins, to which I added niacinamide, 500 mg t.i.d.; selenium, 200 mcg per day; and increased ascorbic acid to 1 gram t.i.d.

Six weeks later he reported he had improved steadily, was much better, his colitis was much better and he had more energy. Six months before he could hardly step up a curb, but now he would walk up stairs with no difficulty. His lesion was healing so well that he was much more confident his operation could be reversed. He was well on his way to recovery.

*Summary of Treatment*
1. Elimination diet.
2. Vitamins, selenium.

### G. S.: Crohn's Disease, Year of Birth 1948

About ten years earlier this man developed pain on urination, apparently his first symptom of Crohn's disease. Two years ago he developed severe pain and required surgery. At operation his bowel and bladder were found to be adherent. After that he had little difficulty with his bowel but was very anxious over a possible recurrence. In addition he was very concerned over his marital problems.

I started him on a sugar-free diet and advised him to add ascorbic acid, 500 mg t.i.d.; vitamin E, 400 IU b.i.d.; zinc sulfate, 220 mg o.d.; and a multivitamin tablet.

One year later he was well, with no evidence of any resurgence of Crohn's.

*Summary of Treatment*
1. Elimination diet.
2. Vitamins, zinc.

### C. W.: Crohn's Disease, Year of Birth 1948

About four years before I saw her, C. W. developed severe diarrhea, cramps and bloody stools. Six months later she was diagnosed as having Crohn's disease and started on Clineral and Salazopyrene. She had had several flare-ups since. If she went off this medication, her diarrhea returned. Her diet was not bad except for a huge intake of milk, six glasses per day.

I advised her to eliminate milk slowly over a three-week period, to go sugar-free, and to add niacinamide, 500 mg q.i.d. (for arthritis); ascorbic acid, 1 gram t.i.d.; pyridoxine, 250 mg o.d.; zinc sulfate, 220 mg o.d.; vitamin E, 400 IU b.i.d.; and selenium, 200 mcg o.d.

She went through a four-day withdrawal period with loss of energy and then felt much better. Her mood was normal and after one month she was on the road to recovery.

*Summary of Treatment*
1. Elimination diet.
2. Vitamins, selenium, and zinc.

Three cases of Crohn's disease, who had been ill four to 11 years, were treated successfully. One required antifungal antibiotic treatment. Four cases of chronic diarrhea were well or nearly well in a few months. The other four responded equally well.

I do not conclude I have treated a sample that represents all cases. This sample was not selected by me and consisted of failures to other treatments in a few who were motivated to seek nutritional help. Many had already started their own treatment, learning from friends and their own reading, and had achieved most of the improvement before they saw me. They merely wanted medical support for what they had done and any additional advice that might accelerate their recovery.

These are illustrative cases, anecdotal, of course, as are all medical case records, but with findings recorded as they were gathered with consultation letters going back to the referring physicians. There are many more similar cases who could be helped and probably easily, since diseases treated early are more apt to respond quickly than diseases already chronic. The double-blind experiments, which Dr. H. Osmond and I were the first to run in North America in 1952, I now consider unethical and will never conduct again.

## SUMMARY OF TREATMENT RESPONSES
## TO ORTHOMOLECULAR THERAPY

|       | Disease | Duration | Diet | Treatment Vitamin | Other | Response |
|-------|---------|----------|------|---------|-------|----------|
| G. A. | Crohn's | 11 years | yes | yes | anti-fungal | well |
| L. B. | Diarrhea | several | no | no | aspirin | well |
| R. B. | Nausea and vomiting | ½ year | yes | yes | — | well |
| D. C. | Diarrhea | 7 months | yes | yes | — | nearly well |
| A. K. | Constipation | 7 years | yes | yes | — | nearly well |
| P. L. | Colitis | 15 years | yes | yes | — | well |
| P. P. | Diarrhea | 6 months | yes | yes | — | well |
| E. S. | Diarrhea | about 20 years | yes | yes | — | well |
| J. S. | Ulcerative colitis | 1 year | yes | yes | — | improved |
| G. S. | Crohn's | 10 years | yes | yes | surgery | improved |
| C. W. | Crohn's | 4 years | yes | yes | — | much improved |

## CHAPTER REFERENCES

Adatia, A. (1975), "Dental caries and periodontal disease." In *Refined Carbohydrate Foods and Disease*, eds. D. P. Burkitt, & H. C. Trowell, 251–277. New York: Academic Press.

Altschul, R., Hoffer, A., & Stephen, J. D. (1955), Influence of nicotinic acid on serum cholesterol in man. *Arch. Biochem. & Biophysics* 54:558–559.

Burkitt, D. (1975), "Hiatus hernia." In *Refined Carbohydrate Foods and Disease*, eds. D. P. Burkitt, H. C. Trowell, 161–172. New York: Academic Press.

Burkitt, D. P., & Trowell, H. C. (1975), *Refined Carbohydrate Foods and Disease*. New York: Academic Press.

Cleave, T. L., & Campbell, G. D. (1966), *Diabetes, Coronary Thrombosis, and the Saccharine Disease*. Bristol, England: John Wright and Sons.

Cleave, T. L., Campbell, G. D., & Painter, N. S. (1969), *Diabetes, Coronary Thrombosis and the Saccharine Disease*. 2d ed. Bristol, England: John Wright and Sons.

De Liz, A. J. (1975), Administration of massive doses of vitamin E to diabetic schizophrenic patients. *J. Ortho. Psych.*, 4:85–87.

Eaton, S. B., & Konner, M. (1985), Paleolithic nutrition. *NEJM* 312:283–289.

Heaton, K. (1975), The effects of carbohydrate refining on food ingestion, digestion and absorption. In *Refined Carbohydrate Foods and Disease*, eds. D. P. Burkitt, & H. C. Trowell, 59–68. New York: Academic Press.

Mandell, M., and Scanlon, L. W. (1979), Dr. Mandell's 5-Day Allergy Relief System. New York: Thomas Y. Crowell.

Phillips, S. F. (1983), Symposium: Pathological basis of chronic diarrhea. *Ann. Royal Coll. of Phys. Surg. Canada* 16:670–674.

Price, W. A. (1989), *Nutrition and Physical Degeneration: A Comparison of Primitive and Modern Diets and Their Effects*. New Canaan, Conn. Keats Publishing.

Trowell, H. C., & Burkitt, D. P. (1981), *Western Diseases, Their Emergence and Prevention.* Cambridge, Mass.: Harvard University Press.

Warburg, O. (1967), The prime cause and prevention of cancer. Lecture at meeting of the Nobel Laureates on June 30, 1966, at Lindau, Lake Constance, Berlin-Dahlem. English edition by Dean Burke, Konrad Triltsch, Würzburg, DBR.

# CARDIOVASCULAR SYSTEM

• • • • • • • • • • • • • • • • • • • • • • • • • • • • • •

The function of the circulatory system, including the heart, is to keep the blood flowing to all parts of the body, to withstand the stresses of minor pulsations and movements, and to repair itself when damaged. It allows nutrients and waste products to traverse its walls. It must grow with tissues and regress as tissues regress. The heart is a specialized section of the circulatory system.

The vascular system has a set of internal and external controls to maintain the correct blood pressure whether we are sleeping or sprinting. When certain areas of the body require more blood, this is provided. In normal brains, frontal lobes receive more blood when awake, less when that person is sleeping. In schizophrenics, this normal pattern is disturbed; their frontal lobes have relatively less blood flow and this flow does not increase when they are awake.

Failure in the circulatory system occurs when vessel walls become too fragile or too rigid, or when homeostatic controls fail. Hypertension may develop.

The blood itself must maintain the correct viscosity or liquidity, must be able to seal off bleeding vessels, and be able to maintain the correct proportion of cells of various types to fluid.

A discussion of the vascular system should include reference to vessel walls, blood pressure control and the blood, but I will deal only with those aspects where orthomolecular medicine promises to make a contribution.

## CARDIOVASCULAR DISEASES

The main problem facing our cardiovascular system is to maintain the integrity of the vessels. The walls must retain their elasticity and strength and their responsiveness to stimuli that control blood pressure. The most common attack on the vessel walls is atherosclerosis. Plaques form in the vessel walls, and this decreases the size of the lumen, decreases blood flow and increases the possibility of thrombus. Thrombus in turn increases the probability that a coronary, cerebral or other large artery will rupture. The main medical problem is to prevent atherosclerosis and to reverse what has already developed. We must prevent other aging changes as well. As the major problem is atherosclerosis, the major factor is lipid metabolism, for if lipid or fat metabolism remained normal we would have no atherosclerosis.

## BLOOD LIPIDS

### Cholesterol

Two main types of blood fats are involved in cardiovascular disease: cholesterol and triglycerides. Cholesterol is a rather complex, four-ringed molecule, a sterol. It is the precursor of a number of important sterols leading to various hormones, such as corticosteroids and 17-keto steroids. The body can make cholesterol from the products of sugar metabolism and can use the cholesterol available in food. If more is available from food, less is made in the body. If a person lost the ability to make cholesterol, it would then be like a vitamin, i.e., an essential supplement. Because it can be made in the body, there is no strong relationship between the amount of cholesterol in blood and the amount in food. The food would have to contain more than the daily requirement, and more than the body could dispose of, before it would begin to accumulate in the body.

Of the two main sources of cholesterol, the quantity in food and that made in the body from sugar, the second source has been neglected. The Saccharine Disease diet, being high in sugar, probably plays a major role in the creation of too much cholesterol in the body. When a large amount of sucrose is eaten, much of it is promptly converted into fat and cholesterol. The Saccharine Disease diet is thus responsible not only for excess calories leading to obesity, but for the elevated blood fats that may also be found. Fiber itself can decrease blood cholesterol. Fiber deficiency, typical of the Saccharine Disease diet, is thus another reason for the elevated cholesterol levels.

Cholesterol is one of the main components of atherosclerotic plaques. It has been a prime suspect for many years, but by itself it must be only one of a number of factors. This is why there will never be a very high statistical correlation between blood cholesterol levels and atherosclerosis. But it is certain that if cholesterol levels are too low, say around 100 mg per 100 ml, it would be very difficult for any to accumulate in the plaques, and if the levels are very high, say over 400 mg, it would be very surprising if it did not settle down in plagues, as it does deposit in skin, or example.

Heated cholesterol in food is more toxic than unheated cholesterol. Prof. R. Altschul (1964) found he could not produce high blood cholesterol in his rabbits with uncooked egg yolks. The egg yolks had to be baked into a special cake, and this rapidly caused hypercholesterolemia when fed to his rabbits. He later found that feeding these rabbits nicotinic acid rapidly brought their cholesterol levels back to normal. I would assume that the higher the temperature, the more toxic the effect; boiled eggs are thus safer than fried eggs.

Three factors have to be examined as they are all interrelated: (1) atherosclerosis and blood fat; (2) blood fat and fat in the diet; and (3) atherosclerosis and fat in the diet. These relationships are extraordinarily complex, since they include at a minimum the quantity of fat in the diet; its quality, i.e., degree of unsaturation; how much lecithin is present; how the food has been processed; the amount of fiber and sugar in the diet; the amount of exercise the person habitually engages in; the hormonal state; and probably several other factors. No study I know of has even attempted to take all these factors into consideration, and perhaps it will never be possible to do so.

On the orthomolecular diet, there is no need to be concerned about getting too much fat. This becomes possible only when processed foods or artifacts such as butter, plant oils and margarine are used. With a balanced orthomolecular diet, it should be very difficult to get too little fat, as even starch-rich foods contain some fat. In addition, with a good diet one need not be concerned about the ratio of saturated fat to unsaturated fat, as a blend of animal and vegetable food will ensure that neither too little nor too much of either fat is consumed. This diet consists mainly of complex polysaccharides, a small quantity of simple carbohydrates found in fruit, and a few sweet-tasting vegetables. It will contain much more fiber than is found in the Saccharine Disease diet. Of the eight definite factors I have listed, a good diet will provide five. If the food is not overly heated, the diet provides six. If enough exercise is obtained, only one factor remains not under the person's control, i.e., the hormonal balance. Other unlisted factors include a genetic factor for hypercholesterolemia, which may override other factors or which merely makes the person unusually sensitive to the Saccharine Disease diet.

## Triglycerides

These are fatty acids attached to glycerol at each hydroxyl group. Most discussions of this fat ignore the three-carbon glycerol base. The fatty acids range in length from four-carbon chains to over-20 chain molecules. They may be fully saturated, such as butyric acid, or unsaturated, such as linoleic acid.

Triglyceride levels have been related to atherosclerosis. In an attempt to define sharper relationships, the fat-protein complex or lipoprotein found in blood has been divided into groups according to the way they separate blood in the ultracentrifuge. These are the high-density lipoprotein particles and the low-density lipoproteins.

The discussion of cholesterol and its relation to food will apply to triglycerides as well.

Finally, it is possible that the basic problem is fat and carbohydrate metabolism in general, engendered by the Saccharine Disease diet, and that elevated blood fats and artherosclerosis are both end results of the same process. To reduce blood fats without removing the main pathological process may be a futile medical procedure.

As I see them, the main factors in causing atherosclerosis are: (1) the Saccharine Disease diet, which is too low in fiber and too rich in sugars and refined carbohydrates; (2) mechanical trauma in areas where the bloodstream undergoes increased turbulence; and (3) decreased ability for self-repair of intima, the innermost lining of the blood vessels.

The relation between cholesterol, fat, and protein is beautifully elegant and complex (Brown, Kovanen and Goldstein 1981). The blood has six different lipoprotein transport systems that bind cholesterol and distribute it throughout the body. Cells take up cholesterol from the carrier system and there it is bound to new lipoprotein carriers. It is lost from the body after being transported to the liver by incorporation into bile salts. Much is reabsorbed; some is lost in feces. Because the cholesterol is recirculated, coming originally from food and from synthesis in the body, there is no simple relationship between plasma cholesterol and diet, except for a few rare conditions such as familial hypercholesterolemia.

Lipoproteins carry two classes of lipids: triglycerides and cholesteryl esters. The fatty acids and cholesterol are released by hydrolysis. Triglycerides are delivered to adipose (fat storage) tissues and to muscle, where the fatty acids are stored. Cholesteryl esters go to the body cells to be used in building membranes and other molecules such as steroid hormones and bile salts.

The cholesterol cycle begins in the intestine, where fat from the food is converted into large globules called chylomicrons. These are secreted into the lymph and poured into the blood. They are too large to leave the blood and are metabolized by lipoprotein receptors, which remove the triglycerides. These receptors line the capillaries of adipose and muscle tissue. As the triglycerides are continuously removed, the chylomicrons become smaller and smaller, becoming remnants. The shrunken chylomicron or remnant is released from the lipoprotein receptor and is carried to the liver, where it is metabolized. The residual cholesterol from the chylomicron is transferred to a high-density lipoprotein particle (HDL). HDL, when elevated in blood, is associated with a lower incidence of coronary disease. The liver, which has absorbed the remnants, secretes cholesterol as bile salts.

Most is reabsorbed by the intestine and some, about 1,100 mg, is lost each day. About 250 mg of cholesterol is derived from food; the rest is made in the body.

The liver synthesizes triglycerides from carbohydrates. Sucrose is particularly effective. The lipids are deposited into very-low-density lipoproteins (VLDL). These are adsorbed by the lipoprotein receptors, which release triglycerides. As VLDL particles lose fat they become smaller and smaller and the particles become intermediate-density lipoproteins (IDL). As with chylomicrons, the excess phospholipids and cholesterol from these particles is incorporated into HDL. The excess cholesterol in HDL is in turn incorporated into IDL, which loses more triglyceride and becomes low-density lipoprotein particles (LDL), which are mostly cholesterol. LDL delivers cholesterol to liver cells. LDL is also removed by scavenger cells, which become more active as LDL levels rise. When overloaded, they become foam cells, components of atherosclerotic plaques.

Three of the six lipoproteins that carry lipids rapidly produce atherosclerosis in humans when present in increased amounts (shrunken chylomicrons, IDL, and LDL). Chylomicrons and VLDL are neutral, while HDL reduces the tendency for atherosclerosis.

A large number of factors are involved in keeping the arterial walls free of atherosclerosis. These include:

1. Substances within the blood, including lipoprotein carriers, cholesterol, triglycerides, platelets, endothelium, muscle cells in arterioles and macrophages, and the number of lipoprotein receptors.
2. Genetic factors.
3. Environmental factors, such as Saccharine Disease-producing diet or smoking.
4. Other diseases, such as high blood pressure and diabetes.
5. Cholesterol-lowering substances.
6. Vitamins, especially nicotinic acid, pyridoxine and ascorbic acid.

If anything interferes with the mechanics of the fat distribution system, atherosclerosis will develop. Liver lipoprotein receptors allow large amounts of cholesterol to be removed from blood. Normal people are thus resistant to dietary cholesterol. If lipoprotein receptors do not function, then dietary cholesterol will affect plasma cholesterol levels more directly. In familial hypercholesterolemia there is a defect in the LDL receptors, and LDL is not metabolized adequately. These patients have very high blood cholesterol even on cholesterol-free diets.

In Western countries many people have too much LDL in blood. This is probably due to too much sugar and calories and perhaps fat. This could be responsible for overproduction of VLDL, which is converted to LDL in amounts greater than can be metabolized by LDL receptors. Sucrose is rapidly changed into fat.

The receptors can be increased by increasing the liver's demand for cholesterol. This can be produced by a combination of a bile acid binding resin, i.e., Colestipol, and an inhibitor of cholesterol synthesis such as nicotinic acid (Illingworth, Roger, Phillipson, Rapp and Connor 1981). These researchers treated 13 patients who had familial hypercholesterolemia (FH) with low-cholesterol, low-fat diet; with diet and Colestipol; and with diet, Cholestipol and nicotinic acid. Cholesterol levels were 415 for diet alone, 327 on Colestipol plus diet, and 246 with nicotinic acid, Colestipol and diet—a decrease of 47 percent below the best-controlled levels. HDL was the same for diet and diet plus Cholestipol, but increased to 53 when nicotinic acid was added. For most of these FH patients, this combination gave them normal cholesterol levels. The results are shown on the following table.

Up to 8 grams of nicotinic acid were used. The typical flush was moderated by giving aspirin, 120 to 180 mg, with each dose, for four to six weeks. Liver function tests re-

| Treatment | Total Cholesterol | | VLDL | | LDL | | HDL | | Triglycerides |
|---|---|---|---|---|---|---|---|---|---|
| | Mg | % | Mg | % | Mg | % | Mg | % | % |
| Diet | 415 | - | 31 | | 337 | | 40 | | 159 |
| Diet and Colestipol | 327 | -21 | 33 | -0 | 256 | -24 | 43 | +7 | 160 |
| Diet, Colestipol, and nicotinic acid | 246 | -40 | 18 | -42 | 177 | -47 | 53 | +32 | 104 |

mained normal. Bile acid binders increase breakdown of LDL, lowering cholesterol levels, but increased synthesis limits the decrease achieved. Nicotinic acid decreases LDL synthesis. The combination provides for the first time a method for protecting FH patients from premature development of atherosclerosis. They will also find that they will receive additional benefits from this remarkable vitamin.

Theoretically, if elevated cholesterol levels force the development of atherosclerosis, decreasing these levels should be therapeutic, and preventing their elevation should be preventive. Nicotinic acid should be both preventive and therapeutic. But theory may not always predict fact. For this reason two types of studies have been required: (1) a study of whether substances such as nicotinic acid lower cholesterol safely and consistently over many years; and (2) a study of whether this is therapeutic in subjects who have already suffered from atherosclerosis. If it is, it should be evident in lowered death rates and increased longevity. The relationship between nicotinic acid, cholesterol and longevity is shown in the results of a recent re-evaluation of the National Coronary Drug Project, which was conducted between 1966 and 1975. About 8,500 men after one myocardial infarct were randomized into groups and given placebo, thyroid, estrogen (two levels), Clofibrate (Atromid), and nicotinic acid. By the end of the study it was clear that thyroid and estrogens should not be used as they increased mortality. The group given nicotinic acid fared slightly better than the group given Atromid.

About two years ago Canner (1985), reviewed the survivors at the end of the study (1975), to determine if any of the patients had been damaged by any of the treatments. It was a toxicity review. To everyone's amazement, the niacin group had an 11 percent decrease in mortality and a two-year increase in longevity compared to placebo and Atromid. The mortality in the Atromid group was greater than that of the placebo group. Thus, nine years or less on niacin (not all nicotinic acid patients remained in the study the whole nine years) provided a benefit to these patients over the next nine years. Had they remained on nicotinic acid, the beneficial effect would have been better, perhaps approaching E. Boyle's (1968) results. With 90 patients followed 10 years while on treatment, he found a 90 percent reduction of mortality—from 60 who would statistically have been expected to die, to 6 who actually did die.

The Coronary Drug Project establishes the fact that nicotinic acid increases longevity and decreases mortality. But it may have proved that this is not due to the decreased cholesterol levels—Atromid, which also lowers cholesterol levels, had no such benefit. This research suggests nicotinic acid operates at a more basic level in decreasing atherosclerosis. The distinction is important for scientists investigating cholesterol metabolism, but practically speaking it should make little difference to clinicians.

As a result of this and other studies, the

## VALUES FOR SELECTING ADULTS AT MODERATE
## AND HIGH RISK REQUIRING TREATMENT

| Age | Moderate Risk | High Risk |
|---|---|---|
| 20 to 29 | Greater than 200 mg per 100 ml | Greater than 220 mg per 100 ml |
| 30 to 39 | Greater than 220 mg per 100 ml | Greater than 240 mg per 100 ml |
| 40 and over | Greater than 240 mg per 100 ml | Greater than 260 mg per 100 ml |

National Institutes of Health (NIH), Washington, D.C., recommends that, when cholesterol levels are elevated, attempts should be made to decrease cholesterol by diet, and when this fails physicians should use substances such as nicotinic acid. The working dose is 1 to 2 grams three times per day. In other words, general practitioners now know they are following advice from high places. NIH has become a promoter of megavitamin (nicotinic acid) therapy.

The table above lists the values of cholesterol with moderate or high risk.

Prevention and treatment must take these factors into account. For prevention only two measures are required: the orthomolecular diet and a program of physical work and/or exercise. People with a genetic potential for hypercholesterolemia should take additional precautions as soon as their blood fats begin to rise, including the use of nutrients such as niacin, ascorbic acid, pyridoxine, vitamin E and zinc.

Treatment is usually more difficult. It includes first the orthomolecular diet and weight reduction. Since this is apt to be rather slow, supplements should be used to reduce elevated blood fats quickly. This also reduces the sludging tendency of the blood and may be life saving. The supplements used are nicotinic acid in doses of 3 to 6 grams per day in three divided doses. If a slow-release preparation is used, 1.5 to 3 grams per day may be adequate. As I have noted earlier, nicotinic acid is an effective, broad-spectrum hypolipidemic agent that normalizes blood cholesterol (elevates it when too low, lowers it when too high); lowers total triglycerides; lowers low-density lipoproteins; and elevates high-density lipoproteins. Nicotinic acid also improves circulation by preventing sludging. It increases the rate of vascularization of injured tissues and decreases frequency and intensity of anginal pain (Altschul 1964). The beneficial effect of nicotinic acid begins in a few days. Our first study (Altschul, Hoffer and Stephen 1955), required only 48 hours of treatment with nicotinic acid for its hypocholesterolemic nature to be established.

Ascorbic acid is used to pull cholesterol out of the atherosclerotic plaques (Ginter 1977), but this requires several months. It tends to restore metabolism and allows blood fat levels to drop. It must also have a beneficial effect on the ability of the intima to heal itself, as does nicotinic acid. At least 3 grams per day should be used.

Pyridoxine has been found to be important in disturbed fat metabolism and should be provided. The Saccharine Disease diet tends to be low in pyridoxine. I suggest at least 100 mg per day be used, but much more may be required. It is a good idea to supplement with zinc gluconate, 50 to 100 mg per day, or zinc sulfate, 110 to 220 mg per day. Finally, I would recommend vitamin E, at least 800 IU per day, because of its antioxidant properties. If heating fat increases its atherosclerotic properties, it is prudent to use antioxidants to protect against excessive oxidation, since cooking food will always remain the main processing technique. Perhaps selenium will one day also be used to reinforce the antioxidant properties of vitamin E.

Exercise needs to be used as well. This is described in our book on senility (Hoffer and Walker 1980).

There is nothing we can do about mechanical stress on our vessels, which must remain, but by keeping the rate of repair of the intima high, by keeping the blood fluid fats normal, and by decreasing our heart rate by good physical fitness, we have gone about as far as we can go. The rest is up to our genetic inheritance and acts of God.

### THE HEART

The heart is a specialized portion of the vascular system. This generates special problems and treatments. As far as coronary disease is concerned, this is merely the formation of plaques with thrombosis, such as can occur anywhere in the body. The extraordinary technology of modern medicine and surgery would be markedly improved if physicians and surgeons were to use orthomolecular medicine before, during and after treatment. It is very likely that fewer heart transplants and other cardiac surgery would be necessary if orthomolecular medicine had been practiced several years before.

There are many problems associated with heart transplants that are not within the field of orthomolecular medicine. But the general question of placing a portion of the circulatory system—a heart which is still free of atherosclerosis—into a person whose entire metabolism has caused atherosclerosis, must be discussed. If the rejection of the new heart is prevented, it too will fall prey to athero-

sclerosis as did the first one. It makes sense that, coincidental with the transplant, orthomolecular treatment should be instituted to protect the new heart from the ravages imparted to the old one by that body. Ideally, people on proper nutrition would need no heart transplants, and those who did become candidates should be placed on orthomolecular treatment immediately. Some may not need anything else. Patients awaiting transplants should be on the full orthomolecular treatment and should continue after the operation.

### THE BRAIN

Artherosclerosis can affect any vessel, including those in the brain. A stroke is a thrombus in a vessel of the brain, probably due to atherosclerosis, but it may come from other causes as well, such as embolus. What I have written about blood vessels in general and the heart also applies to the brain. But there is one main metabolic difference between the brain and other organs—an interruption of the blood supply to the brain is much more serious than it is in any other organ, for the brain has no alternative to glucose and aerobic respiration to survive. This is why more than a few minutes of anoxia will lead to death or to great damage to the brain, so that death might be preferable. This is the reason that body temperature is lowered in some operations when the brain must be anoxic for awhile. At lower temperatures energy utilization is decreased. The brain uses almost 20 percent of all the oxygen consumed by the body at rest, even though there are only 2.5 to 3 pounds of brain compared to 100 to 200 pounds of body. Total blood flow through the brain is relatively constant, awake or asleep, thinking or not thinking. It goes down until consciousness begins to decrease.

Recently it has been shown that anoxia need not be as serious if hypoglycemia is prevented. Monkeys deprived of oxygen survived without permanent impairment twice as long if they were not given glucose. Thus a stroke shortly after a sugar-rich meal and a large increase in blood glucose will be more apt to cause permanent damage. Myers (1977a, 1977b, 1977c).

## HYPERTENSION

Blood pressure must be controlled within narrow limits. Systolic pressure is a measure of the maximum pressure following each contraction of the heart and diastolic pressure is a measure of the constant pressure. The veins have much less pressure. Arterial blood pressure is the one physicians are concerned about.

Any general textbook on medicine will describe factors which control blood pressure. Here I will discuss only factors susceptible to nutritional treatment.

For many years, sodium has been considered one of the main villains in causing hypertension. Millions of patients have been placed on salt-free or very low salt diets, including pregnant women for whom this was an attempt to prevent preeclampsia or eclampsia. This may have done more harm than good.

Recently, exciting evidence has appeared linking hypertension to calcium deficiency, not with sodium excess. Dr. D. McCarron, Division of Nephrology and Hypertension, Oregon Health Services, has stated: "For too long we've assumed that the problems with blood pressure in humans are related to an excess of something. . . . Salt has been the culprit nailed repeatedly. But we are frankly amazed at how poor the data base is that links sodium intake to blood pressure" (McCarron et al. 1984). Dr. McCarron, on the contrary, concludes hypertension is related to a deficiency of calcium. The less calcium in the diet, the higher the blood pressure. In a recent study, 170 patients, of whom 65 percent were hypertensive, were randomly given either 1 gram of calcium or placebo each day for eight weeks, then the treatment was reversed. Half the hypertensives on entering

the study were on medication to control high blood pressure. Forty-five percent became normal on calcium alone. That is, half the hypertensives placed on calcium will no longer need drugs for control of their high blood pressure.

Further, salt restriction lowers high blood pressure in only 5 percent of any hypertensive population, and many hypertensives are already on a low-sodium diet. Finally, a few animal studies show that giving animals sodium lowered their blood pressure.

Calcium appears to be the most important single factor, but animals must also be given sodium and potassium in order to obtain the full benefit of the calcium.

A nutrition study on 21,000 people showed a very strong correlation between calcium intake and hypertension. It was the only nutrient out of 17 which distinguished normal subjects from hypertensives. A further study in California on 2,000 subjects showed that dairy product consumption and blood pressure were inversely related. American blacks have a high incidence of lactose intolerance, and thus have a reduced intake of milk and calcium; this may be a factor in their high incidence of hyptertension. Finally, the elderly often suffer from calcium deficiency, which may be a factor in hypertensive cardiovascular disease in the aging population.

Calcium and magnesium should be in balance. About two parts calcium to one part magnesium are required. I conclude that a diet which provides at least 1 gram of calcium, 500 mg of magnesium and normal amounts of sodium and potassium will be most apt to keep blood pressure normal. The orthomolecular diet supplemented with calcium-magnesium supplements will provide these quantities of essential minerals (see also Altura et al. 1984; McCarron et al. 1984; Whang et al. 1982; and Whitescarver et al. 1984).

## CORONARY DISEASE

The two aims of treatment for coronary

disease are to (1) reverse atherosclerosis, and (2) reduce tissue aging.

(1) *Atherosclerosis*. The main treatment is nutritional, i.e., the orthomolecular diet. With this disorder one depends upon a wide variety of whole, fresh foods to provide optimum amounts of calories and a balance between various types of essential fatty acids. Ideally, caloric intake should keep one at the ideal weight or slightly less. The diet will provide adequate amounts of protein, carbohydrates and fats while avoiding sugars, processed oils, and other food artifacts. This diet alone will keep many people free of atherosclerosis. When other factors make this impossible, one can use supplements to lower fat levels (niacin), to protect vessel walls (ascorbic acid), or to prevent accumulation of lipid (pyridoxine).

One or more of the following supplements are used:

*Niacin*. A minimum of 1 gram t.i.d. of standard tablets or 0.5 gram t.i.d. of slow-release preparations is required. Occasionally this dose will have to be doubled. This will lower cholesterol, lower low-density lipoproteins and triglycerides, and elevate high-density lipoproteins. In time some plaques will diminish in size and the lumen will enlarge. Niacin also decreases the tendency of red cells to sludge. Niacin has been very helpful in diminishing or abolishing angina.

*Ascorbic acid*. This generally has no effect on cholesterol levels but it does improve the health of vessel walls and will, after a year or so, decrease the size of plaque. Perhaps it does so because of its antioxidant or healing effect. It is a good idea to use bioflavonoids as well, because they are effective in reducing edema and inflammation and help keep ascorbic acid in its reduced state.

*Pyridoxine*. This has been implicated in the formation of atherosclerotic plaque. I would use 100 to 250 mg per day.

*Vitamin E*. The medical profession gave the Drs. Shute a very rough time after they claimed vitamin E, in at least 800 IU per day doses, was effective in treating patients with heart disease. This was based upon the unusual medical fallacy that nothing works unless one understands how it works. Vitamin E was thought to have no useful properties. Practically, more physicians began to use it for themselves and for a few of their patients because it did help. Today we have an explanation—vitamin E is a very important fat-soluble antioxidant. Antioxidants are drawing much more attention as free radicals are being invoked in the causation of aging, of immune diseases, and of schizophrenia. We now have a mechanism even though it may not be correct. Coronary disease is a form of aging, with accumulation of old age pigment. It is associated with free radical formation. Vitamin E can deal with these fat-soluble free radicals. Having a rationale, at last, there is no doubt vitamin E will move very quickly into medicine and the Shutes will be recognized for the importance of their work.

*Zinc*. This should be given to enhance the effect of pyridoxine. In many cases there is a double deficiency of pyridoxine and zinc.

*Calcium and Magnesium*. One gram per day of calcium and 500 mg per day of magnesium will decrease the incidence of hypertension and thus decrease the load on the heart.

*Tissue Aging*. The program designed to prevent atherosclerosis is also an antiaging program. The only other nutrient I would add is selenium, because it is a good antioxidant, potentiates the effect of vitamin E, and decreases the probability of developing cancer.

## CEREBROVASCULAR DISEASE—STROKE

The same program is used. It will decrease the chances of developing stroke, and if a stroke does occur, it will hasten recovery and enhance the ability of the undamaged part of the brain to take over some function. I have seen patients after stroke show an acceleration of improvement after beginning on such a program.

## CASE HISTORIES

The following case histories represent an approach which has been helpful to my patients.

### M. B.: Year of Birth 1923

In February 1982, M. B. had a coronary occlusion requiring two weeks in the hospital. He appeared to have recovered but the following year remained very tired, even though he participated in a cardiac fitness program. He suffered shortness of breath on walking up stairs but not when walking on the level. Also it was much more difficult to cope with stress and this impaired his ability to function as well in a senior management job. Before seeing me he had improved his diet.

I started him on a sugar-free diet, adding nicotinic acid, 1 gram t.i.d.; ascorbic acid, 1 gram t.i.d.; vitamin E, 400 IU b.i.d.; pyridoxine, 100 mg b.i.d.; and zinc sulfate, 220 mg o.d.

One month later he was almost normal, with more energy, a greater feeling of being free of tension, and he had no further problem coping with stress.

### C. M.: Year of Birth 1932

In March 1980, C. M. complained of chest pain, present three years, not related to stress. For five months before being seen, the pain was worse and more frequent. Investigation showed a 50 percent reduction in coronary blood flow. He was recommended for surgery but wished to try a medical approach first.

I advised him to try a sugar-free diet, nicotinic acid, 1 gram t.i.d.; ascorbic acid, 1 gram t.i.d.; pyridoxine, 250 mg o.d.; zinc sulfate, 220 mg o.d.; and vitamin E, 400 IU b.i.d.

Two months later he was much better, having had only three episodes of severe pain in two months, compared to two episodes per week before.

After four months there was little pain, but he had started to flush after taking nicotinic acid and his skin burned. I discontinued the nicotinic acid.

I saw him again July 1982. He had had a coronary bypass operation (four vessels) and had since then suffered more pain, especially in the left side of his neck, and he had suffered one bout of pneumonia. Because of his previous flushing with nicotinic acid, I started him again on 500 t.i.d., plus the other vitamins.

In this case the orthomolecular approach decreased pain significantly, but, due to his intolerance of nicotinic acid, he could not continue with an adequate hypocholesterolemic dose, i.e., 3 grams per day, and he required his bypass operation.

### Other Cases

R. K., age 44, had a coronary two months before I saw him. One artery was blocked, which was cleared by angioplasty. He remained well but was very concerned about a possible recurrence. He had had diabetes for 27 years, which was under good control. He also had been operated on for left carpal tunnel syndrome; the same condition was developing on the right side.

He was advised to eliminate sugar, to increase complex carbohydrates and to supplement with niacin, 1 gram three times per day; ascorbic acid, 1 gram three times per day; pyridoxine, 250 mg per day; and zinc, 30 mg per day.

One month later he reported he was able to follow the program. Niacin had not altered his insulin requirements.

N. C., age 68, complained of intermittent claudication, which was present for two years. The left leg hurt more than the right one. Pain was extending to her knee. She was started on a sugar-free diet, niacin, 1 gram three times per day; ascorbic acid, 500 mg three times per day; vitamin E, 400 IU three times per day; a multimineral and a multivitamin preparation.

One month later, zinc gluconate, 50 mg,

was added because her blood copper was too high and zinc was too low. But she could not tolerate the mineral or zinc preparations.

Six months later she still suffered pain but her legs were warm. She could not tolerate niacin, which was replaced by inositol niacinate (Linodil in Canada, a nonflushing niacin preparation). Two months later she was at last able to tolerate zinc. After two years it was still difficult to find a program that was free of side effects. Niacin, 3 grams per day, brought down her cholesterol levels but caused ankle edema. She eventually could tolerate 1.5 grams of Linodil and 1.5 grams of niacin per day for a while, but later she could tolerate only 2 grams of niacin, a slow-release preparation, and Linodil, 1 gram. She was now well, free of pain, and not depressed. Her cholesterol levels are shown in the following table.

On niacin, 3 grams per day, her cholesterol was 208, HDL 62, and the ratio was 3.4. These are normal values. Off niacin her values were 293, 41, and she had a ratio of 7.1. Thereafter, because she could not take this dose, values have been higher. But, in spite of the higher value, this patient is free of intermittent claudication.

W. C., age 48, suffered severe chest pain after swimming to shore from an overturned boat. After angioplasty his blood flow in one artery increased from 5 percent of normal to 70 percent. His cholesterol levels were moderately elevated. He was advised to follow a diet which was free of sugar and milk products, supplemented by niacin, ascorbic acid, pyridoxine and zinc sulfate.

Two months later he reported he was better than he had been in many years. He will remain on this program for the rest of his life.

| Date | Cholesterol | High Density Cholesterol | Ratio |
| --- | --- | --- | --- |
| February 1984 | | | |
|   Before treatment | Very high | | |
| March 1984 | | | |
|   On niacin | 208 | 62 | 3.4 |
| February 1985 | | | |
|   Off niacin 10 days | 293 | 41 | 7.1 |
| April 1985 | 177 | 41 | 4.3 |
| October 1985 | 236 | 45 | 5.2 |
| January 1986 | 248 | 38 | 6.5 |
| May 1986 | 332 | 39 | 8.5 |
| June 1986 | 248 | 34 | 7.3 |

## CHAPTER REFERENCES

Altschul, R. (1964), *Niacin in Vascular Disorders and Hyperlipidemia.* Springfield, Ill.: Charles C Thomas, Publishers.

Altschul, R., Hoffer, A. and Stephen, J. R. (1955), Influence of nicotinic acid on serum cholesterol in man. *Archives in Biochemistry and Biophysics* 54:558–559.

Altura, B. M., Altura, B. T., Gebrewold, A., Ising, H., & Gunther, T (1984), Magnesium deficiency and hypertension: Correlation between magnesium-deficient diets and microcirculatory changes in situ. *Science* 223:1315–1317.

Boyle, E. (1968), "Niacin and the heart." In *The Vitamin B3 Therapy: A Second Communication to A.A.'s Physicians from Bill W.,* Bedford Hills, New York: P.O. Box 451.

Brown, M. S., Kovanen, P. T., & Goldstein, J. L. (1981), Regulation of plasma cholesterol by lipoprotein receptors. *Science* 212:628–635.

Canner, P. L. (1985), Mortality in Coronary Drug

Project patients during a nine-year post-treatment period. *J. Am. Coll. Cardiol.* 5:442.

Ginter, E. (1977), Vitamin C and cholesterol. *Int. J. Vitamin Nutritional Res.* 16(53).

Hoffer, A., & Walker, M. (1980), *Nutrients to Age Without Senility*. New Canaan, Conn.: Keats Publishing.

Illingworth, D. R., Roger, D., Phillipson, B. E., Rapp, J. H., & Connor, W. E. (1981), Colestipol plus nicotinic acid in treatment of heterozygous familial hypercholesterolemia. *Lancet*, 1:296–297.

McCarron, D. A., Morris, C. D., Henry, H. J., & Stanton, J. L. (1984), Blood pressure and nutrient intake in the United States. *Science* 224:1392–1398.

Myers, R. E. (1977), Brain damage not caused by lack of oxygen. *Medical Post*, Canada, March 29, 1977.

Myers, R. E. (1977), Lactic acid accumulation as cause of brain edema and cerebral necrosis resulting from oxygen deprivation. In *Advances in Perinatal Neurology*, eds. R. Korobkin, & C. Guilleminault, New York: Spectrum Publishing.

Myers, R. E. (1977), Report to Second Joint Stroke Conference. Reported in *Medical Post*, March 29, 1977.

Whang, R., Chrysant, S., & Dillard, B. (1982), Hypomagnesia and hypocalcemia in 1,000 treated ambulatory hypertensive patients. *J. Amer. Coll. Nutr.* 1:317–322.

Whitescarver, S. A., Ott, C. E., Jackson, B. A., Guthrie, G. P., & Kotchen, T. A. (1984), Salt-sensitive hypertension: Contribution of chloride. *Science* 223:1430–1432.

# CHAPTER 6

## ARTHRITIS

The joints of our bodies are particularly susceptible to mechanical wear and tear. The ends of the long bones must rub against each other without destroying themselves and must bear the weight of the body. The joints are surrounded by tough connective tissues, ligaments and muscles, which bind the bones together in a tough but flexible unit permitting movement, often against great force. When any of the tissues in and around the joints fail, arthritis is said to be present. The pathology may affect any or all of the tissues, resulting in excessive wear, undesirable deposits, swelling, redness, pain, restriction of movement and eventually permanent fusion or immobility and deformity.

Arthritis affects a very large proportion of the population, many lightly, many with recurrent attacks, and some so severely that they are left crippled. But in spite of its frequency, the causes and treatment are only dimly comprehended. Orthodox medicine includes the following causes: infections, both acute and chronic; trauma; immunological and other factors. Hormones have been implicated. The era of "wonder drugs" was introduced in 1950, when cortisone and ACTH became available and dramatically "cured" severe cases of arthritis. But the wave of enthusiasm was soon replaced by doubt and pessimism, as it was found that not only were the cures remarkably ephemeral, but also the side effects were remarkably hazardous.

Aspirin remains the only palliative treatment. The other treatments include some modern corticosteroids, injections of gold salts, and a few newer synthetics such as Indocid. But millions of arthritics remain victims of this painful, debilitating disease.

The wonder drugs of the 1950s, even though they are no longer used, left a permanent imprint on the treatment of arthritis, which has prevented any serious examination of the nutritional causes of arthritis. Nearly every rheumatologist since 1951 has been unable to free himself from the hormone model. It was the only model of arthritis examined and is the only model used in treatment. The allergy model is receiving some consideration, but no treatment has come from it so far, at least not from classical immunology. All the classic treatments are palliative and all cost the patient dearly in terms of side effects and toxicity.

It is tragic for millions that even the arthritis societies, which ought to be exploring every new avenue of treatment, have followed the same conservative approach. They still declaim that there is no relationship whatever between nutrition and arthritis. It is tragic because two other approaches developed simultaneously with the wonder drugs: (1) the use of large dosages of Vitamin B3 and; (2)

the use of special elimination diets, including fasts. But both of these approaches or treatments are orphan treatments. North American drug laws were based on the principle that only drug companies would develop new treatments. If a physician discovered a new treatment, it had little chance of success unless the drug could be patented. If it could not be patented it could not be developed, for no drug company will sponsor a drug that is not protected by patent. A drug which cannot be patented remains an orphan drug. It has no parents to fight for its survival. Had vitamin B3 been patented, there is little doubt it would today be one of the main treatments for arthritis.

In 1943, Dr. William Kaufman published a little book, *The Common Form of Niacin Amide Deficiency Disease: Aniacinamidosis*. Herein he described in careful clinical detail the many manifestations of vitamin B3 deficiency. These included the following:

1. Tension, irritability, impatience.
2. Impaired memory, distractibility, a feeling as if the patient were in a mental fog, difficulty in comprehension.
3. Unwarranted anxiety and fear.
4. Lack of initative.
5. Paranoid personality.
6. Depression or inappropriate moods.
7. Insomnia.
8. Poor balance.

And many more.

In 1943, the practice of adding niacinamide to flour had not yet become established. Dr. Kaufman's book documents how widespread was subclinical pellagra. One chapter of this valuable book dealt with arthritis. He wrote: "In persons suffering from aniacinamidosis there occurs a progressive clinical pattern which, in its final stages, is diagnosed arthritis." Kaufman summarized the clinical response of 30 patients with "classical arthritis"

treated with niacinamide: "Many patients of this group had been treated previously without striking benefit, by a variety of methods including diathermy, fever cabinet treatment, X-ray therapy, infrared and ultraviolet radiations, massage, hydrotherapy, transfusion of whole blood, intravenous typhoid injections, intramuscular milk injections, bee stings, sulfur injections, gold injections, high oral and parenteral dosages of thiamin hydrochloride and of vitamin C and high oral dosages of vitamin D." Four of these treatments are still being used today: infrared, massage, hydrotherapy, and gold. The improvement he observed using dosages less than 1,000 mg per day of niacin was remarkable. But patients had to continue taking niacinamide continuously or the arthritis would return. This little book was ignored almost completely.

In 1949, Dr. Kaufman published his second book on arthritis, *The Common Form of Joint Dysfunction*. By this time the common forms of subclinical pellagra had more or less been conquered by the addition of small quantities of niacinamide to white flour. But the arthritis was still prevalent, except that much larger quantities of vitamin were required—up to 4 grams per day in three or four divided doses. Then the responses were equally good. The addition of the vitamin to flour had provided enough for the group whose diets were deficient, but a large number of patients required much more than any diet could ever provide—these are in the vitamin-dependent group. For reasons unknown, these people have extra requirements of Vitamin B3. Dr. Kaufman had discovered that a major portion of all patients suffering from arthritis were vitamin B3-dependent. In other words, the arthritis for these patients is one of the major symptoms of subclinical pellagra.

Both of these classic books on arthritis and vitamin B3 are still available from the author, Dr. William Kaufman, 395A Ottawa Lane, Stratford, CT 06497.

Dr. Kaufman based the conclusions in his

second book on 455 patients ranging from four to 78 years of age, treated between March 1945 and February 1947.

It is very difficult to quantify subjective symptoms such as pain, but since arthritis has a limiting effect on movement at joints, it occurred to Dr. Kaufman to measure the amount of joint movement. He assumed that a normal joint would allow a full range of movement. He, therefore, developed a simple, accurate measuring device for determining the amount of movement at all the joints. These figures were then converted into a single index called the "Joint Range Index."

The relation of the index to joint dysfunction is shown in the following table.

### JOINT RANGE INDEX

| Index | Degree of Dysfunction |
|---|---|
| 96 to 100 | none to normal |
| 86 to 95 | slight |
| 71 to 85 | moderate |
| 56 to 70 | severe |
| 55 or less | extremely severe |

As patients improved, their scores rose. In the table below I show some of the responses he observed with niacinamide therapy by September 1948.

In each group there was steady improvement with time. Undoubtedly many more of the older groups would have entered into the slight category.

Kaufman recognized that not every arthritic suffers from aniacinamidosis. He also described cases of arthritis caused by allergies. His diagnosis and treatment of these forms of arthritis can hardly be bettered and are very similar to techniques used by clinical ecologists today.

But this pioneer work remained unknown and almost forgotten except by a few internists who accepted his evidence seriously and began to see the same results in their patients. Vitamin B3 is an orphan drug. It has no drug company as a parent and its use is not patentable; therefore, there is no incentive for any drug company to test, promote and distribute it. This is perfectly comprehensible and the drug companies are not to be blamed any more than the patent laws which shape these decisions. However, if any company could have gotten a patent on vitamin B3 for arthritis, there is little doubt it would be one of the standard treatments today, and millions of sufferers would have greatly benefited. But the societies that were created to promote the interests of the arthritics cannot be absolved so easily. Had they allied themselves more with their suffering members and less with the rheumatologists advising them, they could have promoted large-scale trials that would quickly have demonstrated the therapeutic value of vitamin B3. Every orthmolecular physician today has witnessed exactly the same improvements so aptly described by Dr. Kaufman nearly 40 years ago.

Kaufman (1943, 1949, 1981) began practic-

### SEVERITY OF JOINT DYSFUNCTION

| Ages | Before Niacinamide[1] | After Niacinamide[2] |
|---|---|---|
| 1 to 10 | slight | none |
| 11 to 50 | moderate | slight |
| 51 to 60 | severe | slight |
| 61 to 80 | severe | moderate |

(1) 455 patients
(2) 367 patients

ing medicine in 1941, before vitamins were added to white flour. He quickly recognized that deficiency of niacinamide (and/or niacin) was very common. He defined it as follows: "Aniacinamidosis encompasses the whole range of pellagrous disease. It includes severe, potentially lethal, florid pellagra, as well as the less severe and more chronic forms which cause protracted ill health and which have been called pellagra sine pellagra, atypical pellagra, pre pellagra, subclinical pellagra, incipient pellagra, sub acute pellagra and prodromal pellagra. It is a multisystem syndrome of ill health caused by the lack of niacinamide in adequate amounts for optimal functioning of all the cells of the body. The multisystem symptoms and signs of aniacinamidosis are ameliorated when the patient is treated with adequate amounts of niacinamide and recur when the patient again subsists soley on his or her diet. This syndrome included psychiatric symptoms such as mood changes, personality changes, excessive startle reactions to noise, impaired sense of balance, paresthesias and other sensory impairments. It included changes in skin, gastrointestinal tract, liver disorder, *IMPAIRMENT of muscle strength and maximal muscle working capacity, impairment of joint mobility, periosteal and cartilage tenderness to digital pressure.*" (The italicized portion is a description of the muscular-skeletal symptoms of the arthritides).

With the addition of niacinamide to white flour, many of the symptoms of aniacinamidosis became much less frequent. But the arthritic symptoms did not. This proved that different tissues required different amounts of niacinamide, that the musculo-skeletal tissues—bones, cartilage, fibrous, and muscle tissues—needed more than was provided even by diets containing the added vitamin in flour.

Between 1943 and 1964, Dr. Kaufman found that 95 percent of all his patients had some degree of impaired joint mobility; 65 percent had impaired strength and impaired maximum muscle working capacity; 45 percent had

impaired balance sense; 10 percent of those over 55 were depressed; and 5 percent were hyperactive.

Three of the common symptoms were muscle weakness, decreased maximum muscle working capacity and increased fatigability. They responded most quickly to niacinamide. Kaufman used a gripmeter for measuring strength and a special tally register for measuring the other two variables. It required a pound of pressure to depress the tally; patients tried to depress the tally as quickly as possible for one minute. Normal people could depress the tally bar 220 to 260 times per minute with no pain. Muscular fatigue became evident when the rate of pressing fell off. The moving dial was read every 15 seconds. Time of onset of discomfort or pain was recorded.

Kaufman recorded many cases. One 52-year-old woman was below normal in strength, her total strokes were 176 (20 percent below the lower limit of normal) and at 10 seconds pain started, and severe pain and cramping in her right forearm started in thirty seconds. Thirty minutes after swallowing 100 mg of niacinamide there was no pain for 30 seconds and mild discomfort for the other 30 seconds. One hour later her score rose to 188 pain-free strokes. After six weeks of 100 mg of niacinamide three times a day her score was 260. One week after starting on niacinamide, she no longer required extra rest, was no longer tired by housework, and lost all of her mild anxiety and tension symptoms. These responses were unique to niacinamide, for the addition of any other vitamins did not alter the recovery rate. But 30 percent of subjects did not respond.

Niacinamide also improved joint mobility. The following table relates Kaufman's Joint Range Index to clinical state and amount of niacinamide required. Low scores were associated with severe loss of joint mobility.

JRI scores increase with treatment. Because niacinamide is rapidly excreted, it must be

| Joint Range Index | Clinical State | Dose Schedule | Range of Dose, Mg per day |
|---|---|---|---|
| 96 to 100 | Normal | — | — |
| 86 to 95 | Slight joint dysfunction | 150 to 250 mg every 3 hours for 6 doses | 900 to 1,500 |
| 71 to 85 | Moderate joint dysfunction | 250 mg every 3 hours for 6 doses, or 250 mg every 2 hours for 8 hours | 1,500 to 2,000 |
| 56 to 70 | Severe | 250 mg every 2 hours for 8 doses, or every 1.5 hours for 10 doses | 2,000 to 2,500 |
| 55 or less | Extremely severe | 250 mg ever 1.5 hours for 10 doses, or 250 mg every hour for 16 doses | 2,500 to 4,000 |

*Source:* Kaufman 1949,

given frequently. Kaufman found that 250 mg every three hours was more effective than 500 mg every six hours.

Chemical abnormalities disturb metabolism in cartilage. Microscopic lesions show reduction in chondrocytes, fatty degeneration, changes in collagen, and irregularities in the articular surface. This is followed by localized surface softening. Movement, especially with great force, abrades the surface more. Later, cartilage is eroded with exposure of underlying bone. New bone is formed, seen as spurs on an X-Ray. Adverse changes in articular cartilage in response to wear and tear of joint movements are a primary cause. When cartilage can no longer repair itself at a rate equal to the deterioration, the product is arthritis.

Kaufman's explanation of why vitamin B3 works is the one I used in 1954 when I suggested to Prof. R. Altschul that he try nicotinic acid to repair atherosclerotic damage to the vessel walls of his experimental rabbits. I had concluded that it increased the ability of tissues in my tooth sockets to repair the minor trauma caused by chewing. I suspect vitamin B3 is necessary for everyone for tissue repair and that one of the earliest symptoms of deficiency is a decrease in the rate of repair.

Rheumatoid arthritis is more complex, involving these changes but also allergic, immunologic, and endocrine factors.

Dr. Kaufman concluded:

Just imagine for a moment what things might be like today if patients now 'warehoused' in nursing homes and geriatric hospitals had received (starting two, three or four decades earlier) the benefit of adequate niacinamide therapy alone or in combination with other vitamins. They would now have improved joint mobility, improved strength, improved maximum muscle working capacity, improved balance sense and freedom from certain mental symptoms.

I am convinced, on the basis of my large clinical experience, that there would have been extraordinary human benefits and comparable economic benefits to the individual and society. The whole syndrome of old age as we know it today would have been modified for the better. Geriatric persons would have been able to be independent much longer, would have developed fewer and less severe infirmities and would have required much less paraprofessional and professional medical care than is now the case.

As early as 1953, I had seen similar responses using either niacinamide or niacin for treating people with either rheumatoid or osteoarthritis (see Hoffer 1959). I consider them both effective, but of course most people prefer niacinamide, which causes no flushing. Many orthomolecular physicians, unaware of Kaufman's or my early observations, have told me of the responses they have seen in their patients who were being treated for other conditions. They later reported with surprise how their arthritic symptoms had also cleared.

In our book on senility (Hoffer and Walker 1980), we discussed using vitamin B3 as one of the major components of the antisenility program. We also concluded that much of senility and its social consequences could be prevented. A good diet, supplemented with vitamins and minerals when needed, will retard aging and the wear and tear changes with which it is associated.

Rheumatic fever is another form, more common in younger patients. It, too, can be treated with nutrition and vitamins. I suspect adequate quantities of ascorbic acid would prevent rheumatic fever.

But vitamin B3 is not the only vitamin useful for arthritis. Pyridoxine, and a combination of vitamins A and D3, also play an important role, and the mineral zinc has recently been shown to help some arthritics. Allergies undoubtedly cause arthritis in many, and fasts have been used with success (Mandell 1983). What this implies is that arthritis is not a single disease caused by one deficiency, but is a syndrome characterized by joint pain, inflammation and limitation of movement. The most effective treatment must include a combination of good nutrition (absence of food artifacts or junk), and a search for the appropriate nutrient supplements: vitamin B3, pyridoxine, vitamins A and D3, and/or the appropriate minerals, i.e., zinc or calcium and magnesium.

Attention to the pyridoxine treatment of arthritis was drawn by Dr. John M. Ellis in his book, *The Doctor Who Looked at Hands*, Vantage Press, 1966. He also reported pryidoxine was an effective treatment for edema of the fingers, especially when associated with the menstrual cycle.

Dale Alexander has found that cod liver oil (rich in vitamins A and D3) emulsified in milk was very effective in the treatment of arthritis. This program is similar to the one proposed by Dr. Carl Reich, who uses vitamins A and D3 combined with calcium as a treatment for allergic conditions, such as asthma, and also for arthritis.

Dr. P. Simkin, (*Lancet*, 2:539, 1976), found that 220 mg of zinc sulfate three times per day was helpful in the treatment of refractory rheumatoid arthritis. None of these patients had responded to salicylates, Prednisone, maintenance gold injections, Indomethacin, Chloroquin, Chlorambucil or Oxyphenbutazone. Patients had been on these medications an average of 11 years.

The evidence so far forces the conclusion that the arthritidies are orthomolecular diseases. When this condition is studied more carefully in the future, we will undoubtedly find that a variety of deficiencies or dependencies may attack the joints with less emphasis on the rest of the body. There must be a systemic involvement in every case. I consider arthritis only one of the most unpleasant symptoms of a generalized disease of malnutrition. We still do not know why the connective tissue around the joints is attacked in many people, while other systems occur in other people.

All these nutritional factors must be considered. Rational treatment of arthritis must include good diagnosis, i.e., ruling out those forms which are components of other diseases such as gout and infections. When there is no evident reason, or when the rheumatologist recommends nonspecific therapy such as aspirin, gold, etc., then the patient should examine his or her nutrition and, with the help of a nutrition-oriented physician, begin to explore the supplements and diet referred to here.

*Orthomolecular Nutrition*, by Hoffer and Walker (1978), details what we consider to be an optimum way of eating. If no physicians can be found, then each person must try on his own, after having studied vitamins, minerals, etc. Not being able to find a physician is no excuse for inactivity. In the same way, when anyone is hurt and bleeding you try to stop the bleeding even if there is no doctor around.

## TREATMENT OF ARTHRITIS

Modern treatment of arthritis should take advantage of all the treatments that have been found useful, provided they are not going to harm the patient. The less toxic treatments should take preference over more toxic drugs. One should aim to relieve pain as quickly as possible since pain is very stressful, increases loss of water-soluble nutrients, and decreases capability of our immune defense system. At the same time the treatment should be aimed at causes, so that drugs normally not found in the body are used as little as possible. When joints have been permanently damaged, eroded or deformed, then medical-nutritional therapy will help, but surgical repair will be necessary. Generally surgery will not be needed if joint mobility is possible with little pain. Treatment should be directed at all the causes. If an infection is present, it should be treated. If allergies are present, appropriate treatment is essential, including elimination diets, rotation diets or other measures used by clinical ecologists.

### General Treatment

NUTRITION

Orthomolecular nutrition and elimination of foods to which the patient is allergic. Nightshade plants (potatoes, tomatoes, peppers and tobacco) may be a factor in up to 10 percent of arthritics. Elimination for a couple of months greatly improves the patient if the nightshades are a factor.

SUPPLEMENTS

1. *Vitamin B3*. Niacinamide taken in four doses per day should be tried at optimum levels, usually starting with 500 mg q.i.d. Occasionally nicotinic acid is more effective. A few arthritics enjoy the flush which warms their joints. If neither form is tolerated, one can use inositol niacinate, called Linodil in Canada, with which there is very seldom any flush or gastric distress, as the nicotinic acid is released in the body very slowly.

2. *Ascorbic Acid*. Starting with 1 gram t.i.d. can be very helpful. This vitamin is essential for the health of collagen tissue and intervertebral discs in the back, and it tends to relieve low-back pain.

3. *Pyridoxine*. This can be very helpful and should be used if there is clinical evidence of a need for extra quantities.

4. *Zinc*. This mineral should be used with pyridoxine. Zinc sulfate, 220 mg, is usually well tolerated.

An ideal combination antiarthritic tablet would contain 250 mg of niacinamide, 250 mg of ascorbic acid, 50 mg of pyridoxine, and 10 mg of zinc. This tablet would be taken four to five times daily.

5. *Vitamins A and D3*. A combination of vitamins A and D3 with calcium and magnesium is used by Dr. C. Reich. He has treated many patients with arthritis successfully. His program is shown in the table on the next page.

The usual antiarthritis drugs would be used for quick relief of pain. These include aspirin,

## DOSAGES OF A AND D VITAMINS AND MINERALS

| Product | Average Initial Amount Prescribed | Dosage of Vitamins | |
|---|---|---|---|
| | | Vitamin A | Vitamin D2 and D3 |
| Aquasol A & D | 3-Year-Old Child<br>2 to 3 drops b.i.d.-t.i.d. | 5,000 to 12,000 IU | 1,000 to 2,400 IU |
| Bone meal | ½ tablet b.i.d. | 0.5 gram | |
| Aquasol A & D | 15-Year-Old Adolescent<br>5 drops t.i.d. | 20,000 IU | 4,000 IU |
| Halibut liver oil capsules | 1 b.i.d.    Total | <u>10,000 IU</u><br>30,000 IU | <u>800 IU</u><br>4,800 IU |
| Bone meal | 1 tablet b.i.d. | 1 gram | |
| Aquasol A & D | 150– to 175-Pound Adult<br>6 drops t.i.d. | 24,000 IU | 4,800 IU |
| Halibut liver oil capsules | 2 t.i.d.    Total | <u>30,000 IU</u><br>54,000 IU | <u>2,400 IU</u><br>7,200 IU |
| Bone meal | 1 t.i.d. | 1.5 grams | |

NOTE: If Aquasol A & D is not available, other natural or synthetic A and D vitamins may be substituted. It is possible, however, that the results I attain are dependent on the use of this aqueous solution of these vitamins.*

*[Table and Note taken from Reich (1971)]

the more modern antirheumatic drugs, and, if essential, steroids or gold. One of the great advantages of nutrients is that they are compatible with all medications, do not interfere with any therapeutic effect, and in fact accelerate all healing processes; and the xenobiotic medications can be slowly eliminated, allowing diet and nutrients to maintain health.

### CASE HISTORIES

I have seen about 30 patients who had arthritis as one of their main complaints. A number of them were seen only once. In every case they were asked to come back to be seen if in three months they were not satisfied with the degree of improvement. I assume they were much better if they did not seek another appointment.

### R. B.: Year of Birth 1921

R. B.'s arthritis had come on very suddenly

13 years before. Her hands and feet became swollen and painful. That fall her whole body was affected and she was treated with Prednisone. She improved rapidly but was left with chronic pain in her hands and feet. She had received every known treatment, including gold injections, all of which started out being helpful. In each case she became sensitive to the treatment and developed severe side effects. Her sedimentation rate gradually increased to over 80.

Three years before, her arthritis deteriorated following separation from her husband, but that year she recovered to the point that she could walk and eat by herself. Later she was given a three-week juice fast at an arthritis clinic. She went to the clinic in a wheelchair and came out walking. On resuming food, she quickly deteriorated. She then completed a 10-day fast, once more feeling much better. She had eliminated milk and sugar from her diet with no relief. Tea rapidly increased swelling.

I advised her to eliminate sugar and every other food she thought made her worse, including tea, coffee and chocolate. In addition she was given niacinamide, 500 mg t.i.d.; ascorbic acid, 1 gram t.i.d.; pyridoxine, 100 mg t.i.d.; bioflavonoids, 1 gram t.i.d.; and zinc sulfate, 220 mg o.d.

Two weeks later she reported it was easier to walk and her elbows moved more freely. She had increased her ascorbic acid to 3 grams t.i.d. Four weeks later her sedimentation rate suddenly dropped from 104, where it had been for four weeks, to 68.

### D. B.: Year of Birth 1921

Thirty-five years before this patient saw me, she had fallen down stairs while six months pregnant. Since that time she had had a sore back, which had been slowly worsening. Occasionally she found it very hard to walk. Several years before I saw her, she developed arthritis, which affected her back, fingers, and ankles and feet. She was also diagnosed as having osteoporosis.

The patient knew she was allergic to dust, mold and milk. The latter caused sinus problems and mucus in her throat, which was eased by ascorbic acid.

I advised her to eliminate sugar and milk and to take niacinamide; ascorbic acid; pyridoxine; zinc sulfate, dolomite, six tablets per day; cod liver oil, three capsules per day; and superoride dismutase, one tablet t.i.d.

Four months later her arthritis was not improved but she was sleeping better. She was then started on a diet eliminating nightshade plants.

### J. C.: Year of Birth 1962

For seven years this man had suffered pain in his joints on movement and had had to give up sports. For two years before I saw him, he had received 14 X-ray examinations per year to try to locate the source of his problem.

As a boy he had suffered severe growing pains. He did not tan evenly and had severe acne on his back and face. He consumed six glasses of milk per day.

I started him on a diet eliminating sugar and milk, and his diet was supplemented by niacinamide, 500 mg q.i.d.; pyridoxine, 250 mg b.i.d.; ascorbic acid, 1 gram t.i.d.; zinc sulfate, 220 mg o.d.; and 3 halibut liver oil capsules per day.

One month later he was better. His joints did not lock as much and were stronger, and his acne was better. The month after that he continued to improve. His joints made fewer creaking sounds. The white areas in his nails were clearing.

### N. G.: Year of Birth 1944

One year before, while under severe stress, N. G. had suddenly developed arthritis and was in and out of the hospital for six months. At one time she was almost immobilized by the pain. She failed to respond to a variety of drugs, and aspirin had almost made her deaf. Two months before, she was started on Naproxen and Prednisone and felt much better, but she developed extreme hunger and could not stop eating. She also retained fluid.

I started her on a diet eliminating sugar and nightshade foods, with supplements of niacinamide, 500 mg q.i.d.; ascorbic acid, 1 gram t.i.d.; pyridoxine, 100 mg o.d.; and zinc sulfate, 220 mg o.d.

One month later she was less confused. She was to return in three to six months if not well, but did not return.

### C. H.: Year of Birth 1933

C. H.'s main complaint was distortion of his sense of taste and smell following severe flu nine months before. Everything tasted peculiar, i.e., chicken tasted like rubber. Three months before he came to see me he began to take Surbex 500 and slowly began to feel better, and chicken again tasted like chicken. However, wine tasted and smelled like apples. But this is not why his case is presented here. As a minor problem he had suffered low-back pain for several years. This is an example of rapid response of pain that is not severe to begin with. He had evidence of zinc and pyridoxine deficiencies, i.e., white spots in his nails.

He was asked to increase the Surbex to one tablet t.i.d. and was also given zinc sulfate, 220 mg o.d., plus pyridoxine, 250 mg b.i.d.

Two weeks later his sense of taste and smell improved but his pain was not improved. One month later the pain was gone. Three weeks after that he was almost normal.

### J. H.: Year of Birth 1940

For a year and a half all of J. H.'s joints except her hips were very painful. She was diagnosed as having rheumatoid arthritis but failed to respond to Valdene, aspirin or Naproxen. Her elbows and wrists were especially painful, to the point that she could not even fasten her brassiere at the back. The pain was worse before her periods and she suffered from water retention. If she sat still, she froze and had difficulty starting to move. Her feet were swollen and painful and she had to take eight Bufferin tablets per day.

She was started on a sugar-free, nightshade-free diet, supplemented with niacinamide, 500 mg q.i.d.; ascorbic acid, 1 gram t.i.d.; pyridoxine, 100 mg t.i.d.; zinc sulfate, 220 mg o.d.; and vitamin E, 800 IU o.d.

Three weeks later she was better in spite of very severe stress from learning of her mother's cancer. She was able to sleep without being awakened by pain, had more energy, less stiffness and required less Bufferin. But she suffered increased allergic reactions from spring flowers and grass. I added bone meal, 3 tablets; magnesium oxide, 500 mg t.i.d.; and cod liver oil, 2 capsules t.i.d. One month later she was much better. The pain in her shoulders was gone but her ankles and toes were worse. Three months after that she was free of pain everywhere except in her feet

and at the back of her knees. I added niacin, 500 mg q.i.d.

### V. K.: Year of Birth 1922

This woman was the sickest arthritic I have ever seen in 35 years of practice. The first symptoms struck in 1952 and she was diagnosed arthritic in 1957. She had exacerbations and remissions until she was finally confined to a wheelchair most of the time in 1962, which became a permanent situation in 1973. For awhile she was able to propel herself in her chair using her feet, but for many years she had to be pushed. For the past three years before seeing me, her husband, occasionally helped by a homemaker service, had nursed her.

When I saw her she was in a wheelchair, severely deformed, sitting with her feet crossed under her as they could not be extended. Her hands were horribly deformed and misshapen. She suffered severe, continuous pain in her arms, hips, and back, and her legs were swollen. She wore pressure stockings to try to keep the edema down. She claimed she could still feed herself but it must have taken heroic effort to do so. She could not write. She had not been able to sit up in bed unaided for 15 years. She had just come through a suicidal depression, thinking her husband would be better off without her. He had to provide 24-hour total nursing and home care.

She told me she realized I could probably help her very little, but she hoped I could relieve her of the dreadful pain in her back.

I started her on a sugar-free, nightshade-free diet plus niacinamide, 500 mg q.i.d.; ascorbic acid, 500 mg q.i.d.; pyridoxine, 250 mg o.d.; zinc sulfate, 220 mg o.d.; linseed oil, 2 tablespoons per day; and cod liver oil, 1 tablespoon per day.

One month later she was wheeled in, smiling, by her husband, who was also smiling. Her back pain was much less severe and her hips were free of pain. She was able to sit in her chair with her feet dangling. Her bowels no longer bled, she no longer bruised and her heartbeat was now regular. She was much more comfortable. I added Linodil, 500 mg q.i.d., to her program.

One month later she was even better. She was now able to sit up in bed unassisted for the first time in 15 years. Her depression was gone.

Two and a half months later she telephoned me. I was surprised to hear from her and blurted out, "How did you get to the phone?" She replied it was no problem as she could now get around alone in her chair. She had made steady progress but had called to ask what she could do for her husband—he had the flu and she was nursing him!

I saw her again one year later. She had regained muscle tone and strength. She had some pain in her left arm. She agreed to consult a surgeon to consider the possibility of correcting her severe finger deformities.

This is a remarkable response in a very sick arthritic who had deteriorated steadily for at least 15 years.

### Z. K.: Year of Birth 1946

Four years ago this patient was diagnosed as having Reiter's disease. He complained of pain in his joints, recurrent urethritis, and pain in his abdomen and testicles. He had been given Methotrexate, which caused severe side effects, including confusion and nightmares, and he continually revisualized episodes from his past. He could not tolerate Indocid or aspirin. Because he could not work he was fired from his job. He was paranoid and very anxious, fearful that he had leukemia because of the Methotrexate, and he was very depressed.

I advised him to eliminate sugar and start nicotinic acid, 500 mg q.i.d.; ascorbic acid, 1 gram t.i.d.; pyridoxine, 100 mg o.d.; and zinc sulfate, 220 mg o.d.

One month later he had been better for four weeks but suffered more pain the previous week. I increased the nicotinic acid to 1

gram q.i.d., and added a combination of Amitriptyline, 25 mg, and Perphenazine, 2 mg, before bed.

Two months later he was better, less paranoid, and no longer worried about leukemia. After another month he was much better. One year later he reported that he had not been able to follow the program because he had too little money. A rash had come and gone that spring and he had a hemorrhage in his right eye, so that he was just aware of light. He had stopped his drugs as they made him feel strange. His arthritis was very bad. I started him on niacinamide, 1 gram t.i.d. only. Two and half months later he was better, more outgoing and less depressed. He reported he felt better whenever he took the niacinamide.

### M. L.: Year of Birth 1930

About eight months before I saw her, M. L. suddenly became ill. Three months later all her joints were affected. Her hands were puffy, walking was very painful and she was weak and tired. She had failed to respond to Devil's Claw root, special diets, or aspirin; but Climesteron, 0.2 mg per day, relieved pain and stiffness. When I saw her she was able to play the piano again but both wrists were painful, and she remained weak. DMSO applied to the joints had been very helpful.

No dietary change was recommended, but she was given niacinamide, 500 mg q.i.d.; ascorbic acid, 1 gram t.i.d.; pyridoxine, 250 mg o.d.; zinc gluconate, 100 mg o.d.; and a multimineral preparation.

After one month she was no longer weak and the pain had diminished. After six months she was able to play the piano for many hours with only some pain in her left wrist.

### A. R.: Year of Birth 1931

In 1947, this patient developed pain in her hips which had not been relieved, although it varied in intensity. In 1957, she was bedridden with rheumatic fever. Her hands and feet were badly swollen. The pain was worse two days in a advance of a weather-front change. The Chinook winds in Calgary were particularly hard on her and she moved to British Columbia. Indocid and Entrophen were not very helpful.

Combined with the arthritis, nine months before she saw me she had begun to suffer trigeminal-type neuralgia. Her face felt frozen as if anesthesized and it still tingled.

She was advised to eliminate sugar and nightshade plants and to use nicotinamide, 500 mg q.i.d.; ascorbic acid, 500 mg q.i.d.; pyridoxine, 100 mg b.i.d.; zinc sulfate, 220 mg o.d.; and cod liver oil, 1 capsule t.i.d.

One month later the pain was less severe. Her gums were swollen and she had a faint pink rash around her mouth. She had stopped Prednisone, 10 mg per day, two days before and had also stopped taking Indocid, Entrophen and a diuretic. One month after this she was only on vitamins and was much better. Her face had regained its normal shape and felt well. She had to use a few aspirins over the month.

### E. S.: Year of Birth 1915

About 25 years before she was seen, E. S. suffered pain in her back, which had since eased; but since then she had suffered recurrent episodes of arthritis. The last episode was already present one year when I saw her. Her knees hurt when she stood or sat, her legs were weak, and she was uncertain when walking.

She had been avoiding milk products and coffee. She was able to deal with her pain but wanted to try a vitamin program, as a neighbor had been helped about 25 years ago by niacin.

I advised her to continue to eliminate milk and sugar and to use the same three vitamins and zinc. One month later she was pleased with the response and was convinced she would now regain her health. She was not as weak and her legs were more flexible.

### B. T.: Year of Birth 1948

Four years ago, early in her pregnancy, B. T. suddenly developed severe low-back pain, weakness, and great difficulty in walking. Following that her toes began to hurt and she began to suffer intermittent diarrhea. She was treated in a hospital for two months. She was diagnosed as having spondylitis and given Prednisone, which helped. The rest of her pregnancy was uneventful, but two months later her arthritis flared up, affecting joints previously not touched. One year later she stopped the Prednisone, as she was worried over its side effects. Two years later she had another recurrence and was given Feldene and Prednisone once more. After another six months there was another recurrence, which continued until I saw her. Her right hand, wrist and thumb were swollen and her right knee was swollen and tender. She was very tired and could not carry on with the activities she'd engaged in when she was well.

On a four-day fast before her arthritis first hit, she had felt marvelous.

I started her on a sugar-free, nightshade-free diet and added nicotinic acid, 500 mg q.i.d.; ascorbic acid, 1 gram t.i.d.; pyridoxine, 250 mg o.d.; zinc sulfate, 220 mg o.d.; and 1 tablespoon of linseed oil per day.

One month later she had more pain, especially with diarrhea. She was unable to take ascorbic acid. I asked her to try ascorbic acid again, 500 mg t.i.d., and I added nicotinamide, 500 mg q.i.d., and eliminated milk. She had gone back onto potatoes, etc. I asked her to go back to Prednisone. After another month she was much better. She did not like the taste of linseed oil so was advised to use fish oil capsules instead. One month later she had been free of pain for three weeks, the first time since becoming ill. She had been off Prednisone eight days, was off Naprosyn, and was to go off Feldene. She felt normal.

### M. W.: Year of Birth 1920

About sixteen years before, M. W. had developed arthritis three months after an injury, when he tore a ligament. Since then he had been ill, having been treated in a hospital once and with a variety of medications. He had taken kelp on his own and was convinced this had helped more than anything else. When I saw him he had little pain but his joints were stiff, both hands had the typical deformity of rheumatoid arthritis, and his fingers were deformed with ulnar deviation. For a number of years he and his wife had been carefully avoiding "junk."

He was advised to avoid sugar and nightshade plants and to supplement with nicotinic acid, 1 gram t.i.d.; ascorbic acid, 1 gram t.i.d.; pyridoxine, 250 mg o.d.; zinc sulfate, 220 mg o.d.; halibut liver oil, 2 capsules t.i.d.; bone meal tablets, 2 t.i.d.; and thyroid, 60 mg o.d.

He could not tolerate the full doses of nicotinic acid and ascorbic acid and had reduced them to one-third the prescribed dose. When I saw him after one month he was much better and had no problem with any arthritic symptoms but still felt cold. He was then asked to continue on 1 gram per day each of nicotinic acid and ascorbic acid and to reduce bone meal to two tablets per day.

These 13 cases represent a cross-sampling of the kinds of cases I have seen, and also represent the type of response. It was impossible to do one year follow-ups in most cases, but I assume that had these patients not become well or improved to the point of reasonable comfort, they would have come back for further advice. They were highly motivated to come in the first instance. They had been advised to come back if they were not content with their state of improvement. Once a vitamin program begins to work, it continues to do so, but when the program is discontinued the arthritis may come back.

Unfortunately, I do not see acute arthritics and, therefore, have not been able to test this nutritional approach on this group. There is a remote probability that my group, who had all failed to respond satisfactorily to the usual antiarthritic drugs, may have been unusually responsive to the nutrient approach. It is more probable that acute arthritics would respond even more quickly than do chronic failures.

Ideally one should first try nutritional therapy, but if severe pain and swelling are present, it could be combined with Prednisone or other drugs. This would combine the rapid effect of these drugs with the good, sustained effect of the diet and vitamins. Once the patients are comfortable, the drugs can be withdrawn slowly. Best of all, if everyone were on the proper diet with supplements at the first indication of joint or muscle pain, arthritis would likely vanish.

The doses I have used in my cases are good starting doses, but they have to be adjusted up or down, depending upon the efficacy of the program and the side effects. After the patient is well he or she should experiment with doses to determine the minimum doses that will keep the patient well.

My views about the value of double-blind controlled experiments are well known: that they are much less valuable than many suppose. But clinical observation, no matter how reliable and thorough, is denigrated by labeling it *anecdotal*. I note, however, that this evil word is slowly being rehabilitated. More and more authors refer without shame to their anecdotal observations. Recently, allergy arthritic studies (anecdotal) have been entering the double-blind controlled (scientific) state. Only those who have never used this approach will have been surprised. Darlington, Ramsey, and Mansfield (1986, 236–238) summarized their report thus:

In a blind, placebo-controlled study of dietary manipulation therapy in outpatients with rheumatoid arthritis there was significant objective improvement during periods of dietary therapy compared with periods of placebo treatment, particularly among good responders.' Possible explanations for improvement include reduced food intolerance, reduced gastrointestinal permeability, and benefit from weight loss and from altered intake of substrates for prostaglandin production. A proportion of the improvement was due to a placebo response, but this was not sufficient to explain the whole improvement.

## CHAPTER REFERENCES

Darlington, L. G., Ramsey, N. W., & Mansfield, J. R. (1986), Placebo-controlled, blind study of dietary manipulation therapy in rheumatoid arthritis. *Lancet* i: 236–238.

Ellis, J. (1973), *Vitamin B6: The Doctor's Report.* New York: Harper and Row.

Hoffer, A. (1959), Treatment of arthritis by nicotinic acid and nicotinamide. *Can. Med. Assoc. J.* 81:235–238.

Hoffer, A., & Walker, M. (1978) *Orthomolecular Nutrition.* New Canaan, Conn.: Keats Publishing.

——— (1980), *Nutrients to Age Without Senility.* New Canaan, Conn.: Keats Publishing.

Kaufman, W. (1943), *The Common Form of Niacin Amide Deficiency Disease: Aniacinamidosis.* Bridgeport, Conn.: Yale University Press.

——— (1949), *The Common Form of Joint Dysfunction: Its Incidence and Treatment.* Brattleboro, Vt.: E. L. Hildreth.

——— (1978), Niacinamide: a most neglected vitamin. *Fifth Annual Tom Spies Memorial Lecture.* Int. Acad. Prev. Med Fall Conference, Chicago, Ill. Reprinted from *New Dynamics of Preventive Medicine*, Vol. VI. Edited by L. R. Pomeroy, 1981. Available from International Academy of Preventive Medicine, 10409 Town and Country Way, Suite 200, Houston, TX, 77024.

Mandell, M. (1983), *Dr. Mandell's Lifetime Arthritis Relief System.* New York: Coward-McCann.

Reich, C. J. (1971), The vitamin therapy of chronic asthma. *Journal of Asthma Research* 9:99–102.

## CHAPTER 7

# NEUROLOGICAL DISEASES WHICH PROBABLY HAVE A NUTRITIONAL BASE

Some of the neurological diseases are clearly related to nutritional problems and respond to nutritional and nutrient treatment. Pellagrologists discovered this soon after it was shown that vitamin B3 cured some forms of pellagra. Many patients suffering from organic confusional psychoses and neurological symptoms recovered when treated with large enough doses of niacin, even when these patients had no history of poor diet.

I was familiar with this literature when I began to treat schizophrenics with large doses of vitamin B3 in 1951. As soon as an opportunity arose, I began to treat a number of these neurological conditions.

Early in 1952 I had to treat a middle-aged man for depression and serious confusion. He had been given a series of electroconvulsive treatments (ECT), which had relieved the depression but had left him confused and severely memory impaired. He was able to function at home with the help of his devoted wife. As there was no known treatment and as I could not leave him as he was, I started him on niacin, 3 grams per day, in three divided doses. One month later, to my amazement, he was well. The vitamin had removed the negative effects of the ECT and allowed its positive effects to remain. Since then I never use ECT on patients without also giving them at least two vitamins: Vitamin B3 and ascorbic acid. I am convinced my patients then respond much better to ECT and have fewer undesirable side effects.

Over the past 33 years I have treated the following neurological conditions with nutrition and supplements: senility, epilepsy, post-stroke cases, patients with organic brain changes following trauma, and Huntington's disease. They do not all respond, but many do and are able to lead more useful lives. These patients are not noted for having spontaneous recoveries, each patient providing his or her own control. Double-blind controlled experiments would only prevent a few patients on placebo from getting well.

## SENILITY

Aging and senility are related to each other but are not synonymous. But aging and senility flow along the arrow of time at different rates and arrive at their inevitable destination at different times. A much larger proportion of women and men over age 65 will suffer the infirmities of age, compared to an equal number whose age is under 30. Yet many are senile either physically or mentally before they reach 50, and many are not senile by age 90. There is thus a crude but not perfect relationship. However, it is true that, as the number of years accumulate, both aging and senility approach each other. Perhaps they meet somewhere above 120 years. If so, everyone older than 120 can expect to become senile. About 5 percent of any population in the industrialized world is senile at age 65 years; by age 80 20 percent is senile. If we assume that the relationship between age and senility is linear, which it may not be, we can extrapolate to age 120, when over 80 percent will be senile. If the relationship is curvilinear upward, more than 80 percent will be senile. This conclusion is pessimistic or optimistic depending upon one's point of view. Individuals are doomed to die, but the species would be doomed to extinction if we were immortal; a species' life depends upon birth and death.

Our objective, therefore, is to prolong useful life so that a much greater proportion reach our limit with not enough senility to handicap us. Carl Pfeiffer's (1975) term "useful longevity" is very apt. From what we know now this is feasible for most aging people. Unfortunately, this is known only to a few, and the vast majority of physicians and nutritionists and the public remain ignorant of how we can achieve much greater useful longevity. We cannot stop the years, but we can change the speed with which we reach the end of our useful longevity.

There is evidence from which we can conclude that senility can be prevented, reversed, or inhibited in most people:

1. Not everyone becomes senile at the same rate.
2. The correlation between brain pathology and senility is not one-to-one. Many people senile at death have pretty normal brains, while many brains with a lot of pathology at autopsy did not make their owners senile.
3. Senility can be accelerated or decelerated. One year in a Japanese prisoner-of-war camp during World War II hastened senility by five years. Patients suffering from accelerated senility were restored to normal by taking nicotinic acid. The psychosocial-malnutritional stress which had accelerated senility was neutralized by this vitamin when 1 gram was taken three times per day. There are a large number of accelerating and decelerating factors.

4. It may not be true that the brain cannot replace neurons. It is generally accepted that the 10 to 100 billion neurons with which we are endowed at birth are lost slowly over our lifetime and are never replaced. This was considered a universal mammalian property. Recently, Nottebohm (1984) demonstrated that male song birds grow large numbers of new neurons each spring during the breeding season and lose them again in the fall. If true in birds, is this also true in mammals and people? Is senility a race between neuronal loss and replacement? If so, removal of noxious factors will slow neuronal loss and allow neuron genesis, while positive health factors will decrease neuronal loss and increase new growth.

### GENETICS OF AGING

Aging involves every tissue and organ, but not each to the same degree. It is a general phenomenon, which means it is a pathological alteration of a large number of chemical reactions. No one reaction can be blamed and no single theory will account for it. Every reasonable theory or hypothesis should be examined. They are not contradictory. It will be found that some account for the facts better than others. It may also be found that some theories lead to better treatment. A genetic theory may be better established than a cross-linkage theory, but there is little we can do to change our genes. However, a great deal can be done to decrease cross-linkages. The best theories are the ones which lead to better treatment.

It is wrong to consider any disease solely genetic—genes do not operate in a vacuum. Genes order or direct biochemical processes in which one molecule is converted into another. Each gene is surrounded by a molecular environment of many thousands of chemicals. It is equally true that every disease is genetic because genes and their molecular environment interact continually. We can consider that a disease is mostly genetic if a normal diet cannot provide all the essential nutrients. Scurvy is a genetic disease for man because we cannot make ascorbic acid in our bodies; it is not a genetic disease for mice or rats, who can make all they need. Pellagra is a genetic disease and would appear in everyone if there was a deficiency in food, but it is not considered a genetic disease. In the same way, we can discuss genetic theories of aging, but only if we do not forget that aging genes, if there are any, have certain biochemical needs and many remain inactive if these needs are met. This is the basic problem in aging research. Are there aging genes, as there appear to be, and if there are, what are their specific needs and can they be met, or has nature really programmed us to become aged or senile before we die?

There is little doubt that genetic factors are very important. There are long-lived families and short-lived families. I. S. Wright (1978) described a family where in four generations everyone had lived to 85 and two had lived to be over 100. Twin studies provided further genetic evidence (Falek, Kallman, Lorge and Jarvik 1960; and Jarvik, Falek, Kallman and Lorge 1960). A comparison of identical (one-egg) against fraternal (two-egg) twins showed that one-egg twins were more alike in life span compared with a six-year difference in two-egg twins. But 12 years later the difference in one-egg twins had widened to five years. There was no change in two-egg twins. These findings provide some evidence for both genetic and environmental factors. Two-egg twins are already divergent in both, but one-egg twins are more and more subject to environmental factors, which decrease the uniform effect of their genetic structure. Had the one-egg twins lived in similar environments and used the same type of nutrition, it is likely their life spans would have remained more similar than those of the two-egg twins. This data suggests that environmental factors might completely cancel out genetic factors, since the one-egg and two-egg twins were no longer different at the end of the 12-year study.

I am now treating a one-egg pair of female twins, which also shows the effect of environment. They were born in October 1901 and first seen by me in September 1984. Doris was confused, suffered severe memory loss, and was disoriented. She and her sister had been moved into a small, special facility housing 10 people three months before. This is a well-run facility with very competent, concerned nurses in charge. Before moving there they had both been deteriorating and were suffering from malnutrition. At the new home they were given good food and improved substantially. Doris was aware that her memory was bad and was concerned about it, but at the new home she slept better and was more alert. When I saw her she also suffered a "pins and needles" sensation in one shoulder. She had a slight tremor and sometimes staggered. Gladys, her identical twin, was even worse, not even knowing she had a problem. I had difficulty telling them apart. They were both started on niacin, 500 mg per day; ascorbic acid, 500 mg per meal; folic acid, 5 mg per day; vitamin B12, 1 mg per week intramuscularly; phenylalanine, 500 mg per meal; and a mineral mixture. Blood zinc and copper levels were 42 mcg/dl and 134 mcg/dl for Doris, and 50 mcg/dl and 134 mcg/dl for Gladys.

October 4, 1984—Doris was better and knew what year it was. The nurse agreed her memory was better and her mind clearer. There was no change in Gladys. I added cod liver oil and zinc sulfate, 220 mg per day.

December 6, 1984—Doris was even better, more active, more responsible. Her nurse was very pleased with her response, but Gladys was no better. She had refused to take niacin because she flushed with it and had been off it for three weeks. Gladys was started on inositol hexaniacinate (Linodil).

January 2, 1985—Doris had also decided she did not like the flush and was promptly given Linodil instead. She had continued to improve. Her oral temperature was 36.2°C. She was now easily distinguishable from her sister because she looked healthier and was more cheerful. Gladys no longer objected to the pills as there was no flush and she too had started to improve. Her appetite was better and she slept better, but she was still tired. She felt cold all the time; this information was volunteered by Doris, who did not feel cold. Gladys's oral temperature was 35.6°C.

## FACTORS WHICH ACCELERATE SENILITY

### Nutritional and Psychosocial Stress

The relation between disease and accelerated aging is so obvious it does not excite any attention. There must be few who have not seen friends or relatives age almost visibly as they fight a serious disease. This is one type of stress. Another is psychosocial stress—prolonged exposure to severe stress. This was very obvious during the Great Depression 50 years ago, when many men and women aged very rapidly even when their food supply was adequate. Concern over jobs, loss of money, and forced relocation took their toll and accelerated aging. Society recognizes this in its stories and myths. Who has not heard of someone whose hair turned white overnight? My father, terribly concerned about our farm, loss of crops, no income, the need to educate his family, and our community, of which he was one of the leaders, turned gray—not overnight but within a few months.

Severe malnutrition and/or starvation also accelerate aging. Starving infants look aged. But the clearest experiment that demonstrates the accelerating effect of stress on senility occurred in World War II, when all three forms of stress were combined in the European concentration camps and the Japanese Far East prisoner-of-war camps. The severity of stress is best judged by the death rate in the same way the toxicity of a chemical is measured by the LD 50 test, that is, the amount of chemical given to a series of animals which will kill half of them in a given period of time. Selye defined the degree of stress on his rats as that factor or measure or operation that, applied to a population of rats, would kill 10 percent. The Romans considered that an engagement that killed 10 percent of the soldiers *decimated* them; also a measure of stress or mortality. The death rate in the concentration camps and in the Japanese prison camps was much higher, ranging from 25 to 50 percent over a period of 44 months.

I first became aware of this in 1960 when I met George Porteous. He was manager of a center for infirm and retired men and women. I wanted to study the effects of nicotinic acid on aging, and this center had a large number of men and women suitable for such a study. By then I knew nicotinic acid lowered cholesterol levels (which should inhibit development of atherosclerosis) and had antiaging properties. I had used it on about a dozen elderly people and had found it very effective (Hoffer 1962). But this had been a pilot or preliminary experiment and I hoped to be able to do a much larger controlled study. I discussed this with Mr. Porteous and he agreed this would be worthwhile. He agreed to cooperate, provided each person's physician was informed of the study and agreed we could provide his patient with niacin. He also agreed to discuss the vitamin with his guests, reassure them and let them know about the nicotinic acid flush. If any person or their doctor were concerned or negative, they were excluded.

About two weeks before the vitamin tablets were to be distributed, Mr. Porteous asked me whether he could start taking nicotinic acid, whether it would be harmful to him. I reassured him on the safety of the vitamin and wondered why he wanted to take it. He explained that it would make it easier for him to explain the vasodilation (flush) to his guests if he were able to experience the flush and how it had gradually subsided over a few weeks.

In the fall of 1960, Mr. Porteous came to my office at the University Hospital, Saskatoon. He said he needed about an hour to discuss a personal matter. Then he informed me he had been a member of the Canadian division which had been sent to Hong Kong in 1939, at the request of the British government, in order to bolster Hong Kong's defenses. A few weeks later his division was captured by the rapidly advancing Japanese. They spent the next 44 months in war camps. There they suffered cruel and inhuman punishment from their Japanese guards. They suffered severe starvation and malnutrition, resulting in diarrhea, beriberi, pellagra, scurvy and a number of other serious diseases. When they were released in 1944, nearly one-third of the Canadian soldiers were dead. The remainder had lost one-third of their body weight and were close to death. They were shipped home in hospital ships, given food, treated for old and recent injuries, and given vitamin supplements such as rice bran extracts —in 1944 few synthetic vitamins were available except from research laboratories. Their physicians assumed this treatment would restore their health, but it did not.

Mr. Porteous then described what had happened to him from 1944 to 1960. He had regained his healthy weight but not his health. He suffered from severe chronic arthritis with severe pain and limitation of movement. He could not lift his arms higher than his shoulders. Each morning the combined efforts of his wife and himself were needed to get him out of bed and mobile. He suffered severe heat and cold intolerance. Before the war he had been a physical education instructor for the Y.M.C.A. After the war he was also a psychiatric patient, and suffered from many fears and obsessions; for example, he could not sit in any room unless he was in a corner facing the door. He was very anxious and tense and suffered from insomnia. To the Department of Veterans' Affairs physicians he was a nuisance. He was given bottles containing hundreds of tablets of barbiturates to help him sleep and amphetamines to help him wake up.

In 1957, he was sent to a veterans' psychiatric hospital, where he was diagnosed as having anxiety neurosis. When he came home he was worse, because now the anxiety was reinforced by the burden of the diagnosis, superimposed on his chronic complaints, which had not improved. He now received out-patient psychotherapy from a kind, friendly psychiatrist who removed the pathology added to his burden by the previous psychiatric treatment. He was restored to his previous sick state.

Early in 1960, two weeks after he began to use nicotinic acid, he was normal. He was surprised and delighted but did not tell me until six months later when he was certain the recovery was sustained. He had expected no improvement, he had really wanted only to experience the flush so he could advise his guests better.

Between 1944 and 1960, his file with the Department of Veterans' Affairs had grown to 10 pounds and was kept in two cardboard boxes. From then on it almost ceased growing.

This aroused my interest in using large doses of nicotinic acid for treating patients with similar histories. I was able over the next 20 years to treat about two dozen ex-prisoners of war, concentration camp victims, and others who had suffered long periods of starvation and malnutrition in countries occupied by Germany during World War II. The response in over 90 percent was equally good. These patients had developed a permanent need for large doses of nicotinic acid, i.e., a vitamin B3 dependency.

The Department of Health and Welfare in Canada, sponsored a study to determine if the general chronic illness in Hong Kong prisoners of war was also found in soldiers who had not been treated so harshly. In this "brother's study," brothers were selected, one was a Hong Kong veteran, the other served in Europe. A careful comparison showed there was vast difference. The Hong Kong veterans suffered from a high death rate, arthritis, heart disease, premature blindness, and at least one-quarter of the survivors suffered from serious psychiatric and neurological diseases. The permanently destructive effect of the Japanese incarceration was recognized officially and every Hong Kong veteran was placed on a full disability pension. I have estimated, as have other physicians who have studied these veterans and similiar ones in the U.S.A. and elsewhere, that one year in such a camp aged each prisoner five years.

Mr. Porteous remained well until he died 17 years later while serving as lieutenant governor of Saskatchewan, except for a two-week period in 1962, when he went on a holiday for two weeks and forgot to take his nicotinic acid with him. When he returned, he had relapsed into his previous state.

I have concluded that very severe stress, including malnutrition and starvation, causes a vitamin B3 dependency; that a vitamin B3 dependency accelerates senility; and that the more severe the stress and the vitamin dependency, the more rapidly will senility be accelerated.

We will undoubtedly see huge numbers of prematurely senile individuals among the survivors of the prolonged famine and malnutrition in Africa.

A former deputy minister of health in Canada, an ex-prisoner of war as well, and a close personal friend of Mr. Porteous, when informed of Mr. Porteous's remarkable recovery, flippantly remarked that distilled water would have been as good (the placebo effect). Yet thousands of remarkably active "placebos" (amphetamines and barbiturates) and a stay in a psychiatric hospital with expert psychotherapy had been ineffective. This remarkably cynical retort condemned thousands of Canadian ex-prisoners of war to continued premature senility and concomitant ill health.

## WHAT IS SENILITY?

According to D. Harman (1956) senility and aging are due to the accumulation of free radicals. This free radical theory is probably the best theory we have today, for it encompasses many of the other theories and relationships that have been found. Free radicals are very reactive molecules, usually arising through oxidation by oxygen molecules, which rapidly combine with other molecules in their vicinity. Many substances go through a free radical phase before their final conversion to a more stable, less toxic compound. An example of free radical formation is the oxidation of tyrosine to melanin with a number of free radical molecules in between. Another example is the browning of apples or potatoes exposed to air.

The formation of free radicals from molecules requires an oxidizer (usually oxygen or one of its active forms). The reactions are accelerated by enzymes and by metal catalysts such as copper, iron and mercury, and the reaction is inhibited or decelerated by reducing substances, including vitamin C, vitamin E and others. But even more, the vitamins combine with and so destroy the free radicals already formed and so minimize the damage. Thus, one vitamin E molecule can protect a thousand large lipid molecules from free radical damage. If senility is a function of free radical formation, it follows that: (1) all factors that increase free radical formation will accelerate aging, while on the contrary (2) all factors which decrease free radical formation and minimize free radical damage will decelerate senility.

*Factors which Increase*
*Free Radical Formation*
*and Accelerate Senility*

1. The presence of compounds (substrates) that can be oxidized. All living tissue contains chemicals which are easily oxidized. The rapidity with which a freshly sliced potato or apple turns brown illustrates this. Sugar, fatty acids, some amino acids, and many other substances readily combine with oxygen. The problem faced by living tissue is to slow down and control the rate of oxidation so that it does not overheat or burn up in flames. Of particular interest are the substances derived from phenylalanine and tyrosine. They are all oxidized via a series of free radical intermediates to relatively stable colored pigments called melanins. Tyrosine is changed to dopamine, noradrenalin and adrenalin. From tyrosine onward each substance is changed to a pigmented indole that is highly reactive. In turn these are rapidly converted into polymers called melanin. This is a large complex molecule containing huge numbers of indoles linked to one another. There are two main types of melanin: neuromelanin, found in the pigmented areas of the brain; and melanin, found in skin. Neuromelanin, according to Barr, may be present in every neuron, but it accumulates mainly in the pigmented areas such as the red nucleus. Neuromelanin is derived from dopamine, noradrenalin and adrenalin. Melanins in skin are primarily derived from tyrosine. Heart muscle accumulates melanin from noradrenalin and adrenalin via noradrenochrome and adrenochrome. Beamish and colleagues (1981) have shown that adrenochrome is a factor in causation of fibrillation.

Barr, Saloma and Buchele (1983) do not believe melanin is merely a waste product of sympathomimetic amines (dopamine, noradrenalin and adrenalin). They have gathered evidence which shows that melanin plays a large number of important functions in the development and control of life processes. One of its functions is to capture free electrons and neutralize them. It is an electron trap. In the skin, for example, brown pigment is laid down to protect against the sun. The excited electrons formed by ultraviolet radiation are trapped and we are protected against sunburn.

Life has developed remarkably efficient ways of coping with chemical stress. It makes good sense not to waste the amines but to use them to construct a super molecule, melanin, which absorbs electrons, reduces free radical formation, acts as a scavenger depot and is an excretory organ. All undesirable molecules—organic or heavy metals, such as mercury that are trapped in skin or its appendage hair—in the melanin are carried out of the body as the outer dead hair and skin are shed. In the same way, deciduous trees rid themselves of unwanted chemical garbage by shedding their used leaves. Melanin accumulates in old cells as old age pigment of lipofuscin. Excessive oxidation of amines, because there is too much, or because it is oxidized too quickly, will cause the accumulation of too much neuromelanin, which by its sheer bulk will interfere with cell function. But unlike the skin, the brain has no way of shedding old cells too full of melanin. Is this a factor in aging and senility?

Other oxidizable substances, when present in excess, may play a role in aging. These include free sugars, unsaturated fatty acids and amino acids.

2. The presence of substances that increase oxidation. These are oxidases (enzymes which accelerate oxidation); metals such as copper, mercury, silver, gold, and oxygen; and oxygen-bearing substances such as hydrogen peroxide. The effects of these oxidants have been described by Levine and Kidd (1985).

I believe there is a clear relationship between senility and increased copper levels in blood. Over the past year I have measured blood copper and zinc in nearly 100 patients, ranging in age from 30 to 85. Patients age 40 or less have about 120 mcg of copper per 100 ml. I believe this is too high due to our soft water and copper pipes. I would prefer to see it around 100. After age 40 there is a steady increase, reaching about 160 at age 65 and over. This is not a universal metal phenomenon, since zinc levels showed no age increase, remaining about 100 for the entire group. Elderly senile patients tend to have more copper than nonsenile patients of the same age.

It is impossible to test the effect of oxygen pressure on human subjects developing senility. All other factors being equal, I would expect that people living at higher altitudes might live longer. The optimum altitude would be that which still provided enough oxygen required by our cells while minimizing the tendency to cause peroxidation. Is this at sea level, at 5,000 feet, or at 15,000 feet? Do mountain dewellers live longer than their genetically similar relatives, all receiving the same quality and quantity of food? The effect of oxygen could be tested on small mammals.

### Factors which Decrease Free Radical Formation and Decelerate Senility

1. The decrease in availability of oxidizable substances. The amount of amines released can be reduced by decreasing stress or by increasing our ability to cope with stress. People who are relaxed presumably release less adrenalin. People who avoid alcohol, smoking and free sugars (simple sugars such as glucose, fructose, sucrose and syrups) will have a smaller number of oxidizable molecules. They should live longer and be less senile. Thus stress management, counseling, and psychotherapy should enhance useful longevity.
2. The decrease in metals which increase oxidation. There are few scientists who disagree that we would be healthier with less mercury, copper, lead, cadmium and perhaps flouride in our bodies. We need some copper but most of us get too much in our water from copper plumbing. Fluoride excess reproduces almost all aspects of aging in very young people (Yiamouyiannis 1983).
3. The increase in antioxidants. These are organic molecules such as beta-carotene, vitamin A, vitamin C, vitamin E and metals such as zinc, which antagonize copper, manganese and selenium in small quantities, which in turn antagonize mercury, etc.

### Pathology of Excess Free Radical Formation

Free radicals are involved in formation of cancer, in our immune defense system, in schizophrenia, perhaps in other psychiatric conditions, and in senility. Free-radical theories of cancer and immune deficiencies have been adequately treated in the medical literature. The free radical theory of schizophrenia was first presented by Hoffer, Osmond and Smythies (1954) as the adrenochrome hypothesis. It is reviewed by Hoffer and Osmond (1967), and more recently by Hoffer (1981). Adrenochrome is now known to be a derivative of adrenalin in vivo and will be examined as a factor in schizophrenia when neuroscientists at last bethink themselves to investigate what happens to dopamine, noradrenalin and adrenalin in the body and especially in the brain.

Bjorksten (1960, 1963, 1964, 1968, 1971, 1976) showed the result of free radical formation when he developed the cross-linkage theory of aging. As usual, his theory was accepted very slowly but now seems to be generally accepted as a reasonable explanation of some of the aging changes. Free radicals avidly combine with molecules that have active electrons. By combining with them free radicals create new bonds or linkages. If two long molecules each combine with one free radical, each large molecule becomes attached to the other, losing some of its freedom or mobility. This is what happens when rubber is vulcanized. In its native state the rubber in the tree sap, or latex, is present in small spherical particles, similar to milk's small spherical particles. When rubber is vulcanized the long rubber molecules are pulled out of their spherical or coiled up state by atoms that combine with them. This sets the new polymer into a more rigid but elastic state, which develops the peculiar elasticity characteristic of rubber. If the rubber is overly oxidized the final product is very rigid, much like our modern car tires. Even milk can be polymerized to produce a more rigid, slightly elastic product known as cheese. The combination of long linear molecules to each other by means of reactive smaller molecules is known as cross-linkage and occurs in aging tissues. The best example is skin, which with age become harder, more inelastic and more brittle. This process is accelerated by excessive oxidation caused by overexposure to sun. It also occurs in bone, connective tissue and the internal organs. It must occur in most cells. Where movement or elasticity is essential, the effects of cross-linkages or excessive polymerization can be devastating. When arteries become rigid and can no longer pulsate in unison with the heart, they are much more apt to break. Our coronary and cerebral arteries develop this rigidity, which is called atherosclerosis or arteriosclerosis. The results are devastating. Since the brain is less vulnerable to mechanical friction or wear and tear than is the rest of body, it is likely that cross-linkages play a more important role in tissues outside the brain. Free radical formation probably plays an equal role in all tissues and organs.

## OPTIMUM BRAIN NEEDS

Ideally the brain requires those conditions that our bodies adapted to during our evolution. From a biochemical point of view, our brains require oxygen and removal of carbon dioxide. The brain must have enough water to prevent shrinkage but not enough to produce edema. It must be given all the essential nutrients, and metabolic waste chemicals must be removed. Given these requirements, and starting with a normal brain, the brain can carry on its function. The brain should be the last organ to go, for it is least subject to wear and tear due to motion, trauma and fluctuations in the environment.

To maintain these needs the body provides a service function. The respiratory apparatus gathers oxygen and releases carbon dioxide. The circulatory system carries gases and nutrients to the brain. The digestive system breaks down food into its nutrient components and the excretory system removes waste products. Thus all these systems must be maintained in optimum health. A failure or deficiency in any of these major systems will accelerate aging and senility.

Chemical reactions with or without catalysts (enzymes) are temperature dependent. Each increase in temperature of 10°C. doubles the rate of a reaction. Our body has a constant temperature of 37°C. (98.6°F.). Brain function depends upon maintaining this constant temperature.

Chemical reactions are inhibited, blocked or diverted by impurities. In the same way, strange chemicals (xenobiotics) interfere with normal reactions in the body. The body does have mechanisms for detoxifying and removing these substances, but this requires energy and diverts normal processes into scavenging activity. Is this why so many patients living on high-junk diets suffer so much chronic fatigue?

*Treatment*

1. Maintain the body's service functions. This means that all the physical or pathological problems need to be corrected or improved. Sometimes this is not possible. A patient suffering from severe emphysema will never be able to deliver enough air to his brain unless he lives on pure oxygen.

2. Water. On the average, each person needs six to eight glasses of fluid per day, not including alcoholic beverages, coffee or strong tea. If the body loses excessive fluid, more will be required.

3. Food. The food should be nutritious, aiming at food that is as good as what we have been adapted to during evolution. This food can be described as whole, alive (fresh), nontoxic, variable, indigenous, and scarce (see Hoffer 1983). *Whole* means we eat the entire edible portion of plants and animals. It means we increase our use of organ meats and do not fractionate our vegetables and cereals to inferior products such as white flour, sugar, etc. *Alive* means our food is fresh—whole grains, vegetables, fruit and nuts are alive. Meats should be derived from recently alive sources. Obviously this will be impossible for everyone most of the time or sometime, but it is a useful ideal. Frozen storage under proper sanitary conditions is next best, followed by canning and preserving without additives. When food is fresh one minimizes problems caused by spoilage, infestation and contamination. *Nontoxic* means food is free of additives that are xenobiotic and harmful to the body. *Variable* means we eat a wide variety of foods; we do not depend upon a few staples. Most people eat large quantities of a few staples such as wheat, milk products, sugar, beef and so on, with monotonous regularity. *Indigenous* refers to the foods raised and grown in climate areas similar to what we live in. Canadians should depend on foods grown and caught in Canada for example. This will provide the proper balance of omega-6 and omega-3 essential fatty acids (see Rudin 1981; and Horrobin 1977). Cold weather calls for increased amounts of omega-3 essential fatty acids. Adequate amounts are not found in exotic foods (foods grown in different climatic zones). *Scarce* refers to the fact that during our development surplus food was rare. Only after cropping and herding developed was it possible to accumulate and store surplus food. Only modern industrialized societies can suffer from too much food—a form of affluent malnutrition. We are better off to keep fit and to keep our weight at mean levels or perhaps at levels slightly below mean. When 25 percent of any population is obese they distort mean values upward. Insurance tables relating life expectancy to weight are a better guide. We should aim at these levels plus or minus 5 percent.

A few simple rules will yield a diet which approximates these six guides. The food should be junk-free, i.e., free of additives including sugar, unless it is known that these additives are safe. Examples of safe additives are nutrients, such as vitamins and minerals, added to food, as in enriched flour. This will improve the quality of these foods somewhat but will not restore their preprocessing levels. The second rule is to avoid or decrease the consumption of foods to which we are allergic or which are toxic for us.

4. Vitamins. Most of the vitamins should be available in our food, which must be looked upon as the major source of all supple-

ments. We use extra supplements only when the amount present in food is insufficient to meet the needs of the aging individual. These needs go up with age as our biochemical reactions become less efficient.

Aging individuals become more dependent on some vitamins, especially the B vitamins, as they age. This process is accelerated under severe prolonged stress, as occurred with ex-POWs in the Far East and elsewhere. Perhaps it is a general phenomenon for all nutrients. A number of good Ph.D. dissertations await imaginative nutrition students. They should trace the relationship between dependency and age for each nutrient and for combinations of nutrients.

*Vitamin A*. It is necessary to maintain health of body surfaces, skin and internal membranes. Either vitamin A or its precursor, beta-carotene, have anticancer properties. Aging and incidence of cancer are related. It is thus prudent to ensure enough vitamin A is available. The best sources are fish liver oils, synthetic vitamin A and leafy and green or other colorful vegetables. Ten to 50 thousand units of vitamin A are safe. The toxic dose of beta-carotene is unknown in humans. One should examine for specific evidence of deficiency, such as night blindness and skin problems.

*Thiamin*. Fewer people need extra thiamine (B1), since it became a food additive in our flour. However, a very large proportion of our population induce thiamin deficiency in themselves through overuse of alcohol and sugar. Elderly individuals with such a history may need 100 mg per day or more. Thiamin is safe and at these levels there are hardly any side effects. The amount present in modern antistress formulas or B vitamin complex preparations is generally adequate.

*Riboflavin*. I have not found patients with vitamin B2 dependency. Usually less than 100 mg per day will be adequate. These amounts, as with thiamine, are available in B complex preparations. This yellow fluorescent vitamin colors urine yellow. This provides a good test whether the tablets have been digested and the vitamins absorbed. There is, however, a population at risk for deficiency. Patients who are medicated with phenothiazines (tranquilizers) may develop a deficiency. These compounds have some chemical similarity to riboflavin and may cause a deficiency by competing for riboflavin receptor sites.

*Vitamin B3* (niacin and niacinamide). Vitamin B3 plays a particularly important role in preventing or treating senility. Niacin especially is valuable because of its pronounced beneficial effect on the vascular system. It lowers cholesterol, triglycerides, low-density lipoproteins, and elevates high-density lipoproteins. This decreases the development of atherosclerosis and decreases mortality from vascular accidents. Niacinamide has no effect on blood fats and lipids.

The optimum dose of niacin varies between 3 and 6 grams per day in three divided doses. This may be started suddenly or one may start with smaller doses and slowly increase them as the patient becomes adapted to and comfortable with the reaction. Very few will not have a pronounced vasodilation (flush) beginning in the forehead and extending downward. Most flush very little after a period of days or weeks. If the flush remains a problem, the niacin may need to be discontinued. It may then be replaced by a niacin derivative such as Linodil (inositol niacinate) if the beneficial vascular effect is essential, or by niacinamide if it is not. Or the flush may be moderated by using aspirin, one tablet before each dose of niacin for a few days, or by using antihistamines. Tranquilizers decrease the intensity of the flush. Very few people flush with niacinamide.

Vitamin B3 is relatively safe. It is certainly safer than any xenobiotic such as tranquilizers, etc. The proof is present in any medical compendium describing drugs and vitamins; simply count the number of lines that describe side effects, toxicities and contraindications and compare this with the number of lines that describe uses or indications. The most important toxicity is jaundice, which affects about one in 2,000. It is an obstructive jaundice which clears when the vitamin is discontinued. Other side effects are dose related and disappear as the dose is lowered (see Hoffer 1962, 1969). After the optimum therapeutic dose is established it is continued forever, or until evidence becomes clear that more or less is needed.

I have found vitamin B3 very effective in restoring memory, in improving energy, in lessening the need for sleep, and in increasing alertness. Dr. W. Kaufman (1943, 1949) found it particularly helpful in treating arthritis. This is one of the common afflictions in the malnourished elderly or those who require extra amounts due to dependency. Vitamin B3 also tends to restore skin elasticity, i.e., it may be an inhibitor of cross-linkage formation.

For many years I have been convinced that niacin will prolong useful longevity by witnessing what it has done for my patients and for elderly members of my family. It was particularly satisfying to have this confirmed by a very large, rigorously controlled clincal experiment carried out in the U.S.A. between 1966 and 1983 (Coronary Drug Project Research Group 1975). Canner (1985) found that only the group of patients given niacin experienced a decrease in mortality (11 percent) and an increase in longevity (two years), compared to placebo and Clofibrate. Since then the

Consensus Conference (1985) and the National Institutes of Health (1985) have recommended that attempts should be made to lower elevated cholesterol levels by diet, and when this is not successful to use agents such as niacin to do so. They recommend Clofibrate not be used.

*Pyridoxine.* This vitamin (B6) is intimately related to B3. A deficiency of B6 decreases formation of vitamin B3 from tryptophan and may cause pellagra. On the other hand, too much pyridoxine may also create a deficiency of vitamin B3. Dr. M. Coleman et al. (1985) reported that doses of B6 greater than 2,000 mg per day caused neurological changes in a small number of people. The proportion among such a high dose who develop these changes is not known. Dr. Coleman reported that these symptoms were due to an induced deficiency of vitamin B3. This will explain why orthomolecular physicians have not seen any such side effects; they also usually use vitmain B3 as a supplement. Also, we seldom use more than 2,000 mg per day of B6. The usual dose is under 1,000 mg per day. Children may need extra magnesium with the B6 to prevent the development of irritability or restlessness.

*Pantothenic Acid.* Roger Williams found that pantothenic acid, another B vitamin, increased longevity in animals. It is likely it is also beneficial for humans. It is one of the safest vitamins. The usual dose is under 1,000 mg per day. There is no data relating pantothenic acid to senility.

*Folic acid and B12.* Most surveys have found that aged populations have lower blood levels of these two companion B vitamins than do normal people. These two compounds are so potent that very little is required, but this slight amount may make the difference between disease and recovery. A few elderly people with an intention hand tremor—a tremor occuring when a definite movement is attempted—find this is gone within a week of taking folic acid, 5 mg per day. One patient could not sign her name because of severe tremor. One week after starting on folic acid she was normal.

Vitamin B12 may be given orally or by injection. The usual parenteral dose is 1 mg. It may be given daily or less often, depending upon the response. The best form is hydroxycobalamin, as this is the natural form in the body, making up about 70 percent of all the vitamin in the body. Cyanocobalamin, the form usually used, is slightly more toxic. B12 may be needed even though blood levels are within a normal range. The therapeutic test is still the best indicator. The usual response is an improvement in feeling of well-being, more energy, and less fatigue.

*Vitamin E.* Any nutrient that promotes healing, reverses vascular pathology, especially intermittent claudication, and improves cardiac efficiency ought to be a useful antiaging substance. For just by promoting these healing functions it must be useful for prolonging useful longevity. It is a powerful fat-soluble antioxidant and should protect against excessive oxidation and free radical formation.

*Vitamin D3.* This is essential for maintaining calcium metabolism. It is also essential in providing balance with magnesium and aluminum. There is growing evidence that aluminum absorption is facilitated by a calcium deficiency and is deposited as aluminum silicate in the neurofibrillary tangles and plaques of Alzheimer's disease. It is prudent to add vitamin D3 as fish liver oils or in synthetic form.

5. Minerals. All essential minerals are needed

from conception to death. Aging individuals do not absorb minerals as well and should be given mineral supplements. A few have particular importance. These are support or structural elements, such as calcium and magnesium, and antioxidant elements, such as zinc, manganese and selenium.

*Calcium and Magnesium. Osteoporosis.* Osteoporosis is much more common in women past menopause. Most physicians accept the relationship between bone repair and calcium metabolism. This involves hormones that control bone loss and repair and vitamin D3. For optimum calcium metabolism these hormones and vitamins are essential, plus 1 to 1.5 grams per day calcium intake. Men and premenopausal women need around 1 gram, and post menopausal women from 1.5 to 2 grams. If we assume the average diet contains 500 mg, the rest should be taken as supplements. Most physicians do not realize that calcium and magnesium are intimately related. Lack of magnesium can cause calcium deposits in muscles and in kidneys. This is one reason for kidney stones and is probably the reason there has been an increase in frequency of kidney stones with the increasing use of modern foods. Kidney stones are not caused by ascorbic acid (Hoffer 1985). The National Academy of Sciences in the U.S.A. recommends that the average adult ingest 800 to 1,200 mg per day of calcium. They also recommend we ingest about 350 to 450 mg per day of magnesium, i.e., they recommend a ratio of about 2 to 1, calcium to magnesium. Keen gardeners who realize how important magnesium is for the plants in their garden should have the same interest in their own health. Green vegetables contain magnesium (in cholorphyll). This may be one reason greens have anticancer properties, i.e., because of their magnesium content.

A good source of both calcium and magnesium is dolomite. An American report that commercial dolomite contained too much lead made many people fearful. It is important that dolomite be lead-free, as it is in Canada, where the Health Protection Branch monitors this carefully.

*Zinc, Manganese and Selenium.* Zinc is an essential element which is now in short supply; for a complete discussion see Pfeiffer (1975). When zinc levels are too low, excessive copper may accumulate. This may cause confusion in the elderly. Every aging person should be examined for evidence of zinc deficiency. Look for signs such as skin changes (stria), brittle nails with white spots, depigmented brittle hair, joint pain, slow wound healing, and loss of taste and smell. An average person requires 15 mg of zinc (as elemental zinc) per day. Several preparations are available which will supply 15 mg and more per tablet. Each person will have to find that preparation they can tolerate.

Manganese is deficient in our diet for the same reasons other trace elements are deficient. It is synergistic with zinc. We need about 4 mg per day. As it is safe, more can be taken to make sure we have enough. Pfeiffer (1975) recommends that both zinc and manganese be taken. Anywhere from 5 to 30 mg per day may be needed.

Selenium is another water-soluble essential mineral. We need about 200 mcg per day. Aging individuals would do well to take this amount. For special conditions such as cancer or premature aging, 200 to 400 mcg are used as supplements. Selenium has good antioxidant properties and potentiates the effect of vitamin E.

## TOXIC METALS AND AGING

Toxic elements such as aluminum, mercury, copper, fluoride, cadmium and lead produce symptoms also found in aging individuals. Aluminum has been associated with Alzheimer's disease. In my series of patients, blood copper levels increased with age. I think it is likely that aging is associated with an accumulation of all toxic metals and elements that are excreted with difficulty. The body adapted to an environment that was relatively free of toxic elements, which were all buried deep in the earth or present at the bottom of our oceans. Only after man discovered how to extract metals and to use them did we begin to bring to the surface large amounts of a multitude of heavy metals that are dumped into our air, water and soil. Over the past 600 years there has been a gradual accumulation of lead in our soils. Today our environment is rich in all these metals. If gold and platinum were as cheap as lead and had widespread industrial use, we would find these elements dispersed in our environment as well.

We have placed a new problem on our bodies. How can we eliminate these metals fast enough so they will not accumulate? Some is excreted in urine, a lot is bound to fiber in our feces (if we eat fiber), and some is deposited in our skin and hair. As skin and hair are shed, these minerals are removed from the body. A person with a lot of hair is better able to eliminate these metals. Are bald-headed men therefore more vulnerable to aging than their hairy colleagues? Is this one reason women live longer? Do men with heavy beards remain healthier?

I am convinced that one should examine the relationship between all toxic elements and aging. These toxic elements are fluoride, aluminum, lead, mercury, iron, copper, cadmium, and any mineral which tends to accumulate. Hair analyses will be helpful, as will blood analyses, for copper and zinc.

Any treatment that removes these heavy metals is called chelation treatment. The toxic elements are bound to larger molecules and thus solubilized and swept out of the body. This is how nature does it, using vitamin C, fiber in the gut and some amino acids. Physicians use vitamin C in large doses and also chemicals that have similar properties. Penicillamine is used to remove excess copper from patients with Wilson's disease. It may produce a vitamin B6 deficiency. Ethylenediaminotetraacetic acid (EDTA) has similar properties and is safer. It is used in an intravenous solution in a controversial treatment called chelation therapy. There are two opposing views. One, held by physicians who use it, is favorable; these physicians were all persuaded to use it by learning of favorable responses and, once they began, were convinced by the responses they saw. They have retained this conviction in spite of massive harassment by the established medical associations. The opposite point of view is held by physicians who have never used it and are unfamiliar with the literature. I have seen patients who have received chelation and am persuaded that it is a useful treatment.

In March 1985, I interviewed an elderly man one month after he had received his last of 20 chelation treatments. He had had Alzheimer's disease. According to his wife he had deteriorated to such a degree he could no longer speak intelligently, was disoriented in space, and could not be left alone in a city for even a few seconds, as he wandered away and became lost. An avid golfer who had played on many of the world's golf courses, his handicap had gone up from seven to 27. He was still able to play.

After 10 treatments he was no longer disoriented in space. About this time he seemed to awaken from a sleep. I asked him what was his memory of the condition he had been in. He replied he could not remember what it was like but he recalled that sometime during the last 10 treatments he had awakened. When I saw him he spoke well, tended to be garrulous, but showed no evidence of any Alzheimer's speech disorder. He believed he was poor but his wife assured me they were not. His golf handicap decreased to seven. Here is an objective measure of the value of chelation. I was very impressed. I hope any critic will not immediately demand a double-blind controlled experiment until he is prepared to direct me to the literature that shows the spontaneous recovery rate is more than 0 percent. One recovery in a disease where there have been none before is surely very significant. What we must know is what proportion of Alzheimer's sufferers will respond; is this related to metal intoxication, and, if it is, which element is most significant?

Chelation physicians are practicing physicians, and they do not have the time or money with which to conduct clinical studies. The research institutes are too busy with their own interests. (McDonagh, Rudolph and Cheraskin 1985).

*Resume of Treatment for Accelerated Aging*
1. Correct all physical abnormalities.
2. Maintain fluid balance, 6 to 8 glasses per day.
3. Orthomolecular diet; junk-free, high fiber.
4. Vitamins (one or more):

> Vitamin A about 25,000 IU/day;
> Thiamin—25 to 100 mg/day;
> Niacin—up to 3 grams per day, more if cholesterol very high;
> Pyridoxine—100 to 250 mg/day;
> Pantothenic acid—250 to 500 mg/day;
> Folic acid—5 mg/day;
> Vitamin B12—up to 1 mg parenterally per day;
> Vitamin E—400 to 800 IU/day;
> Vitamin D3—400 to 800 IU/day.

5. Minerals:

> Calcium—1,000 to 1,500 mg/day;
> Magnesium—500 to 750 mg/day;
> Zinc—15 to 100 mg/day;
> Manganese—4 to 30 mg/day;
> Selenium—200 to 600 mcg/day.

6. Chelation therapy.
7. Treat any psychiatric disease specifically.
8. Psychosocial.
9. Speculation.

Evidence is accumulating which links mental changes in aging people to body temperature. The brain is a highly complex, high-energy organ that works best in a constant environment, including temperature. When the brain's temperature is too high one develops delirium; at temperatures of 104°F. and over this is not uncommon. When the temperature is too low the body sinks into a coma. Every chemical reaction is controlled by temperature. Each 10-degree change in Centigrade temperature doubles the rate of reaction. An increase from 36.8° C. to 46.8° C. would double the rate of reaction and kill the patient. A decrease from 36.8°C to 26.8°C. would halve the rate of reaction and lead to death unless special hypothermia conditions were met. Fever is not common but mild hypothermia is.

If brain temperature decreases to 35°C. there will be an appreciable decrease in rates of reaction. Experiments have shown that these minor variations have an appreciable effect on cerebral function. I have found that a significant number of seniles have three-minute oral temperatures below 35°C.

Cerebral hypothermia (brain hypothermia) is common with subclinical hypothyroidism (see Barnes and Galton 1976). The temperature is restored by using dessicated thyroid gland, which is more effective than pure thyroid hormones. Yet modern doctors appear to know nothing about this dried preparation, which has been used for so many decades. Elderly patients should be given thyroid if their temperature is low. It is also a good idea for elderly individuals not to be exposed to low external temperatures and, if they are, to be sure they keep their heads covered, especially if they are bald. An enormous amount of heat is lost from the head.

## EPILEPSY

Nicotinic acid and nicotinamide have anticonvulsant properties, but they are not good enough to be used as the sole anticonvulsant. They potentiate the anticonvulsant action of standard anticonvulsants. I have given them to several epileptics who were not under good control with the usual medications; to achieve good control they needed so much anticonvulsant medication that they were drowsy and sluggish and could not function normally. By adding vitamin B3, 1 gram t.i.d., it was possible to obtain better control with half the dose of anticonvulsant. They were then able to work and to function in the community (Hoffer 1962).

The anticonvulsant dose is not reduced until the patient has been on nicotinic acid (or nicotinamide) for several months. Then the dose of anticonvulsant is slowly reduced while monitoring carefully for frequency of *grand mal* or *petit mal* seizures and degree of sedation. In my book, *Niacin Therapy in Psychiatry*, (1962), I described how vitamin B3 potentiated effects of the anticonvulsant. It also potentiates the effects of tranquilizers. I also reviewed the literature that showed that vitamin B3 by itself had anticonvulsant properties. This work has been established by additional work. Bourgeois, Dodson and Ferendelli (1983) reported on the antiepileptic activity of niacinamide. They summarized their work as follows:

> Summary: Nicotinamide is a ligand of the benzodiazepine receptor and has been reported to have anticonvulsant activity. In addition, our previous clinical experience has raised the possibility that it may also potentiate the action of barbiturates. Therefore, we have examined the anticonvulsant activity and neurotoxicity of nicotinamide alone and in combination with phenobarbital in mice. Nicotinamide had its maximal anticonvulsant effect 15 min. and its maximum sedative effect 45 min. after intraperitoneal injection. At 15 min. the

median effective dose was 586.5 mg/kg against bicuculline and 2,019 mg/kg against pentylenetetrazol. Nicotinamide was ineffective against maximal electroshock. It had a sedative effect, with a median toxic dose of 874.8 mg/kg by the Rotorod Toxicity Test at 45 min. At doses that were ineffective by themselves (0.01 effective dose) nicotinamide potentiated the anticonvulsant activity of phenobarbital against bicuculline and pentylenetetrazol, but the toxicity was not potentiated and therefore the therapeutic index of phenobarbital was improved by nicotinamide. These results suggest that nicotinamide may be useful as a therapeutic adjunct for the treatment of epilepsy with phenobarbital or primidone.

It is important to note that nicotinamide improved the therapeutic index of anticonvulsants, meaning the therapeutic effect was enhanced but the toxicity was not. No other anticonvulsants have been shown to do so.

## INFANTILE SPASMS (HYPSARRHYTHMIA)

Infantile spasm is a rare, serious form of epilepsy in infants, usually coming on in the first year of life, but it may occur up to three years of age. The prognosis is grave. The spasms disappear between ages three to five to be replaced by other forms of generalized seizures; 90 percent of victims become mentally retarded.

The original treatment with ACTH was developed by F. Gibbs. Parents of his infant patients were so impressed with the results they organized a research foundation to sponsor further research.

Corticosteroids are now used, using 2 mg per kg for eight to 10 weeks, and then slowly decreasing the dose. ACTH is also used. A few infants have responded to pyridoxine.

The seizures start with sudden flexion of the arms, forward flexion of the trunk and extension of the legs. The episode lasts a few seconds and may occur frequently.

On November 9, 1983, I saw an infant born October 13, 1982, who had been diagnosed by her family physician and neurologist as suffering from infantile spasms.

The EEG was normal at birth but abnormal at five months of age. She was flaccid, moved very little, and slept most of the time. Two months later the diagnosis was established. She suffered recurrent continuous spasms, except when she was nursing. She was started on ACTH and Prednisone, receiving 30 mg per day of the latter and heavy doses of ACTH. After she was immunized at three months of age and again at six months, she was much worse for the following month. When I saw her, her EEG was abnormal and she manifested her seizures by frequent eyeblinks. The Prednisone dose was down to 5 mg per day. She had had one *grand mal* seizure during the previous stay in the hospital.

She slept all day except when eating, could move her arms and legs, but had stopped rolling around. She babbled but knew no words. She was also getting cranial massage from a chiropractor.

At this time I started her on a multivitamin preparation with minerals available from Kirkman laboratories, P.O. Box 3929, Portland, Oregon, 97208-3929. She was to be given one-quarter teaspoon per day containing:

Vitamin A—1,000 IU
Vitamin C—125 mg
Vitamin B1—6 mg
Vitamin B2—6 mg
Vitamin B6—50 mg
Niacinamide—8 mg
Niacin—6 mg
Pantothenic acid—20 mg
Lecithin—100 mg
1 glutamic acid—50 mg
Vitamin E—61 IU
Folic acid—70 mcg
Biotin—16 mcg
Calcium—40 mg
Magnesium—40 mg

Zinc—2 mg
Manganese—2 mg
Inositol—16 mg
PABA—16 mg
Molybdenum—12 mcg
I added dimethyl glycine—12.5 mg three times per day to her program

On December 22, when I next saw this baby, she had had flu for two weeks. Until then she had shown significant improvement, was vocalizing more and had started to gain weight. By February 8, 1984, she was able to eat much better, vocalized much more, had learned one word, "dada," and had been free of all seizures since December 22. She had also received acupuncture treatment on three successive days from a physician acupuncturist early in February.

I used the multinutrient preparation as she was so malnourished, but I did not expect this would have influence on the spasms. The main anticonvulsant was dimethyl glycine (DMG).

Roach and Carlin (1982) reported that DMG reduced the frequency of seizures from 17 *grand mal* per week to one to two per week, within a few days, when the usual anticonvulsant medication had had no effect. Several of my patients have shown a similar beneficial response. However, in a further report, Roach and Gibson (1983) tried DMG again on five epileptic patients refractory to treatment. Using 270 mg in three daily doses they found no significant improvement in this very sick group.

DMG (known as vitamin B15 or pangamate) is available in health food stores and is considered by most physicians to be a worthless and even dangerous preparation. It has not been established to be a vitamin. Nevertheless, it has been used on a large scale by many people who believe they have been helped, and it is used therapeutically by many physicians in other countries.

Several years ago, Dr. Allan Cott told me

that DMG had accelerated speech development in a few mute children. This was my experience as well. I am convinced it can do so, but there has been no explanation for this activity. The newly discovered anticonvulsant properties of DMG provide a possible explanation.

The infant I treated was not developing speech. In fact, motor development was regressing. Also, she was so passive and indifferent it is unlikely she could have interacted enough with her parents. Speech cannot develop without this interaction. The continuous seizures would account for this inattention and difficulty in learning. How could anyone with continuous seizures learn anything? Once the seizures ceased she was able to start learning.

It is possible children who are mute, who do not learn to speak, suffer from subclinical seizures that are not visible. Not having clinical seizures it would be unlikely they would have EEG studies. Even if they had these studies, it is possible to have deep seizure activity, not apparent with surface electrodes. Many years ago I observed Dr. R. Heath with schizophrenic patients who had deep electrodes implanted. These deep areas suffered an electrical storm, whereas on the surface electrodes did not indicate any EEG abnormality.

If these infants do have subclinical epilepsy, we would have an explanation for DMG's ability to restore speech, but therapy must be started while the brain is still plastic and able to learn speech.

Another child similarly unable to walk or speak is also showing a significant response. This girl was born January 1979 and breastfed until age 14 months. She was beginning to walk and speak. A severe cold terminated nursing and she was started on milk and solid food. Two months later she began to deteriorate: her walking deteriorated, speech stopped, and toilet training was lost. At two years the only physical abnormality was frontal arrhythmia. Infantile autism was suspected. By that time she was completely withdrawn.

In desperation her mother tried a three-month fruit diet with no improvement. Later she was given Deaner and a tranquilizer, which made her dopey, and she developed tardive dyskinesia. Her mother discontinued this contrary to the neurologist's advice and started her on small doses of vitamins. Two and a half months before I saw her an osteopath started cranial manipulation. Following this there was some improvement for the first time.

When I saw her in April 1983, she could say one word, "mama," was very restless, ground her teeth continually, and slept 12 hours per day. She liked being held by her mother, enjoyed affection, and could stand near a table but could not walk alone.

I placed her on a sugar- and milk-free diet plus nicotinamide, 500 mg after meals; ascorbic acid, 500 mg after meals; pyridoxine, 250 mg once a day; halibut liver oil, 3 capsules per day; and DMG, 50 mg after each meal.

Six weeks later she was more active and responsive and vocalized more. After six months she was babbling more and was better socially. She was more attentive, was able to toss and turn, and learned more quickly. I increased DMG to 300 mg per day and replaced the niacinamide with an equal quantity of inositol niacinate. I also started her on a multivitamin-multimineral preparation called Nu Thera, available from Kirkman Laboratories. After eight months she was able to walk a little, hanging onto her mother's hand.

When last seen, 11 months after starting on my program, she was improved in every area. She was more attentive, cried appropriately to get attention, did not grind her teeth, stood well and would walk alone holding onto an object if she did not realize her mother was no longer holding her other hand. Her appetite was better. Her mother was much healthier, no longer looking haggard and stressed, and she felt more optimistic.

This child has never had any convulsions and therefore does not have epilepsy. However, the EEG abnormality showed she was having some kind of electrical storm in her frontal area. Were these the sensory equivalents of infantile spasms, and is this why she is responding to treatment at last? Niacin has anticonvulsant properties. It is impossible to decide which product, inositol niacinate or DMG, is the major anticonvulsant here, if in fact she had a sensory equivalent to epilepsy. I suspect it is the DMG but will know once she has stabilized and I can begin to withdraw one.

One case of infantile spasms proves that out of a general class of patients with infantile spasms one began to improve. I doubt anyone will suggest this 12-month-old infant responded because of her faith in me or my medication, nor has anyone shown that placebo is an effective treatment for infantile spasms. It is highly unlikely that I have seen the only case which will respond, when in fact this is the only case I have ever seen.

It is essential that physicians who have infants with spasms try this treatment on their patients. In this way we can determine how many similar infants can be helped.

DMG is a normal body constituent formed in the metabolism of homocysteine to methionine. Glycine may be involved in seizures. Is DMG in fact a natural anticonvulsant nutrient? Since it can be made in the body it does not qualify for the term "vitamin," (vitamin B3, vitamin D3 and vitamin A are made in the body, but they were classed as vitamins before this was known).

Infantile spasms may be caused by interfering with brain metabolism. Coleman, Sobels, Bhagavan, Coursin, Marquardt, Guay and Hunt (1985) reported that hydroxytryptophan given to a population of children with Down's syndrome caused infantile spasms in 14 percent of that group. This compound elevated serotonin levels. Perhaps DMG helps correct this type of abnormality.

## POST-STROKE AND POST-TRAUMATIC

Brain tissue does not regenerate once it has been destroyed, but the brain itself has remarkable recuperative powers and can recover some function, perhaps by switching lost function into different areas. Whatever the mechanism, I have seen patients following brain damage from stroke or trauma who had stabilized and began to show significant improvement when started on an orthomolecular program. This improvement was appreciated by the patients who had not expected any. One case was a woman around 60 who had prided herself on her good memory. It was helpful to her in her study of English literature. I saw her about a year after she had a stroke. She was then anxious, frustrated and depressed because her memory was no longer reliable and she was able to compare it with what it had been like before her stroke.

After six months on nicotinic acid, 3 grams per day, and ascorbic acid, 3 grams per day, her memory was so much better she was able to live with the residual defect without anxiety and depression. When I first saw her she told me her doctor had advised her she would have to live with her defect and get used to it. She added she would sooner die.

Another case seen recently was D. B., age 38. Two and a half years before I saw him he was struck on the head by a 1,000-pound object. He was in a coma for several days and in a hospital several months. Six months later he could read at a third grade level. Before his accident he had been an avid reader and had been in the ninetieth percentile level for intelligence. Six months after he was in the thirtieth percentile.

By the time I saw him he had improved substantially but he had started to follow a program involving a number of vitamins in large quantities. An EEG did not reveal brain damage. His main complaints were that he had not regained his normal reading skills and could not concentrate because of severe fatigue and headaches. He described himself as thinking like an old person.

He was advised to take niacin, 1 gram three times a day; ascorbic acid, the same dose; vitamin E, 800 IU; and selenium, 200 mg per day. One had a half years later he was much improved. He had improved his diet by eliminating milk and decreasing coffee. It was much easier for him to read and concentrate but he still suffered from pain, which was controlled by Motrin three to four times per day.

For any brain-injured patient one should try niacin and ascorbic acid as a basic program, combined with the orthomolecular diet. Other nutrients will be needed, depending on the history and other symptoms and signs.

## WERNICKE-KORSAKOFF SYNDROME

A small proportion of alcoholics develop Wernicke-Korsakoff syndrome after many years of intense alcoholism. The neurological component, Wernicke's disease, was first described in 1881 by Dr. Carl Wernicke. Two of the first three patients were chronic alcoholics. Six years later Dr. S. S. Korsakoff described the psychiatric component of this syndrome, a unique organic psychosis with amnesia, delirium, confabulation, anxiety, fear, and depression. Confabulation is the term applied to the patients' habit of answering questions with totally inappropriate replies, as if they have a compulsion to answer even when they do not know the correct answer.

For many years both conditions were looked upon as separate diseases, but gradually it became clear they were different aspects of the same organic disease, usually alcoholism. The evidence is outlined by Victor, Adams and Collins (1971). Wernicke's disease is the neurological component due to identifiable pathological anatomical changes in the brain. Korsakoff's syndrome is the psychiatric component arising from these changes and from vitamin deficiency.

Early investigators believed inflammatory and toxic causes were at work, but a nutritional cause was suggested by Dr. H. T. Pershing (1892) before the word *vitamin* had been coined. He suggested the disease was due to a toxic substance arising from perverted nutrition. His treatment was frequent and systematic feeding. Today, thiamine deficiency is believed to be the main problem; Wernicke-Korsakoff syndrome is therefore a form of beriberi induced, usually, by chronic alcoholism. Vitamin B3, nicotinic acid or nicotinamide, should be investigated as a factor. Because of the pronounced effect of vitamin B3 deficiency (pellagra) on memory, it is probable the amnesia is due to a double deficiency of thiamine and vitamin B3. Folic acid may also be involved, since 40 percent of all patients have anemia of the folic-acid type.

Wernicke-Korsakoff syndrome usually comes on after many years of drinking combined with grossly bizarre nutrition. It usually comes on after age 20; peak incidence for men is between ages 50 to 59, for women about 10 years earlier. However, with alcoholism developing earlier, the peak incidence may come sooner. In the Victor et al. series (1971) about 1 percent of the alcoholics had the syndrome, and in nearly every case the patient had suffered severe malnutrition for many months or years. They rarely ate, some going months without a meal.

But alcoholism is not the only cause. Ebels (1978) examined 29 patients with Wernicke-Korsakoff syndrome, none of whom were alcoholic. Five were gynecological patients; 13 suffered from gastrointestinal disorders such as ulcers, pancreatitis and cancer; five had cancer in other areas; and six suffered from anorexia nervosa, severe self-neglect and some were on hemodialysis.

The early symptoms were usually confusion, memory loss, staggering gait, and visual changes such as staring, a blank look or crossed eyes. Patients were apathetic, disoriented, and had marked memory problems including confabulation.

Wernicke-Korsakoff is a preterminal condition with a high death rate. Only about one-fifth in Victor et al.'s (1971) series recovered, requiring up to two years of treatment. Other common complications have been delirium tremens and rum fits.

Thiamine plus a nutritious diet with other B vitamin supplements is the treatment. The neurological symptoms, the Wernicke portion, clear much more rapidly than the Korsakoff symptoms. Even with thiamine, memory may clear very slowly. Victor et al. recommended thiamine, 50 mg per day intramuscularly, and 50 mg by mouth.

It is not surprising that these patients suffer from an induced thiamine dependency, as this vitamin is essential for the metabolism of sugars. It is converted into an enzyme component called cocarboxylase. The conversion of glucose and also alcohol into energy requires it. Giving some alcoholics intravenous infusions of glucose without vitamins in the fluid has precipitated Wernicke-Korsakoff syndrome; Victor et al, caution against this practice. I would add that any intravenous infusion of glucose should contain the water-soluble vitamins B Complex, and vitamin C. The longer the patient must remain on intravenous fluids, the more important this is.

It is likely that any nutritional regime that increases the need for thiamine or any nutrient without any compensating increase in the quantity of the essential nutrients will eventually lead to a variety of deficiencies which, if long continued, will in turn lead to nutrient dependencies. Wernicke-Korsakoff is a classical example of very severe malnutrition and is rare. However, large segments of our population suffer from less severe forms of malnutrition. This is most apt to be found in that segment of our population that lives on the Saccharine Disease-producing diet, i.e., a diet high in sugar, white flour and other junk foods, and low in fiber (Cleave et al. 1969).

Beginning in 1952, Dr. Humphrey Osmond and I began to treat the less severe forms of alcoholism, such as delirium tremens, with large doses of niacin and ascorbic acid, both orally and intravenously (Hoffer 1962). Even delirium tremens untreated can have up to a 20 percent mortality rate. With these two vitamins alone we saw very rapid recoveries with no deaths. Patients were not given thiamine, but they were fed good food, which must have provided enough to prevent the Wernicke-Korsakoff syndrome. Reasoning from this clinical response and from the observation that many Wernicke-Korsakoff patients have had DTs, this suggests that the proper treatment for this syndrome should include a good, junk-free diet, thiamine, 100 mg per day intramuscularly as well as 500 mg by mouth after each meal, combined with niacin, 3 to 10 grams per day. Magnesium and zinc should also be provided. This is an orthomolecular program using more thiamine than Victor et al. (1971) recommended, but then they were totally unfamiliar with orthomolecular theory and practice.

## TARDIVE DYSKINESIA

Both phenothiazines and butyrophenones, classes of tranquilizers, cause a large number of serious side effects and toxic reactions. Of these, one of the more serious is tardive dyskinesia. For a long time psychiatrists avoided recognition of this condition. They did not find it in many patients or tended to underrate its seriousness, but the accumulation of cases has forced psychiatry to look at the issue at last. Frank J. Ayd, (1977) editor of *The Medical-Moral Newsletter*, suggests that the continued use of tranquilizers is justified if mild symptoms of tardive dyskinesia are present, because the good (control of symptoms) outweighs the side effects. But he cautions that physicians are ethically and legally bound to obtain informed consent from the patient, or from the family if the patient is too ill, before undertaking therapy that is to last for more than three months. Failure to do so may be the basis of malpractice liability, even

if the drug was prescribed for valid reasons, according to Ayd (1977).

But what of severe tardive dyskinesia, which may be found in up to 50 percent of patients over the age of 60 who have been treated with these drugs over three years? In many it comes on much sooner. The prominent symptoms are rigidity, akathisia and other muscular movements. Disturbed muscular movements are the main problem; if these are rapid it is called chorea, if they are slow, athetosis. If prolonged spasms occur, it is a dystonia. Choreiform movements are very common. One patient who recently came under my care had been injecting tranquilizer for several years. He required one injection each week to control his psychotic behavior. Nearly every voluntary muscle in his body quivered and moved, and his whole body quivered and shook. Only when he slept could he rest. Not surprisingly, he was very tired.

Tardive dyskinesia does not respond to anticholinergic drugs which are used to protect patients from Parkinsonian-like effects of tranquilizers. There is no generally acceptable treatment and it is considered irreversible for a large proportion of patients.

By the middle of 1973 over 2,000 cases of permanent central nervous system damage and tardive dyskinesia had been recorded in the medical literature. Since most physicians do not publish this kind of data, a much larger number are affected. The FDA recommends that the tranquilizers be used as sparingly as possible and that they be stopped at the first sign of abnormal movement of the muscles, the tongue, the lips or any other part of the body. The FDA bulletin recognized the untreatable and irreversible nature of the disease. Anti-Parkinsonian drugs often make the condition worse.

Unfortunately, many psychiatrists and nurses are unfamiliar with the clinical expression of tardive dyskinesia, and when it is present they assume the movement is neurotic or psychotic in origin. They tend to blame the patient, or the underlying conflict, or they increase the amount of tranquilizer.

Tranquilizers are essential for the treatment of many schizophrenic patients, even if they do not cure patients or do no more than dampen down the more troublesome symptoms. It has been shown very clearly that patients treated with tranquilizers only do not have a better outcome than patients treated before tranquilizers were developed. What tranquilizers do make possible is to maintain patients outside of hospitals who otherwise would have to be kept inside these institutions. It is possible that these hospitals would revert back to the level of care we found so depressing and inadequate in 1950. Orthomolecular therapists use tranquilizers more sparingly, as adjuncts to nutrient therapy, and so fewer new cases of tardive dyskinesia are developing. Most psychiatrists remain unconvinced of the benefits of orthomolecular treatment, mainly because they have not tried it and are restricted to the use of one or another tranquilizer.

The first major breakthrough in the treatment of tardive dyskinesia was reported by Kunin (1976). He concluded that tardive dyskinesia might be due to manganese deficiency caused by the tranquilizers. The tranquilizers are complex molecules that could chelate with manganese and carry it out of the body. Manganese is an essential trace element that is deficient in many people's diet since, like other minerals, it is present in richest amounts in bran. Bran, in one study, had 119 parts per billion while white flour had only 5 ppm. Mental hospitals tend to provide diets rich in food artifact, and these are most apt to be low in manganese. The combination of low-manganese diets and tranquilizer therapy may account for most cases of tardive dyskinesia.

The part of the brain which prevents abnormal muscular movements, the extrapyramidal system, should be rich in manganese. Kunin decided to restore manganese lev-

els. One case responded dramatically: "I did not have to wait long," he wrote, "before a young man consulted me because of tardive dyskinesia due to fluphenazine enanthate (Prolixin). This had been administered over two months earlier at a university psychiatric service in two doses of 100 mg intramuscularly, a week apart, plus 30 mg orally for four days, and 45 mg for four days. He still exhibited masklike facial expression, Parkinson's posture and gait, and severe tremor and rigidity of the extremities. These symptoms had persisted in spite of previous treatment with diphenhydramine (Benadryl), diazepam (Valium) and nicotinamide, 1,000 mg three times per day. Manganese chelate, 10 mg three times per day, was now started. After one day the tremor and rigidity were much improved. After two days he was entirely free of dyskinesia. There was no recurrence."

Altogether, Kunin reported the results of treating fifteen patients. Ten were also given vitamin B3. In four there was a dramatic and almost immediate cure. In nine there was definite improvement in two to five days. Only one patient did not respond.

In one case unresponsive to manganese the addition of nicotinamide caused a dramatic improvement. In eight of nine other cases given nicotinic acid, there was an improvement in mood and clarity of thought.

The combination of manganese and vitamin B3 improved 14 out of 15 (93 percent) of the patients suffering from tardive dyskinesia. This is really a remarkable achievement for a disease generally recognized as irreversible and untreatable. So far no further reports have appeared in the medical literature. This is due to several factors: (1) few psychiatrists read the *Journal of Orthomolecular Psychiatry* (now called the *Journal of Orthomolecular Medicine*) where Kunin's report appeared; (2) most psychiatrists do not believe reports written by orthomolecular psychiatrists; (3) and once a disease is labeled untreatable by establishment leaders (i.e., the FDA), it becomes impossible to believe that something as simple and benign as manganese and vitamin B3 could be a treatment. Nor will the drug companies have the profit motive to examine these substances, since they are not patentable. They are orphan drugs.

Recently I published a letter to the editor of the *Canadian Medical Association Journal*, drawing attention to Kunin's pioneer work. This raised a flurry of interest. Since then one physician to a nursing home on Vancouver Island in British Columbia has added manganese to the program for patients on medication, and tardive dyskinesia is no longer a problem there. Following that a psychiatrist colleague gave manganese to his patients with improvement ranging from dramatic to good. A controlled study is now underway.

Tragic numbers of patients will become ill and suffer needless pain and discomfort. The patient who consulted me was started on vitamin B3 and drops of one-half percent manganese sulfate solution. I decreased the frequency of his injections to one every two weeks. In one week his tardive dyskinesia was gone. It became apparent he required injections every seven days, but in spite of this he has since remained free of tardive dyskinesia.

Kunin also examined manganese levels in hair. Tardive dyskinesia patients had 0.46 ppm, compared to normal levels of 0.8 ppm. When manganese was given, hair levels came up to normal values.

The idea that tranquilizers can remove manganese from the body opens up the unhappy prospect that other essential minerals may also be depleted. Perhaps some of the numerous side effects of drugs are due to an induced deficiency of zinc, copper, chromium, etc. It will be necessary to do assays of blood and hair before and after treatment with tranquilizers. Unless this is done, we may well discover a number of unusual syndromes considered untreatable and irreversible.

The production of tardive dyskinesia by a deficiency of manganese suggests that other neuromuscular diseases such as Huntington's disease or Friedreich's ataxia should be studied for trace element deficiency due to dietary deficiencies or because of increased requirements or dependency.

Kunin's work suggests that tardive dyskinesia is an orthomolecular neurological disease; recent work with choline reinforces this idea. Studies by two groups of investigators with choline, a precursor to acetylcholine, point to the same conclusion. Davis et al. (1976) found that very high doses of choline partially reversed tardive dyskinesia. This was also found by Wurtman (1978). Choline is difficult to take in the quantities required in a pure form, and it may have a stimulant effect by promoting excessive synthesis of acetylcholine. This suggests it should be used carefully, if at all, for epileptics.

Domino, May, Demetriou et al. (1985) treated nineteen patients with tardive dyskinesia with either placebo or 30 grams per day of phosphatidylcholine for six weeks. Five received it for 12 weeks. There was no difference in therapeutic response. Plasma and blood red cell choline levels were elevated about 350 percent. Thus it is clear that elevating choline levels in blood without any other nutrient intervention is unlikely to be helpful.

It would be prudent to prevent tardive dyskinesia by ensuring that all patients on tranquilizers have adequate amounts of manganese, vitamin B3, and choline. Foods rich in these nutrients should be used, with supplements when required.

I recommend that each tranquilizer tablet contain enough manganese to prevent any leaching out of manganese from the body. The amount will have to be determined. The usual therapeutic dose is around 5 mg per day of manganese sulfate. I would estimate that one-tenth that amount per day would protect patients, and this could be provided by adding 0.1 mg of manganese per tablet of tranquilizers, when about three to nine tablets per day are required. Undoubtedly drug companies will not be willing to spend the immense sums of money required to prove the safety and efficacy of manganese to the FDA, and millions of chronic patients will suffer tardive dyskinesia.

Manganese tablets are available in health food stores. I use 0.5 percent solutions of manganese sulfate on prescription, giving 3 to 5 drops t.i.d. I have seen no toxic reactions in the past seven years.

Orthomolecular physicians are unfamiliar with tardive dyskinsia because it does not appear in their patients. Tkacz and Hawkins (1984) examined charts on over 10,000 schizophrenic patients who had been treated and could not find a single case. Recently, Hawkins (1986) collected evidence from a number of other orthomolecular physicians and again found tardive dyskinesia to be very rare. In my own practice, since 1955, I have not seen cases unless they had already developed by previous treatment. The orthomolecular approach may act by decreasing the amount of tranquilizer needed, by decreasing the loss of manganese and in many cases by the addition of manganese.

Physicians may well be exposed to legal suit for allowing their patients to develop tardive dyskinesia.

## ALZHEIMER'S DISEASE

Alzheimer's disease has not responded to orthomolecular treatment. I have treated five cases over the past 10 years using large doses of niacin, ascorbic acid, as well as other vitamins. This treatment has been effective in the senile states not caused by Alzheimer's. Nevertheless, I still consider it to be a disease of malnutrition brought on by chronic malnutrition or other factors. Abalan (1984) suggests it is caused by malabsorption. Thus, in his experience, normal serum albumin levels are achieved only with massive protein feeding.

The unusual variety of neurological, psychiatric, and biochemical findings can be ac-

counted for if there is a massive malabsorption. This will also explain why large doses of nutrients have been ineffective.

A recent finding is consistent with Abalan's hypothesis. Alzheimer's brains are unable to make enough tetrahydrobiopterin ($BH_4$). $BH_4$ is a cofactor in the synthesis of the neurotransmitters dopamine, noradrenalin and serotonin. A deficiency of $BH_4$ causes several neurological and mental abnormalities. In Alzheimer's there is a decrease in synthesis of $BH_4$ from dihydroneopterin triphosphate due to a defect in the enzyme that eliminates phosphate. Alzheimer's brains have more neopterin and much less $BH_4$ than controls.

The conversion of $BH_4$ requires NADPH, yet large doses of niacin have not helped.

When $BH_4$ becomes available, it should be tried, yet there may be a problem getting it into the brain.

Another lead is to use a blood thinner, Warfarin (coumadin). Dr. Arthur C. Walsh (1987) has pioneered the use of Warfarin for treating senile dementia, with good results. He has also treated an Alzheimer's case successfully. Recently, he described a 56-year-old lawyer/engineer executive who could not be cared for at home. He was extremely confused and could not walk because he was so weak. After one week on anticoagulant he was physically much better, could walk alone, and was cooperative. In preparation for sending him to a state hospital, the anticoagulant was stopped. Within a few days he had regressed to his earlier condition. On two more occasions it was stopped with some immediate regression. In the state hospital the Warfarin was stopped. He soon became bedridden and died in three months. Autopsy confirmed Alzheimer's.

I believe the heavy metal toxicity hypothesis of Dr. C. C. Pfeiffer (1975) should be investigated. One should look not just for aluminum but for excess copper, lead, mercury, cadmium and silver. If they are present in excess amounts, methods can be developed to remove them. Chelation therapy will be needed using specific chemicals to bind these metals and remove them.

## CHAPTER REFERENCES

Abalan, F. (1984), Alzheimer's disease and malnutrition: A new etiological hypothesis. *Medical Hypotheses* 15:385-393.

Ayd, F. Discussion. APA Meeting, Toronto, 1977.

Aziz, A. A., Leeming, R. J., & Blair, J.A. (1983), Tetrahydrobiopterin metabolism in senile dementia of Alzheimer's type. *J. Neuro., Neurosurg. and Psych.* 46:410-413.

Barnes, B. D., & Galton, L. (1976), *Hypothyroidism: The unsuspected illness.* New York: Thomas Y. Crowell.

Barr, F. E., Saloma, J. S., & Buchele, M. J. (1983), Melanin: The organizing molecule. *Medical Hypotheses* 11:1-140.

Beamish, R. E., Dhillon, K. D., Sinsal, P. K., and Dhalia, N. S. (1981), Protective effect of sulfinpyrazone against catecholamine metabolite adrenochrome-induced arrhythmias. *Am. Heart J.* 102:149-152.

Bjorksten, J. (1960), A common denominator in aging research. *Texas Reports on Biology and Medicine* 18:347-357.

———(1963), Aging, primary mechanism. *Gerontologia* 8:179-192.

———(1964), Chemical causes of the aging process. *Proc. Scientific Section of the Toilet Goods Assoc.* 41:32-34.

———(1968), The crosslinkage theory of aging. *J. Amer. Geriatrics Society* 16:408-427.

———(1971), The crosslinkage theory of aging. *Finska Kemists Medd.* 80:23-32.

———(1976), The crosslinkage theory of aging: Clinical implications. *Comprehensive Therapy* 2:65-74.

Bourgeois, B. F. D., Dodson, W. E., & Ferendelli, J. A. (1983), Potentiation of the antiepileptic activity of phenobarbital by nicotinamide. *Epilepsia* 24:238-244.

Canner, P. L. (1985), Link niacin to longevity after an M.I., American College of Cardiology Annual Meeting, Anaheim, CA, 1985. *Medical Tribune*, April 24, 1985. Abstract only: *J. Amer. Coll. Cardiol.* 5:442.

Cleave, T. L., Campbell, G. D., & Painter, N. S. (1969), *Diabetes, Coronary Thrombosis and the Saccharine Disease,* 2d. ed. Bristol, England: John Wright and Sons.

Coleman, M., Sobels, S., Bhagavan, H. N., Coursin, D., Marquardt, A., Guay, M., & Hunt, C. (1985), A double blind study of vitamin B6 in Down's syndrome infants, Part 1, Clinical and biochemical results. *J. Ment. Def. Res.* 29:233-240.

Consensus Conference, (1985), Lowering blood cholesterol to prevent heart disease. *JAMA* 253:2080-2086.

Coronary Drug Project Research Group, (1975), The Coronary Drug Project: Clofibrate and niacin in coronary disease. *JAMA* 231:360-381.

Davis, K. L., Hollister, L. E., Barchas, J. D., & Berger, P. A. (1976), Choline in tardive dyskinesia and Huntington's disease. *Life Science* 19:1507.

Domino, E. F., May, W. W., Demetriou, S., Mathews, B., Tait, S., & Kovacic, B. (1985), Lack of clinically significant improvement of patients with tardive dyskinesia following phosphatidylcholine therapy. *Biol. Psychiatry* 20:1174-1188.

Ebels, E. J. (1978), How common is Wernicke-Korsakoff syndrome? *Lancet* 2:781-782.

Falek, A., Kallmann, F. J., Lorge, I., & Jarvik, L. F. (1960), Longevity and intellectual variation in a senescent twin population. *J. Gerontology* 15:305-309.

Hamon, C. G. B., & Blair, J. A. (1987), Pathogenesis of Alzheimer's disease. *J. Royal Society of Medicine* 80:127-128.

Harman, D. (1956), Aging: A theory based on free radical and radiation chemistry. *J. Gerontology* 11:298-300.

Hawkins, D. (1986), The prevention of tardive dyskinesia with high dosage vitamins: A study of 58,000 patients. *J. Ortho. Medicine* 1:24-26.

Hoffer, A. (1962), *Niacin Therapy in Psychiatry.* Springfield, Ill.: Charles C Thomas.

———(1969), Safety, side effects and relative lack of toxicity of nicotinic acid and nicotinamide. *Schizophrenia* 1:78-87.

———(1981), The adrenochrome hypothesis of schizophrenia revisited. *J. Ortho. Psych.* 10:98-118.

———(1983), Orthomolecular nutrition at the zoo. *J. Ortho. Psych.* 12:116-128.

————(1985), Ascorbic acid and kidney stones. *Can. Med. Assoc. J.* 132:320.

Hoffer, A., & Osmond, H. (1967), *The Hallucinogens*. New York: Academic Press.

Hoffer, A., Osmond, H., & Smythies, J. (1954), Schizophrenia: A new approach. II. Results of a year's research. *J. Ment. Sci.* 100:29.

Horrobin, D. (1977), Schizophrenia as a prostaglandin deficiency disease. *Lancet* 1:936-937.

Jarvik, L. F., Falek, A., Kallman, F. J., & Lorge, I. (1960), Survival trends in a senescent twin population. *Amer. J. Human Genetics* 12:170-179.

Kaufman, W. (1943), *Common Form of Niacinamide Deficiency Disease: Aniacinamidosis*. New Haven: Yale University Press.

Kaufman, W. (1949), *The Common Form of Joint Dysfunction: Its Incidence and Treatment*. Brattleboro, Vt.: E. L. Hildreth.

Kunin, R. A. (1976), Manganese and niacin in the treatment of drug-induced dyskinesias. *J. Ortho. Psych.* 5:4.

Levine, S. A., & Kidd, P. M. (1985), *Antioxidant Adaptation: Its Role in Free Radical Pathology*. San Leandro, Calif.: Biocurrents Division, Allergy Research Group.

McDonagh, E. W., Rudolph, C. J., & Cheraskin, E. (1985), The psychotherapeutic potential of EDTA chelation. *J. Ortho. Psych.* 14:214-217.

Moran, C., Whitburn, S. B., & Blair, J. A. (1983), Tetrahydrobiopterin metabolism in senile dementia of Alzheimer type. *J. Neuro., Neurosurg. and Psych.* 46:582.

National Institutes of Health (1985), Lowering blood cholesterol to prevent heart disease. *Consensus Development Conference Statement*, 5 (7).

Nottebohm, F. (1984), Reported in Research News. *Science* 224:1325-1326.

Pershing, H. T. (1892), Alcoholic multiple neuritis with characterized mental derangement. *Int. Med. Magazine* 1:803-809.

Pfeiffer, C. C. (1975), *Mental and Elemental Nutrients*. New Canaan, Conn.: Keats Publishing.

Roach, E. S., & Carlin, L. (1982), NN dimethylglycine for epilepsy. *NEJM* 307:1081-1082.

Roach, E. S., & Gibson, P. (1983), Failure of NN dimethylglycine in epilepsy. *Ann. Neur.* 14:347.

Rudin, D. O. (1981), The major psychoses and neuroses as Omega-3 essential fatty acid deficiency syndrome: Substrate pellagra. *Biol. Psychiatry* 16:837-850.

Tkacz, C., & Hawkins, D. R. (1984), A preventive measure for tardive dyskinesia. *J. Ortho. Psych.* 10:119-128.

Victor, M., Adams, R. D., & Collins, G. H. (1971), *The Wernicke-Korsakoff Syndrome*. Philadelphia: F. A. Davis.

Walsh, A. C. (1987), Treatment of senile dementia of the Alzheimer's type by a psychiatric-anticoagulant regimen. *J. Orthomol. Med.* in press.

Williams, A. C., Levine, R. A., Chase, T. N., Lovenberg, W., & Calne, D. B. (1980), CSF hydroxylase cofactor levels in some neurological disease. *J. Neuro., Neurosurg. and Psych.* 43:735-738.

Wright, I. S. (1978), Can your family history tell you anything about your chances for a long life? *Executive Health*, February.

Wurtman, R. J. (1978), Food for thought. *The Sciences* 18:6.

Yiamouyiannis, J. (1983), *Flouride. The Aging Factor*. Delaware, Ohio: Health Action Press.

# CHAPTER 8

## *METABOLIC STRESS*

Medicine began thousands of years ago, when the first human associated discomfort with something visible or palpable like a boil or swollen ankle or fracture. A local condition was connected with consequent discomfort. Much of today's medicine must still include this simple cause-and-effect medicine, except that we have sophisticated technology and can make visible the pathology that could not have been visualized several decades ago. We use X-rays, CAT scans, and even more technologically advanced machine to show us where internal structures are abnormal, i.e., too dense or not dense enough.

Local, topical, or organ medicine treats a fraction of the illnesses, and perhaps only a minor fraction. The rest of medicine must deal with metabolic reactions that affect the entire body, even though the major problem may arise from one organ such as the thyroid, pituitary or adrenal glands. Metabolic abnormalities may be genetic, expressing themselves very early, like Down's syndrome, or they may come late, as does Huntington's disease. They may arise from nutritional deficiencies such as scurvy, beriberi, pellagra, zinc deficiency; or from toxic reactions due to heavy metals such as mercury, copper, nickel and cadmium; or to halogens such as fluoride or chlorine. They follow invasions of the body by viruses, bacteria, fungi, including yeast, and large parasites. Distortions of the immune defense system also cause generalized metabolic stress reactions. Shock, both physical and psychological, also perturbs the body's metabolism for as long as those stressors operate.

These general or systemic diseases differ from local ones because they cannot be seen as bumps or anatomical changes. They must be inferred from the nature of the illness and symptoms, or by the use of laboratory tests on various body fluids or tissues, such as blood, urine, stools and biopsied or pathological specimens.

There is another major difference between local and systemic diseases. Local diseases much more frequently produce a unique constellation of signs and symptoms, i.e., a syndrome. When such a syndrome is present, it points back to that local disease. Thus angina pectoris, pain in the chest on effort, points to the heart as a source of the discomfort. Systemic diseases seldom have a specific syndrome. A listing of all the possible signs and symptoms of any systemic disease would require many pages. Mercury poisoning causes a variety of neurological, medical and psychiatric signs and symptoms. Fluoride intoxication may cause as wide a range of symptoms. But pellagra may provide a similar set of problems. For each type of metabolic dysfunction there may be a unique marker among the wide variety of afflictions. Thus mercury intoxication may appear as a discoloration of the gums or teeth, and scurvy will cause obvious degeneration of connective tissues. But often these markers are not obvious and always they are too late, for every metabolic disease becomes more difficult to treat successfully the longer it has been present.

With local conditions one will ask where is the lesion, while with systemic conditions one must ask what has caused the whole body to be sick. Local conditions usually cause a narrowly defined syndrome that can be severe in nature and cause severe pain and discomfort. Systemic conditions are more apt to cause a widely diffuse set of complaints ranging from fatigue and vague aches and pain to vague gastrointestinal disorders, skin irritations, and so on. When such a patient must be diagnosed, one can then rule out fairly quickly local causes and begin to search for the systemic causes. It would be costly and inefficient to examine each patient for every possible systemic cause. The first examination should be based on the most probable cause. This is obtained from the history. The common factors such as nutrition and the environment are examined first. In my experience, up to 75 percent of the systemic conditions I have seen are caused by problems in adjusting the body's need for nutrients to what is available to the body. There is a disharmony between what we have adapted to over a million years of evolution and our present food supply. Removing the disharmony should restore that patient's health. If it does not, one must search for other factors such as chronic candidiasis or heavy metal poisoning. Thus each person is like a research program, where both patient and physician work together to determine the probable cause and test this by therapeutic trial, gradually increasing the number of potential causes until, if necessary, every possible cause is examined. Fortunately, very few patients have more than two major casual factors.

It is probably wrong to divide diseases into specific (local) and systemic, since every insult to the body attacks the whole body and elicits a general as well as a local reaction. Many pathological conditions involve the whole body: more than a boil or a wart or a sore eye or a swollen wrist. They invoke a massive reaction of the entire defense mechanisms of the body. If this fails, the person will die. The best current example of such a massive failure is AIDS.

Metabolic stress (hereafter I will use only one word—stress) is caused by a number of factors:

1. Malnutrition and starvation.
2. Invasions (by living organisms).
3. Trauma, fracture, burns.
4. Allergies and sensitivities.
5. Toxic reactions:
   a) Metals.
   b) Organic molecules.
   c) Halogens—chlorine, flouride
   d) Venoms and plant poisons.
6. Psychosocial.

No one can doubt that a healthy person can withstand insults better than one who is less healthy. The natural defenses of our bodies must be maintained at their optimum efficiency. When this is the condition, it is likely many of the diseases will not even occur— the arthritidies will not come, there will be a much smaller probability of developing diabetes, and invasions by bacteria, virus, etc., will have less chance of becoming established.

There are really two issues. The first is whether malnutrition decreases the body's immune defenses below what they would normally be. The evidence for this is conclusive —any form of malnutrition, from protein and calorie deprivation to any vitamin or mineral deficiency, increases the likelihood of developing infections, of not healing as fast after trauma, surgery or burns. It is becoming well known that these forms of malnutrition ought to be treated vigorously.

The second issue is whether improved nutrition as is recommended by orthomolecular nutritionists increases the body's defenses above what they commonly are. About this issue there are two divergent camps. We believe that enhanced nutritional health will increase defenses to the point that the incidence of a large number of diseases is decreased, and if disease is already present then healing is accelerated. However, the majority of physicians do not believe that enhanced nutrition is necessary, for they believe that most people are already nutritionally healthy.

The arguments in favor of nutritional enhancement arise from observations made by many physicians. The first set of observations has been discussed in this book. I have shown how a number of conditions respond to orthomolecular treatment. The fact of this improvement leads to the conclusion that the body's defenses are revitalized. If vitamin B3 improves arthritis, then increasing vitamin B3 intake should prevent arthritis. This is what Kaufman found. The addition of relatively small quantities of niacinamide to flour greatly decreased the number of his patients suffering from a variety of symptoms, including joint problems. There is no question that scorbutics are much more prone to various infections. Enhancing nutritional states from very poor conditions thus improves defenses.

A lead story in *The Medical Post*, March 4, 1986, reads: "Malnutrition, rampant among surgical orthopedic patients, is greatly increasing the number and severity of complications suffered by these people." Studies of orthopedic populations in university and private hospitals have shown patient malnutrition of 42 percent and 68 percent. In one study, 85 percent of Symes amputations performed on malnourished patients failed, compared to 86 percent success among properly nourished patients. The report in *The Medical Post* concludes: "General surgeons have long known that the morbidity and mortality associated with operations on malnourished patients is markedly elevated. . . . Yet very few references concerning the importance of nutrition appear in the orthopedic literature. This study has shown that malnutrition is much more common among surgical patients than most people believe."

The second set of observations arises from experiments in which nutritional supplements have been used in animals and man to test immune defenses. For example, leukocytes can engulf many more bacteria in a medium richer in ascorbic acid. But the most convincing evidence comes from the clinical data summarized by Klenner (1973), Stone (1972), Pauling (1970) and Cathcart (1985).

Ascorbic acid at optimum doses is very effective in helping the body heal itself even when invaded by massive quantities of bacteria, viruses, etc. Often optimum doses are sublaxative or bowel tolerant doses. The B vitamins are very important. For example, vitamin B3 will enhance the body's defenses against tuberculosis and bacteria. As a general rule, any deficiency or relative deficiency reduces our ability to protect ourselves effectively against invasion.

A few organisms are able to protect themselves against the body's defense system, or at least to render it less effective. Leprosy is a slowly growing chronic infection that the body tolerates too well. Large amounts of ascorbic acid have been found helpful in controlling leprosy. Tuberculosis is another slow-growing infection. It can be contained more effectively when vitamin B3 is used. I suspect ascorbic acid is very important here.

Chronic candidiasis has become a major problem. A number of current medical practices increase the hazards of a mild yeast colonization becoming a major infection, (Truss 1978, 1981, 1983). Truss found that a large number of patients with chronic illnesses of different types did not get well until their yeast infection had been contained. These included many allergic reactions, depression, schizophrenia, multiple sclerosis and more. Factors which create chronic yeast infection are diets rich in sugar and the use of antibiotics, corticosteroids and birth control medications. A diet rich in sugar provides an ideal food for intestinal yeast. A few people have such a heavy infestation of yeast that they have become drunk on the alcohol generated in their intestines by the yeast organisms. Antibiotics kill the helpful lactobacillus in the intestine and allow yeast overgrowth. Chronic use of antibiotics makes the problem worse. Corticosteroids and anticancer drugs inhibit the action of the immune defense system and also increase yeast growth. Birth control pills do the same.

Chronic yeast infection causes chronic metabolic stress. Treatment includes the antistress program plus a direct attack on the candida. Diet should be sugar-free. In some cases no food at all, i.e., a fast, is required to empty the gastrointestinal tract.

All systemic diseases are very stressful to the body. Subjectively the patient feels sick, tired, disinterested, may have chills or fever, all combined with symptoms unique to that individual. There are objective changes as well, such as increase in body temperature, increased or decreased pulse rate, elevated sedimentation rate, changes in white blood cell count and other biochemical changes. There is an increased outpouring or loss of nutrients into the urine. The water-soluble vitamins and minerals especially are lost. This shows that the body in dealing with stress mobilizes these essential nutrients but in the process loses a lot. When the vitamin can be made in the body there is a marked increase. Thus, animals which retain the ability to make ascorbic acid may increase the production four to five times when under severe stress. Under stress the amount of ascorbic acid in the adrenal glands drops sharply. There is also an increase in the amount of oxidized ascorbic acid, and the ratio of reduced to ascorbic

acid falls precipitously. As I have shown in the ascorbic acid section, this ratio can be used to measure the degree of stress.

Ascorbic acid is essential for normal leukocyte activity. Leukocytes can engulf and destroy many more bacteria when they contain enough ascorbic acid. They are very avid for this vitamin. This is why many of the symptoms of leukemia are really scorbutic. The leukocytes sequester what little ascorbic acid there is in the body, leaving the other tissues deficient. It can take as much as 7 grams per day to satisfy the needs of all the leukocytes in cases of leukemia.

After severe burns there is a marked loss of essential nutrients in the exudate as well as into the urine. During gastrointestinal diseases there will be a similar loss of nutrients.

An antistress program is thus one of the most important parts of any treatment. It must include optimum supplies of:

1. Calories, but using only the orthomolecular diet.
2. Protein of high quality to prevent tissue loss and to make repair possible.
3. Ascorbic acid in sublaxative doses.
4. Multivitamin preparations emphasizing the major B vitamins. The current antistress formulas being promoted by drug companies are very good, as they contain vitamin C plus the major B vitamins such as vitamin B3 and vitamin B6.
5. Essential minerals such as zinc. Most people are on marginal levels of zinc intake, and with the increased loss during stress may easily be thrown into a deficiency. Even the rather mild stress of a fast can elicit symptoms of zinc deficiency, such as the white chalky areas under the nail.

In addition to the antistress nutritional treatment, one will use measures to alleviate anxiety, to eliminate or reduce pain and to protect the patient from further stress.

Additional nutrient treatment will be required for special diseases.

## BURNS

With burns one must contend with loss of fluid, protein and many essential nutrients. The greater the area burned, the more serious is the condition. Burn units today are aware of the importance of restoring fluid and protein and treating the burned area with grafts, etc., but, in addition to this, and the antistress formula, I am convinced one should use generous quantities of vitamin E, both internally and applied to the surface of the burned area. The use of vitamin E for burns is described by Shute and Shute (1956). The clinical descriptions and photographs of "before" and "after" treatment are very impressive. I have seen small, deep burns heal so completely that it was impossible to detect which area had been burned. The only treatment was surface application of vitamin E.

There is also a rationale for using vitamin E. In a burned area, the tissue is exposed to the air and to oxidation, much as is a cut apple or potato. Because of impaired blood circulation, the body's antioxidants (free radical scavengers) are not very effective. Vitamin E is a good antioxidant, and applied to the burned surface should decrease the formation of these free radicals. Since ascorbic acid is also an antioxidant, a mixture of sodium ascorbate and vitamin E, which could be sprayed on the area, would be very valuable.

Niacin decreases the exudate from burned skin and for this reason should be used.

## INFECTIONS

In addition to the antistress formula, ascorbic acid in very large doses should be used. This may require large doses given intravenously. It is helpful for improving defenses against all infections and does not interfere with the use and action of antibiotics. It is especially valuable against viral infections for which we have no antibiotics, because ascorbic acid promotes the production of interferon in the body.

Ascorbic acid's role in coping with viral infections has already been described in the section on vitamin C. The amount needed is directly related to the severity and toxicity of the infection. A simple viral cold may only require up to 10 grams per day; viral hepatitis may require up to 100 grams per day, most of it given by vein as ascorbate. One of the persistent viral infections, herpes, will also yield to ascorbic acid. Genital herpes and shingles will require additional treatment. For these infections I use a combination of l-lysine, 250 mg q.i.d.; ascorbic acid to bowel tolerance; and vitamin B12 by injection up to 1 mg every day. I will illustrate treatment of both types.

1. Facial shingles with severe intractable pain. The patient complained of severe facial pain present for several months. She had been unable to obtain any relief and had been advised by several physicians that nothing more could be done. I started her on ascorbic acid, 6 grams per day; l-lysine, 1 gram; and vitamin B12, 1 mg injection i.m. twice each week. When I saw her a month later she reported that 24 hours after she started on the program all the pain was gone and the open sores on her face had begun to heal.

2. Genital herpes. The treatment of genital herpes is essentially the same as the treatment of any virus infection, as it depends upon using adequate doses of ascorbic acid. But the response is slower and patients may still have recurrences that are not as painful nor as prolonged.

In February 1984, K. D., age 29, consulted me, complaining of chronic pain in her right leg following an accident three years earlier. After six operations her knee remained unstable and was very painful. She began to drink excessively but four months before seeing me had joined AA. She had also suffered from venereal herpes since age 18. She was started on 3 grams of ascorbic acid; lysine, 250 mg four times per day; B12, 1 mg i.m. every week; pyridoxine, 250 mg o.d.; and a multivitamin preparation three times per day. On her next visit one month later naicinamide, 500 mg four times per day, was added, plus vitamin E, 200 IU, and vitamins A and D.

In May the herpes was gone and her hair had stopped falling out. Her knee was still painful.

May 1985 she reported she had had two outbreaks of genital herpes and had had a candida infection. Because niacinamide caused nausea, it was replaced by niacin, 1 gram three times per day.

October 1985 she reported attacks of herpes came on every six months but the lesions were smaller. They were still painful. She had also reached two years of sobriety.

Antiobiotics kill bacteria in the intestine but are not as effective in containing E. coli and candida. For this reason, many patients who require antibiotics also risk being overcolonized by candida and other undesirable organisms. This can be controlled by using parenteral antibiotics when they are required for a few days, and by ensuring that the diet does not promote yeast growth. The orthomolecular diet should be used as it is sugar-free and high in fiber-rich carbohydrate foods. One may have to use antifungal or anticandida drugs such as Mycostatin concurrently with the antibiotic. This may be very essential for patients who require chronic antibiotic medication.

Finally, acidophilus may be used to colonize the intestine with the normal flora. One can use foods rich in these organisms, such as sour milk (if the patient is not allergic to milk), naturally fermented yogurt, or sauerkraut, or the lactobacillus variants available from drugstores (Bacid), or from health food stores. They should be taken with each meal and continued for a week after the antibiotic has been stopped.

## TRAUMA

Contusions, abrasions, fractures and surgery are all are very traumatic even though pain is readily controlled. Modern surgery is relatively painless and patients do not suffer as they did before anesthetics were introduced. But surgery and after-surgery in most hospitals is still very traumatic to the body, more than is necessary, since hospitals generally are unaware of the need for optimum nutrition or how to achieve it. I have treated a large number of patients who dated the onset of their general fatigue, tension, and general discomfort to the time they had last been in the hospital, usually for surgery, up to several years before. Patients who are aware of the importance of good nutrition, who have been in the hospital, know how bad that food is even if it is served hot or cold as required, is packaged attractively and tastes good (sweet or salty). Fortunately, I have not been in hospitals as a patient for many years, but I have seen the food brought to others. To my surprise, soft drinks, jello puddings, white bread, sugar, and cold (tinned) chicken soup are still considered food by modern hospitals. If every patient admitted to a hospital was prepared for surgery or other treatment with the antistress formula and continued after treatment, they would recover more quickly. The economic saving would be enormous, simply by reducing the number of days in the hospital and by reducing posttreatment complications.

## ALLERGIES

The antistress formula is used for allergies. For certain allergic reactions some of the nutrients play a special role. In every case an attempt is made to localize the substances the patient is allergic to and to manipulate the diet and use antiallergic treatments. These may be all that is required.

Some of the vitamins have antiallergy properties.

## Niacin

The niacin flush is really a histamine flush. Over 30 years ago I ran an experiment on twelve schizophrenic patients using increasing quantities of histamine by injection (Hoffer and Parsons 1955). The flush which followed each injection was identical to the niacin flush. Niacin releases histamine from its storage sites. There cannot be another flush until they are recharged. This is why the first flush is the most intense and does not regain its original intensity until a period of several days without taking niacin. On a maintenance dose of niacin there is much less stored histamine. What is released into the blood has a half-life of 90 minutes. One would reason that since less histamine can be released while on niacin, acute allergic shock reactions should be less intense. Dr. E. Boyle told me that guinea pigs sensitized and then given an anaphylactic dose later on did not die if they were receiving niacin. The unprotected animals were killed by the reaction, as one would expect.

I have found that large doses of niacin can decrease allergic reactions to foods. Before I incorporated cerebral allergies into my practice, I often had to use 12 grams per day or more of niacin for recovery. Then I found that the same patients, well on 12 grams per day, if taken off a food to which they were allergic, could no longer tolerate the same dose of niacin. They required thereafter 3 grams, and sometimes 6 grams, per day. I now suspect that any person who can tolerate the high dose, 12 grams or more, has one or more food allergies. I would expect that most people using niacin at nonflush levels will react much less intensely to all histamine-mediated allergic reactions.

Niacin also releases heparin or heparinoids from the same storage sites. This has a half-life of several days. Heparinoids have remarkable scavenger properties for a large number of molecules. One day, not too far away, we will have oral heparinoid preparations that have no effect on blood clotting but have

valuable clinical properties (Jaques 1979). They may be valuable antihistamine or antiallergy substances.

## Ascorbic Acid

Ascorbic acid and histamine destroy each other. With ready access to ascorbic acid, the histamine molecules released are destroyed. This explains why large doses of vitamin C are effective against insect bites. The bitten area is less edematous and does not itch as much (see also Klenner 1973).

## Pyridoxine

Philpott (1974), has found vitamin B6 helpful in quickly relieving allergic reactions, especially when given intravenously.

## Other Drugs

Vitamins are compatible with all drugs. If antihistamines are needed, they should be used.

## Combination of vitamins A and D3

This has been described for asthma (Reich 1971). I consider it a very valuable treatment.

### TOXIC REACTIONS

## Metals

Most cases of metal poisoning come from our dentists, who use amalgams, and from the lead in our gasolines. Public health officals and governments are aware of the latter and are forcing a slow reduction in the amount of lead added to gasoline, but it will take many years before this source of lead contamination is gone. Children are the major sufferers. They are closer to the ground, where the heavy lead particles settle, and they are more apt to have soil contaminated with lead in their mouths. Elevated lead levels in teeth and hair in children are associated with learning disorders and behavioral problems. Lead also comes from flaking paint.

Very few people are aware that the fillings in our teeth are a major source of heavy metal contamination. Dental schools teach that amalgam fillings are safe, and they are widely used. For example, 200,000 pounds of mercury are used each year in filings in the United States. Dental magazines downplay any hazards from amalgams, even when the main body of the report accurately describes what these hazards are. The *Journal of Orthomolecular Psychiatry* was one of the first to carry information about the dangers of mercury (wrongly called silver) amalgams. Betsy Russell-Manning (1983) compiled an amazing amount of information about the various metals used by dentists, their effects on the body, how to diagnose them as a problem, and what to do about it. Dentists will have to stop using these dangerous metals, even if only a small proportion of people react adversely. If even 10 percent of all people with metals in their mouth are adversely affected, this would account for many millions of sick people. A mercury amalgam consists of a metallic mix of silver (65 percent minimum), tin (25 percent minimum), copper (6 percent maximum) and zinc (2 percent maximum). This is mixed with an equal part of pure mercury so that mercury is the main component.

Mercury is the most toxic ingredient because it vaporizes easily into the mouth, is inhaled, absorbed and converted to organic mercury compounds. These are powerful enzyme poisons and, of course, mercury causes dreadful reactions in the body. The metal also travels through the teeth into the gums, bone, and other tissues. Contrary to what most people think, mercury does not remain in a stable metallic pocket, the filling. Examination of fillings which have been drilled out show empty spaces where mercury once existed when examined under the microscope.

Mercury amalgams have been found to be responsible for a number of diseases such as migraine, multiple sclerosis (Huggins 1982), immune diseases and so on. I will not list the immense number of signs and symptoms which vanish from many people when their metallic amalgams are removed.

If there were no choice, then one could justify using amalgams since it is so important to preserve our teeth. However, there are nonmetallic filling materials which are as good and can be used more readily. Or one can use gold, which is the least soluble and thus least toxic metal.

Metals can harm simply by electrolytic action. They create miniature batteries in the mouth which can generate an appreciable current. This by itself can cause difficulty in a few people.

General practitioners should be aware of the possible relationship between fillings and disease when they have patients who have unusual complaints that do not respond to standard treatment. They should not conclude that the patients are neurotic or have psychosocially caused diseases without further evaluation.

General practitioners should examine the mouth carefully, record the number of amalgam fillings or other metallic structures and determine when the fillings were placed. They might ask the patient to bring in a dental assessment from their dentist. There are very few dentists who are interested in and skillful in assessing metal damage. However, one can advise patients not to allow any further fillings with amalgams and in some advise that the amalgams be replaced. In the meantime, the antistress formula will help neutralize some of the toxic reactions and increase elimination.

A high-fiber diet is helpful, as heavy metals bind to the fiber. A high-fiber diet will protect birds against cadmium poisoning. Vitamins will counteract some of the poisoning effect on enzymes. Ascorbic acid will bind with mercury and other minerals and increase their excretion. The process of drilling out mercury amalgams releases a lot of mercury particles and vapor. Extra ascorbic acid should be taken before and after visiting the dentist.

Finally, patients should be advised to avoid all amalgam fillings, to avoid nickel bridgework, and to use only nonmetallic fillings, or gold, or a high-grade stainless steel very low in nickel. Even better, proper diet and oral sanitation will reduce the need to have fillings put in.

### Organic Toxins

These are carbon-containing compounds such as carbon tetrachloride, insecticides and plant growth inhibitors. They are enzyme poisons and increase the production of free radicals in the body. Excessive oxidation causes a number of chronic reactions ranging from acceleration of senility and cancer to increasing the prevalence of allergic reactions. Modern water in many cities is recycled and contains traces of organic chemicals that are not removed. Chlorine, added to sterilize the water, combines with these to form chlorinated organic compounds that are very toxic and accumulate in the body.

The best treatment is the antistress formula, but in addition one may need large doses of vitamin E. Ascorbic acid will destroy the water-soluble free radicals and vitamin E the fat-soluble free radicals. If the water is heavily contaminated, it should be filtered through activated charcoal to remove these chlorinated organic compounds.

### Halogens

The only halogens we need to worry about are chlorine and fluoride. The former is added to our water to sterilize it and the latter to reduce caries in teeth. If no better system is available, chlorine must be used, for the alternative of no sterilization is much worse. Some countries are using ozonization to purify water, which seems better to me, especially if no excessive quantities of hydroxyl ions are present in the treated water.

Patients may be sensitive to the chlorine. I have known a few who did not recover until they began to use unchlorinated water. The chlorine can be removed by filtering it out and also removing chlorinated hydrocarbon molecules, or by converting it to sodium chloride by the addition of traces of ascorbic acid

to each glass of water before it is drunk.

It is impossible to remove fluoride from fluoridated water, so this water is best avoided. I suggest that each city run two water systems, one for those who want fluoride and the other for those who do not. The purer water should be cheaper since it has not been processed by the addition of fluoride.

### Venoms and Plant Poisons

These include snake and insect bites, bites or stings of a few fish species, and toxic or stinging plants such as poison ivy. They are best treated by the antistress formula, using huge quantities of ascorbic acid and specific antipoisons or antivenoms when they are available. Dr. Klenner (1973) described the use of large doses of ascorbic acid for neutralizing insect and snake bites successfully. It can be life saving. For plant toxins an antihistamine can be very helpful.

In 1954 I was stung by a wasp. In amazement I watched the sting site on my arm grow into a hive. Within a few minutes I swallowed one gram of ascorbic acid powder, which I then considered a large dose. Then I observed my hive. It kept growing for about ten minutes and was by then large, red, shiny, and very itchy. Suddenly it stopped and almost as quickly began to recede. One hour after the bite it was very difficult to see the site and all the itching was gone.

About five years ago while in Grand Cayman, a friend touched a very vicious plant called "cow itch." Within a few minutes he suffered excruciating pain on his arm, chest and neck, areas which had been in contact with this common stinging plant. I promptly gave him 5 grams of ascorbic acid by mouth and a Benadryl tablet. Within one hour he was comfortable, the itch nearly gone.

Ascorbic acid destroys histamine, which may explain its beneficial effect in dealing with these toxins. I think it is prudent for any person apt to be exposed to these stings and bites to take substantial daily doses of ascorbic acid and to increase these doses as soon as possible after such contact. The more dangerous the venom, the larger must be the dose, which may have to be given intravenously as the ascorbate salt in doses up to 100 grams per day.

## *Psychosocial Stresses*

These are dealt with in the usual human way by providing support, reassurance, counseling if it is requested, and antianxiety medications, antidepressants or mild tranquilizers to temporarily shut the patient away from most of the stress. But the physician must remember as well that stressed people require the antistress formula in greater doses than when they are unstressed.

## FOOD SENSITIVITIES

There has never been a time when a few physicians have not known that some foods make a few people sick. Some of the folklore is based upon this; for example, in folklore milk is considered to be a mucus-forming food. In fact, milk will very frequently form mucus in people allergic to it. Common symptoms are sinus drip, postnasal drip, phlegm, and often what appears to be a cold. Often one does not "catch" a cold, one eats it. Yet most people do not find milk a mucus-producing food for them.

Over 60 years ago, Walter Alvarez described the effect of foods in causing anxiety, irritability, mental confusion and other symptoms. Dr. Theron G. Randolph described how certain allergic reactions caused neuroses and psychoses in a number of reports, and he presented his findings to a World Congress of Psychiatry in Montreal. But he and previous investigators were ignored. It wasn't until about ten years ago that William Philpott (1974) studied clinical ecology under Dr. Marshall Mandell and introduced it into orthomolecular psychiatry. Most of us had already moved from being orthodox to orthomolecular psychiatrists, but we were still convinced that allergies had little to do with psychiatry.

But the Philpott-Mandell reports and demonstrations were convincing, and today most orthomolecular physicians examine their patients for allergies. Soon after Dr. Philpott's reports, I had 160 of my schizophrenic patients fast for four days. All were partial or total failures on megadose vitamin therapy and standard therapy. Over 100 were normal at the end of the fast. Within months the whole pattern of my practice changed. I used to have a long waiting list of patients for admission to hospital for ECT, but, once I began to consider allergy as a factor, my waiting list vanished and I had to use ECT very rarely. From around 50 patients per year (out of about 500 seen in a year), I found only about five to 10 required ECT. I am now convinced that no psychiatrist should ignore the role of allergies.

Classical allergists are more impressed with immunological tests than they are with patients made sick. They wish to reserve the term "allergy" for certain types of responses. I have seen a few almost livid with rage at the thought that foods could cause allergies. This is their problem. Orthomolecular physicians need not apologize to anyone for using the term "allergy" to describe undesirable reactions to food, unless it is known there is a direct toxic reaction (contaminants, additives, etc.) unrelated to allergies.

There are a number of excellent books describing allergies or clinical ecology such as Crook (1980), Gerrard (1973), Kaufman and Skolnik (1984), Mandell and Scanlon (1979), Philpott and Kalita (1980), Randolph and Moss (1980), Rapp (1979), and Smith (1981).

Crook, W. G. (1980), *Tracking Down Hidden Food Allergy.* Jackson, Tenn.: Professional Books.
Gerrard, J. W. (1973), *Understanding Allergies.* Springfield, Ill.: Charles C Thomas Publishing.
Kaufmann, D. A., & Skolnik, R. (1984), *The Food Sensitivity Diet.* New York: Freundlich Books.
Mandell, M., & Scanlon, L. W. (1979), *Dr. Mandell's 5-Day Allergy Relief System.* New York: Thomas Y. Crowell.

Philpott, W. H., & Kalita, D. K. (1980), *Brain Allergies: The Psychonutrient Connection.* New Canaan, Conn.: Keats Publishing.

Randolph, T. G., & Moss, R. W. (1980), *An Alternative Approach to Allergies.* New York: Harper and Row.

Rapp, D. (1979), *Allergies and the Hyperactive Child.* New York: Cornerstone Library.

Smith, L. (1981), *Foods for Healthy Kids.* New York: McGraw-Hill.

Reading these books will prepare any physician to introduce clinical ecology into his or her practice. This will benefit many patients, increase the satisfaction of helping more patients recover and will undoubtedly increase the practice as well.

Allergies are sensitivities to foods and other foreign molecules, and whether airborne, in water, or in food, they are diagnosed in the usual way. The patient's history should determine whether allergic reactions were present during infancy and what happened after that. The presence of symptoms doctors do associate with allergies such as asthma, hay fever and rashes, will suggest that other diseases in these patients are also allergies. I have found that patients with depression have a very high incidence of these recognized somatic allergic reactions. The nutritional history should also focus on food allergies. Patients' likes and dislikes are very helpful, especially when combined with frequency lists showing what are the most common foods causing these reactions.

Finally, clinical and laboratory tests are used. They all have advantages and disadvantages.

1. *Elimination Diets, Including Fasts.* When foods which cause reactions are eliminated long enough, the body stops responding, i.e., the symptoms clear. This will usually happen during a four-day fast; or suspected foods may be eliminated individually or in groups. Once symptoms are gone the foods are individually reintroduced as a challenge. If the symptoms are reproduced, one has established a food allergy for that person.

The advantage of the elimination diet is that it is an actual test of foods and is fairly reliable, but many patients will not or believe they cannot fast, and it takes several weeks to complete food testing. It is very economical. For overweight patients, losing weight is another advantage. Finally, the fast can be a very dramatic illustration to the patient of how foods can bring on symptoms. Once one had experienced a four-day "cold" after drinking a glass of milk, milk is not nearly as appealing.

2. *Intradermal Tests.* Food extracts are injected intradermally using different dilutions. A dilution less than the most dilute required to elicit a reaction can be used to neutralize a reaction. These can then be combined to develop solutions which can be given weekly to desensitize the patient.

This technique requires much more effort on the part of the physician and staff of technicians, and therefore is more expensive. For many it is easier than fasting and the subsequent food testing. In my opinion it is not as accurate as the fasting technique. It works best for patients unable or unwilling to follow the careful testing or dietary program called for by fasting and special diets because the physician does the testing, and the desensitizing treatments allow patients to carry on with a minimum of dietary change from their previous patterns of eating. This is the more traditional way followed by orthodox physicians and their pious patients (a pious patient is one who believes everything the doctor tells him and follows the medical advice religiously).

3. *Sublingual Testing.* This is in principle similar to intradermal testing but is more

accurate, probably because it is more physiological—normally we do not eat through our skin but through our digestive mucosa. Its main flaw is the subjective element, which may cause a problem, but when used skillfully it is very helpful.

4. *Radio-Allergo-Sorbent Test (RAST)*. This test measures the amount of immunoglobulin E present in blood. If IgE antibody levels are high for a specific substance, this indicates the patient is allergic to that substance, but a low level does not prove an allergy is not present.

5. *Cytotoxic Test*. In this test, white blood cells are mixed with food extracts. Food extracts that are toxic to the leukocytes will destroy them. This is seen by microscope. The degree of damage is given a rough quantitative rating. One sample of blood can be used to test up to 200 different food extracts. One assumes that if this type of toxicity (cytotoxicity) can be seen in vitro, a similar destuctive effect occurs in vivo.

When the foods are identified, the patient places himself on an elimination diet, avoiding all the foods that tested positive. Following a period of adjustment to the new diet, that person should become well since the leukocytes are no longer under continuous attack. Clinically this is what happens. Patients do recover. To prevent the formation of new allergies, they follow a four- or five-day rotation diet. After a period of months, forbidden foods may be introduced in the rotation. Many patients may eventually be able to eat everything, but on a rotation system. These diets are described in the books referred to in this section.

According to Kaufman and Skolnik (1984), the reproducibility of the test is high, i.e., when two samples of blood are drawn about the same time, very similar results are found. This is a test of the skill of the technician reading the results. The cytotoxic test does not measure allergies as defined by most allergists, but it may measure food sensitivity. Reliability of a test is a measure of its relevance to the clinician. Here too as measured by clinical response it is fair.

The cytotoxic test has many advantages. It is easy for patient and physician.

Since leukocytes are part of our defense against invaders, cancer, etc., I wonder if a patient placed on a diet generated by this test might have a better prognosis for a wide variety of diseases. It seems only prudent to me to reserve our leukocytes for the more important job of keeping us alive rather than to have to deal with foods we can avoid.

Many patients will need no tests and can discover their major food sensitivities by history and a few simple eliminations. Others may require one or more tests, and I expect some may well need all of them.

### Treatment

Once the allergies and sensitivities are established, treatment is relatively simple. The foods must be eliminated until the body regains the ability to digest these foods without reactivating the original reaction. Some can resume eating these foods in a few months. In a few cases that food will always cause a reaction. I had a patient who developed hives after eating tomatoes when 15 years old, and again when she tried them once more at the age of 65. This is called a fixed allergy. Patients will discover their own allergies once they understand the connection between foods and their own health.

I said that the treatment is relatively simple. I meant that it is simple to give correct advice, but it may be very difficult for patients to follow the program. The transition between the old and new diet can be very difficult. Patients need support, encouragement, and counseling. Even then they will frequently fail and become frustrated. For patients sensitive to sweets, holidays, especially Christmas, can be particularly trying. January is relapse month for adults. Eventually patients who are motivated will establish the dietary program they need for their health.

During the initial phases of the elimination diet, many patients enter a supersensitive phase when even small amounts of the food will elicit a severe reaction. For six months after I eliminated milk and all its derivatives, I was in this phase. Even a touch of butter or cheese would bring on a runny nose. Perhaps this is fortunate, for it reinforces patients' determination not to consume what they are allergic to.

The antiallergic nutrients have been described earlier. Unfortunately, there are a few orthomolecular physicians who know little about allergies and an even greater proportion of clinical ecologists who know as little about vitamins and minerals. But wide spectrum clinicians will combine the best of both. Several clinical ecologists, once totally opposed to the use of vitamins, have started to use them. They found, to their surprise, that their results were much better. There is some evidence that these vitamins enhance the body's ability to clear itself of allergic reactions and to deal with them more effectively.

## AUTOIMMUNE DISEASES

Here the immune defense system fails to recognize its own tissues and attacks them, causing diseases such as lupus or multiple sclerosis. Or the system simply fails to function, causing AIDS as its most definite example. There are a number of reasons why the immune system fails, including nutritional deficiencies; probably heavy metal poisoning, such as mercury leached out of mercury amalgam fillings; chronic infection with Candida,

and perhaps with other fungi or parasites. Perhaps multiple food allergies and sensitivities eventually immobilize our immune defenses. It is likely that excessive free radicals will do the same. Thus, many patients with lupus cannot tolerate the sun. This suggests that they are very sensitive to what the sun does, i.e., create free radicals which are used in darkening our skin.

I will deal with two autoimmune diseases as these are the ones I have treated. These are lupus erythematosis and multiple sclerosis.

### Lupus Erythematosis (L.E.)

I first became interested in using niacin for L.E. many years ago when a patient with severe depression and L.E. was referred to me. Part of the treatment included niacin, which I used, not expecting it to do much for his L.E. To my surprise, his L.E. began to clear and when last seen several months later he was almost well. My second patient responded equally well at first, but after six months the L.E. returned and this vitamin combined with ascrobic acid no longer helped.

Later I read the book, *The Sun is My Enemy*, by H. Aladjem (1972). In this book the author describes how lupus affected her, how it was concluded that there was no treatment, and how on her own she tracked down a professor in Bulgaria who apparently had developed a treatment. He told her that one variety of lupus did respond to niacin given intramuscularly, and he advised her to start and to continue with this at home. Her physician in Boston was very reluctant to give niacin to her or to sanction this, but she persuaded him to carry on. When she published her book, she was well, and when I had lunch with her in New York several years later, she was still well. The dose the Bulgarian professor recommended was 1 cc per day.

About this time I began to correspond with Mrs. Betty Hull in Texas, who had also recovered from lupus. She organized a club, Leanon, for Lupus Erythematosis Anonymous, and began to publish a little newsletter* that contained the latest information about various forms of lupus and treatment. It carried notes about patients and letters from patients describing their disease and response to treatment. There is little doubt that nutritional treatment is extremely important. It may have to be combined with modern drugs. Generally, when nutritional therapy plus supplements are used the response is better, and smaller doses of strong drugs are needed and can be dispensed with earlier.

The treatment for lupus should include an investigation for allergies, an examination to determine if supplements of vitamins and minerals are required, and treatment for these syndromes.

### Multiple Sclerosis

Multiple sclerosis has remained mysterious and very difficult to treat. In 1951 I directed a survey of all MS patients in Saskatchewan. About that time surveys of prevalence had shown that MS was more common in cold countries like Canada. Thus, the prevalence in New Orleans was significantly lower than in Winnipeg. The Saskatchewan figures were about the same as for Manitoba, and recent surveys have shown they are still very bad.

The reasons for the effect of climate have not been discovered. Suggestions have been made that it is due to temperature or to the level of minerals in soil. The North American glaciers covered all of Canada and the northern United States, leaving behind soils rich in metals such as copper. Copper, although essential in trace amounts, is toxic, and it was suggested these copper levels played a role. Perhaps other minerals were involved, since copper toxicity does not cause MS-like symptoms.

The work of Horrobin (1977, 1979) and Rudin (1981) suggests that prostaglandins and their essential fatty acid precursors are in-

volved. Evening primrose oil has been helpful to some patients with MS. Also, R. Swank found that diets low in fats derived from milk products were helpful. This indicates there is a fat involvement, but may also be due to allergic reactions to milk.

If temperature is a main factor, then one can develop a relationship. Animals and plants living in cold areas such as Canada must have more unsaturated fatty acids to increase winter hardiness. That is why fish from cold waters, seals in northern Canada, and plant oils such as linseed oil and canola oil, are richer in omega-3 essential fatty acids (EFA) than animals in warm waters and warm plant oils such as olive, peanut and coconut oils. People living in Canada need more omega-3 EFA, but Rudin (1984) has shown that our modern diet contains only 20 percent of the EFA it contained 100 years ago. The change occurred when industry began to supply all our cooking oils, which are warm oils, low in EFA of the omega-3 type.

What would happen to a person predisposed to MS, living in a cold climate on a diet deficient of omega-3 EFA? Since winter hardiness is a function of the mass of the body, of which the brain is a minor component, then it is likely the limited quantities of EFA will be sequestered by the tissues most in need of winter hardiness properties, i.e., skin, subcutaneous tissues, muscles and ligaments. Any deficiency is apt to be shown in internal organs, including the central nervous system. Is this central deficiency of omega-3 essential fatty acids a key factor in allowing the MS changes in the nerves of the body? Is this a reason why MS is rarer in people living in warm areas, for there the overall need for EFA would be less and there would be less tendency for MS to occur? This hypothesis can be tested by studying dietary habits of patients with MS, compared to their relatives who are well and to people in warm areas. It can be tested further by restoring the balance

---

*Publication ceased in 1984.

between the two main groups of essential fatty acids and saturated fats.

There is significant evidence that there are a number of MS syndromes, perhaps four or more. A few patients recover on an elimination diet, eliminating foods to which they are allergic or sensitive. A second group includes patients who have recovered on the F. Klenner (1973) multivitamin orthomolecular approach. A third group has recovered when treated effectively for chronic candidiasis. A fourth group may be mineral-sensitive. Until pure syndromes can be isolated, it may be impossible to run controlled, double-blind studies. Many patients can be helped, but many do not respond—perhaps because it is difficult to determine which group each patient falls into. I have seen a number of cases and will describe a few here.

I am unhappy with the overall therapeutic response, especially from chronic patients with MS. When the illness is caught early, the results are much better. The patient must be very dedicated and powerfully motivated to follow the complicated treatments that have been used. They must contend with physicians who are opposed and discourage them, with the costs of treatment and with the slow pace of response. When every MS patient can be evaluated carefully using all the diagnostic measures and treated carefully with support from family and community agencies, the results will be much better than those achieved by palliative drug treatment alone.

THE VITAMIN SYNDROME

This was described by Klenner (1973). Undoubtedly there are a number of MS patients who respond to this multivitamin approach. It requires heroic dedication to take all the vitamins required orally and by injection, but some are able to do so and profit. The program consists of the following nutrients:

| | |
|---|---|
| B1 | 300 to 500 mg q.i.d. before meals |
| | 400 mg i.m. o.d. |
| Niacin | 100 to 3,000 mg q.i.d. before meals |
| B6 | 100 to 200 mg q.i.d. |
| | 100 mg i.m. o.d. |
| B12 | 1 mg i.m., 3 per week |
| B2 | 40 to 80 mg o.d. i.m. |
| Crude liver extract | 1 mg daily i.m. |
| Choline | 700 to 1,400 mg q.i.d. after meals |
| Lecithin | 1.2 grams t.i.d. |
| Magnesium | 100 mg t.i.d. |
| Calcium gluconate | 240 mg q.i.d. |
| Calcium pantothenate | 200 mg q.i.d. |
| Glycine | 1 teaspoon in milk q.i.d. |
| Mega-Min | 1 o.d. |
| Ascorbic acid | 2 grams q.i.d. |

One of the most publicized recoveries on Vancouver Island was Mr. D. Humphreys, whom I have met. His recovery is complete. Other patients have also responded, as is shown in the following news report which appeared in *The Victorian*, Victoria, B.C., Monday, January 26, 1976:

*Group of five beat multiple sclerosis*

A group of five people—all victims of multiple sclerosis—are quietly making medical history here in Victoria.

To date, there has been no known medical cure for the crippling disease.

Now, new treatment—using simple vitamins—has brought about definite improvement in all five, and one woman's progress has been described by her doctor as "dramatic."

[JM] . . . a 42-year-old housewife . . . was in a wheelchair. Now she can walk—and even dance.

A mother of three and a wife of a retired serviceman, Mrs. [M] has been on the treatment for only six weeks.

But Mrs. [M] and the rest of the group are lucky. They have doctors in Victoria willing to give the treatment.

Some 13 others in the Greater Victoria area have also found doctors who will help and they are commencing treatment now.

But a further 10 MS sufferers are still seeking medical aid—and being turned down.

The problem—the treatment is new to doctors and not officially recognized by the medical profession.

"There are only seven or eight doctors here who are going along with this," says Dale Humphreys, the man who started it all.

On Nov. 5, 1975, *The Victorian* printed the story of Humphrey's startling recovery from MS.

The 48-year-old music teacher . . . was cured of MS following treatment prescribed by Dr. Frederick R. Klenner of Reidsville, North Carolina.

A medical paper by Klenner, outlining the treatment, was made available through *The Victorian*. MS patients were instructed to take the paper to their doctor if they wished to try it.

The result was astounding. Since then, letters have been coming in steadily from all over the world as the story of Humphreys spreads far and wide.

One Toronto man is flying to Victoria around Feb. 1 to meet with Humphreys in a desperate attempt to find someone who will treat him.

Humphreys, once almost reconciled to a wheelchair, is now 100 percent fit and even able to do two jobs.

Mrs. [M] gives thanks to her doctor—"I'm one of the lucky ones. I asked him to help me and he read Klenner's paper. He said: 'There's nothing to hurt you here' and then he agreed we could go ahead,' " she says.

"I can't understand those doctors who say 'no' to their patients—some of them don't even give a reason."

## CHAPTER REFERENCES

Aladjem, H. (1972), *The Sun Is My Enemy*. Englewood Cliffs, N.J.: Prentice-Hall.

Cathcart, R. F. (1985), Vitamin C: The non toxic, non rate-limited, antioxidant free radical scavenger. *Medical Hypotheses* 18:61-77.

Hoffer, A., & Parsons, S. (1955), Histamine therapy for schizophrenia: A follow-up study. *Can. Med. Assn. J.* 72:352-355.

Horrobin, D. F. (1977), Schizophrenia as a prostaglandin deficiency disease. *Lancet* 1:936-937.

Horrobin, D. F. Oka, M., & Manku, M. S. (1979), The regulation of prostaglandin E1 formation: A candidate for one of the fundamental mechanisms involved in the actions of Vitamin C. *Medical Hypotheses* 5:849-858.

Huggins, H. A. (1982), Mercury: a factor in mental disease. *J. Ortho. Psychiatry* 11:3-16.

Jaques, L. B. (1979), Heparin: An old drug with a new paradigm. *Science* 206:528-533.

Klenner, F. R. (1973), Response of peripheral and central nerve pathology to mega doses of the vitamin B complex and other metabolites. *J. Appl. Nutri.* 25:16-40.

Pauling, L. (1970), *Vitamin C and the Common Cold*. San Francisco: W. H. Freeman.

———(1976), *Vitamin C, the Common Cold and the Flu*. San Francisco: W. H. Freeman.

Philpott, W. H. (1974), Ecologic, orthomolecular and behavioral contributors to psychiatry. *J. Ortho Psych.* 3:356-370.

Reich, C. J. (1971), The vitamin therapy of chronic asthma. *J. Asthma Research* 9:99-102.

Rudin, D. O. (1981), The major psychoses and neuroses as Omega-3 essential fatty acid deficiency syndrome: Substrate pellagra. *Biol. Psychiatry* 16:837-850.

Rudin, D. O. and Felix, C. (1987), *The Omega-3 Phenomenon: The Nutrition Breakthrough of the '80s*. New York: Rawson Associates.

Russell-Manning, Betsy (1983), *How Safe Are Silver (Mercury) Fillings?* Los Angeles: Cancer Control Society.

Shute, E., & Shute, W. (1956), *Your Heart and Vitamin E*. Detroit: The Cardiac Society.

Stone, I. (1972), The natural history of ascorbic acid in the evolution of the mammals and primates and its significance for present-day man. *J. Ortho. Psych.* 1:82-89.

Swank, R. (1972), *The Multiple Sclerosis Diet Book*. Garden City, New York: Doubleday and Co.

Stone, I. (1972), *The Healing Factor: "Vitamin C" Against Disease*. New York: Grosset and Dunlap.

Truss, C. O. (1978), Tissue injury induced by candida albicans: Mental and neurologic manifestations. *J. Ortho. Psych.* 7:17-37.

——— (1981), The role of candida albicans in human illness *J. Ortho. Psych.* 10:228-238.

——— (1983), *The Missing Diagnosis*. Birmingham, Ala.: C. O. Truss.

# CHAPTER 9

## ORTHOMOLECULAR PSYCHIATRY

Orthomolecular psychiatry has the same relationship to orthomolecular medicine as does orthodox psychiatry to orthodox medicine. Every patient with any disease has a psychological reaction or component that may be very minor and not require any psychiatric treatment, or it may be of such severity as to necessitate psychiatric treatment. For many patients, both specialties must work together. Orthomolecular medicine has a much wider sweep, and if it were more popular it would leave orthomolecular psychiatry with a narrower, more sharply defined field. Orthodox medicine tends to think in organic or psychological terms. If a thorough physical examination and tests do not reveal a sufficient explanation of the symptoms, that patient's illness is promptly dumped into the psychiatric area. Even the use of psychosomatic medicine has not altered this, for to most physicians psychosomatic medicine is looked upon as a disease with physical symptoms caused by psychological factors. In short, these physicians lump both psychiatry and psychosomatic medicine together.

Orthomolecular physicians recognize that a large fraction of the psychiatric patients are ill due to physical factors, not due to any organ dysfunction. The usual tests do not reveal pathology. These physical factors are changes in metabolism and/or nutrition. They might be looked upon as humoral factors or as a third category of illness. When they are treated successfully, their psychiatric symptoms clear. Very little pyschotherapy is required, and that can be given by any competent physician. In my practice, I have estimated that if each referring physician were to first place his or her patient on an orthomolecular regime and wait up to three months, I would lose half my practice. Patients who require orthomolecular psychiatrists suffer from prolonged anxiety or depression, or from schizophrenia, or from other disorders that the general practitioner is not equipped to deal with due to lack of time, experience or skill. A few orthomolecular physicians have been very successful in treating large numbers of schizophrenics, most of them failures of orthodox psychiatry, i.e., drug treatment alone (see Paterson 1981; Kowalson 1967; and Green 1970).

The same basic principles apply to orthomolecular psychiatry, i.e., the principle of individuality, the orchestra principle, and very importantly the recognition of the syndromes that comprise psychiatric diagnosis. None of the psychiatric diseases are homogeneous. They are caused by a variety of factors. Psychiatrists have divided schizophrenia into a number of subgroups, such as catatonic, paranoid, etc. This differentiation is based upon the clinical description of these subgroups. These terms are of little value since they do not endure, nor do they help indicate which treatment should be used. Patients may easily shift from one subgroup into another. The syndromes that orthomolecular psychiatrists use are based upon causal factors and do determine treatment.

Orthomolecular psychiatrists use the medical model (Siegler and Osmond 1974). About 1970, orthodox psychiatrists had reached the zenith of a general move away from the medical model. Their emphasis on psychotherapy as the major treatment inevitably led to this position. The American Psychiatric Association did nothing to stem this move. The situation became so bizarre that in some psychiatric centers, psychologists and social workers were all given equal status with psychiatrists. They were the patients' doctors and determined which drugs they would receive; then they would request that an M.D. sign the drug order since society has not yet given these professional groups the right to prescribe drugs. In the past decade there has been an increasing realization that psychiatrists must use the medical model if they are to help their patients recover. But there are many centers that still subscribe to a model muddle. I have seen patients who have been treated who did not know their therapist was not a physician as they had assumed. Most *patients* will adhere to the medical model.

*Orthomolecular*, the word developed by Linus Pauling in 1968 (1968, 1986) describes a system of treatment that uses nutrients and normal constituents of the body in optimum amounts as the main treatment. Orthomolecular physicians use all modern treatments, including drugs, surgery, physical and psychological methods, when these are appropriate; when antidepressants or tranquilizers are needed they are used in conjunction with the nutrients and nutrition. The drugs are used to gain rapid control over undesirable or disabling symptoms and are slowly withdrawn once the patient begins to respond to orthomolecular treatment. Patients with schizophre-

nia remain well after the tranquilizers are discontinued. They do not suffer the debilitating side effects of chronic tranquilizer medication. Surgeons have found that their patients respond more quickly after surgery and suffer fewer undesirable reactions. Since all people are healthier when they eat food only (avoiding junk and artifact), they can resist disease and injury more effectively when they are healthier due to optimum nutrition.

The major emphasis on nutrition and nutrients sets orthomolecular physicians apart from other physicians who seldom show any interest in the nutritional condition of their patients and are generally resistant and even hostile to the use of vitamins and minerals. These physicians depend almost entirely on drugs, surgery, and radiation.

Nonmedical professionals such as psychologists and nutritionists can advise patients about nutrition. Even though they are not allowed to practice medicine, i.e., prescribe drugs, they are able to help many persons regain their health. But the majority of orthomolecular practitioners are physicians, of whom about 10 percent practice psychiatry.

Every division of medicine is bolstered by a set of principles based upon theoretical ideas and practical experience in dealing with patients. One of these principles is individuality, the fact that every person is unique, has different nutrient requirements and responds differently to treatment. Knowledge of individuality is ubiquitous from the time an infant first recognizes mother as different from other women. The facts of physical and anatomical differences are not in dispute. We each have a particular shape, form, color, personality and life history. The use of names recognizes that fact and the importance of individuality.

Physicians are equally aware of anatomical individuality but are less aware that there are wide ranges of need for drugs and even more variation in optimum vitamin requirements. Surgeons hope that an appendix that must be removed is where it is supposed to be, but good surgeons are not surprised when it is not. Physicians know a few patients are eased of their depression with 25 mg of a standard antidepressant, while some require 10 times as much. Nutritionists know nutrient requirements vary, that each person has a unique need for proteins, fats, carbohydrates and micronutrients, but nearly every nonorthomolecular professional grossly underestimates the wide range of variation. Roger Williams' (1956) summary of the vast data for the biochemical uniqueness of people is persuasive, but many years before, Garrod (1902), one of the founders of human biochemistry, wrote in discussing alkapttonuria: "These are merely extreme examples of variation of chemical behavior which are probably everywhere present in minor degrees and that just as no two individuals of a species are absolutely identical in bodily structure neither are their chemical processes carried out in exactly the same lines . . . it is no more surprising that they should occasionally exhibit conspicuous deviations from the specific type of metabolism than that we should meet with such wide departures from the structural uniformity of the species as the presence of supernumerary digits or transposition of the viscera." When any population is examined for any one attribute such as height, weight, shape or color, there is a range in the measurements used to describe them. Height varies from under two feet in infants to over seven in a few adults. Most male adults range between four-and-one-half to six feet tall. When height is plotted against the number of people at that height, one has drawn a frequency distribution curve. Many more men will have a height of five-and-one-half feet than five or six. To give someone a simple estimate of the height of the population we would estimate the average height and also the degree of deviation from it by the standard deviation. This statistic has been so arranged that the mean value plus or minus two standard deviations from

this mean will account for about 95 percent of all that population. About 5 percent of any group will vary beyond this range for biological variables in general.

Normally the curve looks like a bell. The bell-shaped distribution curve applies to other measures, such as daily need for protein and for vitamins or minerals, but for each nutrient the curve will have a different shape. It may be short and broad or narrow, or it may not be bell-shaped. But for each one, at least 2.5 percent will require more than the rest of the population (the 97.5 percent). We can only surmise why this is the case, as there has been little interest in this phenomenon. There may be a problem with absorption in the intestine. Thus, with pernicious anemia, specific areas in the gut which normally absorb vitamin B12 are lacking, or after the vitamin is absorbed it may not be combined efficiently into its coenzyme, or it may be wasted or held too tenaciously by some organ systems, thus depriving other parts of the body. Orthomolecular physicians deal with patients whose needs for nutrients lie beyond the usual distribution. These patients require up to 1,000 times as much of certain nutrients. For practicing with this principle, orthomolecular physicians are subjected to criticism by physicians who are not aware of these matters and who refuse to believe that a number of chronic diseases are present because these extraordinary nutrient needs are not met.

Because the concept of individuality is so basic to this entire work, it is necessary to enlarge our understanding of its enormous role in all human affairs. I assume that few will disagree with the fact we differ in visible attributes such as height, weight, color, configuration, fingerprints and so on. We also differ in physical capability, strength, dexterity, coordination, skill, and in our interests. There is a remarkable search for unique niches or interests. Discoverers want to be first, for only one can be so unique. Scientists fight over priority, for only the first is remembered and honored. Artists strive to be different, to be known for the uniqueness of their creativeness and talent. Uniqueness is often honored and rewarded, but of course it must be the type of uniqueness which society finds acceptable. Some forms of uniqueness lead to imprisonment or involuntary admission to mental hospitals. What few people recognize is that physical, physiological and even psychological factors that are measured as different arise from a metabolic apparatus, our bodies, which are unique. The total of these hidden biochemical factors which create our individuality is much greater than are the visible attributes. Identical twins, who are as alike genetically as it is possible to be, possess many biochemical and nutritional differences. When that one fertilized egg makes an error and divides in two, each of which creates a new individual, there is no perfect division of all the genes or other cellular particles that control life.

Individuality is as pervasive as our atmosphere; we are not aware of it unless it does something dramatic. People are surprised when they see examples where the law of individuality appears not to have been obeyed. When two identical twins walk down the street they will attract more attention than do fraternal twins. Quintuplets attract enormous attention. Perhaps we are so comfortable with individuality because it has shaped our evolution and culture.

What began as a random variation became one of the driving forces of mammalian culture, for this created the possibility of identifying individuals. Identification made it possible to establish a close relationship between mother and child and later father and child, and led to the creation of families, which is one of the bases of human culture.

Human infants usually bond within the first six months after birth, but there must be some who require much more time and some who never do bond. Perhaps some of the behavioral aspects of infantile autism arise from a long-delayed bonding due to some interference in the infant's ability to bond. This could arise from a number of perceptual illusions or hallucinations that would make identification of mother or father impossible.

Being a parent is never easy. It is even more difficult when there is no relationship between mother and child, or when the relationship is faulty, for then the infant cannot or does not reward or compensate mother with appropriate responses. If baby never smiles back at mother, it becomes extraordinarily difficult for mother to smile at baby. One of the enduring characteristics of mothers of depressed or otherwise sick children who do not smile is their own frustration and depression. It is not hard to decide when a sick child has begun to get well by looking at mother. When mothers are cheerful, less haggard and more optimistic, it is almost certain their child has begun to recover. Many mothers have described how they felt the first time their child began to respond normally, something they may never have seen before. One of the enormous burdens psychiatrists placed upon mothers was the facile acceptance of the idea they had made their children sick, either deliberately or, more frequently, under the sway of their own subconscious conflicts. Adding guilt to their burden certainly did not help and in most cases made the problems worse.

Many children with learning and/or behavioral disorders do not respond appropriately to their parents, or they do so only on rare occasions. This is a grave problem with schizophrenic and autistic children. They appear to be disinterested and respond inappropriately to either a warm, positive approach or to punishment or sanctions. This is why techniques used to mold behavior in normal children are so ineffective for autistic and schizophrenic children. Babies will reject being held or cuddled. They will not come when they are called, will not attempt in any way to win their parents' approval. Their main motive is to pursue their own self interest, which may be destructive, bizarre, and usually is difficult to tolerate. Every whim or fancy must be obeyed immediately. When restrained, all hell breaks loose.

The continual burden upon the parents is enormous. An extraordinary effort is needed to keep some semblance of order, to protect brothers and sisters, or to protect the sick child against self-mutilation. The frustration of some of the parents has been so great they developed a fear they would injure their child by beating them, and some have. I am convinced many battered children are ill and unable to respond appropriately to parents, who themselves may have similar tension or depression and respond inappropriately.

It appears these sick children have not bonded emotionally to their parents, perhaps because their sensory apparatus was defective. Some may fail to see their parents as unique individuals; this is a rare symptom patients have described to me. Many years ago a minister brought a very depressed patient to me. He was considering suicide and had made several attempts. He was very worried about a universal plot directed against him. I asked what was his evidence. He replied that wherever he went, he saw the same person near him. On his way to my office, when he stopped at a red light, he noticed this man sitting in a truck alongside him. When he was sitting in the University Hospital waiting room, the same person sat beside him. Often he would see this man following him. He concluded there was a plot and that this person was hired to follow him. Since delusions are often a response to perceptual changes, it occurred to me that he must have lost his ability to identify faces so that every person looked alike, as if the same mask was on every person. When questioned, he reported that faces appeared to him to be vague, diffuse and alike. This is a rare schizophrenic symptom, but in December 1979 I ran across

another example that illustrates the enormous impact of perceptual changes. A woman with schizophrenia no longer recognized her husband and children as her family. They did not look like they had. She became very suspicious and fearful and had to be admitted to a psychiatric ward. The difficulty in bonding in an infant with perceptual illusions is immense if the misidentification prevents recognition of mother as a unique person.

If babies did not recognize their parents, one of the bases for the human family would be absent. Species like turtles, who never see their mother, have adopted different mechanisms to ensure survival. They are produced in large quantities and genetically programmed much more than are mammals.

Uniqueness and identification had such an enormous evolutionary advantage that it quickly became the norm for mammalian species. It has become a function of our inheritance. It is normal and desirable to be unique. With identical twins nature appears to go against this rule. The two individuals who appear to be alike attempt to be different by dressing differently and developing different interests. Their parents will add distinguishing attributes if necessary by clothing or other measures. Only plant and animal breeders go against this trend when they try to breed animals or plants that are as alike as possible, i.e., are purebred. This is easier for plants but can be devastating for both plants and animals.

The visible attributes which make us unique are merely the end result of a large number of biochemical and physiological reactions in our bodies. These, in turn, determine our nutritional needs and how we will respond to the food we eat. The differences between people can be enormous, and the range of variation in nutritional needs will be much greater than it is for measures such as height or weight, but ability and creativity may range a thousandfold. How does one judge the difference between an average violinist and a Yehudi Menuhin?

Orthomolecular medicine is concerned mostly with biochemical and nutritional differences. They are as basic to the production of health and disease as normal biochemical reactions are for the final normal human being. The fact that some people require large doses of nutrients has been hard to accept because the vitamin concept has been accepted too well. Early observations that vitamins were required in small amounts has become dogma—many believe that only small quantities are ever required. This dogma began to break several decades ago when a few sick children were discovered who required very large quantities of pyridoxine, vitamin B6. They were said to be vitamin B6 dependent. The earlier concept only accepted the idea of a vitamin deficiency. The few classical deficiencies such as pellagra, beriberi, scurvy and rickets are rare in industrialized nations, but when they do appear it is due to gross deficiencies and abnormalities of the diet. A child with a pyridoxine dependency would remain ill on a diet that contained enough pyridoxine for most people. Since these early findings, a large number of other dependency diseases have been found. These findings were already foreseen over 40 years ago by pellagrologists who were active before World War II. They reported with surprise that some chronic pellagrins would not remain free of the symptoms of pellagra unless given at least 600 mg per day of vitamin B3. This was an enormous dose at that time, when only 5 mg or so was considered necessary to prevent pellagra, and when the price of vitamins was still very high (at a time when medical research funds were very scarce). Chronic pellagra produced an irreversible biochemical change so that small amounts of vitamin no longer could maintain health. A vitamin deficiency, which we all would suffer from if deprived of small amounts of vitamin B3, had been converted into a vitamin B3 dependency, for which large amounts were necessary each day, forever. I have seen a large number of patients who did not re-cover until they began to take 3 grams per day of vitamin B3. In the past they had suffered from severe prolonged stress and malnutrition. The best examples were those who had survived concentration camps in Europe or prisoner-of-war camps in the Far East. Many ex-prisoners of war today suffer all the ravages of an accelerated aging process because of these dreadful experiences. I have estimated that one year in such a camp accelerated aging by five years. Canadian soldiers kept in Far East camps four years have aged at least twenty years, having an apparent physical and mental health of about 80 years of age when they are only 60. Only niacin, 1 gram taken three times a day, has restored some of them to their normal health.

In my opinion, one of the schizophrenic syndromes is a vitamin B3 dependency. But even amino acids may be required in large quantities. A few people sleep better when they take 1-tryptophan, 1 or 2 grams per evening. Phenylpyruvic aligophrenia may be due to a tyrosine dependency. Isoleucine may be required in large doses for some schizophrenic syndromes.

The question arises, why should even a few individuals require these large quantities? What has allowed these conditions to remain as a small part of our population? What is the biological advantage that has overbalanced the serious disadvantages? Why has evolution not removed any person with these inherited factors, or is nature still proceeding with the very slow process of developing a variety of man much less dependent on certain nutrients? Is scurvy a way of weeding out those of us who cannot survive on tiny quantities of vitamin C? We have no answers, but we do know it is possible for every person to become dependent on a large number of nutrients. Linus Pauling (1968), in his classic paper, "Orthomolecular Psychiatry," showed how energy requirements of any cell created a species of animals unable to make vitamin C. Thousands of years ago, our animal ancestors foraged for food very rich in vitamin C. They may have consumed several grams per day in the green vegetation and fruit. With this type of diet there would be less advantage in making vitamin C in our bodies, as most animals do today. A genetic mutation that removed the capability of making vitamin C from glucose would confer no disadvantage as the vitamin C was available in the food. The energy saved or not required to make vitamin C would be used in other reactions. This energy saving conferred enough biological advantage for the genetic mutation to sweep across the entire population. Once established there was no turning back. We are forever unable to make vitamin C and must depend upon our food and supplements. Since the genetic condition hypoascorbemia became established (see Stone 1972 a, b), man has suffered fantastically from scurvy, one of the enduring great plagues.

Pauling's (1968, 1986) account of the development of hypoascorbemia may be expanded to account for all the nutrients we must receive in our food. They can be divided into two main classes: those which can be made in the body from other nutrients, and those that must be preformed in our food. The first class is very large and includes every chemical in the body that is essential for health; there may be thousands of these. Ordinarily we need not be concerned about them, but if one could not be made, it would become essential. Any diet which failed to provide it would allow a deficiency to appear. The second class is quite small, totaling around 40 to 45. It includes the vitamins, eight or nine amino acids if we include tyrosine as an element that is essential for some, a few fatty acids and some minerals or trace elements. Of the 20 amino acids, eight cannot be made in the body and are thus considered essential amino acids. The remaining twelve can be made in the body from the eight essential amino acids. It is important, however, that we remember that all 20 must be present in the body. The 12 nonessential amino acids are just as essential to metabolism, and when supplied to adequate amounts they spare the body the need to make them from the eight "essential" ones. Biochemists have just begun to examine the relationship of deficiency of nutrients to disease. The vitamin concepts have been restrictive in the past but are being overcome.

At one time, single-celled creatures were neither animal or vegetable, or perhaps they were entirely vegetable, i.e., dependent only upon inorganic salts, water, oxygen and sunlight. Animal life must have developed for the first time when one cell engulfed another and survived, for by this simple step all the energy required by cells to make a host of organic chemicals could be used for other metabolic functions. That first cell which swallowed its neighbor became the parent of all animal life on earth. The energy saved became available for movement and cellular colonies—and for creation of the multicelled animal. If we still had to make everything in our bodies we would probably be plants.

The earliest animal cells must have been able to live on salts, like plants, or by engulfing other cells. Gradually the need to make everything would vanish, and these cells would become more and more dependent on eating other cells. Gradually, the machinery required to make organic molecules would be altered for other purposes. As soon as a nutrient like vitamin C could no longer be made, it would become an essential nutrient. Thus, the molecules that we call vitamins became essential, and of the 20 amino acids that cells need, eight can no longer be made. It would be wrong to believe this process has stopped. Tyrosine may be an essential amino acid for PKU syndrome, but it is difficult to see how PKU syndrome confers any evolutionary advantage. It is unlikely man will ever find a diet that supplies quantities of tyrosine. An examination of relatives of PKU syndrome victims may reveal whether there are any advantages to having the gene for PKU syndrome. Nicotinic acid may be in a transitional phase, i.e., it may be in the process of becoming a vitamin. A vitamin, by definition, is a substance that cannot be made in the body, but the body can convert about 1 to 2 percent of the tryptophan into vitamin B3. Perhaps, in a few people, a much greater fraction can be diverted into the vitamin. Are there a few who cannot divert any tryptophan into vitamin B3? We will never know until a search is made. I believe this search will be most profitable in schizophrenic patients, especially in cases of childhood schizophrenia and infantile autism, for these individuals would be much more sensitive to the quantity of vitamin B3 present in food and would require much more. Any individual who could convert more tryptophan into vitamin B3 would be able to get by on a diet so low in vitamin B3 that it would cause pellagra in other individuals who could convert much less tryptophan. There is a potential advantage in being less dependent on endogenous sources of vitamin B3, provided the diet contained enough; more tryptophan would be available for conversion into serotonin and other intermediate chemicals. Serotonin is important for activity of the central nervous system and probably digestion; it is present in greater concentration in these areas. Perhaps schizophrenia is the price society is now paying for the gradual spread of this phenomenon. There need not be any cost if society ensured that every person had optimum quantities of vitamin B3 in their food from birth onward.

Roger Williams (1977) emphasized another basic concept that he called the orchestra principle. Just as it is impossible to consider one instrument in an orchestra more important than another, so must all the nutrients required by the body be available. They all work together. An excess of one cannot compensate for the deficiency of another. On a practical level, even the best use of nutrient supplements cannot compensate for the continued consumption of foods rich in added sugar and other cosmetic additives.

## QUALITY OF RECOVERY

A source of conflict between orthomolecular and other physicians is their expectation of the quality of recovery. Expectations of recovery depend upon one's experience of the quality of recovery. Psychiatrists who use tranquilizers only expect that they will reduce the intensity of symptoms in nearly every patient, provided they have selected the most efficient dose. But they expect few recoveries, and over the past decade they have learned the cost to patients for the relief they have gained. The cost includes inability to function normally in the community and neurological side effects such as tardive dyskinesia. Tranquilizers work rather quickly. In brief, they rapidly control symptoms but do not recover many patients.

Orthomolecular psychiatrists combine the rapid effect of the tranquilizers in reducing symptoms with the slower effect of the nutrient treatment in reaching recovery. They see a much larger proportion of schizophrenic patients get well to a degree not seen by tranquilizer therapists. The latter group believes that orthomolecular therapists are prone to exaggeration. Tranquilizer physicians with the usual prejudices against nutrients who have seen the results of treatment on their patients are usually astonished at the quality of recovery.

When a patient has recovered, one does not need a questionnaire or scale to decide this. In sharp contrast, tranquilized patients may appear to be better, even though there has been no improvement in their psychosis. For this group, a major industry has developed consisting of psychologists, psychiatrists and instruments for testing to determine whether there has been any change.

I have been using a simple four-point scale to measure recovery:

1. Absence of symptoms and signs.
2. Ability to be normally productive in the community, which means the patient is engaged in work at home or in the work force at the same level of skill as before the illness hit. Income tax paid before and after the illness is a good measure of recovery, except for those whose income is independent of work. Sick patients on or off welfare seldom pay the same taxes as do their peer group.
3. Ability to get on reasonably well with family.
4. Ability to get on reasonably well in society in activities normally tolerated by any substantial portion of that society. Rebels in a society that contains a number of other rebels are not mentally sick people just because they are rebellious, even though rebels probably are paranoid people.

A *recovered* patient has reached these criteria for all four aspects. If only three are reached, the patient is *much improved*. An *improved* patient has reached two, while any patient who has attained only one is described as *not improved*, whether in a hospital or in the community. These are clear-cut criteria, easy to use. Very few chronic patients reach recovered status or even much improved status; most would score 0 or 1 point only. In sharp contrast, most acute and subacute schziphrenics will reach states of improvement greater than unimproved (0 to 1 point). A few examples will illustrate how this scheme is used.

A man, having recovered from a florid schizophrenic breakdown, enrolled in a college of medicine at a prominent Canadian university, graduated, specialized in psychiatry, and has had a successful practice for nearly 20 years. I consider him *well* or *recovered*.

A woman who had been severely paranoid for many years and required many months of treatment in University Hospital, Saskatoon, Saskatchewan, is seldom paranoid but still suffers from anxiety and tension a good deal of the time. I would consider her *much improved*.

She managed her own business until she sold it recently, gets on well with her family and the community. Because of her anxiety and occasional paranoid suspicions, she has not achieved *well* status. Most psychiatrists would consider her within the normal range.

A third patient only occasionally suffers from voices and thought disorder, which are generally well controlled with tranquilizer medication, but he is unable to work because he is too drowsy and lacks initiative. He gets on well with his family, who are supportive of him, and with the community. He is classed as *improved* (2 points).

The fourth patient is free of signs and symptoms of schizophrenia but is unable to work, has no family relationships, and has no friends. He is *not improved* (1 point).

### DIAGNOSIS

An examination of a patient is not complete without a mental state examination. This must be systematic and thorough. From this, one can arrive at a diagnosis and can get some idea of why the patient has certain problems. The mental status examination I follow (see next page) is based on one published by Dr. Karl Menninger over 30 years ago.

In getting at the mental state it is important to ask direct questions. Contrary to the ideas current several years ago, asking patients if they see visions will not cause them to do so. For some years, psychiatrists were afraid to ask these questions because they feared their patients were so suggestible they would be creating a new symptomatology for them. I have not found this to be true. Patients who do not hear voices will not say they do. I exclude malingerers for whatever reason from consideration; they range from sociologists who tell psychiatrists they see visions when they do not, to a few prisoners who might wish to be transferred to a psychiatric ward.

When a patient does have a perceptual symptom, he or she should be asked to elaborate on it. How long does it last? When does

| MENTAL STATE | | |
|---|---|---|
| **Perception—** | Visual | Illusions |
| | Auditory | |
| | Taste | |
| | Olfactory | |
| | Tactile | |
| | Orientation | Hallucinations |
| **Thought Disorder—** | **Thought Content—**Delusions, etc. | |
| | **Thought Process—**Blocking, speech too fast, too slow, no ideas whatever. | |
| **Mood—** | Depression, anxiety | Quality |
| | Manic-depressive | |
| | Euphoria | Quantity |
| **Behavior—** | Hypoactive | Quality—Appropriate/ Inappropriate |
| | Hyperactive | Quantity |

it come? What effect does it have? Does it cause fear or anger? Simply talking about these symptoms will relieve many patients of some of their anxiety. The suicidal young man who had difficulty differentiating faces was much relieved when this was explained to him as a symptom of schizophrenia. After he left my office, the minister asked him what I had said. He replied, "He told me I had schizophrenia. I do not know what it means, but I certainly feel better." He made no more suicide attempts and slowly recovered on orthomolecular treatment.

There are so many perceptual symptoms, so many types of thought disorder, so many variations in mood and behavior, that it may be impossible to adequately cover the entire mental state on the first or second interview. It is important to determine the diagnosis rapidly so that treatment may get underway. Patients should be relieved of their symptoms as quickly as possible. Two perceptual tests have been developed that provide an enormous amount of information quickly, without tiring the patient or the doctor.

The first test, the Hoffer-Osmond Diagnostic (HOD) test, we developed in 1959 (Hoffer and Osmond 1961). It is based upon the fact that diagnosing consists in asking the right questions, which can be answered yes or no.

If a number of yes answers are obtained, it points to a syndrome. Does your chest hurt? Yes. Is it worse on breathing? Yes. Do you feel hot? Yes. Already we know we should look for some chest pathology, perhaps one of the pneumonias. Do you hear voices? Yes. Do you think they are real? Yes. Does it bother you? Yes. Already we know we are dealing with a schizophrenic syndrome.

There is a popular card questionnaire, the Minnesota Multiphasic Personality Inventory (MMPI), which the patient sorts into categories. This test was originally developed as a personality test, but since personality has little to do with diagnosis, it is not surprising that the MMPI has slight relation to diagnosis. To develop the HOD test, Dr. Osmond and I searched the literature written by recovered and still ill schizophrenics; we listened to our patients and examined their clinical records. And we explored the hallucinogens: LSD, mescaline, and the schizophrenogenic compounds adrenochrome and adrenolutin. From this large literature and from our own experiences, we prepared a series of 145 questions, which were placed on cards numbered 1 to 145. A large number of cards contained questions dealing with perception, a smaller number of cards centered on thought processes, mood and behavior. Patients were asked to sort cards into "True" or "False" categories. If they were not sure of an answer they were to place the card in the "False" box. In most cases, 15 to 20 minutes were required. In framing these questions we tried to visualize what it would be like to be schizophrenic. After a large number of subjects had been tested, we examined several groups of subjects for each item. If a question was placed in the "True" box by half of the schizophrenics, and by none of the normal controls, this question would be given extra weight in the scoring. In this way we developed a scoring system which was simple and good for diagnosing schizophrenia. The test is described by Hoffer, Kelm and Osmond (1975), and is available from Rehabilitation Research Foundation, Box BV, University, Alabama, U.S.A. 35486. High scores suggest schizophrenia, low scores do not favor this diagnosis. There is a perceptual score, a thought disorder score, a mood score and a global or total score. Many physicians are using this test and are finding it very helpful. In my opinion, every patient with psychiatric complaints ought to be tested, since their discomfort may be based on perceptual symptoms. The test is not time consuming and can be scored in a few minutes by anyone. Physicians who start using the HOD are surprised at the number of patients they had not been able to help who scored high on the HOD test. They were thereafter able to help them by starting them on vitamin B3 treatment. High HOD score is one of the indications for using this vitamin.

The HOD test may also be used to monitor treatment. If the scores go down, the patient is getting better; if they go up, worse. There is one exception to the latter; a few patients are paranoid and will not admit symptoms, while others are confused and are not aware of many of their symptoms. When they begin to improve, their paranoid ideas are less dominant or they are less confused; consequently, the HOD scores one to three months after treatment has started may be higher than the

original score, but thereafter as improvement continues the scores begin to decrease. If one suspects these two factors have been the reason for the two low initial scores, it is simple to ask the patient. In most cases they will discuss why they did their test in this way. The HOD test may also be used to monitor whether a relapse is beginning. If scores begin to rise after a long period of stability, it indicates a relapse is underway.

The HOD test may be done as often as required. Patients generally do not object if they understand it is designed to help them. I usually show them their scores and sometimes they are charted to show changes that occur with time. Patients are interested and will ask for their scores. The HOD test is a very useful adjunct to diagnosing and is much superior to MMPI.

### USES OF THE HOD

The first test of any new diagnostic test is, How valid is it? Assuming there is a basic, reliable diagnostic test, how will the new test correlate with it? We found that the HOD has a very high degree of validity. It is less subject to observer error; if three psychiatrists examine a patient they are apt to disagree over the diagnosis, but if the same three see the results of the HOD test, they must agree over the scores although they may choose to disregard them. All the published studies where this relationship has been carefully examined conclude that the HOD does discriminate between schizophrenics and nonschizophrenics, which is what we hoped it would do. It is not designed to discriminate between various forms of neuroses or between depressions and neuroses.

Psychiatric diagnosis is imprecise. Since the HOD test results are independent of the psychiatrist, it ought to give a truer picture of the patient's mental state and ought to be a better measure of schizophrenia than clinical judgment alone. In the same way, a thermometer gives us a more accurate measure of the degree of fever than feeling the person with lips or hands. Studies have confirmed this. Dr. David Hawkins compared the HOD test results of patients just after admission with two sets of diagnoses: the admission diagnosis, which is a provisional diagnosis and the discharge diagnosis. At discharge much more is known about the patient, and this should be reflected in the final diagnosis. He found that there was a higher correlation between the admission HOD test results and the discharge diagnosis than with the admission or provisional diagnosis. When I saw these results I was pleased but not surprised, for I had seen the same phenomenon over and over for many years. Patients admitted for depression who had schizophrenic HOD scores would be rediagnosed as having schizophrenia on discharge or subsequent admissions, even though the diagnosing psychiatrist had never seen the results of the HOD test. The results were removed from the ward on completion and were kept in our research files, which were not made available to the residents or medical students.

This property of the HOD has great practical and therefore economic value. A clinic on Long Island, associated with the North Nassau Mental Health Center, used the HOD as one of their intake screening tests. Clients who had high scores (pathological) were referred to Dr. Hawkins' clinic, while others were dealt with by clinic staff. Until then they had had an enormous waiting list and ran large deficits. Too much of their time and money were used in diagnosing. After they incorporated the HOD into their intake, they soon ran through their waiting list, were able to provide prompt help, and no longer suffered from deficits. They saved huge sums of money, for there is no better way of saving money than to know very early which is the correct diagnosis so that prompt treatment can be started.

With the exception of the EWI, there is no psychological test as reliable and valid as the HOD test for schizophrenia. It follows that it will also be useful in measuring change. As the disease worsens, more symptoms should (and do) appear, and HOD scores rise. When patients improve, the number and intensity of symptoms decrease, and HOD scores decrease to normal scores. When there are no changes in scores, there is no essential change in the disease. Every physician who has used the HOD to monitor treatment will confirm these conclusions. The test can be repeated frequently, as long as there is a change in the clinical condition. When the change is slow, there is no point in repeating the test too frequently. Sometimes patients depend upon the change in scores to bolster their own impression and will ask for the test and want to know the scores. This can be very helpful to patients whose various sets of symptoms do not ease at the same rate. Patients judge their own recovery by reference to those symptoms that trouble them most. A patient with both visual illusions and depression may find the illusions more disabling than the depression. This would apply, for instance, to a truck driver whose livelihood depended upon driving, but who found this very difficult because of visual illusions that he was off the road; or if he could not judge the location and speed of oncoming traffic. Depression might be much more tolerable. If the illusions disappeared while the depression hung on, he would still feel improved. If the depression cleared while the illusions remained, he might judge himself not improved. Another patient might find depression much more disabling. Any improvement in illusions without any change in depression would be of little value to the patient. The HOD is very valuable in determining where the improvement has occurred. When this is shown to patients, they immediately become more optimistic, since they can see the improvement in one area, even though the other symptoms have not altered. Evidence for any degree of improvement is helpful and encourages the patient to carry on with treatment.

The HOD test records change in a large number of symptoms, no matter how this is achieved. When the scores do not decrease, it is doubtful whether there has been any real improvement. Tranquilizers are very effective in dampening down symptoms and in reducing their impact upon the patient; visions and voices are not as threatening, paranoid ideas are reacted to less violently. However, for a large number of patients there is no essential decrease in the quality of the symptomatology. I have seen HOD test scores on hundreds of chronic schizophrenics, who are maintained in the community or hospital wards by constant medication with tranquilizers. Their HOD scores have been just as high after tanquilizer therapy as they were before treatment was started. But for a large number of patients, scores do go down. These patients are generally better and can look forward to a time when they will no longer require any tranquilizers or very small dosages. A large proportion of chronic patients with high HOD scores while under tranquilizer control have been placed on orthomolecular therapy. It has been my experience that scores begin to go down and symptoms really leave. Voices that have been undiminished for years slowly decrease in intensity and frequency.

The HOD test is also useful in channeling psychotherapy. It is very helpful to know which symptoms are most disturbing and how they have affected the patient's thinking and behavior.

## HOD SCORES AND THE SCHIZOPHRENIAS

The schizophrenic syndrome is an expression of a metabolic disorder in the brain in response to a large number of factors. We should not expect the HOD to help us decide why the syndrome is present, and it does not.

## HOD SCORES AND PYROLLEURIA (MALVARIA)

We found the HOD test very valuable in establishing the validity of the Malvaria syndrome. After we had found that some nonschizophrenics were positive for kryptopyrrole, while some schizophrenics were negative, we were interested in seeing whether the presence of this abnormal metabolite in urine imposed a particular clinical pattern on the patient. Was the pattern the schizophrenic syndrome, since the metabolite was more closely related to schizophrenia than to any other psychiatric group? Large numbers of positive and negative patients were given the HOD test. The results were clear: Patients with this factor had average HOD scores which were identical with schizophrenic scores, while patients negative for the factor had average, nonschizphrenic scores. This supported our clinical conclusion that Malvaria and schizophrenia were clinically similar. Malvaria is, in fact, one of the schizophrenic syndromes.

## RELATION OF HOD SCORES TO AGE

We found that the HOD scores for subjects in a large high school population were highest at age thirteen and decreased with age. The younger population appeared to be much more unstable perceptually. As they matured they reached adult low HOD scores. However, scoring was not only age related. We also found that students who were behind their peers scholastically had higher scores than their peers. We also found the high scoring students more often had psychiatric difficulties. This suggested that high scoring teenagers were not well, even though they were part of a normal population and neither they nor their families had considered they were ill. Those teenagers who started to improve their nutrition and take the proper vitamin supplements improved and their scores became normal. This large school survey was completed before the use of drugs reached its present state. I would assume a much larger proportion of high school students would be high scorers today. I believe those high scorers were students suffering from affluent malnutrition—from too much sugar and other junk. Perceptual stability in young adults and teenage students is probably a measure of nutritional adequacy.

## HOD SCORES AND MENSTRUATION

Early in our use of the HOD test we found that women tended to have higher scores than men. Since about 25 percent of adult women before menopause are testing just before or just after their period, this could have been an explanation. It is well known that premenstrual tension is common and tends to make any psychiatric syndrome worse. A survey of women followed over their cycle confirmed the relationship. Their HOD scores were lowest during the ovulation phase, increased the closer they came to their period and decreased after that. HOD scores free of this hormonal effect can therefore be obtained only if all women are tested at the midpoint of the cycle. However, in most cases the disease pattern imposes a clear HOD change which overshadows the monthly cycle.

## PATIENT ACCEPTANCE OF THE HOD TEST

Psychologists have seldom taken patients' wishes into account when they developed tests theoretically designed to help patients. Perhaps they simply have been unaware of the medical model or the patient-doctor relationship; or, like most professional people, i.e., architects, they have paid little attention to the users. Few architects designing hospitals have given much thought to patients' needs or consulted them. For this reason, when Prof. J. Izumi gave patients' needs a special role when he designed a psychiatric hospital for Yorkton, Saskatchewan, it was considered revolutionary.

The medical model requires that the patient divulge to his physician subjective information that allows the physician to diagnose

and treat. Nothing else is required, and if it is demanded it is an invasion of privacy that patients should and will resent. For this reason, attitude tests are of little value. It is irrelevant for the vast majority of patients what they think about geography, space, politics, etc.; although for a very small number these may be built into a thought disorder that is essential to be known. In the same way, intelligence tests have little value in psychiatry. Patients are aware that there is no need to divulge everything, and when tests appear irrelevant to their problem they will not do the test or will not answer correctly. A test of the value of any test as perceived by patients is the need for built-in lie detector items.

We have found that the HOD test is very acceptable to over 95 percent of all subjects tested. I can recall only a few out of thousands of my patients who found the HOD unacceptable. However, if the test results were used for nonmedical purposes it would be rejected just as much as any other test so used, and rightly so, since this would be an abuse of the doctor-patient relationship.

The questions asked by the HOD test are the same ones that could be asked by any physician aware of the complete mental examination. Patients find them appropriate and relevant. Of all the tests I have used, the HOD is one of the most acceptable.

## CONTROVERSY

There is no controversy over this test, but perhaps one may arise. So far, those workers most apt to be involved in any debate in the press have simply not bothered to use it. It is used on a wide scale by several thousand physicians and a few psychologists. So far, no clinician using it has written a report critical of it.

The HOD test led to the development of a more sophisticated and accurate test called the Experiential World Inventory (EWI), (El-Meligi and Osmond 1970). This test is better balanced, having the first 200 questions (1 to 200), more or less equivalent to the second two hundred (201 to 400). The patient completes a questionnaire by marking "True" or "False" categories. The scores are obtained by placing a template over the answer sheet. The eight scores are graphed to form a profile. When the profile is in the top half, schizophrenia is indicated. The higher the profile, the more probable the diagnosis. As the patient recovers, the profile drops into the normal range, i.e., the lower half of the chart. This test takes more time than the HOD but yields much more information. Often when the HOD test has not shown evidence for schizophrenia, although clinical judgment suggests it is present, I have used the EWI, which has confirmed the diagnosis. Because of its greater number of questions, it is not as practical for first screening of the patients by physicians. It lends itself more to institutional use by psychologists. Most physicians would find it valuable to use both, reserving the EWI for more difficult diagnostic problems. EWI is available from Robert Mullaly, Ph.D., Intuition Press, P.O. Box 404, Keene, NH 03431.

## SYNDROMES

A syndrome is a constellation of symptoms and signs which point toward one or more causes of the illness, or may point toward an organ of the body or to a functional problem of the organ. Thus pneumonia, a constellation of fever and pain in the chest that worsens on movement all suggest pathology in the lung. This may arise from infection, bacteria, virus, etc., or from an invasion. It is important to determine the cause, since different diseases, even when they cause the same syndrome, require different treatments. This applies to the brain or central nervous system as well as to any other organ.

Psychiatric diagnosis has been based on the idea that the various diseases are due to psychosocial factors. Physical or biochemical factors have begun to receive more attention over the past 10 years, but this is not yet reflected in the recent psychiatric nomenclature. Thus schizophrenia is subdivided into various groups by clinical criteria, which are not related to causes and do not indicate which treatment has the best chance of success. Another outcome is that, in my opinion, psychiatric nomenclature is too complex and unwieldy. I doubt that many practicing psychiatrists use more than a small fraction of all the diagnostic terms that are officially recognized.

I have found a simple scheme that has been particularly valuable and which I believe will be equally helpful to other physicians. This scheme is based on grouping together the main areas of change as determined by the mental state, i.e., by a combination of changes in perception, thinking (thought disorder), mood and behavior. This scheme might be viewed as an operational scheme. It is not influenced by psychosocial factors, which do influence the content of the disorder but not the process.

### The Syndromes

THE SCHIZOPHRENIAS.

Schizophrenia is a combination of perceptual and thought changes. It is a disease of perception combined with an inability to tell that these perceptual changes are unreal. Unreal means they are subjective changes, which are real to the patient but unreal to normal people and unreal to the patient when he or she recovers. Terms such as *hebephrenic, catatonic* and *paranoid* are not needed. The terms *acute* and *chronic* merely describe the duration of the disease. Mood and behavior symptoms are secondary.

MOOD DISORDERS.

Here I include depression, euphoria, excessive swings between depression and euphoria, and anxiety or tension. This syndrome includes any disorder of feeling including not feeling, i.e., the inability to feel emotion. Patients with perceptual changes and thought disorder do not belong here.

THE ADDICTIONS.

These are primarily mood disorders where the person finds that a number of drugs alleviate some of the symptoms. The behavior is determined by the need of the addict to obtain the drug or substance he or she is addicted to. There are two types of reactions: (1) those considered socially acceptable by the vast majority of people, such as eating too much sugar and other junk food, or smoking and drinking—but not to the point of alcoholism—and the use of socially sanctioned drugs (over-the-counter and prescription); and (2) those considered socially unacceptable and often illegal. Here the drugs are not legally available, and to obtain them the addict may, and usually does, resort to any antisocial activity. A vast infrastructure, from growers, to middlemen, to street providers, has developed. Examples are marijuana, heroine and cocaine addiction. If cigarettes were illegal, we would have a problem here as well. I know a few sugar addicts who would commit antisocial acts to obtain sugar.

CHILDREN WITH LEARNING AND BEHAVIORAL DISORDERS.

These children suffer from perceptual changes which impair their ability to learn, with secondary behavioral problems.

BEHAVIORAL DISORDERS.

This includes both children and adults. There are no apparent perceptual changes, no apparent thought disorder, nor does mood appear to be altered. Perhaps we have here an example of a program disorder, i.e., their lifestyles or life experiences have been such that they can behave in no other way. I would include professional criminals here. Of course, people commit crimes for many other reasons.

There are a large number of habits or repetitive acts that range in quality and intensity from those that are acceptable to those that impose a great burden on the person. These include tics, abnormal movements (unless caused by physical disease or drugs), obsessive ideas, compulsive acts, etc. These people do not suffer from thought disorder or perceptual changes and are not antisocial, but they will suffer from anxiety and/or depression, depending on how difficult and disabling their abnormal habit is. Often the mood disorder is primary and provides the spur for perpetuating the motor activity. This group should be in the mood disorders. A number of these patients respond well to some of the tricyclic antidepressants.

THE ILLUSIONOGENIC REACTIONS.

Drugs like LSD seldom cause hallucinations; they are better considered illusionogens because they alter the experience of normal perception. For most people there is no thought disorder except for brief periods. The subject remains aware that he or she has taken a drug and that the perceptual changes are self/drug-induced. These people are not schizophrenic, but if they lose this insight, and they may do so for several days or longer, they then belong with the schizophrenic syndrome.

SENILE CONFUSIONAL STATES.

These patients suffer from profound thought disorder, both in content and process. They are disoriented for person, time, and place, and have severe memory disturbance. These are all due to a grossly disturbed brain that is no longer able to function. Thought content is a random and often inappropriate recall from their lifetime memory banks.

*Causes of the Syndromes*

Each syndrome is caused by several factors. The schizophrenic syndrome can be found in some patients with thyroid disorders, chronic rheumatic fever, some of the neuromuscular disorders such as Huntington's disease, pellagra and in some drug intoxications. All these make up a relatively small proportion of all schizophrenic patients. In the same way, any one of the syndromes described, with the possible exception of the behavioral disorders, is caused by a number of factors.

Orthomolecular physicians have added three additional groups of causes and are studying a fourth. The three are the vitamin dependencies, the cerebral allergies and mineral problems. Amino acid dependencies are being examined as another possible cause. These have already been discussed.

The first step in diagnosing is to determine the syndrome. Before treatment is started one tries to find the cause or provisional cause. During treatment ideas about the cause may have to be reviewed. The exact cause may not be known until the patient has recovered. Treatment must also take into account the syndrome. A depressive is given different orthomolecular psychotherapy than a schizophrenic and usually requires somewhat different adjunctive drugs. The prognosis is different.

## TREATMENT

Orthomolecular treatment for all psychiatric problems includes certain general components, but each patient will require an individualized program. There is no single recipe for every patient. These main components, already described for physically ill patients, are nutrition and supplements, all combined with the best of modern medicine and psychiatry. One combines the rapidity of action of drugs with the enduring therapeutic action of nutrition and supplements.

### Nutrition

This has already been described as a diet that consists of foods that are whole, fresh, variable, nontoxic and indigenous. A diet free of added sugar will approximate such a diet well enough for most patients. It is easy to remember and allows patients the freedom to select the diet that best suits them.

### Diets For People With Food Allergies or Food Toxicities

A large number of people suffer from one or more food allergies. There is a debate between clinical ecologists and allergists as to whether *allergy* is the correct term. Whether or not they are allergies, there is no doubt that some people are made sick by certain foods. I am one, being made ill by all milk products. I believe *allergy* is the correct term, for using an antihistamine will reduce or prevent these reactions in many people.

These reactions may occur with whole foods or may be a reaction to additives in the food. In either case, the problem must be dealt with if the patient is to obtain relief from these reactions.

The type of diet depends upon the foods to which one is allergic. If there are only a few food allergies the simplest program is to avoid these foods while maintaining the food-only, artifact-free program. I avoid all products derived from milk and do not follow any rotation diet. A few people may develop more food allergies if they become heavily dependent on any other food; using rotation diets will decrease this danger. Over 90 percent of all allergies are variable, meaning that in time tolerance will develop to small amounts of the food if it is not eaten too often. Six months or more of complete abstinence from the offending food is required. During the initial few months, that person may be supersensitive to the food, as I was to milk, butter, cheese, or cream. Less than 10 percent of allergies are fixed, meaning one never develops a tolerance.

If the person is allergic to many foods it may be impossible to devise a diet which eliminates them all. Allergists have developed several ways of dealing with this problem. One way is to use a rotation diet (see Mandell and Scanlon 1979). These may be four-day, five-day or greater rotations. A certain class of foods are used the first day, and if on a five-day rotation, repeated on the sixth day. Each food is used every five days. This allows the body to develop a tolerance for these foods. It works best for minor food allergies.

Foods that elicit a strong reaction may have to be eliminated totally. The rotation diet may be used in conjunction with desensitization, using extracts of the foods in various dilutions, which are prepared individually for each person after testing.

Rotation diets may be burdensome for patients or they may not work well. Other techniques under investigation are the use of proteolytic enzymes or antihistamines. The enzymes are usually pancreatic enzymes or derived from plants such as papain. They help break down proteins to their amino acid components. The body does not develop allergic reactions to natural amino acids, but will react to dipeptides and polypeptides, which are chains of amino acids. These protein breakdown fractions may be absorbed into the blood and settle in various tissues of the body, including the brain. This may be one of the mechanisms for these undesirable (allergic, toxic) reactions. By improving the quality of the digestive process, the tendency for these reactions to occur will be lessened. Other measures which improve digestibility include eating slowly, chewing food thoroughly, and provision of acid if it is lacking. Psychologically, a meal consumed in a friendly, relaxed atmosphere will be digested more readily.

Enzymes may not be helpful, perhaps because other nonprotein fractions of partially digested food are involved or because some are allergic to the animal used to provide the enzyme.

One can also use antihistamines, which are helpful provided there are no side effects such as drowsiness. If depression is a major symptom of food allergies, the tricyclic antidepressants are helpful. The optimum dose is used until the depression has cleared, after which the optimum maintenance dose is determined. I have given smaller quantities of antidepressants to patients who were not depressed, and have found that many can then eat foods that formerly caused severe reactions. Modern antidepressants have been developed on the basis of their antiserotonin properties, while their antihistamine properties have been ignored. This was a mistake, since the antihistamine properties are probably the major way in which they are antidepressant. A new preparation, Mianserin, not available in the U.S.A., is claimed to have little effect upon serotonin or dopamine pathways, but is recognized as an effective antihistamine. Another way is to take a substance before meals which will adhere to the antigen antibody receptors and protect the body in this way. Some of the coumarin bioflavonoids will do this, and one, sodium cromoglycate, is already used for allergies.

### Drugs

There are three main classes of drugs, using the most common effect as a criterion: tranquilizers, antianxiety and antidepressant drugs. Members of one class are not all the same type of chemical, nor is their activity only in the one area. There are drugs which can have tranquilizing, antianxiety and antidepressant qualities.

Tranquilizers are mainly phenothiazines and butyphenone drugs like Chlorpromazine and Haldol. They may be taken orally or, less frequently, by injection. Usually tranquilizers are used for very disturbed, agitated schizophrenic or manic patients. In small doses they may help with anxiety. Orthomolecular physicians find that the optimum dose, when combined with vitamins and nutrition, is somewhere between zero and that dose usually recommended in the drug insert. When vitamins are not used, the recommended doses and even higher are most often needed. After treatment is well underway, it is usually possible to decrease the dose of tranquilizer. This is desirable because tranquilizers cause inertia and apathy, which make it very difficult to function normally. The lower the dose, the less restraint there is on normal activity.

Tranquilizers impose an unusual burden on

patients, which is important to understand—no person can become normal while taking tranquilizers. I know of no normal person who will tolerate the major effect of tranquilizers: the inertia, apathy, drowsiness, and sluggishness of thought are too intolerable. Nor would we trust ourselves in the hands of people who we knew were taking tranquilizers. This includes people like pilots, physicians, lawyers, accountants, carpenters, and all other skilled professionals and workers. I certainly would not fly in a plane if I knew the pilot was taking tranquilizers. No skilled person would be in full possession of his or her faculties if on tranquilizers. But for many patients these drugs are very valuable and essential if they are to be treated adequately. They help control symptoms and make life more tolerable for many sick people.

The ideal situation would be to discontinue the use of the drugs as soon as the symptoms are gone, but this cannot be done, since as soon as the drugs are withdrawn, the symptoms reappear. The price of control of the symptoms is the production of other symptoms that at the onset of the illness are essential and at the termination of the illness are intolerable. This is why so many patients will discontinue medication even though they know there may be a relapse. Patients stop taking vitamins also, but the proportion who do so is much less. With good nutrition and vitamins the continued use of tranquilizers does not produce these debilitating side effects. It allows the person to function normally while keeping the disease under control. The difficult choice for the patient on tranquilizers is to suppress the symptoms while suffering another set of drug-induced symptoms, or to be free of drug-induced symptoms while running the risk of relapse. A few alcoholic schizophrenics are faced with the same difficult choice. A patient who was constantly hearing voices discovered that when drunk they were gone; the alcohol acted as a tranquilizer. The need to take alcohol soon made her an alcoholic, but she soon found the chronic drunkenness intolerable and joined AA. One month later, to her horror, the voices returned. Tranquilized schizophrenic patients may be free of voices and visions, but the chronic tranquilized state is similar to that woman's chronic drunkenness, only different symptoms are present.

Orthomolecular psychiatry provides the patient with a solution; when both tranquilizers and vitamins are used in combination, we are able to use the rapid calming effect of the tranquilizer and the slower continuing healing effect of the vitamins. As the patient begins to improve, the amount of tranquilizer is slowly reduced until the level is so low it can no longer exert any harmful effect. In most cases, except for chronic patients, the tranquilizer can eventually be discontinued. I would not hesitate to fly with a pilot who is well by virtue of taking vitamins, or to consult a physician or other skilled person similarly treated.

## ANTIANXIETY DRUGS

These are drugs such as Valium, Librium and similar diazepine compounds. They work quickly and effectively in controlling anxiety. They have anticonvulsant properties and are muscle relaxants. They are generally safe when used in small doses, but it is possible to become dependent on them—a few people have great difficulty discontinuing them. Vitamin B3 increases the effectiveness of barbiturates and these drugs. This was an observation my research group made many years ago. Recently it has been shown that niacinamide reacts with the diazepine receptors in the brain.

## ANTIDEPRESSANT DRUGS

These are used for treating patients whose main symptom is depression. Anxiety is often present but is secondary to the depression. I believe they act primarily as antihistaminic compounds.

## SCHIZOPHRENIA

Usually the patient is interviewed alone, but in many cases no useful information will be obtained unless a responsible adult is also present. Parents or siblings can be very helpful. They are especially important during the discussion of treatment, since these patients are usually so perturbed or confused that they cannot remember much of the discussion. Treatment is best described with a family member present.

After the diagnosis is established, it is discussed in detail with the patient. Since schizophrenia is such a dreadful disease and responds best to early treatment, one should diagnose at the first interview. If necessary, the diagnosis can be revised later on. I describe schizophrenia as a biochemical disorder with mental symptoms. It differs from other metabolic diseases in that the brain is one of the main target organs, whereas other diseases select other organs. I make it clear to the patient that no one must be blamed—neither parents, society nor the patient. It is not caused by bad parents or bad society; these concepts have harmed huge numbers of patients. Psychiatrists with slender evidence spun tenuous hypotheses, which they applied liberally to their patients. Many families have been destroyed by this thoughtless application of a poor idea. Parents and society are involved in this illness, as they are in any medical disease.

I explain to the patient that the term *schizophrenia* is applied to a number of diseases caused by different factors. Treatment will depend upon the relevant cause. When patients know they have schizophrenia they are generally relieved and are better able to cooperate. Many psychiatrists now inform their patients of the diagnosis. When we first began to do so in 1959, it was considered as bad as any heresy, but with the return to the medical model, diagnosis has also come back.

Prognosis is not avoided. Every person wants to know how long they must suffer. Prognosis cannot be precise because it depends upon a large number of factors. The best single predictor is the duration of the illness. Chronic schizophrenia will take more time to heal than acute schizophrenia. The next best indicator is the ability or willingness of the patient to cooperate with treatment. Patients who have no insight and believe they are well are particularly hard to treat. This is logical—few people who believe they are well will accept and cooperate with treatment. The family is very important, and with their cooperation treatment is possible until there is improvement and insight is reestablished.

Assuming the treatment will be followed, it is possible to prognose recovery or near-recovery. This is shown in the following table.

| Duration of Illness | Time required to reach much improved or recovery status. |
|---|---|
| 1 year | 3 to 6 months |
| 2 years | 6 to 9 months |
| 3 years | 9 to 15 months |
| Over 3 years | 1 to 5 years |

The response is monitored by regular clinical examination and by tests such as the HOD and EWI.

Orthomolecular treatment is more sophisticated than simply using one or two drugs. The therapist must know all the drugs, but must also know nutrition and the use of supplements.

Many patients have been on tranquilizers for some time when first seen. If tranquilizers have been effective in containing symptoms, patients are maintained because nutritional treatment is slow. If the drugs are stopped suddenly there may be a relapse before the nutritional treatment begins to work. Psychiatrists hostile to orthomolecular treatment have taken their patients off tranquilizers while allowing them to start on vitamins, usually in inadequate doses. If they relapsed, the psychiatrist blamed it on the vitamins, telling their patients they had made them sick.

Patients may prefer to use tranquilizers only. In British Columbia the Pharmacare plan covers all drugs, but does not pay for vitamins if patients are receiving social welfare. Since tranquilizers are free but patients have to pay for the vitamins, they may prefer not to use them. As a physician in B.C., I can prescribe any drug, no matter how toxic or ineffective, and it will be covered. But vitamins that will help cure the patient are not covered. I have had one or two schizophrenics who elected to be permanently on welfare because they did not want to buy the vitamins. Each patient who fails to recover will cost B.C. $1 million during his or her lifetime. It is a strange economy. In fairness to our government, they simply follow the advice of the B.C. Medical Association. In other matters, the government has been less compliant.

I tell my patients that tranquilizers alone never cure anyone. They merely reduce the intensity of the symptoms and make life slightly more endurable. They create a better behaved, chronic dependent person. Only with orthomolecular treatment can the majority of schizophrenic patients hope to become well and normally independent.

If the patient's diet is inadequate, as most are, nutrition is discussed in detail. The patient is told why he or she must follow a sugar-free or junk-free diet or if one must avoid certain foods such as milk or bread, and why. Often when patients change their diet they go through a withdrawal period lasting one or two weeks. It is usually a minor version of the withdrawal reaction following cessation of smoking or drugs. Occasionally the withdrawal can be very severe. Patients should be told they may have such a withdrawal reaction.

Then the patient is given a list of recommended nutrients. As a minimum they include vitamin B3 and vitamin C. I usually write the the names of the vitamins and the dosages on my prescription sheet and make sure the patient can read my writing and knows what I recommend. If side effects, such as the niacin flush, will occur, these are described to the patient. I also use pyridoxine, usually in combination with zinc, for the following indications: (1) pyrolleuria; and (2) premenstrual tension or any symptoms that are cyclical and related to the period.

For the inexperienced physician I recommend the following way of starting:

*Step 1*—Tell the patient the diagnosis, that it is a metabolic (chemical) disorder and will be mainly treated by nutrition, supplements, and drugs if necessary.

*Step 2*—Describe the sugar-free diet and why it is needed.

Step 3—If there is a history of allergic reactions, estimate which food is likely a factor and eliminate it for a period of four weeks or more.

*Step 4*—Start with vitamin B3, 1 gram t.i.d. If nicotinic acid is going to be used, describe the flush sequence.

*Step 5*—Add ascorbic acid, 1 gram t.i.d.

*Step 6*—If there are indications for pyridoxine, add that.

*Step 7*—If pyridoxine is added, also add a zinc preparation.

*Step 8*—If necessary, use one of the standard psychiatric drugs.

At subsequent visits evaluate any change in the patient by direct observation and, if available, by checking with the family. Make necessary changes in dosages depending upon response and side effects. Because the vitamins are relatively safe, there should be no fear of increasing the dosage while remaining within the recommended dose range.

At first one may wonder why dose changes are to be made, but after experience on a few patients confidence will develop and it becomes relatively easy. A good rule is to have a dose high enough to optimize rate of recovery without unpleasant side effects.

Physicians must be patient when treating schizophrenics, as progress can be very slow. This may be why psychiatrists trained in psychoanalysis make such good orthomolecular psychiatrists—psychoanalysis teaches patience. One must be able to distinguish between rapid response to tranquilizers and the slower, different response to vitamins.

## CHILDREN UNDER AGE 14 WITH LEARNING AND BEHAVIORAL DISORDERS

Elsewhere I have described the treatment of children using optimum doses of vitamins (Hoffer 1971, 1972,); see also Cott 1969, 1971 and 1985; Green 1969; Rimland 1978; Silverman 1973; Von Hilsheimer 1970; and Lendon Smith 1976).

### Diagnosis

A large number of diagnostic terms have been used in describing these children, including retardation, minimal brain damage, hyperactivity, autism and schizophrenia. Several years ago I counted up to 100 different diagnostic terms. Most of them have little significance, more often reflecting the diagnostic bias and interest of the diagnostician than a true syndrome.

I have several objections to these words. *Retardation* is a particularly bad one, for it takes the child away from medical treatment and into a pedagogical stream. This is why hospitals for the retarded became known as "training schools," while better-class residences for the retarded became "campuses." I believe the label is wrong because it is a dead-end. There certainly are children who cannot learn due to a number of metabolic factors that prevent learning, ranging from perceptual illusions and hallucinations to thought and memory problems, hyperactivity and depression. Once these are treated, what appeared to be retardation disappears. The term *retardation* is merely a descriptive term

for children who learn slowly or bizarrely—it is not a diagnostic term.

I also dislike the term *minimal brain damage* because it suggests there has been permanent brain damage. This term is just as frightening to parents as *retardation*, and just as wrong. The trouble with nearly all of the diagnostic terms is that they do not indicate which treatment should be used, with the exception of infantile autism, which indicates that pyridoxine must be used as part of the program; and schizophrenia, which also points to a particular treatment.

Orthomolecular physicians prefer to work with syndromes already described and with causes such as cerebral allergy, vitamin deficiency or dependency, or mineral problems. Each of these broad groups is broken down into more specific groups, according to what is the allergy, and which vitamin or mineral is needed.

The majority of children with problems suffer from metabolic problems induced by nutritional excesses or deficiencies. However, a small group suffers from a variety of psychosocial factors including broken homes, parental brutality or pathology, and so on. In diagnosing, one must determine which area is responsible, for it is as wrong to treat children with psychosocially caused problems with vitamins as it is to treat children suffering from nutritional problems by psychotherapy or family counseling. Unfortunately, the second error has been, and still is, the more common one.

The following diagnostic scheme is helpful for children with learning and/or behavioral problems.

I. Are the causes psychosocial? If yes, a broad range of psychosocial intervention may be necessary.
II. Are the causes metabolic?
1. Cerebral allergies.
2. Vitamin deficiencies and dependencies.
3. Mineral problems.

4. Genetic problems, *e.g.*, PKU.
5. Unknown.

Since 1967 I have been using a simple questionnaire for measuring children's response to treatment. Twenty-seven behavioral items are checked by observation and by discussion with adults who know the child well. Parents and teachers doing this checklist will usually come up with comparable scores. The items are shown in the following list.

1. Overactive.
2. Doesn't finish projects.
3. Fidgets.
4. Can't sit still at meals.
5. Doesn't stay with games.
6. Wears out toys, furniture, etc.
7. Talks too much.
8. Doesn't follow directions.
9. Clumsy.
10. Fights with other children.
11. Unpredictable.
12. Teases.
13. Doesn't respond to discipline.
14. Gets into things.
15. Speech problem.
16. Temper trantrums.
17. Doesn't listen to whole story.
18. Defiant.
19. Hard to get to bed.
20. Irritable.
21. Reckless.
22. Unpopular with peers.
23. Impatient.
24. Lies.
25. Accident prone.
26. Enuretic.
27. Destructive.

Each item is scored: 5 if the symptom is severe, 3 if it is moderate, and 1 if it is not present. The maximum score is 145, the minimum 27. Normal children score less than 45. The mean score for over 800 hyperative children I have tested is around 75. As the child improves, the scores decrease. The behavioral checklist was developed using symptoms that differentiated hyperactive children from normal children in a study report by M. Stewart (1970).

*Treatment*

CEREBRAL ALLERGIES

For many years I was puzzled by what appeared to be an unpredictable response to vitamin treatment. Some children would respond to vitamin treatment, while other children whose clinical symptomatology appeared to be the same, did not. Fortunately, enough did respond to convince me that the treatment was effective. The mystery cleared when the concept of cerebral allergy became part of orthomolecular psychiatric treatment, for then a large proportion of children who had failed to respond to vitamins recovered when the foods to which they were allergic were identified and removed from their diet. The first diagnostic problem is to determine into which group the child falls.

Enough information may be obtained from the history. A history of colic, other gastrointestinal upsets, eczema and other skin problems suggests allergy to milk or sugar or any other food. There may be a history of the pediatrician changing formulas in an attempt to find one that was compatible. Even breastfed babies may have allergic reactions, to cow's milk for example coming through the mother who is drinking milk. Usually the infant becomes better and appears to lose his or her allergies. Several years later, the offending food is reintroduced to the diet, especially if it is milk, because mothers are very often convinced cow's milk is as healthy and important as mother's milk and must be given. In addition they are very concerned about calcium. After a while, most children will be able to drink milk without a resurgence of the original symptoms and all is well. However, after several years, usually before playschool or kindergarten, the child becomes hyperactive and/or develops a learning disorder. This is the cerebral expression of the allergic reaction. It is seldom suspected by parents and even less frequently by the family physician or pediatrician. A history of allergic symptoms followed by a quiescent period that in turn is followed by learning and/or behavioral problems immediately suggests allergies are the cause. In many children, both somatic and psychological problems coexist such as rashes, asthma, hay fever and sinusitis (often called a chronic cold, or appearing as frequent colds). There may also be a family history of allergies.

The final diagnosis is made by elimination diets, which may be as simple as avoiding all milk products and all foods containing added sugar (junk-free) to very complicated rotation diets. If a child is hyperactive because of milk allergy, he or she will be well in a few weeks on a milk-free diet. The changes can be very dramatic. The diagnosis can be established with certainty by challenging the child by reintroducing milk, which will be followed by a prompt relapse. This will nearly always be true during the phase of supersensitivity following withdrawal of an offending food, which may last up to one year. After that the child may be able to tolerate that food every four to five days.

When many food allergies are present it is more difficult to determine the ones responsible, and a one-day fast may be necessary for older children. The fast is followed by introducing individual foods into the diet. The same treatment is used, i.e., avoidance or rotation of foods in a four- or five-day rotation. A substantial number of children respond to special diets, including the Feingold diet (1974). Excellent books dealing with these problems are available, for example Crook (1977) and Smith (1976).

Some of the allergic children also require supplementation with vitamins. The common ones used are ascorbic acid, 0.5 to 3 grams per day. Ascorbic acid is used for its antihis-

tamine properties as well, because the vitamin molecules destroy histamine molecules. Vitamin B3, usually niacinamide, may also be needed, as well as pyridoxine. Milk-allergic children very often require supplementation with pyridoxine and zinc. I have observed a very high association between excessive milk consumption, i.e., three glasses of milk per day or more, and pyrolleuria. This may be due to the chemical composition of cow's milk, which is too rich in protein (thus increasing pyridoxine requirements) and has too little zinc and iron. It is also rich in a sugar, lactose.

As a rule I place all my patients on the junk-free or living diet already described and eliminate certain foods if I suspect there is a problem. I also start them on minimal doses of three vitamins: niacinamide, 500 mg three times a day; the same dose of ascorbic acid; and pyridoxine, 100 to 250 mg per day.

If there is a very rapid recovery suggesting the diet is mainly responsible, I may then consider slowly eliminating the two B vitamins. I believe every child should be on ascorbic acid. If there is no improvement or a very slight one, this suggests the child falls into the vitamin dependency group and will need larger doses of the two B vitamins. But they must always remain on the junk-free diet.

It is easier for a child to follow a program if he or she experiences firsthand why certain foods are to be avoided. A personal, subjective observation is worth dozens of parental injunctions. One invokes the evolutionary adaptation that protects animals from being poisoned twice by the same food. If a coyote eats lamb meat infiltrated with enough lithium to make him nauseated and vomit, but not enough to kill him, that animal will eat that meat only once. Thereafter lambs are avoided. If a rat survives poisoned bait it will not eat any more. This is an important survival mechanism; we learn from experience. But for this mechanism to be invoked there must be a short interval between eating that food and some unpleasant psychological or physical experience. If a migraine headache followed each use of marijuana, there would be no users. The mechanism cannot be invoked if the interval between eating and reaction is too long. In the same way, a child punished immediately for some wrongdoing realizes the connection. If the punishment comes a week later there can be no reasonable association. The same applies to criminals who too often are punished many years after the crime—little is learned.

Food allergies develop slowly and reach a chronic phase where there are symptoms that are unrelated to food. The continual intake of the offending food serves to keep the problem alive. In order to invoke the sharp reaction, the person must first become well and if there is a sugar allergy this may require several weeks or months. Then the use of sugar will cause a sharp, unpleasant reaction. The patient can now experience the full impact of the sugar.

I have used this technique with children who refused to cooperate. They are asked to avoid all junk food for six days, then to eat as much junk as they can on the seventh day, preferably Saturday. In about half the cases there is a violent reaction, which can take any form, including headache, nausea or vomiting. When this occurs they begin to recover on Sunday. Other children experience no physical subjective reaction but become more hyperactive, more violent and more difficult to cope with. Parents are now convinced of the importance of avoiding junk, while the child is convinced more slowly. This is not a characteristic of children only; adults too have great difficulty realizing foods can make them sick. Many must suffer several relapses before the association is firmly learned. January is a common relapse month for adults. September is the common relapse month for children. Holidays like Halloween and Easter are followed by difficult days at school for teachers.

There is a threshold for the allergic response. One of my young patients discovered he would get sick on Saturday if he ate more than three chocolate bars. He therefore restricted his sugar intake to below that level.

After many months it may be possible for the child to have a sweet now and then with no reaction. Fortunately, most young people after being away from sweets for many months have lost their addiction, but it can be reactivated by going back to the pretreatment diet.

VITAMIN DEPENDENCY GROUP

About half the children I see fall into this group. They require more vitamins. The vitamin B3 group needs a minimum of 3 grams per day. The dose is very important. I have seen a large number of children who were given doses which were too low, either as a result of drugstore error or because parents felt less would do just as well, and there has been no response. A child who will recover on 3 grams per day may be totally unresponsive to two grams per day. After the child is well, it is permissible to decrease the dose slowly to determine whether a smaller maintenance dose can be used.

I prefer niacinamide for children. A few cannot tolerate even small quantities and may need niacin instead. They must be warned about the flush. If the maximum tolerable dose is less than 1.5 grams per day of each, I then use Linodil, 1 gram three times per day. If the patient can tolerate 1.5 grams of both niacinamide and niacin, both are used to yield the total therapeutic dose of 3 grams per day.

PYRIDOXINE

This vitamin is especially indicated for infantile autism and for pyrolleuriac children. The usual dose range is 100 to 2,000 mg per day in three divided doses. The optimum dose is measured by studying the clinical response to increasing doses. Pyridoxine most often has to be supplemented with magnesium and/or zinc.

The correct doses of all three vitamins, i.e., B3, B6, and C, is attained when the child improves steadily and is maintained until the child is well. After being well for a long time it may be possible to decrease the dose. It is unusual to have to increase it unless growth into adulthood makes the childhood dose inadequate.

Both parents and children want to know how long they will have to continue on vitamins. The answer is as long as they want the child to remain well. I find it is important to carry the child through adolescence. But it is permissible at any time to go off the vitamins, if the child is placed back on if there is a relapse. The best time to try taking a child off the vitamins is during the summer break, when a relapse is not as serious as during the school year. If there is a relapse the child may respond more slowly to the renewed treatment but should eventually reach the previous healthy state. Girls respond more quickly than boys.

## TREATMENT OF ADOLESCENTS

The same philosophy of treatment is used as with children. However, during adolescence new problems develop which increase the difficulty of treatment. Thus with younger children, the exceptionally sick child has to be admitted to the hospital, but with adolescents the proportion who needs admission is slightly greater. There is also a wider range of difficulty, as more adolescents refuse to accept their illness or the medical model and reject treatment. This is not surprising. If a learning disorder or hyperactivity and antisocial behavior have been present many years, it becomes very difficult to accept that the problem is within that person. Many of these patients have a history of failure, and even though a biochemical problem is easier to accept than personal blame, it still denotes a failure, even if only of the metabolism.

Adolescents are generally ill longer than children and have had more time to develop patterns of thinking and behavior which create difficulty for them. Chronic processes are harder to deal with. Also, adolescents in trouble have more chance to become members of antisocial peer groups which reinforce their antisocial behavior. Hyperactive youngsters must associate with other hyperactives, since normal children find their erratic behavior impossible to deal with. They become involved in street drugs, alcohol, and all the serious fallout from these problems.

In discussing treatment I will not repeat information already in the previous chapter, but there are special problems that need attention.

### Approach to Treatment

This depends upon the adolescent, the parents, and the state of their relationship. The most difficult patients have been sick since childhood and have experienced only a sick relationship. If there are many positive factors, one can work with these. If there are too few positive factors, it may be impossible to treat the patient outside of an institution. If the parents are firm, able to withstand a lot of stress, and able to work with their sick child, the prognosis is much better. Once the adolescent begins to become more normal, this reinforces the therapeutic process.

Generally I deal with these patients as if they were adult. I examine them, advise them where the problem is, and advise them what they can do to get better. No blame is attached to anyone. Parents are involved from the first interview as allies of the patient and physician against the real enemy, the disease.

Once the patient has accepted the treatment and begins to improve, the situation at home and in school improves steadily. There are, however, two crisis periods. The first can come at any time if the patient goes off the treatment either by desire or for other reasons. A relapse may come on rather quickly and it may be very difficult to reinstate the program. The second crisis arises after the patient has recovered. A new sense of confidence develops, especially in schizophrenic patients who develop the idea they are cured and no longer need any treatment. They will discontinue all medication, and may relapse and initiate the illness cycle all over again.

This happened recently to a young man who came to Victoria from Australia. He had been schizophrenic for several years. I started him on a comprehensive treatment program, which he followed under supervison of his own psychiatrist at home. For a year there was no change in his condition, then he slowly began to improve. When I saw him in Australia a few years ago, he had been almost well for a long time, but he had stopped all his vitamins. He refused to go back on because he knew he was cured and that by his own will he would prevent any relapse. A few weeks after I saw him, he killed himself. The suicide rate among adolescent schizophrenics is perhaps 25 times as high as among a normal population.

The longer the patient is on treatment, the less chance there is for a rapid relapse. After five years of being well, if medication is stopped, relapses are generally slower if they do occur and can be dealt with. Also, after the adolescent years these people deal with their problems in a more mature way—they are less impulsive.

### Allergies

I have seen a very clear relationship between diet and behavioral disorders. The diet becomes distorted by addiction to certain foods and junk food. Allergies develop to foods that are used frequently, such as sugar, milk, wheat, etc.; in other words, the staples that are consumed nearly every day in large quantities. With continued use the allergic symptoms become low grade and chronic and an addiction to these foods occurs. Thus, as a rule, if one wishes to quickly discover which foods one is allergic to, enquire about foods hated or loved. Hated foods are no problem because they are avoided. Loved foods are often used to excess and are responsible for much of the problem.

Since we eat those foods we like, the palate determines what we will abuse. This is why sugared products are so dangerous; they taste good and are packaged in appealing colors, flavors and boxes; and they are promoted by massive advertising. The addiction to sugar may start during childhood. I can recall one seven-year-old boy who would eat handfuls of pure table sugar. After being placed on a sugar-free diet, he was once seen during the night, creeping into the kitchen on hands and knees toward the sugarbowl to eat it pure, by the handful. Sugar is as addicting as heroin or morphine, and during withdrawal patients can suffer similar withdrawal symptoms; they have to go off "cold turkey." This can apply to milk or other foods as well. I have seen this in many patients during childhood, adolescence and adulthood.

The addiction to sugar (candy, chocolate, etc.) creates a pattern of antisocial behavior, i.e., behavior designed to meet the craving for sugar. Just as a drug addict will rob and sell to make enough money to buy drugs, children will begin by stealing. If parents provide ample supplies of sugar directly or by the allowances they give, there is no need to steal. But when parents realize what is happening and restrict sugar intake, the child begins to steal, first from parents and siblings because usually families do not hide their money from relatives. These children can steal small sums for a long time before being caught. If the child is caught early in his or her career of petty stealing, if parents realize the cause, and if they use punishment humanely but firmly, this may be the end of the petty thievery. But if the child has been stealing a long time or is caught only a few times, it becomes like a game of chance; being caught 10 percent of the time may be acceptable odds in order to meet the craving, for the money is most often used to buy sweets. Once the pattern is developed it may continue into adolescence to provide money for alcohol, cigarettes, marijuana and other street drugs. I consider the addiction to sugar one of the most important predisposing factors to adolescent antisocial behavior.

Sugar also distorts the judgment of the addict. Under the influence of hypoglycemia, it is much more difficult to control antisocial impulses. I have examined adults arrested for minor crimes committed during such a hypoglycemic phase.

All the studies relating psychiatric, behavioral and physical symptoms to food allergies have been clinical studies. I will not describe them as "anecdotal" because all doctor-patient studies are anecdotes. The only nonanecdotal studies are laboratory tests. The differences between double-blind anecdotal studies and open clinical anecdotal studies are only in the way these clinical histories (anecdotes) are arranged. I see no advantage in double-blind studies, which I have several times described as not proven, expensive, nonclinical studies best used by investigators with a lot of money, little interest in the doctor-patient relationship, and a paucity of ideas. These investigators know that the only reasons for using double-blind experiments are: (1) to obtain research grants; (2) to get their papers published; and (3) to avoid being called anecdotal.

In my opinion, the clinical studies in ecology are every bit as scientific and valid as are double-blind studies. But as double-blinds are more persuasive to nonecologists, it is helpful to have them done, at least once. This kind of study was reported by Egger, Wilson, Carter, Turner and Soothill (1983). This is a carefully controlled, double-blind study. They began with 88 children, all suffering from migraine. After being observed for four weeks, the children were started on a special diet, free of most foods known to cause migraine, and supplemented with vitamins. The children who had one or no headache in the last two weeks were started on foods to be tested, one new food every week. A commercial orange juice drink (three glasses) was given as a source of artificial color and preservative. If

the child had not responded to the fourth week on the diet, he or she was started on an alternate diet.

Each child who responded to foods was asked to enter a double-blind crossover trial. The majority of children developed migraine and associated symptoms when given the foods to which they had previously reacted. Very few reacted to the placebo preparation. This is shown in the following table.

|  | Headaches | Associated Symptoms |
|---|---|---|
| Active food | 26 | 27 |
| Placebo | 2 | 2 |

These children also suffered from other disturbances. They were hyperactive and suffered from a wide variety of physical symptoms. Some were on anticonvulsant drugs.

Four of the five authors had been convinced that any child responding to an altered diet was a placebo responder. After this study they concluded these were true allergic reactions controlled by diet. Their study also convinced them these allergic reactions were not IgE mediated.

I have included this study so readers will have a reply to their colleagues who maintain there have been no controlled studies. Of course, other double-blind studies have been reported, but critics will only accept double-blind studies if conducted by physicians not identified with clinical ecology and published in establishment journals. This study, had it been published in the *Journal of Orthomolecular Psychiatry*, would have been rejected as nonscientific.

### Supplements

The same vitamins and minerals used for children are used for treating adolescents, but minimal doses of vitamin B3 and ascorbic acid are 3 grams per day; and of B6, 250 mg per day. Adolescents who feel they have an illness and are being helped will cooperate. Patients who do not believe they are ill will find a variety of reasons why they cannot take the tablets: They are too big, taste bad, make them sick, etc.; these have to be discussed and where there is a real difficulty, it should be dealt with.

## Drugs

Adolescents are more apt to need some of the modern medications such as tranquilizers, antidepressants and antianxiety compounds. When combined with nutrition and vitamins, these compounds are more effective, so less is required. Tranquilizers are used to reduce agitated psychotic behavior and tension, antidepressants are used for the depressions. A few young patients may require both. It is essential to use as little tranquilizer as possible so the patient can continue to learn, both in school and socially. Some adolescents are so disturbed they may have to be heavily tranquilized either at home or in the hospital, but as soon as possible, the doses should be decreased and eventually eliminated.

## MOOD DISORDERS

There are two major groups of mood disorders: the anxiety-depressions and the mood swings. The mood swing patients fall into several groups depending upon the height of the upswing. If they reach a manic phase, they are called manic-depressive, but most depressions do not hit manic highs and swing more prosaically from deep depression to normal mood.

The anxiety-depressions may fall into two classes with much overlap. Some are basically depressed and develop secondary anxiety because of the depression. Others are basically very anxious and tense and react to that with depression. Treatment with orthomolecular therapy will be very helpful. In my experience a very large proportion of this group suffers from the usual variety of nutritional problems ranging from allergies to dependencies. Depression is described by Ross (1975). An amazing number of men and women with anxiety-depression lose their chronic fatigue, inertia and depression when given proper nutritional treatment. The remainder may require adjunctive drug treatment. When depression is predominant, antidepressants are used. When anxiety is predominant, antianxiety drugs work best. Often it is impossible to be sure which is predominant, but a therapeutic trial will decide. If antidepressant drugs make patients worse, they probably have a primary anxiety state. If Valium or Librium make the patient worse, they probably have a primary depression. A few patients require a combination of antidepressants and tranquilizers. Once the patient is well, the drug is slowly withdrawn. I think it is best for a depressed patient to be well for six months before starting to reduce the doses of antidepressant.

For the second group of depressions, much more dependence must be placed on drugs. These depressions are very deep-seated and are probably not caused by nutritional factors. They are metabolic diseases, but so far their etiology in unknown. The usual drugs are used: tricyclics and newer antidepressants; amine oxidase inhibitors; combinations of both of these in a small number of cases; and for some there is nothing that relieves the depression except electroconvulsive treatment (ECT). The modern procedure, which includes anesthetics and other drugs, is remarkably safe. I have not seen a single fatality in 31 years of psychiatry and I have used it since 1950, when it was the only reliable treatment. The procedure should generate no more fear than having a tooth drilled. Long series of ECT are seldom required. I find anywhere from five to 12 are helpful. I consider less than five a waste of time and usually unhelpful because the depression returns so quickly. If patients are deeply suicidal, ECT is fast, efficacious, and life saving.

Manic-depressive mood swings are more

difficult to treat. The patient prefers the manic state, while the family finds it easier to deal with the depressed state. Treatment for the depressive phase is as I have just described. The problem is that the depression, once removed, may be followed by a manic phase that in turn is followed by another depression. In my experience the primary change is the manic mood, which is followed by a period of exhaustion and depression. If the manic mood swings can be prevented, there will be no ensuing depressed phase. This is why lithium salts can be so helpful. Lithium serves best to protect the patient against another manic attack.

A manic attack may be due to the brain's overproduction of amines, which act as stimulants. The manic phase does have some resemblance to the hyperactivity generated by too much amphetamines. If the brain does generate too much amine, this appears to be followed by an exhaustion of the biochemical synthetic mechanisms, which make these amines, and a deficiency develops. This is probably the basis for the depression that lasts until the production of these amines is restored. If there is an overshoot, too much production, another manic attack will follow. Sometimes one must combine lithium, to prevent the manic episode, with an antidepressant to protect against depression. Manic episodes will also require tranquilizers, often in large doses.

Both depression and mania create a positive feedback system that worsens the condition. Depressed persons commonly retire from stimulation and want to sleep more. Typically they become more seclusive, avoid visitors, go to bed early and sleep late in the morning. These are exactly the factors required to perpetuate the depression or make it worse. It has been shown that lack of sleep tends to counter depression. In one study, 24 hours of wakefulness was no worse than antidepressants. Many people feel good all week except Sunday. On their day of rest they sleep in.

The extra sleep is enough to make them depressed and irritable. Thus depression is aggravated by seclusion, avoidance of stimulation by people and events, by too much sleep and by too little activity. This deepens the depression. Thus we have a positive feedback system. A depressed person should do just the opposite, i.e., he or she should: (1) avoid seclusion; (2) sleep less—go to bed later and get up much earlier; and (3) force more exercise. These measures, combined with orthomolecular treatment, will hinder the development of the depression part of the cycle.

There is an equally detrimental positive feedback in the manic state. Manic patients seek out too much stimulation. They are too excited or busy to sleep and seek out activity that accelerates the manic phase. One of my manic patients under reasonably good control began to develop another episode; he became overly active. Instead of consulting me he flew to Las Vegas, stayed awake three days and nights, drank too much and became uncontrollably manic. He was shipped back to Canada and had to be admitted to a hospital. A manic patient should seek seclusion and try to get more sleep, with the help of medication if necessary. Generally I am not concerned over any patients if they obtain seven or eight hours of sleep per night. However, one cannot depend only on these psychological ways of preventing manic or depressed episodes.

## THE ADDICTIONS

Treatment of all addictions must deal with two phases: (1) the withdrawal phase; and (2) the phase of recurrent desire for more.

### Withdrawal Phase

Withdrawal from all addictive foods and drugs causes an increase in tension, anxiety and other discomfort. I have seen an abrupt withdrawal from milk precipitate a suicidal depression in an adult woman, for which she had to be admitted to a hospital. Withdrawal from sugar can lead to as many "cold turkey" symptoms as withdrawal from heroin. Most smokers have experienced the withdrawal from tobacco. In fact, these withdrawal symptoms will attack up to 100 times per day, leading in each case to another cigarette. I now withdraw patients more slowly if they consume huge amounts of any one food. Obese men and women know what withdrawal symptoms are, even if they do not know that the unpleasant, weak, hungry sensation is a lack-of-food-induced withdrawal state. The first part of most prolonged fasts is characterized by withdrawal symptoms from foods. They are not really hunger, for on the fourth or fifth day there may be no symptoms at all. If these symptoms were actually hunger, one would expect them to get worse. After a much longer fast, real hunger symptoms do arrive.

One does not have to consume huge quantities of a food to be addicted. Several months ago I suddenly stopped drinking coffee. My normal intake had been three to four cups per day of weak coffee. I expected no problem because I was certain I was not allergic to coffee or overcaffeinated. To my surprise I went through a mild, four-day withdrawal, which culminated on the fourth evening in a mild headache. On the fifth day I was normal.

Withdrawal symptoms are aggravated by fear of withdrawal. Drug addicts who have heard about the horrors of cold turkey withdrawal have a more difficult time than those who are less fearful. With reassurance, much of the fear and panic can be prevented.

I have found that a water fast coinciding with withdrawal can be very helpful. During a fast, the hyper- and hypoglycemia swings eventually stop. But if food is eaten during withdrawal, especially if it is the wrong kind, these glycemic ups and downs are greatly exaggerated. One of my addict patients was very fearful of cold turkey withdrawal. I admitted him to a hospital, gave him minor amounts of an antianxiety drug and fasted

him for four days. He was surprised how easy the withdrawal was. The same applies to alcoholics. In 1951, I visited an alcoholic ward in one of the well known Boston hospitals. They were comparing the effect of hormones such as ACTH against other treatment. The neurologist in charge of the study told me they had found nothing better than simply placing each alcoholic in bed and watching until he or she began to ask for food. They were, in fact, being treated by alcohol-induced fasting.

Food addicts (more properly junk food addicts) are treated by withdrawal. The patients are advised that the withdrawal symptoms will not be that bad, that they can cope with them. They are also reassured that no food for a few days will not kill them and will not cause severe hypoglycemic attacks. If they still remain very fearful, they may be withdrawn in a hospital. After many months of abstinence the craving for the food will disappear. It can be readily activated by starting back on the foods they are allergic to. Other factors may do the same. Several years ago I began to treat a woman for anorexia nervosa. She would consume huge amounts of starchy foods (bread, doughnuts), become swollen, feel guilty, and take laxatives. Eventually I began to treat her for yeast infection, candida albicans. Within a month she had lost her passion for those foods. She remained on medication for one year. On my advice she went off this medication. Within a week her old craving for these foods reappeared and she was back in her usual pattern. I started the same antiyeast medication again, and a month later she no longer overate or took laxatives.

Alcohol addiction requires special additional treatment because many years of consuming alcohol, devoid of any useful nutrients except water, markedly distorts the body's metabolism. During withdrawal from alcohol there is serious danger of developing delirium tremens and/or convulsions called "rum fits." The delirium can be treated by massive quantities of vitamins given at first intravenously and then orally. The most important vitamin is B3, either niacin or niacinamide. This treatment was described by Hoffer (1962).

Vitamin C is used to replenish that lost by the stress of alcoholism. Thiamin is required, and a balance of other B vitamins. Since alcohol increases loss of zinc and magnesium, these should also be given. Once all danger of alcoholism's toxic after-effects are gone, the dose of vitamins can be decreased.

Treating the second phase is more difficult. It is inversely related to motivation. The highly motivated patient requires little treatment. Motivation is gained from "hitting bottom." i.e., realizing that the pain and suffering from the alcohol is greater than that experienced when sober. It is also gained by responding to social pressure from family and the community. Motivation is reduced by pain, tension and depression. Treatment is aimed at encouraging the patient to persevere, to improve general health, to reduce depression and anxiety. General health is promoted by the sugar-free, allergy-free diet supplemented with vitamins, especially B3 and vitamin C. Bill Wilson, known as Bill W., cofounder of Alcoholics Anonymous, released the first report on the usefulness of niacin in relieving fatigue, depression, and anxiety. The first medical studies were reported by R. Smith (1974). Antidepressants are useful for depression.

Drug addictions have different problems. Here, also, there are two phases: (1) the withdrawal; and (2) treatment to prevent relapse. I will not describe the use of methadone to replace heroin. I see little medical value in replacing one addicting drug with another, even if there are social advantages in doing so. It would be better to keep the addict on heroin. However, I am convinced addicts can be treated successfully if they will accept orthomolecular treatment.

Withdrawal is easily treated by using junk-free food or fasting if the patient is agreeable, supplemented with vitamins. The two most important ones are vitamin B3 and ascorbic acid. R. Smith (1974) reported that large doses of niacin were very helpful in moderating withdrawal symptoms and in helping addicts get off whichever drug they were addicted to. Ascorbic acid is used by Libby and Stone (1977). They use 30 grams per day supplemented with high protein mixtures and B vitamins. This helps addicts go through withdrawal with no symptoms. After eight to 10 days the dose of ascorbic acid is gradually reduced. During high ascorbic acid treatment there is no desire for the drug they were addicted to. Perhaps B3 and ascorbic acid work because they are both centrally active; niacinamide in the brain acts on the diazepine receptors, while ascorbic acid acts on the dopamine receptors, as do Haldol and other tranquilizers. Large doses of these vitamins are needed because less than 1 percent of the dose gets across into the brain where it can react with these centers.

## NUTRITION AND BAD BEHAVIOR

There can be no doubt that there is a strong link between nutrition and good behavior and nutrition and bad behavior. The best example is the consumption of alcohol, which is the prototype of pure calories, free of any other known nutrient. There has never been any provision in nature for an adaptation between alcohol and our biochemistry. One of the major causes of bad behavior (antisocial and criminal) is alcohol, even in nonalcoholics. This is due either to the toxic effect of the alcohol per se, to the chronic generation of multinutrient deficiencies by the consumption of too many calories as alcohol for long periods of time, and/or to a combination of these factors. People suffering from malnutrition are much more sensitive to alcohol. That is why many alcoholics become more and more sick and can tolerate less and less alcohol. This is also why people who watch their nutrition and use supplements can tolerate more alcohol.

The major cause of bad behavior is pure

sugar (sucrose, glucose, fructose) from which alcohol is easily made by fermentation. One might consider alcohol and sugar as closely related as children and their parents. Sugar does not make people drunk. Its effects are much more insidious, but over decades it is probably much more harmful. Rarely, the sugar can be converted into enough alcohol by yeast in the gut to make the subject drunk. The body has adapted to small amounts of free sugar, i.e., that present in ripe fruit. Ortho-molecular physicians have observed bad be-havior arising from sugar consumption for many years. This is only surprising to other physicians who go along with nutritionists and others who follow the balanced diet myth, i.e., anyone can eat these toxic substances provided a variety of foods are consumed.

Three criminology scientists have been most active in collecting and presenting the evi-dence relating malnutrition to bad behavior. Barbara Reed Stitt, a probation officer, (1983) was one of the first. Alexander Schauss (1979, 1980), has been the most active and has trained many thousands of probation officers and oth-ers interested in criminal behavior. Prof. Leon-ard Hippchen (1978, 1982) worked within the academic field. His two books will one day be recognized as classics wherein there was the first attempt to coordinate nutrition with the sociology and psychology of criminal behav-ior. Psychologists such as V. Rippere (1983 a, b, c), and B. Rimland (1983), (with G. E. Lar-son 1981) have and are making major contri-butions. They are also serving a very useful role as critics who have unmasked the slip-shod and faulty work of those who have claimed to confirm, Feingold (1974) for exam-ple, but have not (Rippere 1983 a, b, c,; Rim-land 1983).

Unbiased observers have long noted an as-sociation between refined carbohydrates, es-pecially the sugars, and bad behavior. I consider unbiased observers people who are naive about the controversy over whether the sugars cause bad behavior, and who have not taken a position based upon some ideological view, such as that a balanced diet overcomes any maladaptive response to any food con-stituent. These people include teachers who have seen what happens to their young stu-dents the day after Halloween, parents who have seen how sweets can alter their chil-dren's behavior within hours, and corrections officers who have seen what sugar does to chronic offenders. Barbara Reed Stitt was a naive probation officer until she observed what sugar did to her and to her offenders.

Controlled studies have corroborated these naive observations. These are summarized by A. Schauss (1982). A number of studies have shown that groups placed upon diets free of sugars and refined flour behaved more nor-mally. The results were most marked in hy-poglycemic inmates, i.e., over 75 percent of the population. Double-blind studies yielded similar results. At the time Schauss wrote his report, every detention center in the U.S. and Canada that reduced sucrose consumption found a significant reduction in disciplinary problems. Sugar may not be the only culprit. The usual diet high in refined carbohydrates is also low in B vitamins. Thiamine, vitamin B3, and B6 are all related to central nervous system function; in their absence behavior may become very bad.

Refined carbohydrates have a deleterious effect not only because they distort the entire diet, but also because they are so often aller-gens and so cause bad behavior. Clinical ecol-ogists have known this for decades. But possible allergens range over the entire spec-trum of foods from tomato juice to lettuce. Usually people become allergic to staple foods, especially those to which they are devoted. In one study, out of 26 chronic juvenile of-fenders, 88 percent had hypoglycemia and the group was characterized by a high inci-dence of known food and environmental al-lergies, allergic rhinitis and skin problems. When milk products and sugar were removed from their diet, sinus stuffiness decreased, their skin improved, they had more energy and their behavior was better. They were less hostile, aggressive, irritable and depressed. Many drank five to 10 8-ounce glasses of milk per day, with excessive consumption of orange juice or high-sugar soda drinks.

Many people are allergic to food additives as well as to foods. Over 3,000 additives are used in North American foods. An average person thus eats close to 10 pounds per year of additives alone. "Average" is misleading as it minimizes the problem; it includes babies as well as 200-pound adults. If babies and those few who deliberately avoid junk foods were removed from this statistic, the mean for the residual group—perhaps 60 percent of the population—would be closer to 20 pounds, i.e., 25 grams per day. Even if we use only the mean of 4 grams per day reported by Schauss, we all consume 5 grams per day. Well-known drugs such as Haldol are active in doses of a few milligrams per day.

Feingold (1974) first reported that additives create bad behavior in children. He was subjected to a barrage of unreasonable and incorrect attack (see Rimland 1983). Orthomolecular therapists have confirmed Feingold, as have thousands of parents. Feingold at first was not aware that sugar was equally bad. Since processed foods that contain added sugar also have additives, placing children on additive-free or sugar-free diets tends to produce the same improvement in diet. This confuses the results of trials. Additives do affect many children. Sugar also affects many. Both together can be devastating. The year before Feingold died, he recognized that sugar was an important negative factor. He and I discussed this several times. Among these additives are phosphates, present in soft drinks. One ounce of soda contains 12 mg of phosphate. The average American consumes 326 cans of soda per year, while adolescents consume 836 cans per year. One can visualize the terrible effect all that phosphate has on calcium and magnesium metabolism.

But American diets do not consist of foods rich only in sugar, or in additives, or in phosophates; all are present. Prinz, Roberts, and Hantman (1980) placed 28 hyperactive children (ages seven to nine) on well-balanced diets. Then their diet was modified as follows:

1. Well-balanced only.
2. Well-balanced diet plus sucrose.
3. Well-balanced diet plus artificial food dyes.
4. Well-balanced diet plus sucrose and food dyes.

Only the last group deteriorated significantly. The effects of the various additives (sugars and dyes) combined are synergistic.

Rippere (1983a, b, c) notes that the view that foods cannot cause bad behavior is very modern. The orthodox position for several thousand years was that dietary factors can provoke mental pathology. Rudin (1984) also refers to our diet as an untested, experimental diet. The sugar and additives have been grafted onto our diet without any controlled studies. In fact, in my opinion, if the FDA in the United States and the FDD in Canada were consistent and had the power to do so, all these modern food preparations would not have been allowed. Rippere (1983 a, b, c) summarized the nutritional approaches to behavioral modification from the point of view of a research psychologist. She concludes:

The ancients maintained that a sound mind existed in a sound body and in enlightened circles there is universal agreement that much of the modern refined carbohydrate, additive-laden convenience food diet is not conducive to either. What is surprising is that the idea that nutritional factors are important to the maintenance of mental functioning met with such intransigent and irrational opposition from official and would-be official bodies. . . . The evidence reviewed here is sufficient to support the conclusion that many sufferers from many mental and behavioral disturbances, who are at present receiving pharmacological, social, psychological, custodial or no treatment might benefit from nutritional modification. In some cases, improved nutrition would obviate or reduce the need for other forms of treatment.

Rimland and Larson (1981) also reviewed the whole field and came to the same conclusions. In addition they reviewed published studies that proved that psychosocial intervention alone was no better than no treatment at all in modifying bad behavior.

No one has claimed that *all* antisocial and criminal behavior is due solely to bad nutrition. Our claim is that there has been almost total neglect of a very important component of bad behavior, while every other form of behavioral modification has been studied and applied on a very large scale. When all the causal factors are examined, and when treatment is applied to deal with the most relevant causal variable, then the results of treatment will be vastly improved.

Recent evidence links criminal behavior to inherited biological factors. Mednick, Gabrielli and Hutchings (1984) examined criminal behavior in Denmark, using data from over 14,000 adoptions. They found a significant association between criminal parents and their children, even when their children had been adopted out. The type of crime of the biological parents was not related to the type of crime committed by the child. They concluded that biological predisposition is involved in some aspect of criminal behavior.

Obviously what must be inherited is an increased sensitivity to the factors in our diet that lead to a decrease in judgment, an increase in impulsive behavior, and an increase in self-centeredness—for criminal behavior consists of acts that are impulsive, lack judgment, or ignore the rights of others relative to the desires of the criminal. Perhaps what is inherited is an increased sensitivity to alcohol, sugar, food allergies and additives.

One of the ways one could deal with the problem would be to pay special attention to vulnerable families. A vulnerable family would be one where one parent had a history of criminal behavior. If one could place their children on a proper diet, perhaps one could break the association.

Alcoholism is a nutritional disease. No one doubts alcoholics are more prone to antisocial and criminal behavior than are nonalcoholics. Alcohol per se is almost a liquid replacement for the simple sugars. Like the refined sugars it is devoid of all the elements of any food, lacking protein, lipids, complex carbohydrates, vitamins, and minerals. It causes generalized malnutrition by forcing a dependence on other foods, for the nutrients required to metabolize and neutralize the effects of alcohol; and alcohol is toxic. The addiction to alcohol is very like the addiction to sugar. Addicts will steal, lie, etc., do anything which will provide them with sugar or alcohol. The alcoholics in our society are derived mainly from the much larger proportion who are addicted to sugar.

There is, of course, a well-known association between schizophrenia and crime. Schizophrenics as a rule are as law-abiding as the general population; but when they do commit a crime it is more apt to be bizarre and incomprehensible, since their actions are based upon perceptual and thought disorder symptoms. If every schizophrenic were cured, there would be a corresponding decrease in the incidence of crime.

The presence of kryptopyrrole (KP) in urine is another marker for a population more apt to engage in abnormal behavior (Hoffer 1966 a, b—there I reviewed the relationship between diagnosis and frequency of patients with this factor of kryptopyrroleuria).

Out of this group, 14 had been charged with a serious criminal offense, more than simply being drunk and disorderly. Ten were positive for KP. The charges were morals offenses [1], public mischief [1], theft [2],

| Group | N | Percent Positive for KP |
|---|---|---|
| Schzophrenia | | |
|    Never treated | Over 200 | 55 to 75 |
|    Treated, well | Over 50 | 0 |
|    Treated, not well | Over 200 | 40 to 50 |
| All neuroses | Over 300 | 20 to 50 |
| All behavioral | | |
|    disorders | Over 200 | 20 |
| Alcoholics | Over 60 | 35 |
| Physically ill | 250 | 10 |
| Normal | 80 | 5 |

Source: Dr. A. Hoffer (1966).

fraud [2], armed robbery [1], intent to wound [1], shooting a police officer [1], disorderly conduct and theft [1]. The four with no KP included one possession and theft, two fraud and one allowing an unauthorized person to drive his car. Seventy-one percent of this group had KP, a proportion as high as the schizophrenic group. Treatment of this condition restored these patients to normal. If every person with KP were treated, there would be another major decrease in crime and antisocial behavior.

## Treatment

I believe that every person who is charged with any crime should be examined. Those who have any one of the biochemical psychiatric disorders so easily treated should be treated by adjusting their diet and using the appropriate nutrients in optimum amounts.

### CHAPTER REFERENCES

Cott, A. A. (1969), Treatment of schizophrenic children. *Schizophrenia* 1:44-59.

———(1971), Orthomolecular approach to the treatment of learning disabilities. *Jo. Ortho. Psych.* 3:95-105.

———(1985), *Dr. Cott's Help for Your Learning Disabled Child.* New York: Times Books.

Crook, W. G. (1977), *Can Your Child Read? Is He Hyperactive?* Jackson, Tenn.: Professional Books.

——— (1983), *The Yeast Connection.* Jackson, Tenn.: Professional Books.

Egger, J., Wilson, J., Carter, C. M., Turner, M. W., & Soothill, J. F. (1983), Is migraine food allergy? A double blind controlled trial of oligoantigenic diet treatment. *Lancet* 2:865-868.

El-Meligi, A. M., & Osmond, H. (1970), *EWI, Manual for the Clinical Use of the Experiential World Inventory.* New York: Mensa Sana Publishing.

Feingold, B. F. (1974), *Why Your Child is Hyperactive.* New York: Random House,

Garrod, A. E. (1902), The incidence of alkaptonuria: A study in chemical individuality. *Lancet* 2:1616-1620.

Green, R. G. (1969), Reading disability. *Canadian Med. Assn. J.* 100:586.

——— (1970), Subclinical pellagra: Its diagnosis and treatment. *Schizophrenia* 22:70-79.

Hippchen, L. J. (1978), *Ecologic Biochemical Approaches to Treatment of Delinquents and Criminals.* New York: Van Nostrand Reinhold.

——— (1982), *Holistic Approaches to Offender Rehabilitation.* Springfield, Ill.: Charles C Thomas.

Hoffer, A. (1962), *Niacin Therapy in Psychiatry.* Springfield, Ill.: Charles C. Thomas.

——— (1966), Quantification of malvaria. *Int. J. Neuropsychiat.* 2:559-561.

——— (1966), Malvaria and the law. *Psychosomatics* 7:303-310.

——— (1971), Megavitamin B3 therapy for schizophrenia. *Can. Psychiat. Assn. J.* 16:499-504.

——— (1971), Vitamin B3 dependent child. *Schizophrenia* 3:107-113.

——— (1972), Treatment of hyperkinetic children with nicotinamide and pyridoxine. *Can Med. Assn. J.* 107:111-112.

Hoffer, A. and Osmond, H. (1961), A card sort test helpful in making psychiatric diagnosis. *J. Neuropsychiat.* 2:306-330.

Hoffer, A., Kelm, H., & Osmond, H. (1975), The Hoffer-Osmond Diagnostic Test. Huntington, N.Y.: R. A. Krieger Publishing HOD test kit available from Rehabilitation Research Foundation, P.O. Box BV, University, Ala. 35486.

Kowalson, B. (1967), Metabolic dysperception: Its diagnosis and management in general practise. *J. Schiz.* 1:200-203.

Libby, A. F., & Stone, I. (1977), The hypoascorbemia-Kwashiorkor approach to drug addiction: A pilot study. *Jo. Ortho. Psych.* 6:300-308.

Mandell, M., & Scanlon, L. W. (1979), *Dr. Mandell's 5-Day Allergy Relief System.* New York: Thomas Y. Crowell.

Mednick, S. A., Gabrielli, W. F., Jr., & Hutchings, B. (1984), Genetic influences in criminal convictions: Evidence from an adoption cohort. *Science* 224:891-894.

Paterson, E. T. (1981), Towards the orthomolecular environment. *J. Ortho. Psych.* 10:269-283.

Pauling, L. (1968), Orthomolecular psychiatry. *Science* 160:265-271.

—— (1986), *How to Live Longer and Feel Better.* New York: W. H. Freeman.

Prinz, R. J., Roberts, W. A., & Hantman, E. (1980), Dietary correlation of hyperactive behavior in children. *J. Consulting and Clin. Psych.* 48:760-769.

Reed, B. (1983), *Food, Teens and Behavior.* Manitowoc, Wis.: Natural Press.

Rimland, B. (1978), Risks and benefits in the treatment of autistic children. *J. Autism and Childhood Schizophrenia* 8:100-104.

Rimland, B.(1983), The Feingold Diet: An assessment of the reviews by Mattes, Kavale and Forness and others. *Journal of Learning Disabilities* 16:331-333.

Rimland B., & Larson, G. E. (1981), Nutritional and ecological approaches to the reduction of criminality, deliquency and violence. *J. Applied Nutr.* 33:116-137.

Rippere, V. (1983), *The Allergy Problem.* Wellingborough, Northants., England: Thorsons Pub.

—— (1983b), Food additives and hyperactive children: A critique of Connors. *Br. J. Clinical Psychol.* 22:19-32.

—— (1983a), Nutritional approaches to behavior modification. *Progress in Behavioral Modification* 14:299-354.

Ross, H. (1975), *Fighting Depression.* New York: Larchmont Books,

Rudin, D. O. (1984), *The Omega Factor and the Life Style Diseases.* Prepublication.

Schauss, A. (1979), Differential outcomes among probationers comparing orthomolecular approaches to conventional casework counselling. *J. Ortho. Psych.* 8:158-168.

—— (1980), *Diet, Crime and Deliquency.* Berkeley, Calif.: Parker House.

Schauss, A. G., & Simonsen, C. E. (1979), A critical analysis of the diets of chronic juvenile offenders. *J. Ortho. Psych.* 8:149-157.

Siegler, M., & Osmond, H. (1966), Models of madness. *Br. J. Psych.* 112:1193-1203.

—— (1974), *Models of Madness, Models of Medicine.* New York: Macmillan.

Silverman, L. J., & Metz, A. S. "Numbers of pupils with specific learning disabilities in local public schools in the United States: Spring 1970." In Minimal Brain Dysfunction, eds. F. F. de la Cruz, B. H. Fox, & R. H. Roberts (1973), *Annals of the New York Academy of Sciences* 205:146-157.

Smith, L. H. (1976), *Improving Your Child's Behavior Chemistry.* Englewood Cliffs, N.J.: Prentice-Hall.

Smith, R. F. (1974), A five-year field trial of massive nicotine acid therapy of alcoholics in Michigan. *J. Ortho. Psych.* 3:327-331.

Stewart, M. A. (1970), Hyperactive children. *Scientific American* 222:94-98.

Stewart, M., Ferris, A., Pitts, N., & Craig, A. G. (1966), The hyperactive child syndrome. *Amer. J. Orthopsychiatry* 36:861-867.

Stone, I. (1972a), The natural history of ascorbic acid in the evolution of the mammals and primates and its significance for present-day man. *J. Ortho. Psych.* 1:82-89.

—— (1972b), *The Healing Factor: Vitamin C Against Disease.* New York: Grosset and Dunlap.

Von Hillsheimer, G. (1970), *How to Live With Your Special Child.* Washington, D.C.: Acropolic Books.

Williams, R. J. (1956), *Biochemical Individuality.* New York: John Wiley and Sons.

—— (1977), *The Wonderful World Within You.* New York: Bantam Books.

# HUNTINGTON'S DISEASE

• • • • • • • • • • • • • • • • • • • • • • • • • • • • •

There is a great surge of interest in this disease, formerly called Huntington's chorea (HD). HD probably existed during the Middle Ages, but it was first described in 1872 by Dr. George Huntington, almost as an afterthought or a medical curiosity. He believed it was a variant of Sydenham's chorea.

It usually begins between the ages of 20 and 50, especially between the ages of 35 and 44, and progresses slowly over the next 20 years. There are no periods of remission, but the disease may stabilize for periods of time before it continues its downhill path. About 70 percent of patients affected die within 15 years of onset. Only 10 percent survive 20 years of illness. In a series of 120 patients, one 87-year-old was found whose first symptoms started when he was 14 (Bruyn 1978).

HD is an autosomal dominant genetic disease—only one defective gene is required for the disease to appear. Thus, every child from one parent with HD has a 50 percent chance of having the gene. A person with no HD genes cannot pass on this disease and, of course, will not become ill. A person cannot be certain he or she is free of the gene until their life is nearly over.

The specific course of HD is not known, i.e., no specific abnormality has been determined that can be used to diagnose or to treat this disease. Recent research suggests genetic markers are present. The general cause is known—it is genetic. This means that bio-chemical reactions determined by that gene require a particular sort of chemical environment within or just outside the cells of the nervous system of those who are at risk. The fact that HD usually develops after maturity suggests that the specific gene requirement is for one or more nutrients. One idea is that something turns the gene on at around age 35 to 45. I believe that the HD gene directs a series of chemical reactions that must have larger than average amounts of two vitamins: B3 and E. In other words, it is a double vitamin dependency condition. As I have explained in the section on vitamins, a dependency may develop slowly or be present at birth. Stress and malnutrition must be present for several years before a typical vitamin B3 dependency develops. Populations must be on a Saccharine Disease-inducing diet for 20 years before the typical disease appears. Persons at risk for HD probably have an increased need for B3 and E, but it requires many years for the disease to develop. The quality of the diet and the amount of vitamin B3 and vitamin E determines when the symptoms appear. If such a person at risk for HD were to live on a junk-free diet supplemented with adequate amounts of these vitamins, I expect the disease would either appear much later or not at all. I would expect that if a cohort of people at risk for HD were to be studied nutritionally, one would find that it would appear earliest in those on the poorest diet and latest in those whose diet most resembled the junk-free diet. HD is more common in lower socioeconomic classes, which also have a higher incidence of other neurological disease, alcoholism, mental deficiency, and other psychiatric diseases.

HD occurs in four to seven people per 100,000. As physicians become more familiar with it, its prevalence goes up. Unless it is suspected, patients may be misdiagnosed as schizophrenic or neurotic or having other neurological disease. In the U.S.A. about 10,000 to 25,000 have HD, and another 20,000 to 50,000 are at risk. HD was brought to public attention when Woody Guthrie died in 1967 after suffering 13 years of the disease. His widow, the late Marjorie Guthrie, founded the Committee to Combat Huntington's Disease, which has played a significant and important role in informing the public about this fearful, crippling disease.

Folstein and Folstein (1981) provide a good description of the diagnosis, disease, and some of the nonnutrient drug treatments that may have to be used.

Physically the disease causes involuntary muscle movements anywhere in the body. Each patient develops a unique set of movements. At the beginning the patients are restless and fidgety and grimace occasionally. Partial openings of the mouth and spasmodic workings of the throat develop and speech becomes dysarthriac. It may become difficult to swallow and breathe. The eye muscles develop a fine tremor and the eyes may move backward and forward on a lateral plane. When the lower limbs are affected, the walk becomes awkward and unsteady. Fatigue becomes common and severe.

Psychiatric symptoms come on before the physical changes are apparent. Perceptual changes are rare but thought disorder is common. Delusions develop but concentration remains normal. Confusional states occur rarely. Mood changes also occur, beginning with anxiety and depression; but later, when the illness is well advanced, moods may be euphoric. Behavior is changed. About 20 percent of patients have been punished for criminal behavior before HD was diagnosed. There are two periods when patients become psychotic: Early in the illness a schizophrenic syndrome is produced, and a second peak incidence comes during the middle of the illness and tends to be like an organic psychosis.

So far no clear biochemical changes have been found. Perry, Hansen and Kloster (1973) found that HD brains had much less gamma-aminobutyric acid (GABA) and homocarnosine in the red colored areas of the brain. They felt this indicated a deficiency of GABA, perhaps due to a deficiency of the enzyme which makes GABA, glutamic acid decarboxylase (GAD). Bird, MacKay, Rayner and Iversen (1973) did find 80 percent reduction of GAD in HD brains.

These red pigmented areas contain pigment made from noradrenalin and perhaps adrenalin and do not come from dihydroxyphenylalanine (dopa). Albinos cannot convert dopa into melanin, but their brains contain the same red pigment. For a discussion of adrenochrome, the oxidized pigment from adrenalin, and its relation to schizophrenic syndromes, see *The Hallucinogens* (Hoffer and Osmond 1967).

There is no known treatment for HD. The symptoms may be partially controlled with modern medication, but the disease continues its way unchecked. In this it resembles Parkinsonism, which also continues to deteriorate the patient whether or not l-dopa is used. So far I have not been able to find a single case reported in the literature where the disease has been reversed or even halted. There is little doubt that, had any physician discovered such a reversal of this progressive, fatal disease, it would have been reported.

In 1973, a man referred to me by his physician appeared with his wife in my office.

They told me he was suffering from Huntington's chorea. They knew much more about it than did I, for I had not seen any patient with HD. But I did recall from my medical training that it was a disease for which there was no cure. It was possible to use palliative treatment directed toward symptoms, which created discomfort, but nothing could halt the progression of this deteriorating disease. I quickly admitted to the patient my almost total ignorance and asked what they expected I could do. They had heard about megavitamin therapy, had already eliminated all junk from their diet, and wished to supplement it with vitamins. But they did not know which supplements to use and hoped I could advise them. They knew HD was untreatable and had minimal expectation of any major improvement. They hoped the vitamin supplementation might slow the rate of deterioration.

There were five boys in the family. Their father had HD and also one uncle (the father's brother). Both had died psychotic in mental hospitals. Of the five boys, two were normal. The eldest of the five was in a nursing home, bedridden and mentally deteriorated. The youngest was even worse in a different nursing home, where he died a year later. The middle son, my patient, had been deteriorating steadily for about 20 years.

My patient (hereafter called Mr. A), was born in 1913. When I first saw him in October 1973 he had been ill since age 40.

His illness began with increased nervousness, which had become worse over the previous year. His weight had been 165 pounds at age 40, but had decreased to 130 pounds when I saw him, due to loss of muscle tissue. He had become so weak it required all his energy merely to survive: to eat, dress and look after himself. He was tired all the time.

Mr. A had no perceptual changes but his thinking was starting to deteriorate. He suffered from blocking (repeated gaps or pauses in his flow of thought), his memory was faulty, his concentration was poor. He was depressed,

irritable, nervous and tense. His walk was jerky, his muscles cramped often and he stumbled a lot.

I agreed to supervise his vitamin supplementation, but it was understood that there must be no expectation of recovery on anyone's part. I was concerned that I might be accused of generating false hope in a case where there had never yet been any cure. I had had enough trouble from ignorant critics who claimed that I generated false hope for schizophrenics, when I presented data showing that orthomolecular therapy was superior to the use of standard psychiatric treatment only.

Mr. A was advised to continue his junk-free diet, but also to add to it ascorbic acid, 1 gram after each meal; a preparation called Megavits (containing thiamin, 100 mg; riboflavin, 25 mg; pyridoxine, 100 mg; niacinamide, 200 mg; and ascorbic acid, 500 mg) after each meal; and vitamin B12, 1 mg per week.

One month later he was less depressed, stronger, his concentration was better, and he had been able to work, for the first time in many years, on his roof. I added niacin, 1 gram after each meal; folic acid, 5 mg twice per day; and some magnesium sulfate in solution for his muscle cramps.

Two months later he was still free of depression. He stated that if he felt as well for the rest of his life, even with further deterioration, he would be content. I doubled his niacin level and added vitamin E, 400 IU twice per day.

Four months later there was no additional change; he was bored and considered going back to work.

Six months later he was the same but his weight was 125 pounds. He had lost five pounds in six months of treatment. Because of a history of severe sinusitis and excessive milk intake, I placed him on a two-week dairy-free program.

After seven months he again noted he was more tired. He had felt no better on a dairy-free program and had resumed dairy product consumption. I therefore concluded there had been no real improvement in seven months, even though he felt better and was stronger. His progressive weight loss was ominous and indicated his muscles were wasting as they had been doing for many years. I therefore doubled his vitamin E, to 800 IU twice a day. One month later his weight was steady at 125 pounds but there was no other change. The following month he gained two pounds and at month 11 he was 135 pounds. This was the first time during his illness that weight loss had been reversed. His muscles were regaining their size, tone and power. His chest, which had been falling in, regained its normal shape. All muscle tremor and cramps were gone. Both he and his wife felt the improvement coincided with the doubling of the dose of Vitamin E. I again doubled vitamin E, to 1,600 IU twice per day, and reduced niacin to 500 mg after each meal.

At 13 months his weight, which had reached 139 pounds, had settled down to between 135 and 136 pounds. He had become so energetic that his caloric output kept his weight from increasing. Both he and his wife were pleased with his progress. He felt niacin caused nasal swelling, so this was discontinued and replaced by an equal amount of niacinamide.

At 17 months he reported he was normal, being as well as he had been when he was 40, before the disease struck.

At 22 months he discontinued the niacinamide to see if he still needed it. Within a few weeks he became very restless and tense, and when he walked his legs stiffened. He quickly went back to niacinamide and in a few days was well. When last seen in the summer of 1976 he remained well, nearly three years after treatment was started.

I had several reasons for using these particular vitamins. This kind of polypharmacy, when used by orthomolecular physicians, is frowned upon by our critics. It is curious, however, that they see nothing wrong with using a complex mixture of tranquilizers, antidepressants, and other substances needed to protect patients against their toxic effects. The one drug-one disease model trained physicians to use one drug per disease. If the drug did not work, nothing else was offered. This is considered the scientific approach, especially by proponents of the double-blind method in research. When one is faced with a disease for which there is no treatment, the "scientific" approach calls for using only one compound. If six nutrients may have some value but it is not known which one to use, then there are two ways; first, each nutrient can be studied alone, but this approach will require many years of investigation. The "scientist" need not be concerned because he has nothing to lose, but the patient is in a different position and cannot afford the luxury of the "scientific" approach. However, it is possible to be scientific as well as to give the patient's welfare first priorty; this method is just as scientific and much more humane. This is to start the patient on all the nutrients and hope for a response. Once the patient is well or better, one can at one's leisure withdraw one nutrient at a time to determine if it is an essential component. This is the approach I use in dealing with these hopeless, deteriorating conditions.

I did not have time to continue my study with Mr. A after I left Saskatoon for Victoria, B.C., in the fall of 1976, but in 1982 this patient wrote to me to report that he was still getting on well.

However, I do have another case to add to my series. A series of two in most diseases is too insignificant to be taken seriously, but for a disease as rare as HD I consider it respectable. Two recovered cases must be taken seriously, since no one else has ever reported even one recovery.

The second person to get well did not think she had HD, even though she knew she had a 50 percent chance of having received the gene from her mother (Hoffer 1983).

Mrs. A's husband recovered from schizophrenia on orthomolecular treatment. Her mother was ill with HD in a mental hospital in France. She had concluded that if vitamins could cure a disease as serious as schizophrenia, they might prevent the appearance of HD in children of parents with this disease. She started to use a megadose vitamin approach in December 1978. November 17, 1981, she reported she was taking the following vitamins: vitamin E, 800 IU; niacin, 2.5 grams; vitamin C, 1 gram; and one multiple vitamin tablet. She said she was well. She had for the previous seven years been too tired to work as an engineer, but now was back at work. In addition she had suffered perceptual illusions that kept her from driving, had a number of fears and loss of memory. After one year on vitamins, these were all gone.

Her husband wrote: "The change in [AB] since she started the vitamin treatment and particularly the choline has been nothing short of amazing." A complete description of this case is available (Hoffer 1983).

AB had not been diagnosed as having HD but she had the early symptoms and had also transmitted these genes to one or more of her daughters, who were later placed on vitamin treatment as well with good responses. We have, therefore, a way of determining which children are most apt to have the HD genes and a way of preventing the illness from developing. All at-risk children should be started on vitamins. Those who show a major response probably have the genes and should continue to take the vitamins.

I used vitamin E because of the well-established relationship between vitamin E deficiency and dystrophy in animals. I used vitamin B3 because of its well-known property of preventing perceptual and thinking disorders, and I used vitamin C because of its antistress properties. The other vitamins were used merely to balance the program. However, it is possible some of them have an important role to play as well.

Two recoveries do not prove that every patient with HD will recover, but it does prove that there are others who will respond. It is highly unlikely that the only patients who could recover came under my care or attention. I am convinced that the HD syndrome is caused by several factors, and that one of them is an inherited, slowly progressive dependency on vitamins, perhaps a double vitamin B3 and vitamin E dependency.

I wish I could have run a series of cases, but HD is so rare that one psychiatrist sees very few HD patients, unless some accumulate in chronic mental hospitals. In 25 years of practice I had seen one case. When I submitted my report to the *Canadian Medical Association Journal*, it was rejected out of hand because I had not run a double-blind series. In my correspondence with the editor I pointed out that I could not wait another 150 years to build such a series. He depended on a critic, who suggested I run a series in a mental hospital where there might be a few. In fact, his suggestion meant I should give up my practice and turn to a state institution in the hope I would be permitted to search for and treat a few other HD patients. The recovery of one case, the first ever reported, meant nothing. I therefore reported it in the *Journal of Orthomolecular Psychiatry* (Hoffer 1983).

It seems impossible for physicians who claim they are scientists to repeat accurately research reported by others, even when they have been reminded forcefully of their responsibility to science to at least try to be scientific. I had no doubt they would ignore almost my entire report and latch onto only one component. Caro and Caro (1978) were the first to report that vitamin E does not work, even though they used no dietary controls, did not use any other vitamins and used only 1,200 IU of vitamin E. They said this dose was slightly lower than the dose I had used. I started with 800 IU per day and in a few months increased it to 3,200 IU per day, which was the maintenance dose for several years. I suppose 1,200 IU can be said to be a slightly lower dose. Perhaps Caro and Caro would also consider 20 units of insulin to be "slightly" lower than 50 units for a diabetic who requires 50 units.

I here take the liberty of recording a letter submitted to the *British Medical Journal* by Mrs. Majorie Hall:

> As a nutritionist who brought notice of the great improvement in Dr. Hoffer's patient to the attention of Combat, I would like to comment on "Vitamin E in Treatment of Huntington's Chorea."
>
> I imagine I am the person in England who "seconded" the work by suggesting dietary regimes for 2 H.C. patients in Great Britain (with cooperation from their G.P.'s). It was not one patient as stated.
>
> The treatment suggested and proved successful by Dr. Hoffer was 3,200 IUs of vitamin E daily (and not 1,200 as stated), plus a carefully controlled dietary regime containing full basic nutritional supplements and removal of valueless or exacerbating foods.
>
> No nutritionist would ever put a seriously ill person on a diet containing one greatly increased supplement without great thought being given to the rest of the dietary regime. In my opinion this would do more harm than good.
>
> Also I have never heard of anyone putting a multiple sclerotic on a gluten free diet only. The remainder of the regime is just as important and must contain long chain oils to supplement essential fatty acids. In spite of all the adverse comments a great many people have made remarkable improvement on such a diet suggested by nutritionists.
>
> It is a great pity that doctors during their training do not learn something more than the rudiments of nutrition. It is my view that if they did there would be fewer degenerative illnesses when caught in the early stages, and that includes Huntington's chorea (Hall 1978).

Several recent reports indicate that the use of nutritional therapy is gaining ground. Charles N. Still (1979, 1980–81) found that HD and pellagra are much alike when they are compared clinically. Both are chronic progressive disorders of the central nervous system, invariably leading to cachexia and death. Both usually develop during the second half of life. Both have similar symptoms. Both are similar genetically. When both parents have pellagra, about half their children will also. This observation is based on these families eating the typical pellagra-producing diet. It shows that some people are much more prone to develop pellagra, even when all eat the same diet that is deficient in vitamin B3 and tryptophan. Neither disease has unique neuropathologic changes and they resemble each other. Dr. Still concluded that pellagra was a good clinical model for HD, which showed a nutritional approach should be tried. Claude Bernard stated that when there is a disease for which there is no treatment, i.e., HD, and when a physician claims that he or she has been able to treat some, it is ethically imperative to try that new treatment provided it does the patient no harm (orthomolecular treatment). Furthermore, since pellagra is a multinutritional disease requiring good food and vitamin supplements, the same approach should be used in treating HD. Still thus emphasized adequate calories, supplements with amino acids, vitamin E, and other vitamins.

Still used 400 to 800 IU of vitamin E each day, given 30 minutes before meals. Vitamin E is an antioxidant and will decrease peroxidation of polyunsaturated fatty acids. He also used ascorbic acid, 1 gram per day, to enhance the role of vitamin E. He did not recommend more ascorbic acid as it might enhance peroxidation. He also used small quantities of all the B vitamins, extra protein (50 to 100 grams per day) in a liquid nutritional supplement, and polyunsaturated fatty acids combined with lecithin. Using this program, Still was able to halt weight loss.

The Committee to Combat Huntington's Disease reprinted and distributed a report from *Let's Live* magazine, July 1980*. Several patients with HD described how nutritional therapy helped. Elaine described her two brothers who died by age 40, one weighing 118 pounds at six feet tall when discharged from the hospital. In addition to the drugs prescribed, she gave him nutritional drinks rich in protein; vitamin E, 3,200 IU; ascorbic acid, 9 grams; 250 mg each of B3, B6 and pantothenic acid; with other B vitamins, vitamins A and D, calcium, magnesium, manganese and zinc. In one year his weight increased to 160 pounds. The other brother did not respond as well, but he had cancer in addition to HD. Both brothers became more alert. The handwriting of one became legible. Dr. Charles N. Still (1979, 1980–81) is quoted in the article as saying: "What is involved, I believe, is an accelerated form of aging due to one or more central nutrient defects . . . we know that it helps weight. We can stabilize weight in both men and women. We are definitely altering stamina and vigor in the patients who are not already damaged to the extent that they cannot make use of the increased energy."

## TREATMENT

### Basic

The basic treatment is nutritional. It must be started as soon as possible and must be the first treatment used, not the last, since no other treatment has any rationale nor has been shown to help even one patient. Subjects at risk should start on preventive treatment during adolescence, if not earlier. Ideally every infant born to a family at risk must be fed sugar-free or junk-free food. The progression of treatment follows:

A. *For All Children Born to Families at Risk*
1. Orthomolecular nutrition.

---

*I knew Mrs. Marjorie Guthrie only a few years. She was very interested in the nutritional approach but told me she had been rebuffed by the medical advisors to the association.

2. Supplementation if required, i.e., vitamin B3 and B6 for hyperactivity or learning disorders, vitamins A and D for allergies such as asthma or hayfever. The usual indications used by physicians for all orthomolecular diseases are followed.

B. *For All Adolescents in At-Risk Families*
1. Orthomolecular nutrition.
2. Supplements (in three divided doses);
    (a) Niacinamide, 100 to 500 mg per day.
    (b) Ascorbic acid, 1,500 mg per day and higher.
    (c) Pyridoxine, 100 to 300 mg per day.
    (d) Vitamin E, 800 IU per day.
    (e) Zinc preparations yielding 30 mg of zinc per day.
    (f) Manganese, 50 mg per day.
    (g) Selenium, 100 mg per day.

C. *For Patients Having HD*
1. Orthomolecular nutrition. It is important to determine any food allergies and to avoid these foods.
2. Supplements (in three divided doses):
    (a) Vitamin B3: This is especially important when psychiatric symptoms are present. Nicotinic acid is used to lower blood lipids. Nicotinamide is tolerated better by many patients. The dose is 1 to 3 grams per day.
    (b) Ascorbic acid: A minimum of 1 gram, three times a day, is used. In some cases the dose may have to be increased until a sublaxative level is reached. If pure ascorbic acid is too sour, any one of its salts, such as sodium ascorbate, calcium ascorbate or potassium ascorbate may be used.
    (c) Pyridoxine: 250 mg per day. More is needed if there is clear evidence of pyridoxine or zinc deficiency.
    (d) Vitamin E: I prefer the d-alpha tocopherol form. The dose should be increased from 400 IU twice daily until weight loss is halted. Changes

are made every month. Up to 4,000 IU (4 grams) may be required.

(e) Zinc salts are used, either zinc sulfate, 220 mg once or twice per day, or zinc gluconate, 100 mg used in the same way. If one salt causes nausea, the other should be used.

(f) Manganese preparations, 50 mg per day.

(g) Selenium, 200 mg per day.

(h) Essential fatty acids, especially the omega-3 ultraunsaturated series. The best sources are linseed oil, wheat germ oil, and evening primrose oil. Fish oils (not fish liver oils) are a good source but are difficult to obtain in North America. Linseed oil is used as salad oil. One to six tablespoonsful per day are used. It is rich in calories, which is helpful to HD patients to prevent weight loss. Wheat germ oil is less potent. Evening primrose oil is very rich.

These nutrients are used for the following reasons:

*Vitamin B3:* To treat psychiatric disorders, which are common in HD.

*Vitamin C:* To improve immunological defenses, to improve tissue and cellular repair and for its general antistress properties.

*Pyridoxine:* For its antineurotic properties.

*Vitamin E:* As a specific antioxidant, which has been shown to protect animals against neuromuscular diseases.

*Zinc:* For its general healing properties. Zinc deficiency is very common.

*Manganese:* For its antitremor properties. It is specific against tardive dyskinesia, a tranquilizer-induced disease.

*Selenium:* As an antioxidant to bolster the effect of vitamin E.

*Essential Fatty Acids:* To provide these essential precursors of the prostaglandins.

## CHAPTER REFERENCES

Bird, E. D., Mackay, A. V. P., Rayner, C. N., & Iversen, L. L. (1973), Reduced glutamic acid decarboxylase activity of post mortem brain of Huntington's chorea. *Lancet* 1:1090-1092.

Bruyn, G. W. (1978), Huntington's chorea: Historical, clinical and laboratory synopsis. *Handbook of Clinical Neurology* 6:298-378.

Caro, A. J., & Caro, S. (1978), Vitamin E in treatment of Huntington's chorea. *British Med. J.* 21:1.

Folstein, S., & Folstein, M. (1981), Diagnosis and treatment of Huntington's disease. *Comprehensive Therapy* 7:60-66.

Hall, Margery (1978), Vitamin E in treatment of Huntington's chorea. Letter to the Editor, *British Medical Journal* 1:153.

Hoffer, A. (1983), Latent Huntington's disease—response to orthomolecular treatment. *J. Ortho. Psych.* 12:44-47.

Hoffer, A., & Osmond, H. (1967), *The Hallucinogens.* New York: Academic Press.

Perry, T. H., Hansen, S., & Kloster, M. (1973), Huntington's chorea. *NEJM* 288:337-342.

Still, C. N. (1979), Nutritional therapy in Huntington's chorea concepts based on the model of pellagra. *Psychiatric Forum* 9:74-78.

————— (1980–81), Sex differences affecting nutritional therapy in Huntington's disease—an inherited essential fatty acid metabolic disorder? *Psychiatric Forum* 9:47–51.

Zucker, M. (1980), Looking for the nutritional link to defuse the time bomb. *Committee to Combat Huntington's Disease*, New York.

# CHAPTER 11

## CANCER AND ORTHOMOLECULAR TREATMENT

In Chapter 15 of Irwin Stone's book, *The Healing Factor* (1972), he describes some of the medical literature relating ascorbic acid to cancer. There is a surprising amount of research, very often confusing and conflicting. However, this should have been expected since cancer is very complex and early pioneer investigators were unaware of the optimum doses that might be required. I agree with Dr. Stone's contention that there is more than enough evidence to warrant human clinical trials, but this was not done until Cameron and Pauling published their book, *Cancer and Vitamin C* (1979). This work has received so much world-wide attention there is no need to summarize it here. I am convinced from the evidence presented by Cameron and Pauling, and from my own clinical observations, that vitamin C must be an important component of any program designed to treat and contain many of the cancers. Perhaps with the newer constructive attitude of the National Cancer Institute and the American Cancer Society, proper clinical studies will be carried out. Until then we will continue to use vitamin C because clinical judgment shows that it has great value. When enough physicians are involved, the academics will hasten to start these studies.

Cancer treatment has two main objectives: (1) to destroy the tumor; and (2) to enhance the body's ability to destroy and contain the tumor. Standard cancer treatment has been directed against the tumor using surgery, radiation and chemotherapy. Lately some interest has developed in enhancing the body's cancer defenses, using nutrients such as vitamin A, beta-carotene or the mineral zinc. Following Cameron and Pauling's lead, orthomolecular treatment is aimed primarily at enhancing cancer defenses. There need be no clash between combining both approaches. I believe that chemotherapy will run down our bodies' defenses, as has been pointed out by Pauling, but it is possible that this would not happen if ascorbic acid were taken before and during chemotherapy.

I practice orthomolecular psychiatry but have treated 95 cancer patients since 1976, who were referred to me for psychiatric and nutritional counseling. Before I agreed to accept these referrals, I had decided to follow a number of principles. The first was that I would not directly treat the tumor—this was the province of the referring physician and other specialists. Most of the patients had already been treated by surgery, radiation or chemotherapy, or a combination thereof. I did not reject patients because they had had or were receiving chemotherapy. In some cases I encouraged patients to seek one of these treatments. Usually, if it were explained to them that the only important objective was to improve results of treatment, they would overcome their earlier apprehension. I was not interested in proving that one form of treatment was superior to another. My second principle was to explain to each patient that the use of diet and nutrient supplements was recommended to improve their resistance or immune defenses against the cancer.

Over the past year I have reviewed these 95 patients, and I have concluded that the nutritional counseling did improve the quality of life and survival when patients were able to follow the program.

## TREATMENT

*Nutrition.* Patients are advised to eliminate all junk from their diet. This means they avoid foods containing added sugars and preservatives. They must also avoid foods to which they are allergic and foods which may predispose to certain cancers, such as caffeine, theophylline, and theobromine in coffee, tea and chocolate; as well as milk products. Milk is rich in estrogens and has been linked to precancerous lesions in the breast. I advise a decrease in meats, more dependence on fish, and an increase in vegetables—eaten raw whenever possible. The orthomolecular diet is followed with a swing toward vegetarianism.

### Nutrient Supplements

*Ascorbic Acid.* Dr. R. Cathcart developed the concept of determining the optimum dose by increasing the dose until severe diarrhea and gas develop. The optimum dose is a few grams below this. The bowel tolerance dose he recommends is 15 to 100 grams per day, divided into four to 15 doses per day. When using very high doses one should consider swallowing the powder directly to minimize the amount of fluid consumed. I start with 12 grams per day in three, 4-gram doses.
*Vitamin A.* Up to 50,000 IU per day is safe. Provitamin A or beta-carotene is given, using 30,000 IU capsules, one or two per day.

*Vitamin E.* D-alpha tocopherol, 400 IU twice per day.
*Vitamin B3.* Preferably niacin, up to 1 gram three times per day.
*B-complex.* A good B-complex preparation containing 50 mg each of the major B vitamins, that is, B1, B2, B3, B6 and/or pantothenic acid.
*Zinc.* 30 to 50 mg per day as chelate, gluconate or sulfate.
*Magnesium.* 500 mg per day.
*Selenium.* 400 to 500 mcg per day, preferably in a yeast-free base.

## TREATMENT OUTCOME

Survival data is shown in the table on page 231. I have not included details of the standard treatment given or of the nutrients, but I have listed cases by their ability to follow the program and to take ascorbic acid. My only objective is to compare those who would not or could not follow the program for at least two months against those who could. The latter group are again divided into those who took only 3 grams per day of vitamin C and those who took 12 grams per day or more. The first 41 patients are included.

I saw twelve patients between 1978 and 1980. Of the six able to take enough ascorbic acid, four are alive and well. The remaining eight died. The kind of patient, the kind of cancer and response will be indicated in the following 12 brief histories.

J. C., FEMALE, AGE 57.
In 1966 she had a radical left mastectomy. In 1975 cancer was found in the other breast and metastasis in bones. She received a lumpectomy and one week later an oophorectomy. In 1979 more lumps were discovered and in January 1980 she was given chemotherapy. I saw her eight days afterward. She was unable to follow the program and died in hospital three months later with brain metastasis.

C.B., MALE, AGE 72.
By 1979 a sarcoma with Paget's disease

## TABLE SHOWING SURVIVAL DATA, 1985

| | CONTROL GROUP | | | TREATED | | | | | |
|---|---|---|---|---|---|---|---|---|---|
| Year | N | Months¹ Alive | N Alive | 3G N | M | N | Vitamin C N | M | 12G N |
| 1978–80 | 5 | 7 | 0 | 1 | 10 | 0 | 6 | 53 | 4 |
| 1981 | 3 | 4 | 0 | 1 | 9 | 0 | 4 | 45 | 3 |
| 1982 | 2 | 2 | 0 | 1 | 2 | 0 | 6 | 33 | 5 |
| 1983 | 1 | 2 | 0 | 1 | 24 | 1 | 10 | 20 | 6 |
| Total | 11 | - | 0 | 4 | - | 1 | 26 | — | 18 |

(1) Mean of entire group.

invaded the superior ramus of his left pubic bone. He was treated by surgery and radiation but the tumor, after a transient regression, began to spread again quickly. He was referred to me in January 1980. He started on the program, taking 12 grams per day of ascrobic acid, plus additional intravenous vitamin three times per week. In one month the edema in his left leg was gone. After two months the tumor began to regress. After four months the radiologist noted: "Present study shows marked improvement with some apparent bony reconstitution of his left superior ramus. There has certainly been no further bony destruction in the interim." He is today alive and well.

B. D., MALE, AGE 63.

For six years he suffered recurrent growths on his vocal cords and had six operations. After each operation his voice was normal for a short time. In 1976 he developed severe rheumatoid arthritis, which cleared when he became a vegetarian. June 1979 he began the nutrient program with 3 grams per day of vitamin C. Two months later his voice was normal and he felt well.

In June 1983 his voice was hoarse, cancer was diagnosed and he received 10 radiation treatments. I increased vitamin C to 4 grams three times per day. He continued with radiation, receiving another 15 treatments. Examination in July 1985 showed he was free of cancer. He is alive and well.

R. D., MALE, AGE 61.

R. D. was operated on for glioblastoma and a brain abscess. Surgery left him impaired. He was able to follow the program for two weeks only. He died one year later.

C. H., FEMALE, AGE 53.

C. H., a heavy smoker, got influenza with high fever. On antibiotics she responded slowly. In September 1980 cancer was resected. Secondaries were present. She refused radiation or chemotherapy. In September she started on the program. By year's end her X-ray showed no tumor but three months later she suffered another bout of 'flu, later pneumonia, and later tumor cells in her pleural fluid. During this time she remained on her vitamins in spite of attempts by her physician to discontinue the program. March 1981 she was admitted to hospital and died April 4, 1981, from recurrent adenocarcinoma and pneumonia.

I. L., FEMALE, AGE 73.

In February 1978 cancer of the bowel was resected, leaving her with a colostomy. One year later she developed severe low-back pain. She was given radiation with no relief. She required an electronic device to control pain and later was given Digoxin for her heart. She could not tolerate more than 1 gram per day of vitamin C because of severe pain and nausea, but tried from July 22 to September 15, 1980. She died May 5, 1981.

S. L., FEMALE, AGE 31.

In January 1979, S. L. had a modified left mastectomy and oophorectomy. Following this she received chemotherapy. Throughout she took vitamin C. She did not lose any hair. In March 1980 she was started on my program. Two months later she discontinued all vitamins but would not tell me why. There had been a recurrence in her right breast with secondaries in her chest and she was on chemotherapy. I have not been able to find out what happened after that. She is not included in the table.

E. L., FEMALE, AGE 76.

E. L. had a large, inoperable cancer of the left upper lobe with extension into glands. She received 10 radiation sessions. She was started on my program April 17, 1979 and died November 7, 1979.

A. M., FEMALE, AGE 23.

In May 1977 this patient had severe headaches from brain tumor. It was operated on from base of skull and later received chemotherapy. She was seen September 28, 1977, and died one month later.

A. S., FEMALE, AGE 61.

In May 1978 this patient had jaundice. At operation a tumor was found on the head of the pancreas about the size of a squash ball. The surgeon considered it was inoperable but created a bypass to clear her jaundice. After discharge she started to take vitamin C, 10 grams per day. One month later I increased this to 40 grams. February 21, 1979, a CAT scan was negative. The skeptical physician repeated the scan. Later her obstructed duct opened. The patient has remained well.

N. T., FEMALE, AGE 65.

In 1977 this patient had a left mastec-

tomy. Glands were negative. In August 1980 it had spread into her lungs. She refused chemotherapy. October 1980 on her own she began to use only ascorbic acid, 26 grams per day. I then added the rest of the program. By December 12 her liver was enlarged. She discontinued the program. She died in February 1981.

S. G., FEMALE, AGE 33.

In 1971, S. G. was very depressed and later became anorexic. She was found guilty of defrauding her employer and sent to prison. Three days later she went into a coma for three weeks. Her weight was down to 59 pounds. In I.C.U. she slowly recovered but was left with total amnesia. In 1976 she was operated on for cancer of the lung and had secondaries in her back. I saw her December 23, 1976, when she showed perceptual symptoms, was paranoid with thought blocking and was very depressed. She was started on a vitamin program, including 9 grams of ascorbic acid per day. One month later her memory was better. Two months later her memory suddenly became normal and she was depressed and guilty. In April 1977 she started on Elavil. Two months later pain was less severe. She was still getting radiation for her back. By March 1978 she was mentally competent. She still remains alive and well.

I. S., FEMALE, AGE 58.

In 1974 I. S. received a panhysterectomy for carcinoma of the uterus. In 1976 it had invaded her colon, which was resected. In 1978 it recurred in her aorta and superior vena cava. She was given 19 radiation sessions, receiving the last October 1978. In December 1978 she was started on the program but I gave her only 3 grams of vitamin C per day. Three weeks later she felt less tired, stronger. She died 10 months later.

M. S., FEMALE, AGE 50.

In November 1981 this patient had a mass

in her left breast, one larger, hard lump and one smaller one beneath it, and one in her axilla. This patient refused surgery and the mass continued to grow. She had concluded that neither surgery nor chemotherapy offered her much hope. She then tried a variety of diet treatments, including the Living Diet recommended by Ann Wigmore. For three months on this diet she felt well but the mass continued to grow.

When I saw her in March 1982, she was very ill, emaciated (85 pounds), and terminal. One doctor refused to give her another appointment in a week, telling her she would be dead before then. I could see how he could arrive at this decision, but not his inability to provide her any support.

She started on sodium ascorbate, 4 grams t.i.d. and to bowel tolerance.

One month later she had consulted a naturopath, who advised her to follow a large variety of organ extracts and vitamins in small doses, as well as vitamin A, 1,000,000 IU per day.

In June 1982 she reported her weight had dropped to 79 pounds but then she began to gain. More metastases were found and she was given a six-month prognosis. Because her cancer was still advancing she then received an experimental collagen preparation intravenously for two weeks and orally after that.

On July 6 she was 82 pounds, had more energy and was more optimistic. August 4 she reported she was also receiving I.V. sodium ascorbate as well as using it orally. Her weight was 83.5 pounds, but the cancer had ulcerated to the surface. She felt well.

October 18, 1982, still on vitamin A, her hair fell out and her liver was enlarged. She had fluid in her abdomen and lungs. She was also anemic. I immediately had her discontinue the vitamin A. By November 17 her hair began to grow back but her liver was still enlarged.

On January 20, 1983, she weighed 102

pounds, liver tests were better, her hair was growing, she felt well, but the cancer kept on enlarging. She had no pain. February 21, 1983, her left arm became edematous. I discussed with her the use of radiation, urging her to consider this. On March 22, 1983, her left arm was swollen. On April 19, 1983, the Cancer Clinic in Victoria refused to treat her because they had never seen that type and severity of lesion respond. However, by means of a personal relationship of her husband to an oncologist in Vancouver, they agreed to try chemotherapy and not radiation as I recommended. On June 2, 1983 she had received four sessions of chemotherapy with few side effects, primarily nausea. The tumor was receding, skin was covering the lesion, and the swelling in her arm was gone. She had lost all her hair but felt good and was able to function normally. On July 4, 1983, her weight was 108 pounds. Now she found she could not tolerate ascorbic acid. Bioflavonoids were added, 1 gram t.i.d. On August 2, 1983, the lesion was healing well with only one small local area still open. She was 111 pounds and her hair was coming back. She could not tolerate the bioflavonoids due to nausea. On November 15, 1983, she continued chemotherapy. The entire left breast tissue was gone and her left breast was flat, but the skin had healed and appeared normal. Hair was slowly growing. Her weight was 110 pounds. Her left arm was swollen.

*Brief Outline of Treatment*

*Nutrition.* Sugar-free; junk-free; reduce red meats; increase green vegetables; avoid tea, coffee, cocoa, and milk products.
*Vitamin C.* 12 grams per day to bowel tolerance.
*Vitamin B3.* 1.5 to 3 grams per day.
*Vitamin A.* 25,000 to 50,000 IU per day.
*Beta-Carotene.* 30,000 to 60,000 IU per day.
*Vitamin E.* 800 IU.
*B-complex.* 50s.

*Zinc.* 30 to 50 mg.
*Magnesium.* 500 mg.
*Selenium.* 400 to 500 mcg per day.

Prognosis is very poor unless the patient can follow the program for at least two months.

Recently (1986) Dr. Charles Butterworth, chairman of the Department of Nutrition Sciences, University of Alabama, reported that folic acid, 10 mg per day, and 500 mcg of vitamin B12, reversed precancerous lesions in smokers. This was a double-blind designed trial. All the men had metaplastic cells on deep sputum smears. The presence of these cells correlates with subsequent development of cancer. After treatment all the patients were improved. None of the placebo group were. Also in a few patients with positive Pap smears these vitamins reversed the lesions and they disappeared. This suggests that folic acid should be included in any cancer treatment program. There is no evidence it will reverse cancerous tissue, but it should prevent pre-cancerous tissue from proceeding further.

### CHAPTER REFERENCES

Butterworth, C., as reported in *The Medical Post* by Johnson, Roger: Vitamins might breathe life into precancerous lung cells, December 23, 1986.

Cameron, E., & Pauling, L. (1979), *Cancer and Vitamin C.* New York: W. W. Norton.

Stone, I. (1972), *The Healing Factor: Vitamin C Against Disease.* New York: Grosset and Dunlap.

## chapter 12

# SKIN, ACNE AND PSORIASIS

## ACNE

Adolescent acne is one of the more common afflictions, but it is seldom the main complaint among the patients referred to me.

Rarely is it so severe that it is the primary concern. About 15 years ago, in Saskatoon, a 16-year-old boy was very depressed. His face was hideously covered with huge, irregular, red, oozing bumps and lumps, here and there infected. He told me he could no longer live with his face, that if my treatment did not help he would kill himself. He told me this very calmly and seriously. The acne had ruined his social life.

I have never considered acne a chronic infection and cannot understand why antibiotics help, but they had not helped him. I do consider acne a form of malnutrition. So does Dr. C. C. Pfeiffer. He describes a nutritional treatment for acne in his book, *Mental and Elemental Nutrients* (1975). I therefore started the boy on a sugar-free diet, eliminated all milk products, and added niacin, 3 grams per day; ascorbic acid, 3 grams per day; pyridoxine, 250 mg per day; and zinc sulfate, 220 mg per day. One month later his face was better. The vivid reddening had begun to recede, his face was no longer infected, and his mood was better. He told me he was no longer considering suicide. After three months his face was almost clear. He was cheerful and had begun to resume his social activities at school and elsewhere.

This is a dramatic example. There are very few failures, although the rate of recovery varies enormously. I also advise my patients not to scrub their faces vigorously, and not to squeeze or play with their faces.

I will describe a few cases from a very large number whose acne was their main complaint and was associated with depression and anxiety. Most adolescent cases have minor degrees of acne: a few pimples on their face, shoulders, and back. They do not present it as a problem, but when questioned they admit they are concerned. In every case their acne cleared on orthomolecular treatment.

Susan, mother of three children, had suffered from severe facial acne from childhood, but she had become so skillful with makeup that I was unaware of it, even though I had known her from childhood. Several years ago she complained to me about her acne and asked if nutrition and vitamins could help. I placed her on my standard program. Within six months she was clear of acne. She had not responded to any previous treatment recommended to her by a large number of general practitioners and dermatologists. This remarkable change was very impressive to her father, an excellent physician and a skeptic about megadose vitamin therapy. She remained well but then began to deviate from this program until the acne began to come back. She had been so well she had forgotten what it had been like and had become careless. On resuming the program the acne cleared and she has remained well for the past three years.

S. G., age 29, had suffered from acne since age 13. The only treatment that had helped was tetracycline, 1 gram each day. But every time she began to use this antibiotic it would work well for a while but eventually the acne would return. Birth control medication was not as helpful, and after a while it, too, no longer helped. She had failed to respond to a variety of ointments and had become allergic to some of them as well as to soap. Sunlamp radiation made her face better but her chest worse. She had not responded to vitamin A, 20,000 IU; vitamin E, 400 IU; and B-complex preparation. In addition to her acne, she was troubled by itchy scalp, white areas on her nails and a pungent underarm odor.

As an infant she had suffered colic. She was a heavy consumer of milk products, except for two weeks in Greece—her skin had been very good then, which she credited to the sun.

She was advised to eliminate sugar and milk products, supplemented by niacin, 100 mg three times per day; ascorbic acid, 1 gram three times per day; pyridoxine, 250 mg per day; cod liver oil, 2 capsules three times per day; dolomite, 3 tablets per day; and zinc sulfate, 110 mg.

After a week her acne began to clear. After three weeks her face was better but she had several mild relapses. Three months later she was normal but had to increase her zinc sulfate to 220 mg per day. She has now been clear of acne for eight years.

P. K., age 33, suffered from acne for 12 years and headaches for six years. During her teens she had gone through a severe bout of acne. It reappeared after her child was born. Tetracycline was sometimes helpful. The acne varied from moderate to very severe. In addition she developed bouts of headaches six years before I saw her, each bout lasting three days.

She was advised to follow a sugar-free diet, supplemented by niacin, 100 mg three times per day; ascorbic acid, 1 gram three times per day; pyridoxine, 250 mg per day; and zinc sulfate, 110 mg per day.

Within two months her skin was much clearer, although it was still subject to infection. Her mood was better.

One year later she reported her skin had gotten much worse six months before. She had decreased niacin by one-half because of the flush. She also had developed a vaginal discharge, continuous diarrhea, and a very dry throat. She had also observed that cheese made her worse. I asked her to discontinue niacin and started her on Mycostatin.

One-and-a-half years after she first consulted me she was well. But during that time the vitamin program and diet had to be readjusted. Eventually she remained on niacinamide, 2 grams per day; ascorbic acid, 3 grams; pyridoxine, 500 mg; zinc sulfate, 220 mg. She has remained well for seven years.

I. N., age 25, could not remember when she was free of acne. Tetracycline helped, but, whenever she went off it, the acne recurred. She had several features indicating pyridoxine deficiency, including white areas on her nails, many obvious stretch marks on her body, and severe premenstrual depression. She was placed on a sugar-free program with niacin, 100 mg three times daily; ascorbic acid, 1 gram three times a day; pyridoxine, 250 mg once a day; and zinc sulfate, 110 mg per day. Three months later there was no improvement. Niacin was increased to 500 mg three times per day; ascorbic acid, to 2 grams three times per day; pyridoxine, 250 mg; and zinc sulfate, 220 mg per day. I advised her to discontinue birth control medication. The acne began to improve in one week. Nine months after starting the program she was well. She had consulted another psychiatrist to discuss certain problems but felt no better. Neither did she improve on trycyclic antidepressant medication. She was advised to increase her pyridoxine to 500 mg per day and to double the ascorbic acid. When seen last she was normal and has remained well for seven years.

### Summary

Most patients with mild to severe acne will respond to a diet that eliminates sugar and foods they are allergic to, supplemented by vitamin B3, vitamin C, pyridoxine and zinc; but optimum amounts must be used. These amounts are determined by varying the dose and judging the response. No patients need suffer acne, nor need they be exposed to the harmful effects of chronic use of tetracycline.

Both skin and nervous system are ectodermal structures. Perhaps they have similar nutritional needs. This may explain why so many psychiatric patients have problems with their skin. I have yet to see a person who suffers from acne and is free of mental symptoms. My patients who recover from their psychiatric illnesses invariably note a great improvement in their skin, while acne sufferers lose their depression and anxiety as the acne clears. There is a relationship that accounts for some of the correlation. Simply being freed of acne will remove depression and anxiety. However, I have seen many whose acne was under control with antibiotics who still remained emotionally disturbed. Orthomolecular treatment removed both acne (and the need for tetracycline) and the depression. I assume that any person with severe to moderate acne is not free of psychiatric symptoms. Both are the result of malnutrition.

## PSORIASIS

Psoriasis is so erratic in its distribution and in its remissions and exacerbations that it is very difficult to develop a treatment that is consistently effective. What helps one person may make another person worse. Thus, many years ago, I treated a schizophrenic patient with niacin. One month later he was better, but he insisted on talking about his remarkable recovery—not from his schizophrenia—but from his psoriasis. As he had not told me he had psoriasis, I was very surprised. He told me he was now able for the first time in his life to walk around without a shirt on. His back and chest had been covered with lesions. One month later his skin was clear, Naturally, the next patient who came to me with psoriasis immediately was started on niacin. I informed him how my previous patient had gotten well. One month later when he returned, to my chagrin, his psoriasis was much worse. Since then I have found that niacin may make psoriatics worse. When I have a patient with psoriasis and wish to use vitamin B3, I use niacinamide, which has no effect one way or the other.

I have found that orthomolecular treatment either helps or does not. It does not make anyone worse. The following examples illustrate the treatment and response.

Mrs. C. T.'s (age 42) main complaint was severe migraine headache every week, present since puberty. I also found she had suffered from psoriasis since age 25 on legs, arms, and scalp. She had been treated in the hospital on several occasions. She also had mild arthritis in her wrists and knees.

I placed her on a sugar- and milk-free program supplemented with niacinamide, 500 mg four times per day; pyridoxine, 250 mg per day; zinc sulfate, 220 mg per day.

Six weeks later the psoriasis was improved, her legs were clear, her arms were much better, and her hair was not as dark. The headaches were much less severe, they came every two weeks with less pain in between.

Miss E. S.'s (age 17) main complaint was psoriasis on her elbows and legs, present about seven years. The patchy lesions were made worse when she was hot, and by fatigue and coffee. During July and August the psoriasis usually cleared. Her mental state showed she was on the edge of schizophrenia. She was started on niacinamide, 1 gram three times per day; ascorbic acid, 1 gram twice per day; vitamin A, 25,000 IU per day; riboflavin, 100 mg per day; and dolomite, 1 tablet three times per day.

Two months later she was better both mentally and physically, but there was only slight improvement in her psoriasis. She was improved enough mentally that she no longer needed to be seen.

## TREATMENT OF SKIN LESIONS REVIEWED

The skin is one of the major organs of the body in volume, activity and complexity, and it includes hair and nails. Skin protects us from invasion of growing organisms, from chemical contamination and from excessive sun. It seals our bodies and protects them from loss of water and nutrients. It is part of our thermoregulatory apparatus and is an excretory organ. It is involved in communication between people and animals and is intimately involved in reproduction. It is amazing that people are afflicted with so few lesions. But if skin is to continue to function, it must be properly nourished. It cannot absorb nutrients directly but is nourished by means of its circulatory system. If malnourished it will respond in a variety of ways. These diseases of nutrition which afflict skin will not respond to salves, ointments, lotions and so on, even though they are useful in treating surface infections and contaminations. Dermatologists must become orthomolecular; unfortunately, I do not know of any who have. They still disclaim any connection between diet and acne.

In general, skin lesions are treated, as are other diseases, by eliminating from the diet and the environment substances that are harmful, by providing nutritious food and by using supplements when they are needed.

### CHAPTER REFERENCE

Pfeiffer, C. C. (1975), *Mental and Elemental Nutrients.* New Canaan, Conn.: Keats Publishing.

# INDEX